JUSTICE LEAGUE UNITED

VOLUME 2
THE INFINITUS SAGA

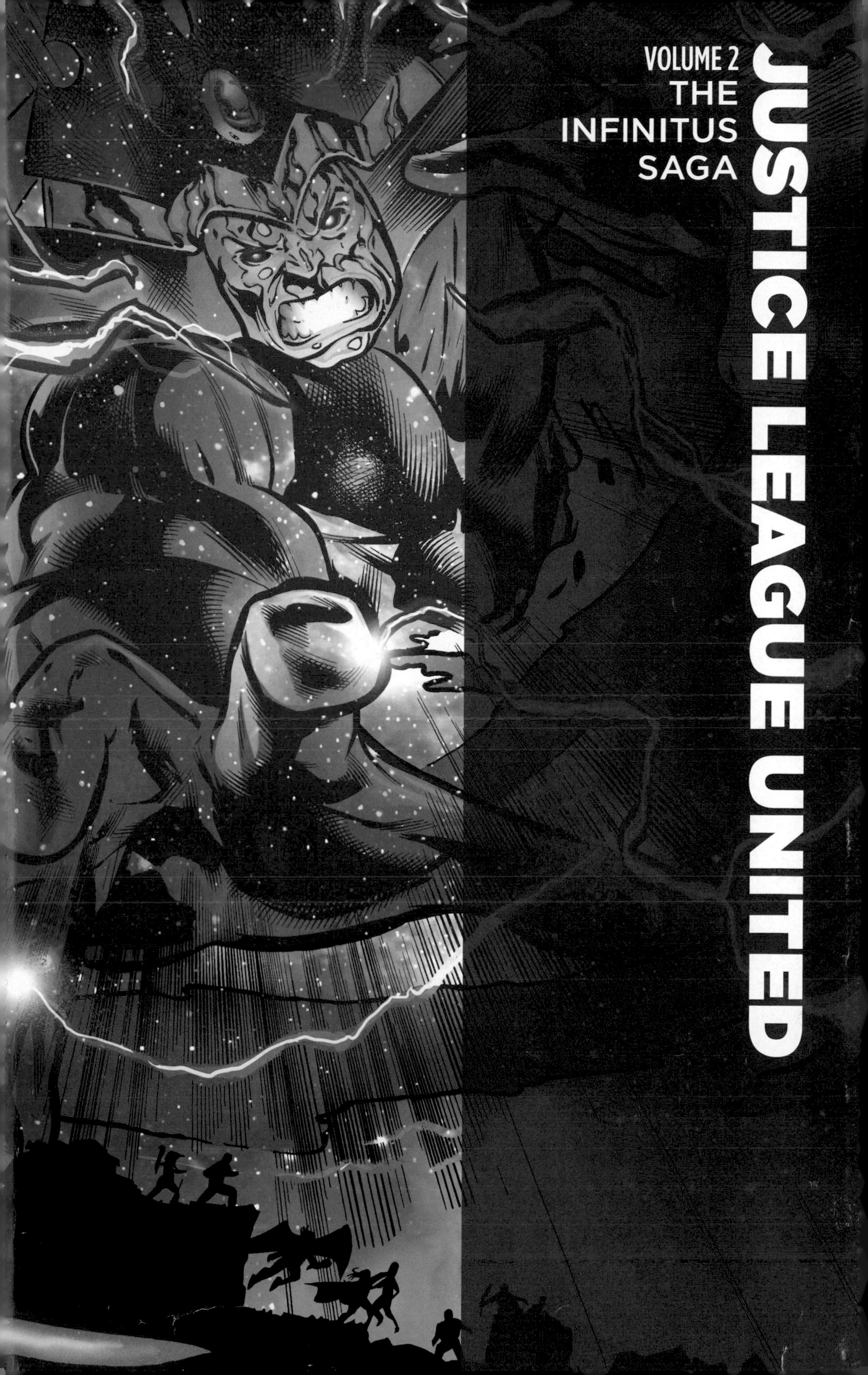

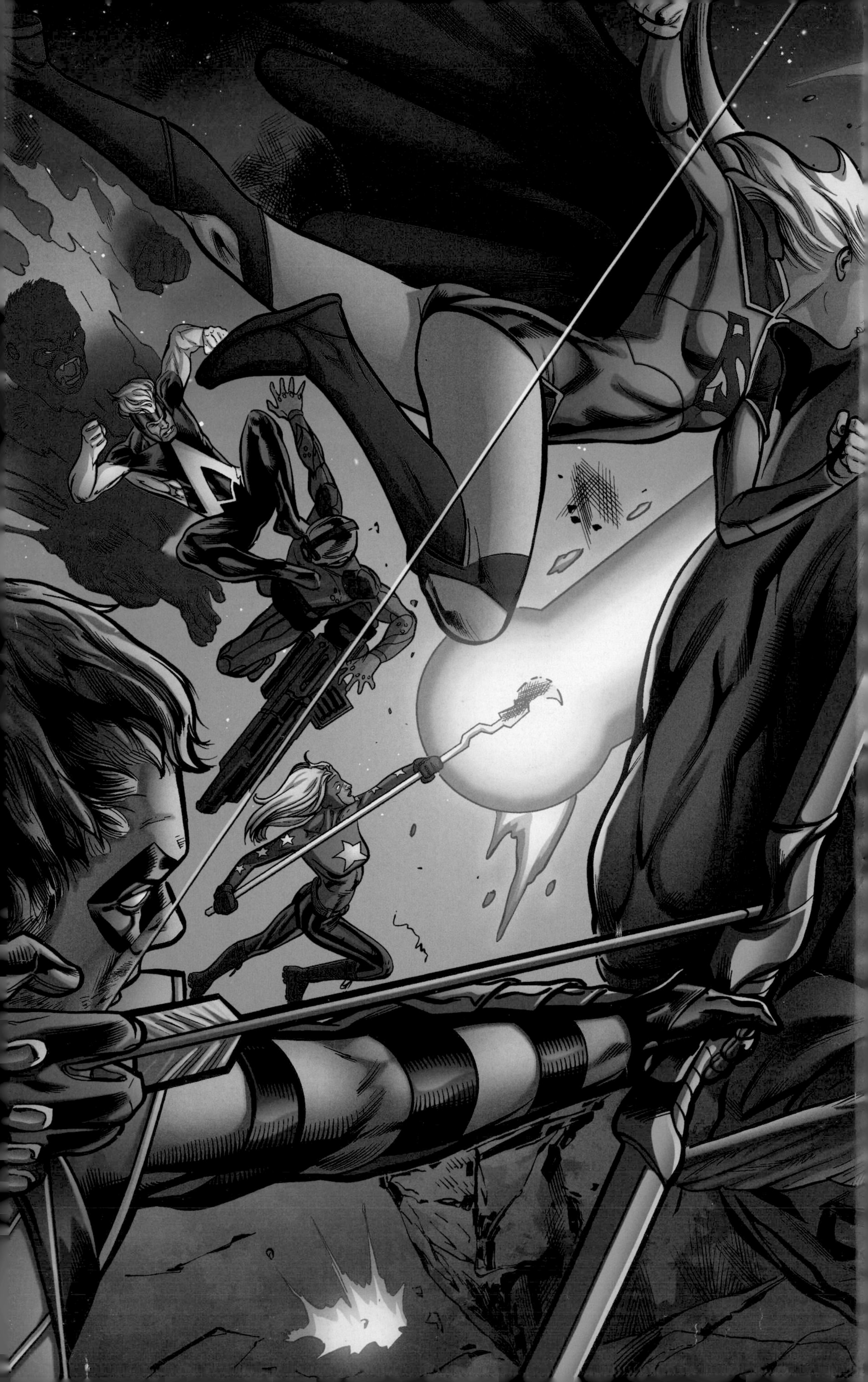

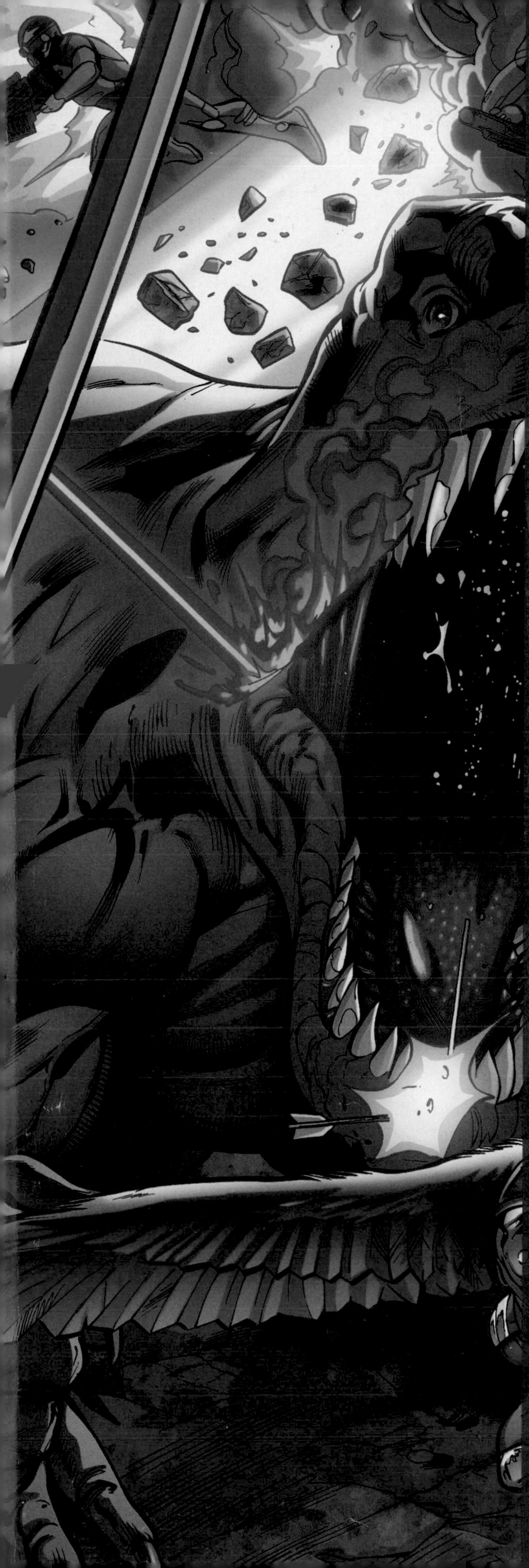

JUSTICE LEAGUE UNITED

VOLUME 2
THE INFINITUS SAGA

WRITTEN BY
JEFF LEMIRE

PENCILS BY
NEIL EDWARDS

INKS BY
JAY LEISTEN
KEITH CHAMPAGNE

"FUTURES END: HOMEWORLD" ART BY
JED DOUGHERTY

COLOR BY
JEROMY COX
GABE ELTAEB

LETTERS BY
DEZI SIENTY
TAYLOR ESPOSITO
TRAVIS LANHAM

ORIGINAL SERIES AND COLLECTION COVER ART BY
ANDREW ROBINSON

FUTURES END COVER ART BY
MIKE McKONE & GABE ELTAEB

SUPERGIRL BASED ON CHARACTERS CREATED BY
JERRY SIEGEL & JOE SHUSTER
BY SPECIAL ARRANGEMENT WITH THE JERRY SIEGEL FAMILY

BRIAN CUNNINGHAM RICKEY PURDIN Editors – Original Series
AMEDEO TURTURRO Assistant Editor – Original Series
JEB WOODARD Group Editor – Collected Editions
ROBIN WILDMAN Editor – Collected Edition
DAMIAN RYLAND Publication Design

BOB HARRAS Senior VP – Editor-in-Chief, DC Comics

DIANE NELSON President
DAN DiDIO and JIM LEE Co-Publishers
GEOFF JOHNS Chief Creative Officer
AMIT DESAI Senior VP – Marketing & Global Franchise Management
NAIRI GARDINER Senior VP – Finance
SAM ADES VP – Digital Marketing
BOBBIE CHASE VP – Talent Development
MARK CHIARELLO Senior VP – Art, Design & Collected Editions
JOHN CUNNINGHAM VP – Content Strategy
ANNE DEPIES VP – Strategy Planning & Reporting
DON FALLETTI VP – Manufacturing Operations
LAWRENCE GANEM VP – Editorial Administration & Talent Relations
ALISON GILL Senior VP – Manufacturing & Operations
HANK KANALZ Senior VP – Editorial Strategy & Administration
JAY KOGAN VP – Legal Affairs
DEREK MADDALENA Senior VP – Sales & Business Development
JACK MAHAN VP – Business Affairs
DAN MIRON VP – Sales Planning & Trade Development
NICK NAPOLITANO VP – Manufacturing Administration
CAROL ROEDER VP – Marketing
EDDIE SCANNELL VP – Mass Account & Digital Sales
COURTNEY SIMMONS Senior VP – Publicity & Communications
JIM (SKI) SOKOLOWSKI VP – Comic Book Specialty & Newsstand Sales
SANDY YI Senior VP – Global Franchise Management

JUSTICE LEAGUE UNITED VOLUME 2: THE INFINITUS SAGA

DC Comics, 2900 West Alameda Avenue, Burbank, CA 91505
Printed by RR Donnelley, Salem, VA, USA. 11/13/15.
ISBN: 978-1-4012-5766-8
First Printing.

Library of Congress Cataloging-in-Publication Data

Lemire, Jeff, author.
Justice League United. Volume 2, The infinitus saga / Jeff Lemire, writer ; Neil Edwards, artist.
pages cm
ISBN 978-1-4012-5766-8 (hardback)
1. Graphic novels. I. Edwards, Neil (Comic artist), illustrator. II. Title. III. Title: Infinitus saga.
PN6728.J87L56 2015
741.5'973—dc23
2015031186

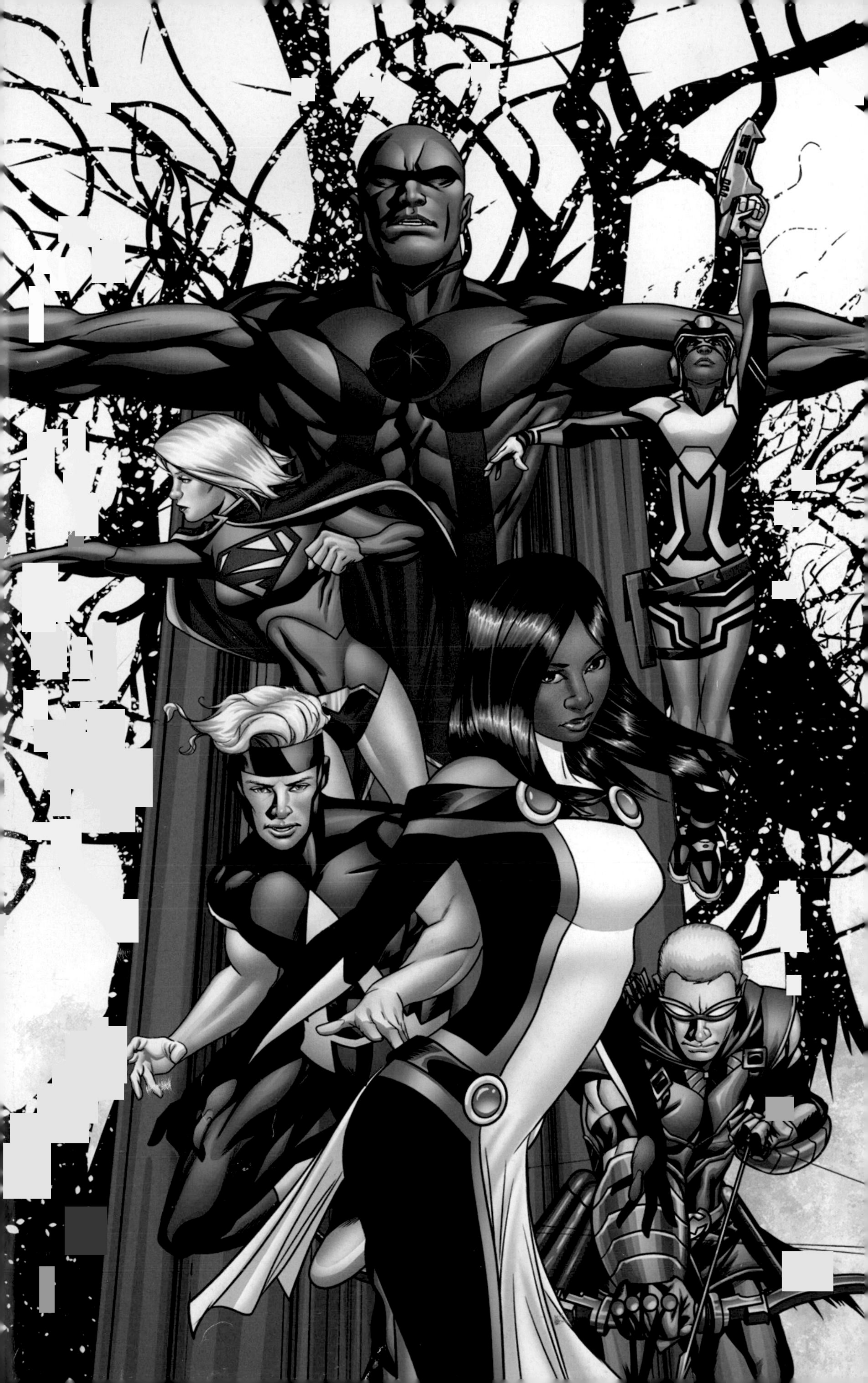

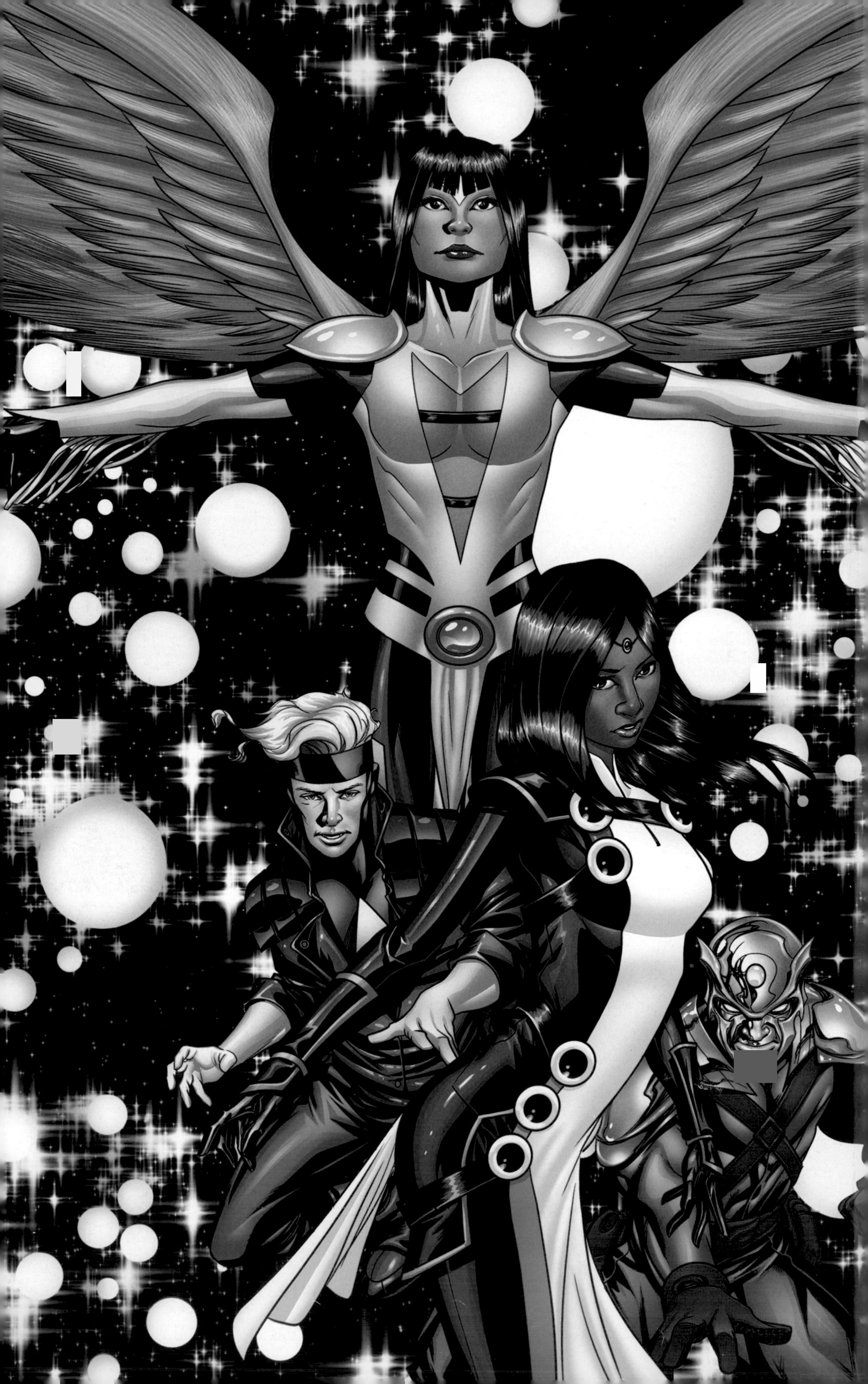

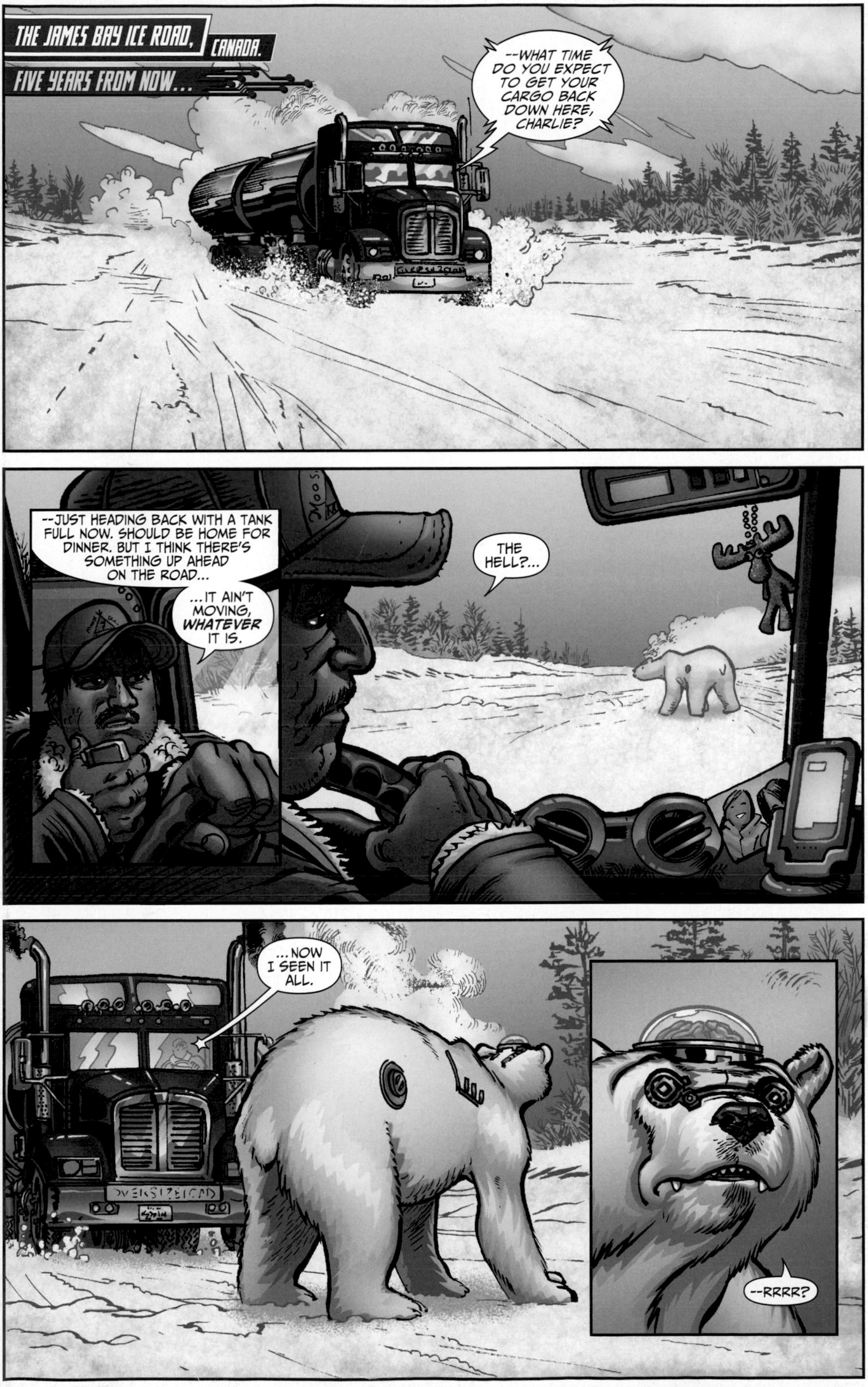
THE JAMES BAY ICE ROAD, CANADA.
FIVE YEARS FROM NOW...
--WHAT TIME DO YOU EXPECT TO GET YOUR CARGO BACK DOWN HERE, CHARLIE?
--JUST HEADING BACK WITH A TANK FULL NOW. SHOULD BE HOME FOR DINNER. BUT I THINK THERE'S SOMETHING UP AHEAD ON THE ROAD...
...IT AIN'T MOVING, WHATEVER IT IS.
THE HELL?...
...NOW I SEEN IT ALL.
--RRRR?

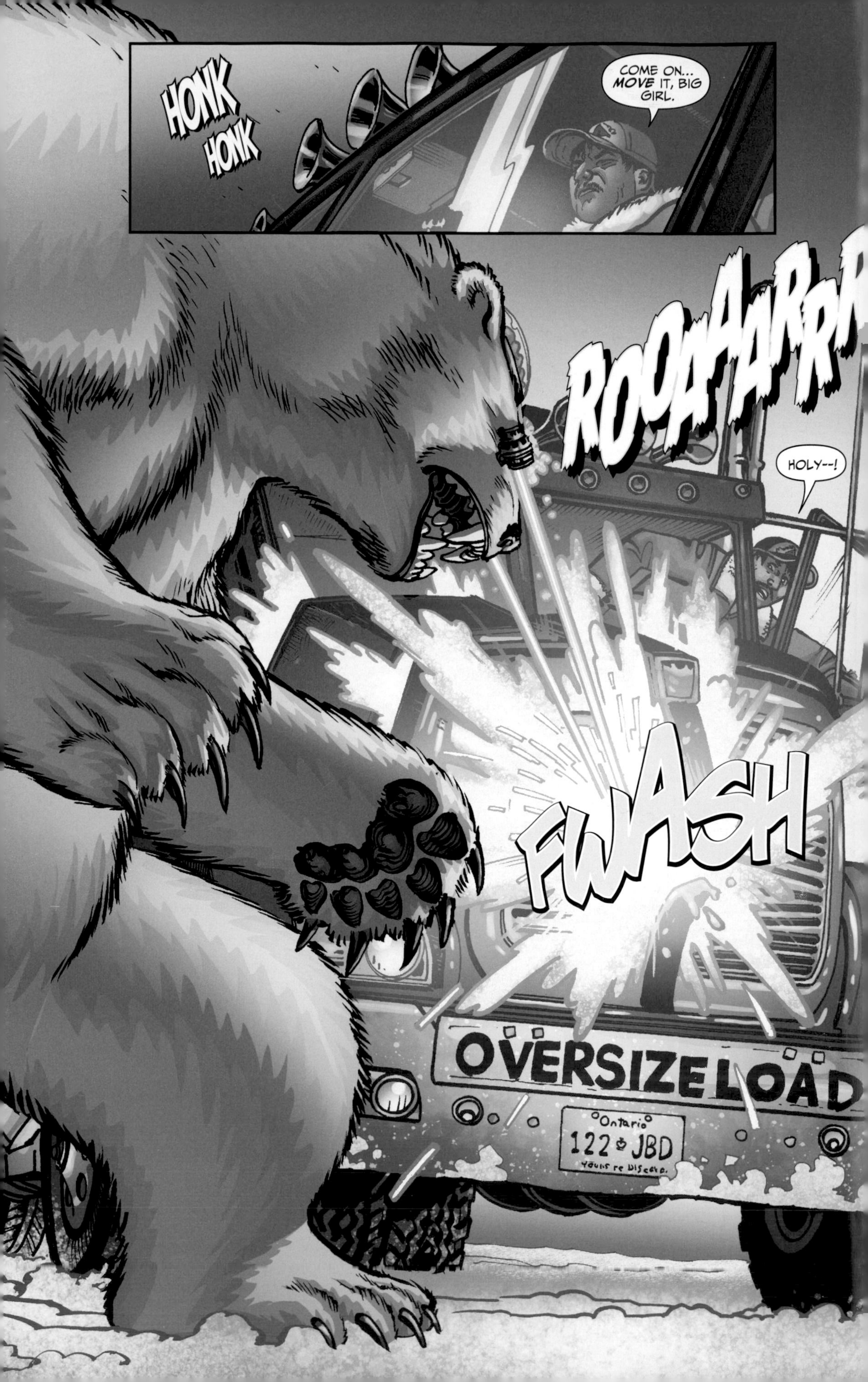
HONK
HONK
COME ON... MOVE IT, BIG GIRL.
ROOAARRR
HOLY--!
FWASH
OVERSIZE LOAD
Ontario
122 JBD

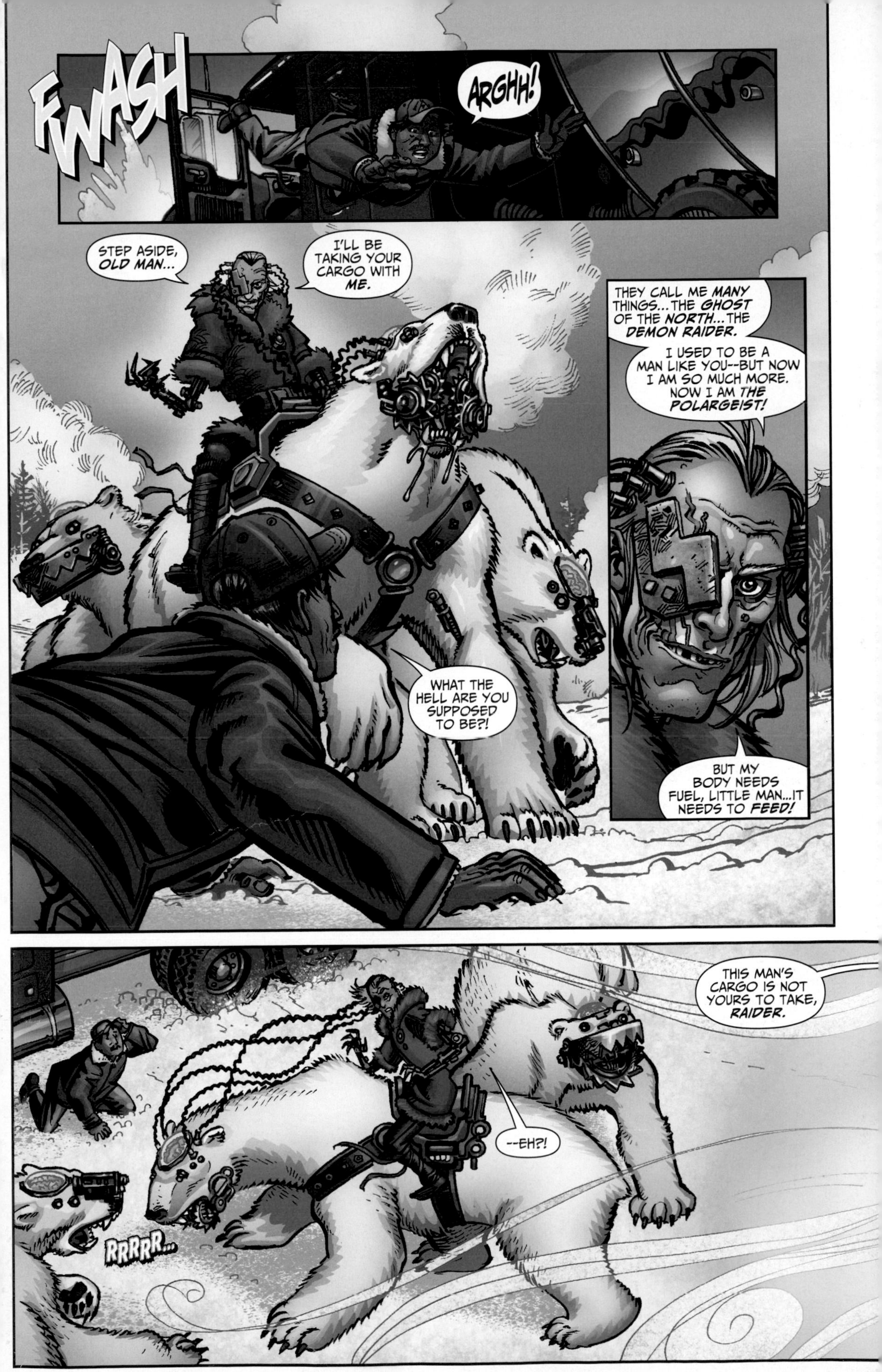
FWASH
ARGHH!
STEP ASIDE, OLD MAN...
I'LL BE TAKING YOUR CARGO WITH ME.
WHAT THE HELL ARE YOU SUPPOSED TO BE?!
THEY CALL ME MANY THINGS... THE GHOST OF THE NORTH... THE DEMON RAIDER.
I USED TO BE A MAN LIKE YOU--BUT NOW I AM SO MUCH MORE. NOW I AM THE POLARGEIST!
BUT MY BODY NEEDS FUEL, LITTLE MAN...IT NEEDS TO FEED!
THIS MAN'S CARGO IS NOT YOURS TO TAKE, RAIDER.
--EH?!
RRRRR...

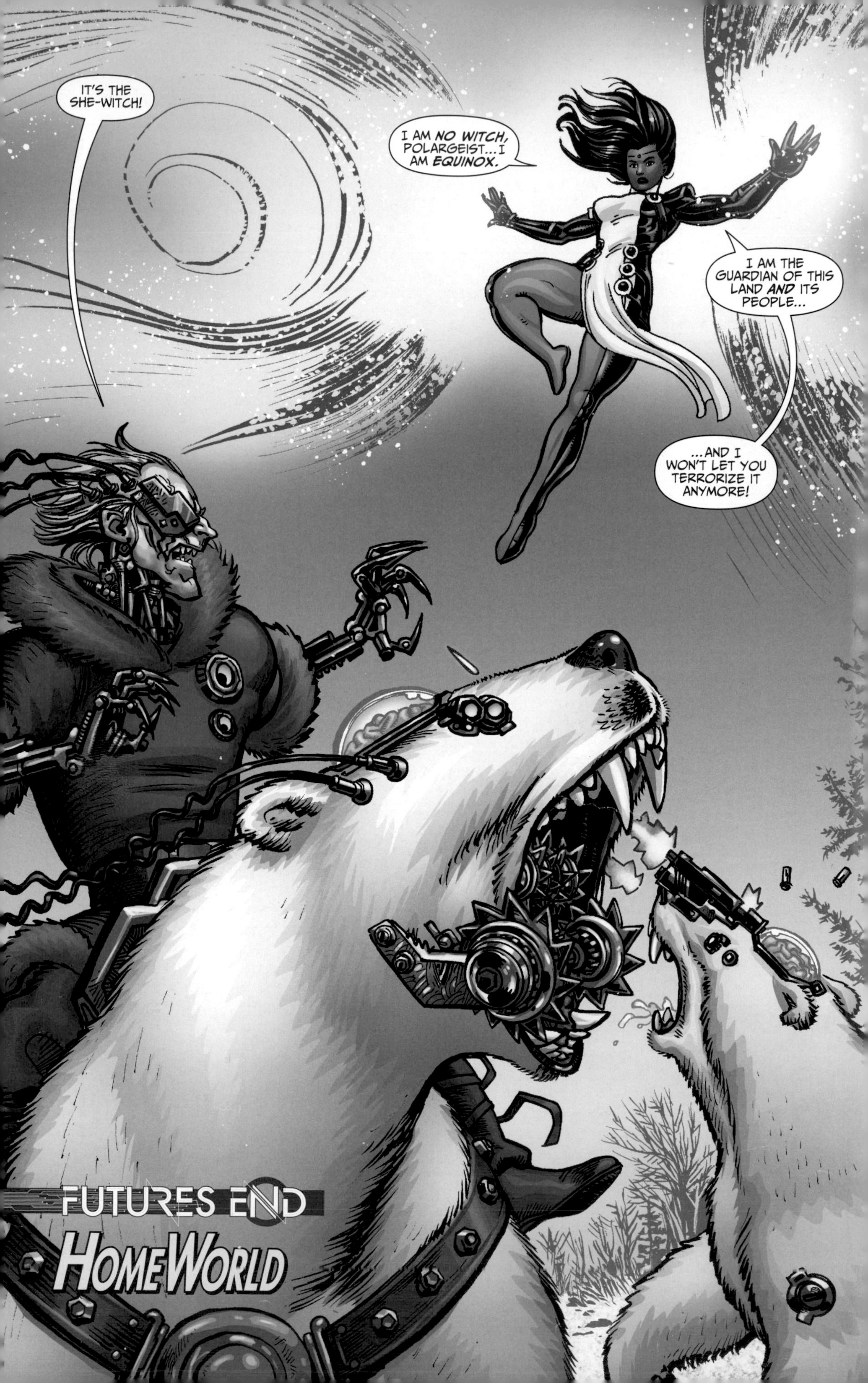
IT'S THE SHE-WITCH!
I AM NO WITCH, POLARGEIST...I AM EQUINOX.
I AM THE GUARDIAN OF THIS LAND AND ITS PEOPLE...
...AND I WON'T LET YOU TERRORIZE IT ANYMORE!
FUTURES END
HOMEWORLD

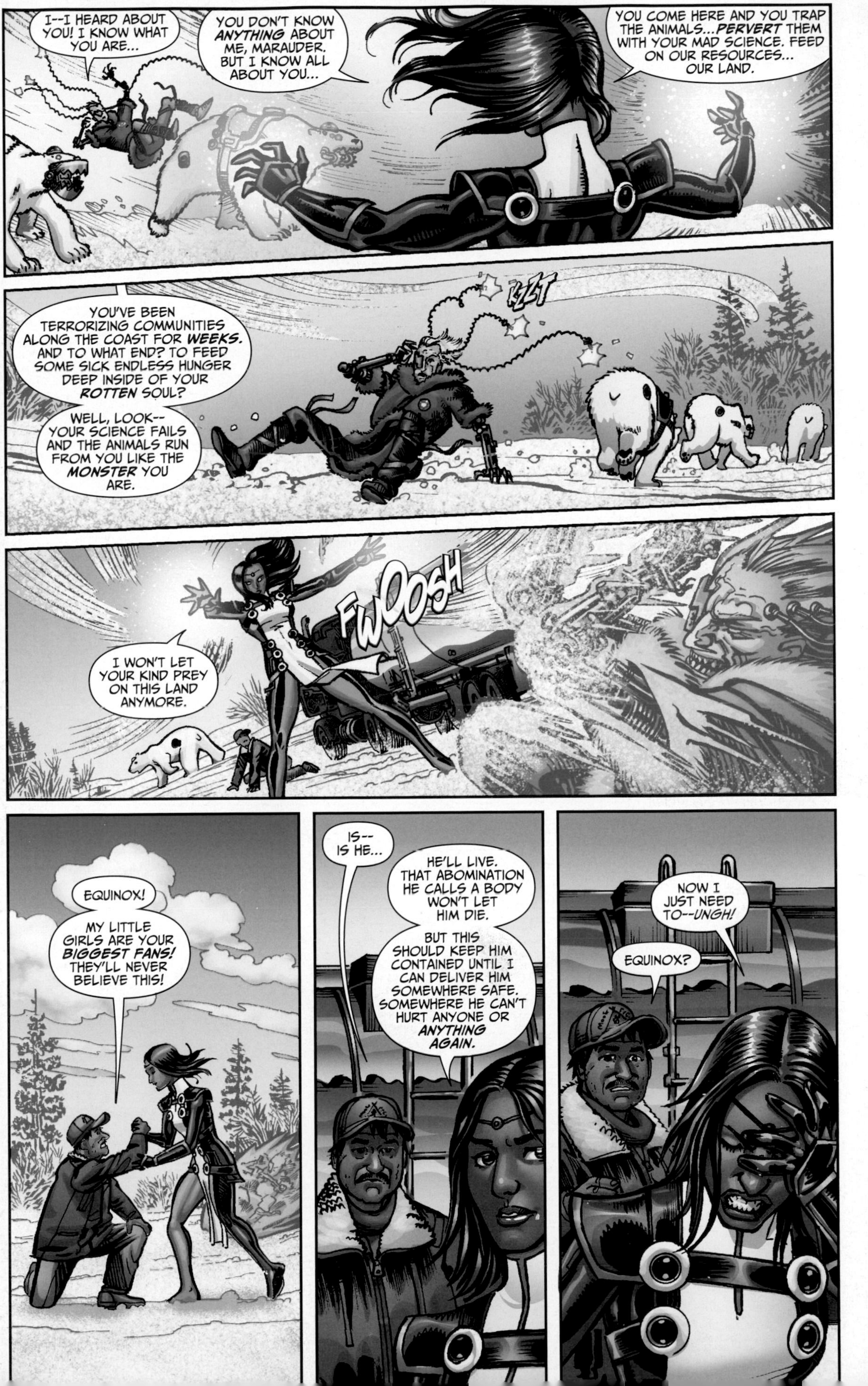
I--I HEARD ABOUT YOU! I KNOW WHAT YOU ARE...
YOU DON'T KNOW ANYTHING ABOUT ME, MARAUDER. BUT I KNOW ALL ABOUT YOU...
YOU COME HERE AND YOU TRAP THE ANIMALS...PERVERT THEM WITH YOUR MAD SCIENCE. FEED ON OUR RESOURCES... OUR LAND.
KZZT
YOU'VE BEEN TERRORIZING COMMUNITIES ALONG THE COAST FOR WEEKS. AND TO WHAT END? TO FEED SOME SICK ENDLESS HUNGER DEEP INSIDE OF YOUR ROTTEN SOUL?
WELL, LOOK-- YOUR SCIENCE FAILS AND THE ANIMALS RUN FROM YOU LIKE THE MONSTER YOU ARE.
FWOOSH
I WON'T LET YOUR KIND PREY ON THIS LAND ANYMORE.
EQUINOX!
MY LITTLE GIRLS ARE YOUR BIGGEST FANS! THEY'LL NEVER BELIEVE THIS!
IS-- IS HE...
HE'LL LIVE. THAT ABOMINATION HE CALLS A BODY WON'T LET HIM DIE.
BUT THIS SHOULD KEEP HIM CONTAINED UNTIL I CAN DELIVER HIM SOMEWHERE SAFE. SOMEWHERE HE CAN'T HURT ANYONE OR ANYTHING AGAIN.
NOW I JUST NEED TO--UNGH!
EQUINOX?

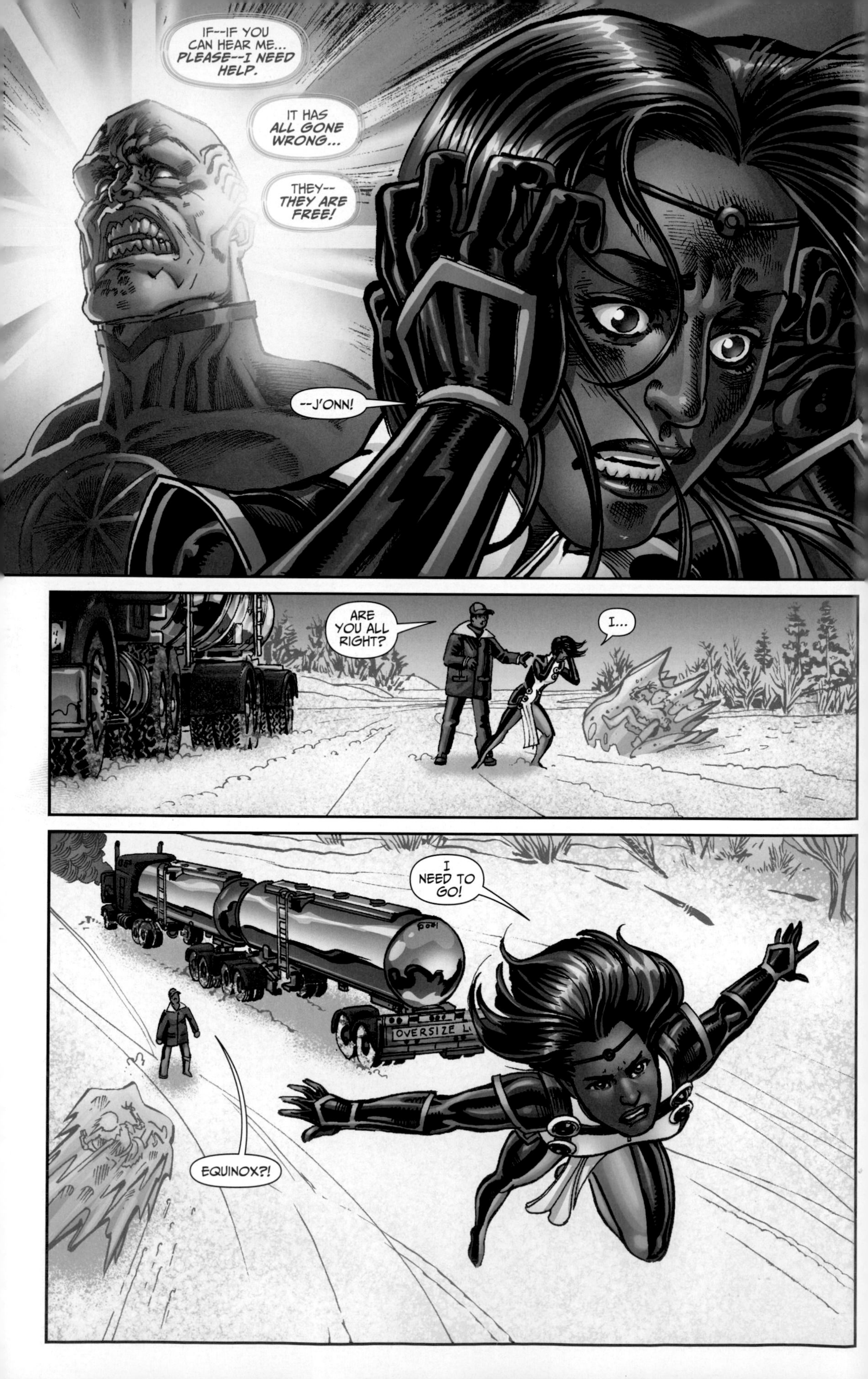
IF--IF YOU CAN HEAR ME... PLEASE--I NEED HELP.
IT HAS ALL GONE WRONG...
THEY-- THEY ARE FREE!
--J'ONN!
ARE YOU ALL RIGHT?
I...
I NEED TO GO!
OVERSIZE L
EQUINOX?!

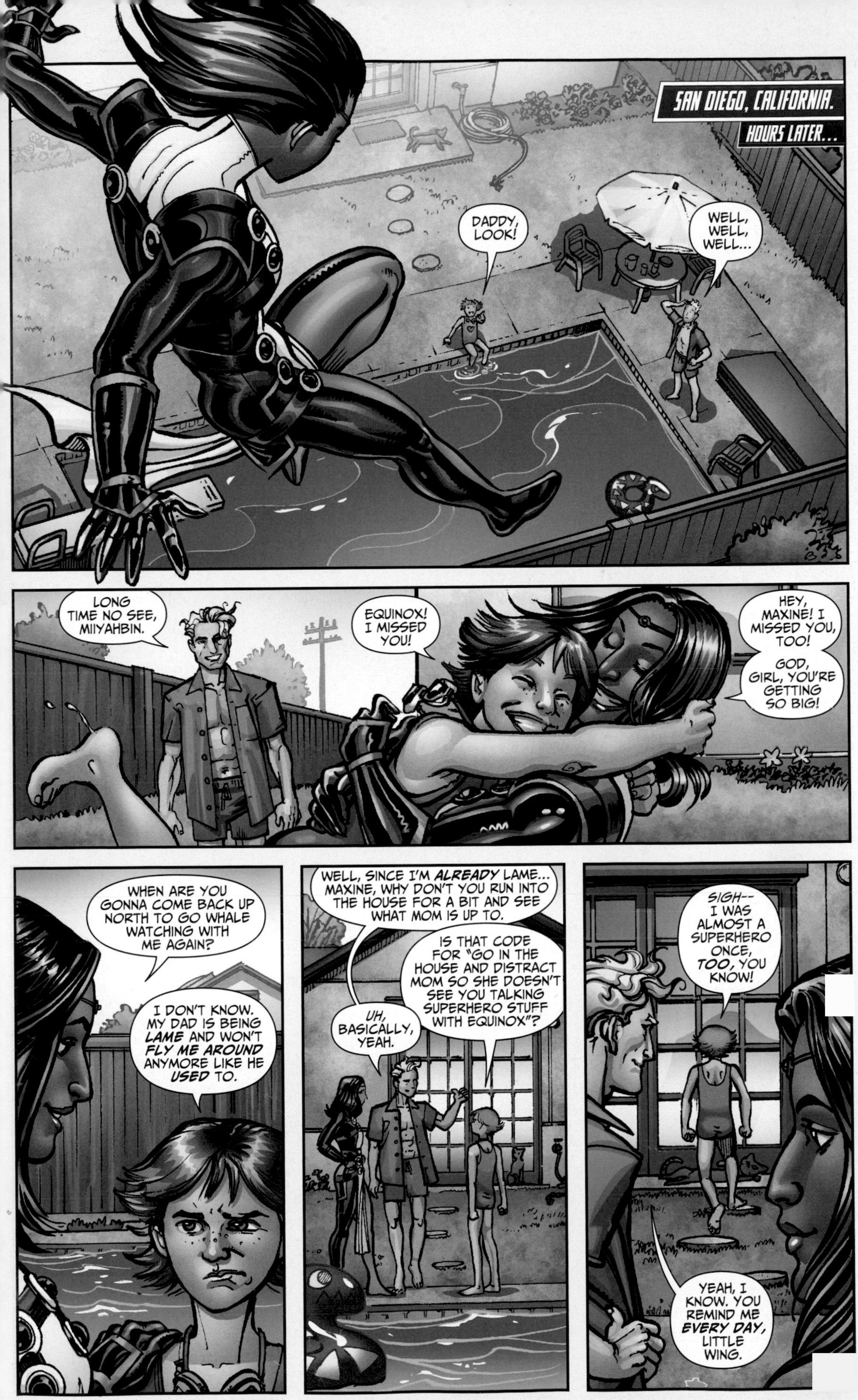
SAN DIEGO, CALIFORNIA.
HOURS LATER...
DADDY, LOOK!
WELL, WELL, WELL...
LONG TIME NO SEE, MIIYAHBIN.
EQUINOX! I MISSED YOU!
HEY, MAXINE! I MISSED YOU, TOO!
GOD, GIRL, YOU'RE GETTING SO BIG!
WHEN ARE YOU GONNA COME BACK UP NORTH TO GO WHALE WATCHING WITH ME AGAIN?
I DON'T KNOW. MY DAD IS BEING LAME AND WON'T FLY ME AROUND ANYMORE LIKE HE USED TO.
WELL, SINCE I'M ALREADY LAME... MAXINE, WHY DON'T YOU RUN INTO THE HOUSE FOR A BIT AND SEE WHAT MOM IS UP TO.
IS THAT CODE FOR "GO IN THE HOUSE AND DISTRACT MOM SO SHE DOESN'T SEE YOU TALKING SUPERHERO STUFF WITH EQUINOX"?
UH, BASICALLY, YEAH.
SIGH-- I WAS ALMOST A SUPERHERO ONCE, TOO, YOU KNOW!
YEAH, I KNOW. YOU REMIND ME EVERY DAY, LITTLE WING.

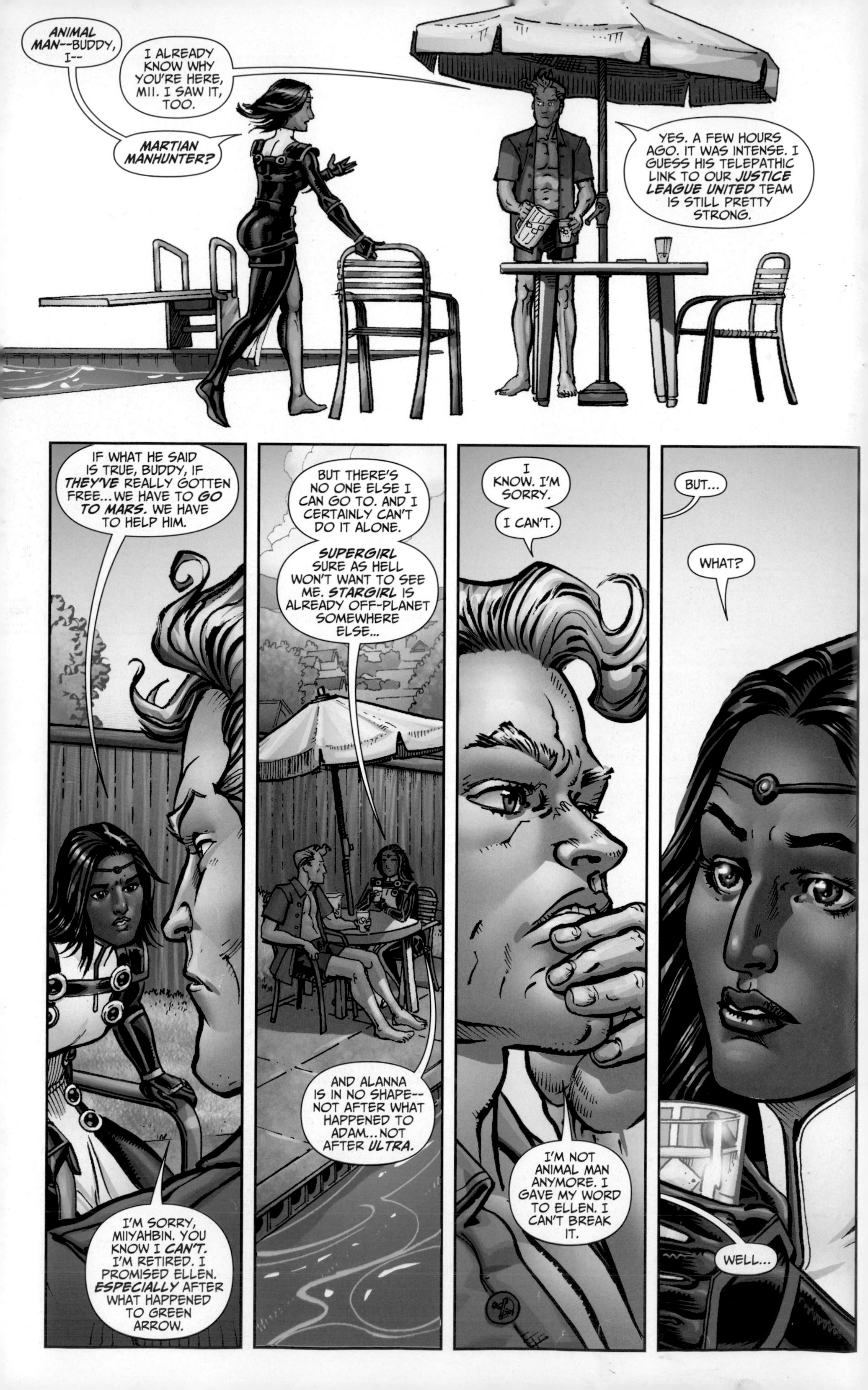
ANIMAL MAN--BUDDY, I--
I ALREADY KNOW WHY YOU'RE HERE, MII. I SAW IT, TOO.
MARTIAN MANHUNTER?
YES. A FEW HOURS AGO. IT WAS INTENSE. I GUESS HIS TELEPATHIC LINK TO OUR JUSTICE LEAGUE UNITED TEAM IS STILL PRETTY STRONG.
IF WHAT HE SAID IS TRUE, BUDDY, IF THEY'VE REALLY GOTTEN FREE...WE HAVE TO GO TO MARS. WE HAVE TO HELP HIM.
I'M SORRY, MIIYAHBIN. YOU KNOW I CAN'T. I'M RETIRED. I PROMISED ELLEN. ESPECIALLY AFTER WHAT HAPPENED TO GREEN ARROW.
BUT THERE'S NO ONE ELSE I CAN GO TO. AND I CERTAINLY CAN'T DO IT ALONE.
SUPERGIRL SURE AS HELL WON'T WANT TO SEE ME. STARGIRL IS ALREADY OFF-PLANET SOMEWHERE ELSE...
AND ALANNA IS IN NO SHAPE--NOT AFTER WHAT HAPPENED TO ADAM...NOT AFTER ULTRA.
I KNOW. I'M SORRY.
I CAN'T.
I'M NOT ANIMAL MAN ANYMORE. I GAVE MY WORD TO ELLEN. I CAN'T BREAK IT.
BUT...
WHAT?
WELL...

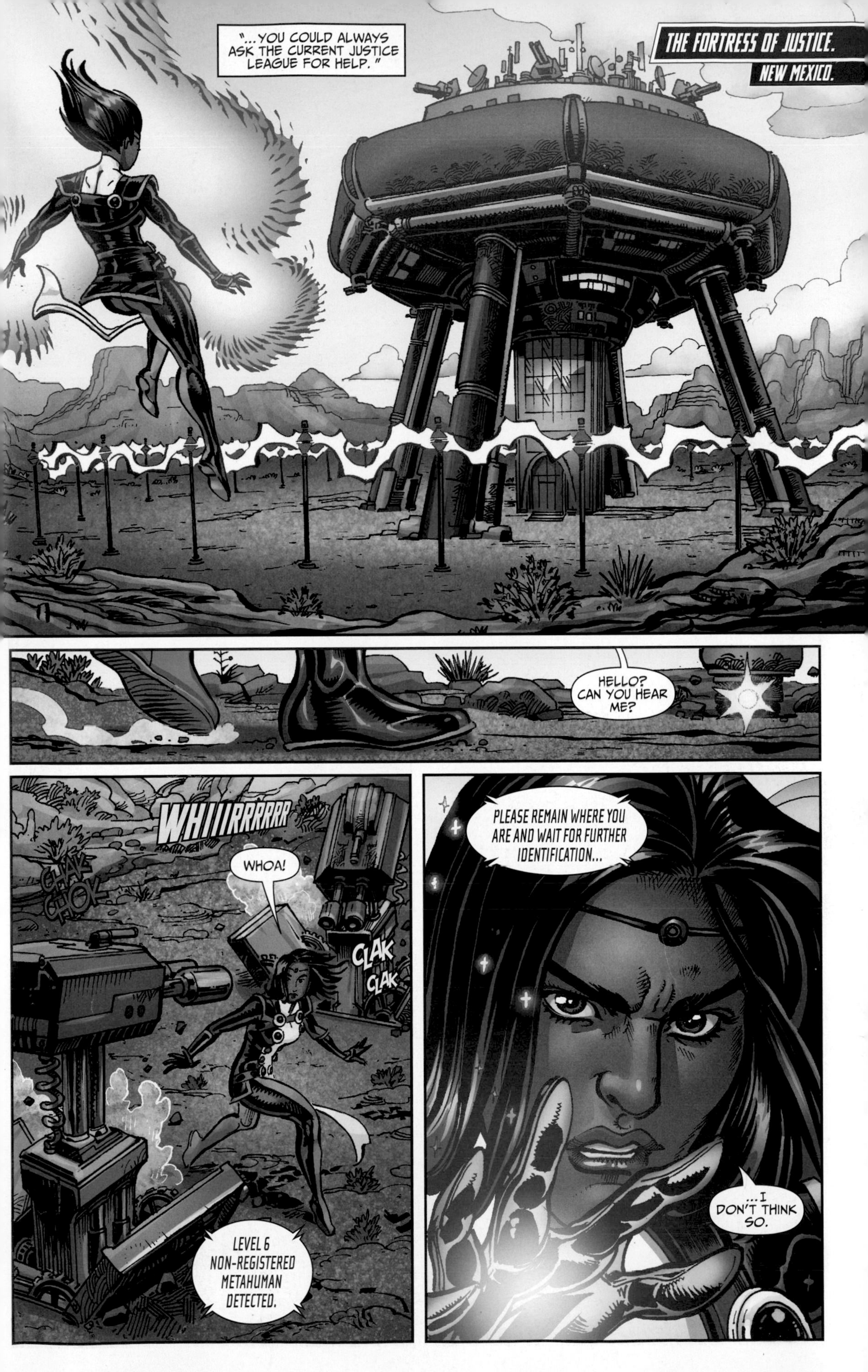
"...YOU COULD ALWAYS ASK THE CURRENT JUSTICE LEAGUE FOR HELP."
THE FORTRESS OF JUSTICE.
NEW MEXICO.
HELLO? CAN YOU HEAR ME?
WHIIIRRRRR
WHOA!
CLAK
CLAK
LEVEL 6 NON-REGISTERED METAHUMAN DETECTED.
PLEASE REMAIN WHERE YOU ARE AND WAIT FOR FURTHER IDENTIFICATION...
...I DON'T THINK SO.

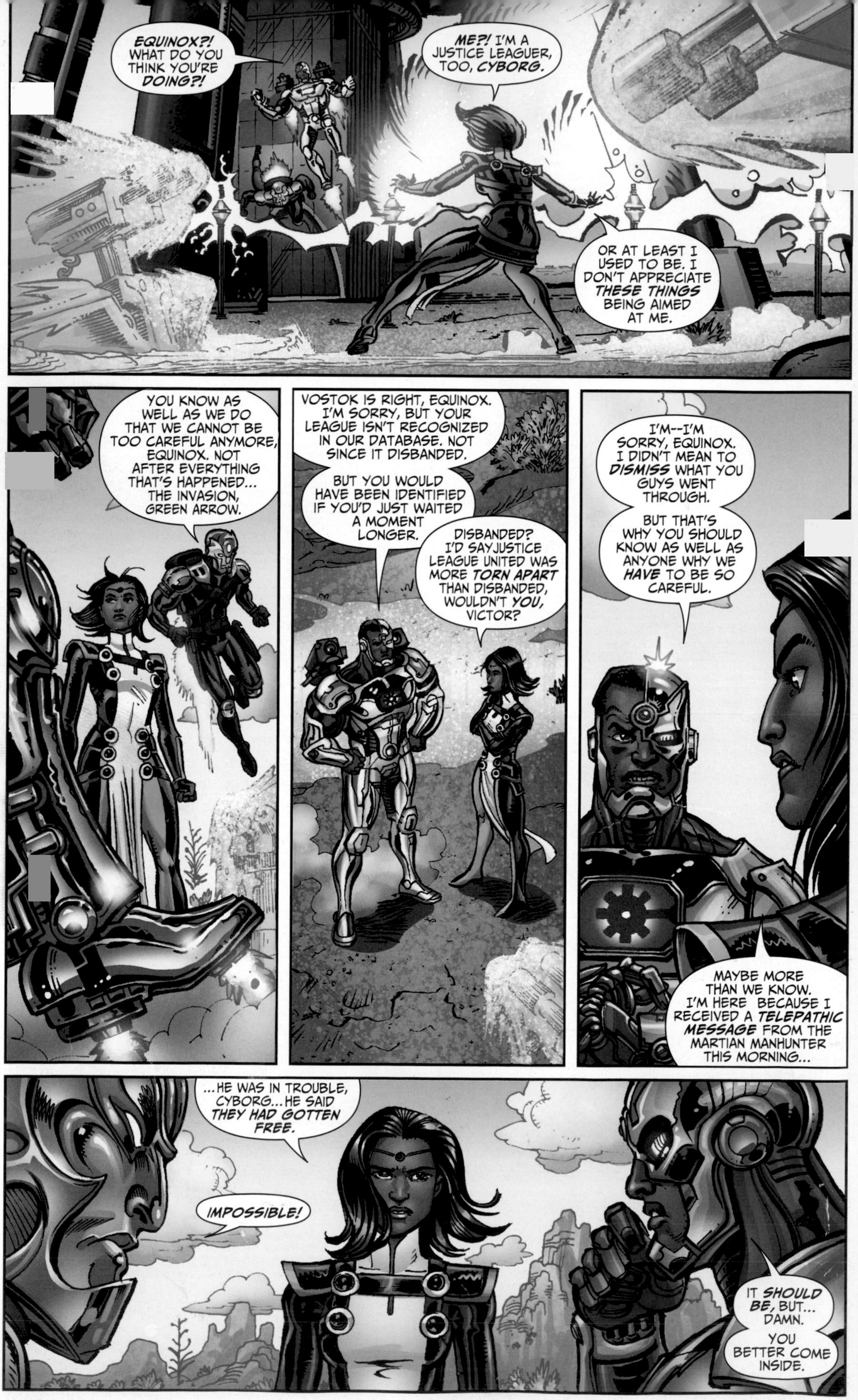
EQUINOX?! WHAT DO YOU THINK YOU'RE DOING?!
ME?! I'M A JUSTICE LEAGUER, TOO, CYBORG.
OR AT LEAST I USED TO BE. I DON'T APPRECIATE THESE THINGS BEING AIMED AT ME.
YOU KNOW AS WELL AS WE DO THAT WE CANNOT BE TOO CAREFUL ANYMORE, EQUINOX. NOT AFTER EVERYTHING THAT'S HAPPENED... THE INVASION, GREEN ARROW.
VOSTOK IS RIGHT, EQUINOX. I'M SORRY, BUT YOUR LEAGUE ISN'T RECOGNIZED IN OUR DATABASE. NOT SINCE IT DISBANDED.
BUT YOU WOULD HAVE BEEN IDENTIFIED IF YOU'D JUST WAITED A MOMENT LONGER.
DISBANDED? I'D SAYJUSTICE LEAGUE UNITED WAS MORE TORN APART THAN DISBANDED, WOULDN'T YOU, VICTOR?
I'M--I'M SORRY, EQUINOX. I DIDN'T MEAN TO DISMISS WHAT YOU GUYS WENT THROUGH.
BUT THAT'S WHY YOU SHOULD KNOW AS WELL AS ANYONE WHY WE HAVE TO BE SO CAREFUL.
MAYBE MORE THAN WE KNOW. I'M HERE BECAUSE I RECEIVED A TELEPATHIC MESSAGE FROM THE MARTIAN MANHUNTER THIS MORNING...
...HE WAS IN TROUBLE, CYBORG...HE SAID THEY HAD GOTTEN FREE.
IMPOSSIBLE!
IT SHOULD BE, BUT... DAMN.
YOU BETTER COME INSIDE.

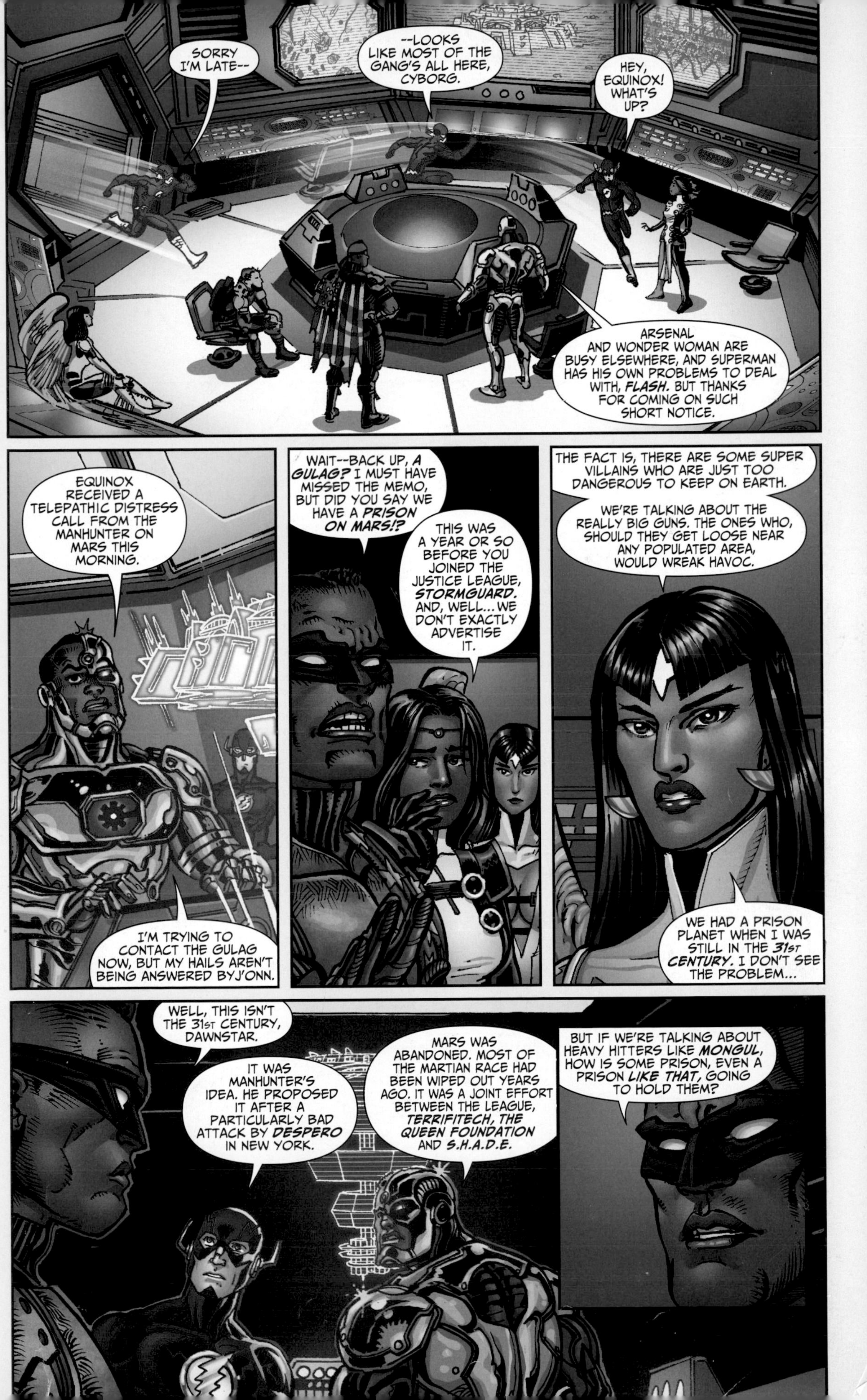
SORRY I'M LATE--
--LOOKS LIKE MOST OF THE GANG'S ALL HERE, CYBORG.
HEY, EQUINOX! WHAT'S UP?
ARSENAL AND WONDER WOMAN ARE BUSY ELSEWHERE, AND SUPERMAN HAS HIS OWN PROBLEMS TO DEAL WITH, FLASH. BUT THANKS FOR COMING ON SUCH SHORT NOTICE.
EQUINOX RECEIVED A TELEPATHIC DISTRESS CALL FROM THE MANHUNTER ON MARS THIS MORNING.
I'M TRYING TO CONTACT THE GULAG NOW, BUT MY HAILS AREN'T BEING ANSWERED BY J'ONN.
WAIT--BACK UP, A GULAG? I MUST HAVE MISSED THE MEMO, BUT DID YOU SAY WE HAVE A PRISON ON MARS!?
THIS WAS A YEAR OR SO BEFORE YOU JOINED THE JUSTICE LEAGUE, STORMGUARD. AND, WELL... WE DON'T EXACTLY ADVERTISE IT.
THE FACT IS, THERE ARE SOME SUPER VILLAINS WHO ARE JUST TOO DANGEROUS TO KEEP ON EARTH.
WE'RE TALKING ABOUT THE REALLY BIG GUNS. THE ONES WHO, SHOULD THEY GET LOOSE NEAR ANY POPULATED AREA, WOULD WREAK HAVOC.
WE HAD A PRISON PLANET WHEN I WAS STILL IN THE 31ST CENTURY. I DON'T SEE THE PROBLEM...
WELL, THIS ISN'T THE 31ST CENTURY, DAWNSTAR.
IT WAS MANHUNTER'S IDEA. HE PROPOSED IT AFTER A PARTICULARLY BAD ATTACK BY DESPERO IN NEW YORK.
MARS WAS ABANDONED. MOST OF THE MARTIAN RACE HAD BEEN WIPED OUT YEARS AGO. IT WAS A JOINT EFFORT BETWEEN THE LEAGUE, TERRIFITECH, THE QUEEN FOUNDATION AND S.H.A.D.E.
BUT IF WE'RE TALKING ABOUT HEAVY HITTERS LIKE MONGUL, HOW IS SOME PRISON, EVEN A PRISON LIKE THAT, GOING TO HOLD THEM?

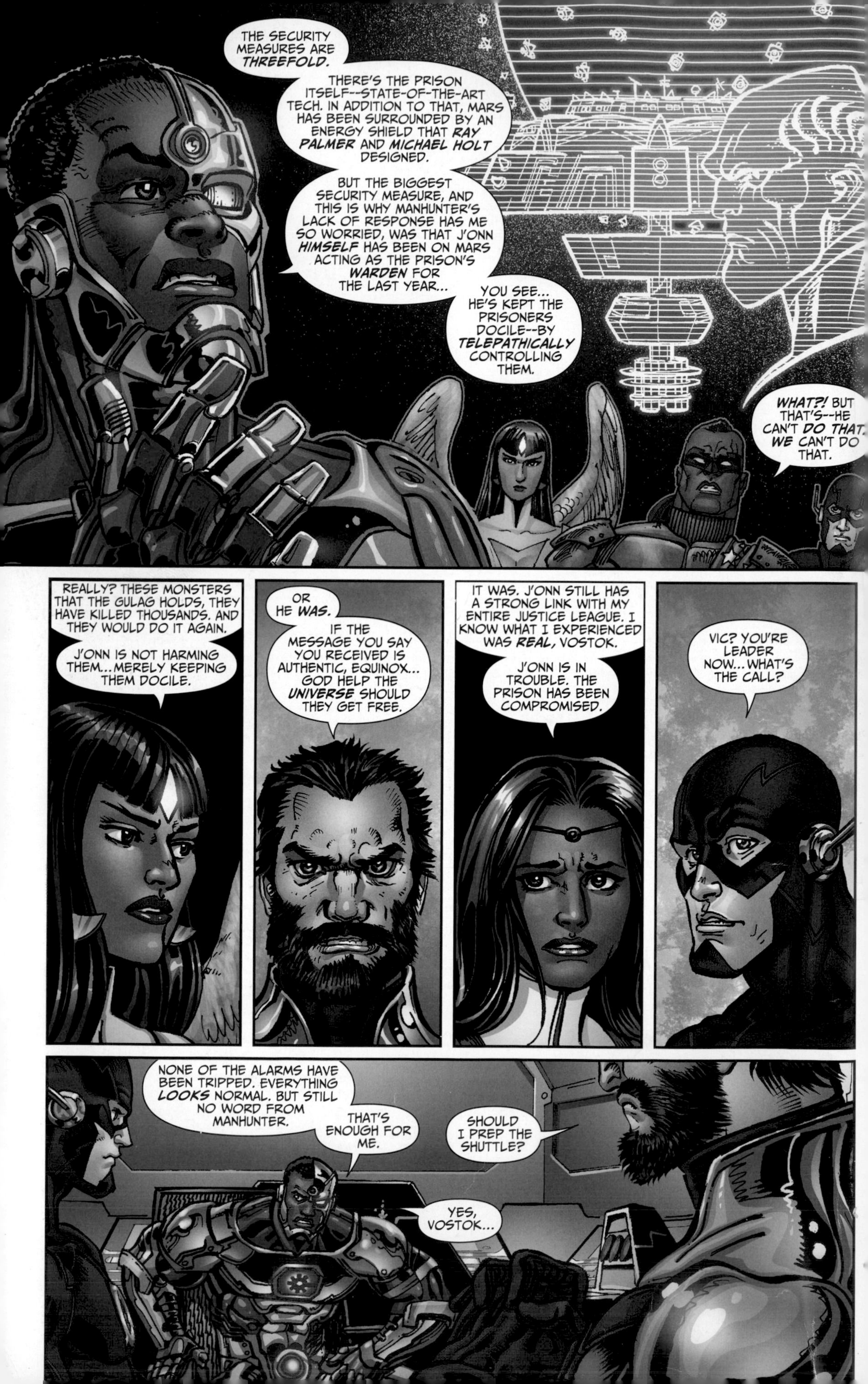
THE SECURITY MEASURES ARE THREEFOLD.
THERE'S THE PRISON ITSELF--STATE-OF-THE-ART TECH. IN ADDITION TO THAT, MARS HAS BEEN SURROUNDED BY AN ENERGY SHIELD THAT RAY PALMER AND MICHAEL HOLT DESIGNED.
BUT THE BIGGEST SECURITY MEASURE, AND THIS IS WHY MANHUNTER'S LACK OF RESPONSE HAS ME SO WORRIED, WAS THAT J'ONN HIMSELF HAS BEEN ON MARS ACTING AS THE PRISON'S WARDEN FOR THE LAST YEAR...
YOU SEE... HE'S KEPT THE PRISONERS DOCILE--BY TELEPATHICALLY CONTROLLING THEM.
WHAT?! BUT THAT'S--HE CAN'T DO THAT. WE CAN'T DO THAT.
REALLY? THESE MONSTERS THAT THE GULAG HOLDS, THEY HAVE KILLED THOUSANDS. AND THEY WOULD DO IT AGAIN.
J'ONN IS NOT HARMING THEM...MERELY KEEPING THEM DOCILE.
OR HE WAS.
IF THE MESSAGE YOU SAY YOU RECEIVED IS AUTHENTIC, EQUINOX... GOD HELP THE UNIVERSE SHOULD THEY GET FREE.
IT WAS. J'ONN STILL HAS A STRONG LINK WITH MY ENTIRE JUSTICE LEAGUE. I KNOW WHAT I EXPERIENCED WAS REAL, VOSTOK.
J'ONN IS IN TROUBLE. THE PRISON HAS BEEN COMPROMISED.
VIC? YOU'RE LEADER NOW...WHAT'S THE CALL?
NONE OF THE ALARMS HAVE BEEN TRIPPED. EVERYTHING LOOKS NORMAL. BUT STILL NO WORD FROM MANHUNTER.
THAT'S ENOUGH FOR ME.
SHOULD I PREP THE SHUTTLE?
YES, VOSTOK...

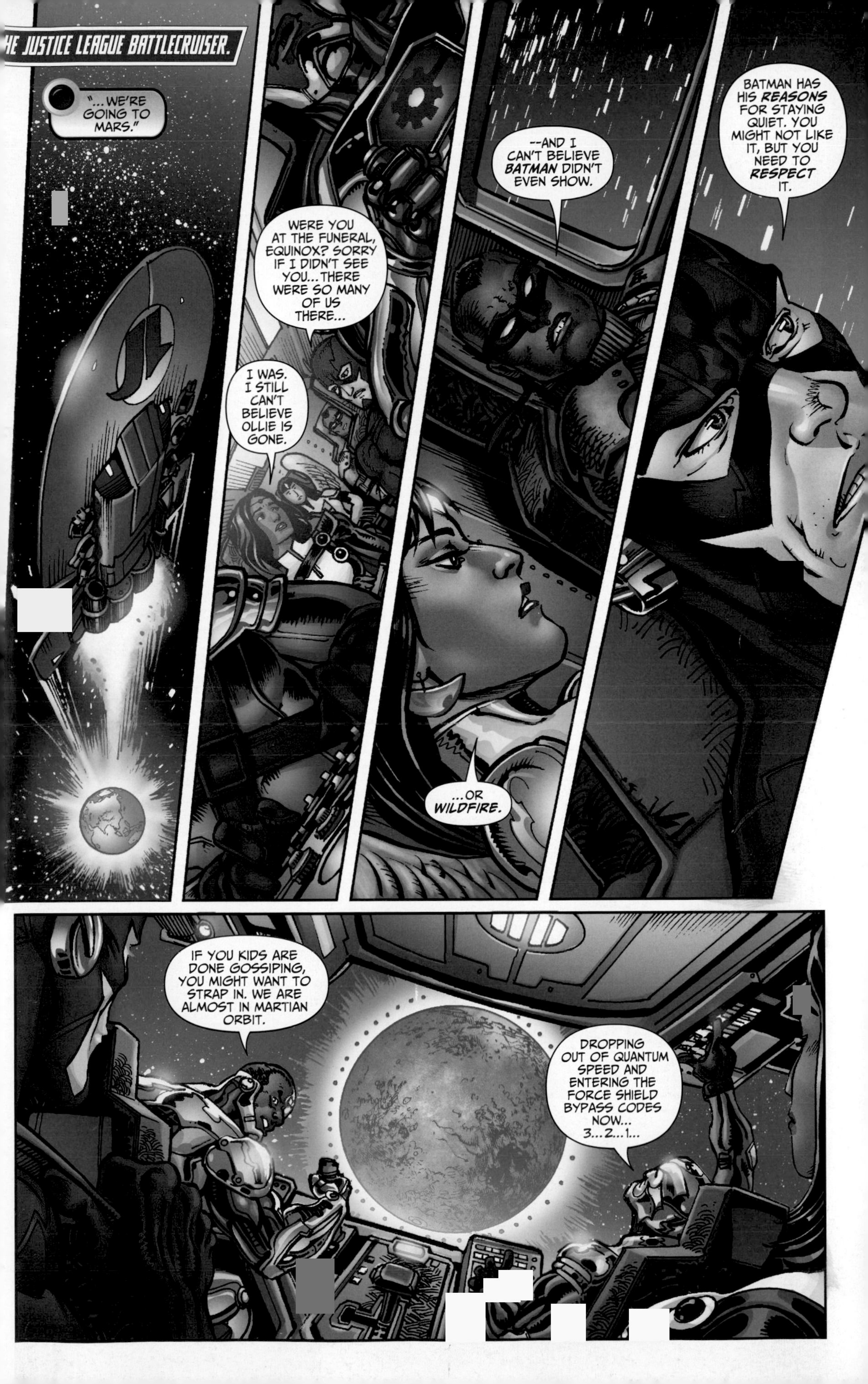

THE JUSTICE LEAGUE BATTLECRUISER.
"...WE'RE GOING TO MARS."
WERE YOU AT THE FUNERAL, EQUINOX? SORRY IF I DIDN'T SEE YOU...THERE WERE SO MANY OF US THERE...
I WAS. I STILL CAN'T BELIEVE OLLIE IS GONE.
--AND I CAN'T BELIEVE BATMAN DIDN'T EVEN SHOW.
...OR WILDFIRE.
BATMAN HAS HIS REASONS FOR STAYING QUIET. YOU MIGHT NOT LIKE IT, BUT YOU NEED TO RESPECT IT.
IF YOU KIDS ARE DONE GOSSIPING, YOU MIGHT WANT TO STRAP IN. WE ARE ALMOST IN MARTIAN ORBIT.
DROPPING OUT OF QUANTUM SPEED AND ENTERING THE FORCE SHIELD BYPASS CODES NOW... 3...2...1...

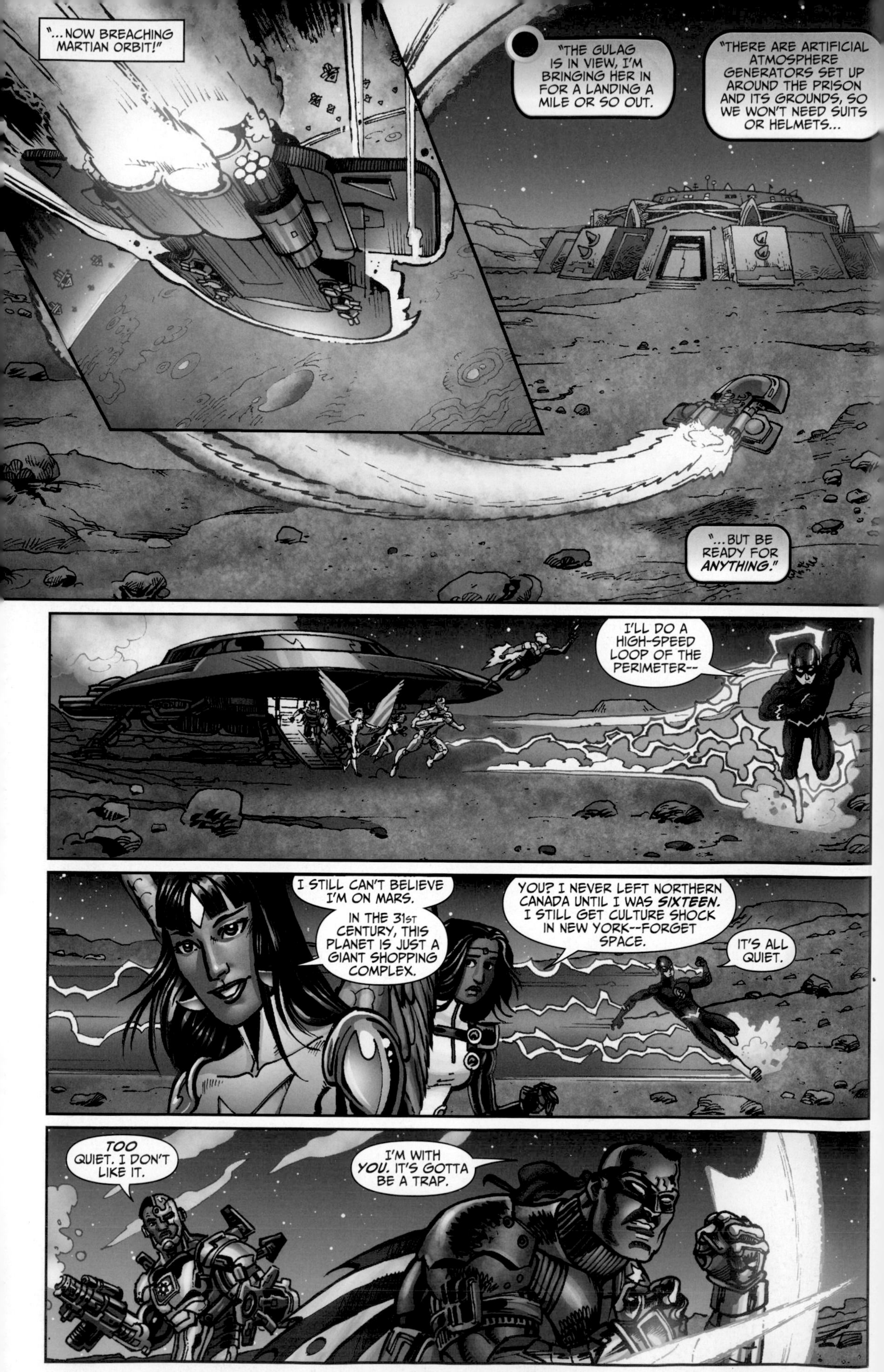
"...NOW BREACHING MARTIAN ORBIT!"
"THE GULAG IS IN VIEW, I'M BRINGING HER IN FOR A LANDING A MILE OR SO OUT.
"THERE ARE ARTIFICIAL ATMOSPHERE GENERATORS SET UP AROUND THE PRISON AND ITS GROUNDS, SO WE WON'T NEED SUITS OR HELMETS...
"...BUT BE READY FOR *ANYTHING*."
I'LL DO A HIGH-SPEED LOOP OF THE PERIMETER--
I STILL CAN'T BELIEVE I'M ON MARS.
IN THE 31ST CENTURY, THIS PLANET IS JUST A GIANT SHOPPING COMPLEX.
YOU? I NEVER LEFT NORTHERN CANADA UNTIL I WAS *SIXTEEN*. I STILL GET CULTURE SHOCK IN NEW YORK--FORGET SPACE.
IT'S ALL QUIET.
TOO QUIET. I DON'T LIKE IT.
I'M WITH *YOU*. IT'S GOTTA BE A TRAP.

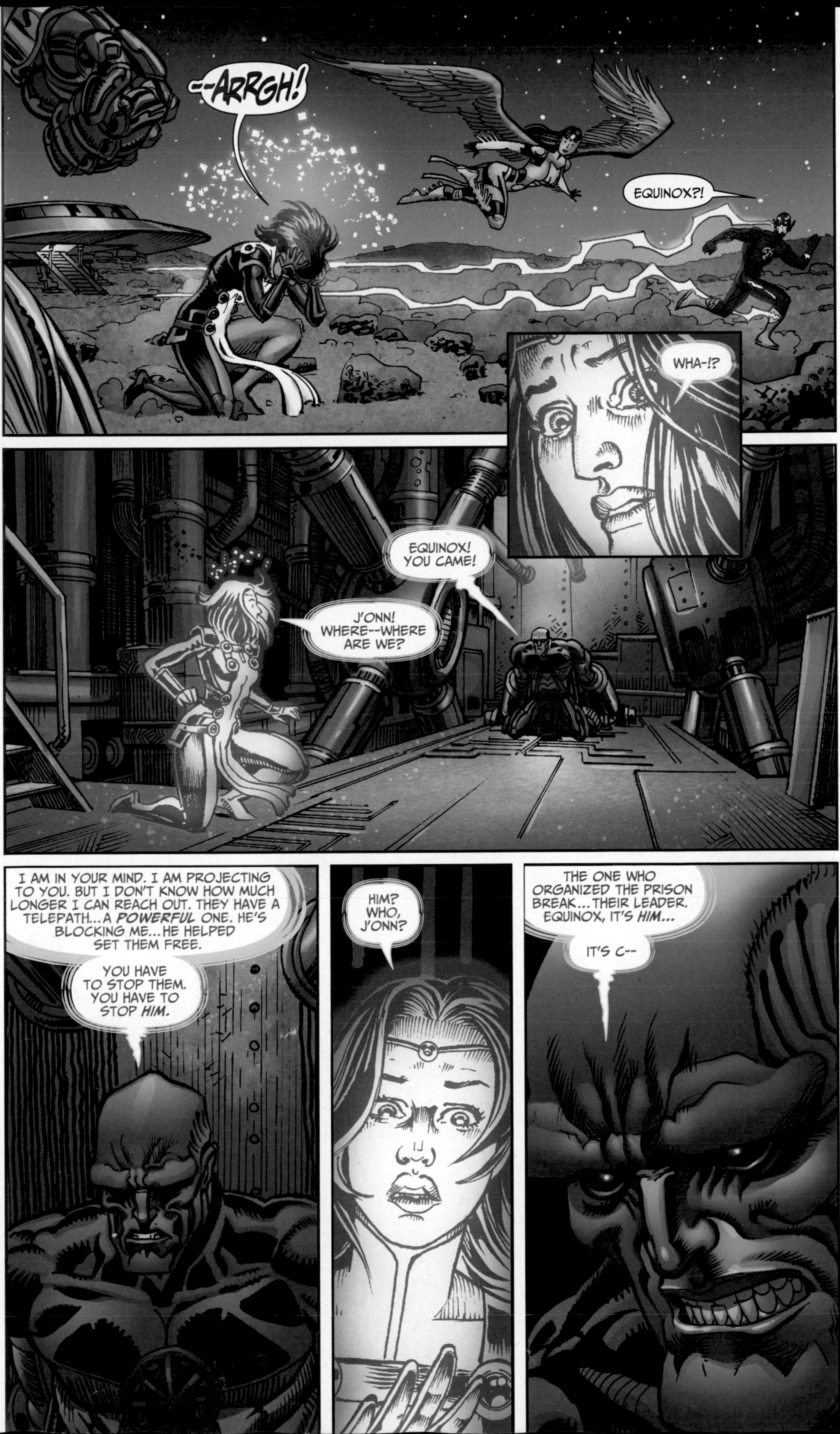
--ARRGH!
EQUINOX?!
WHA-!?
EQUINOX! YOU CAME!
J'ONN! WHERE--WHERE ARE WE?
I AM IN YOUR MIND. I AM PROJECTING TO YOU. BUT I DON'T KNOW HOW MUCH LONGER I CAN REACH OUT. THEY HAVE A TELEPATH...A POWERFUL ONE. HE'S BLOCKING ME...HE HELPED SET THEM FREE.
YOU HAVE TO STOP THEM. YOU HAVE TO STOP HIM.
HIM? WHO, J'ONN?
THE ONE WHO ORGANIZED THE PRISON BREAK...THEIR LEADER. EQUINOX, IT'S HIM...
IT'S C--

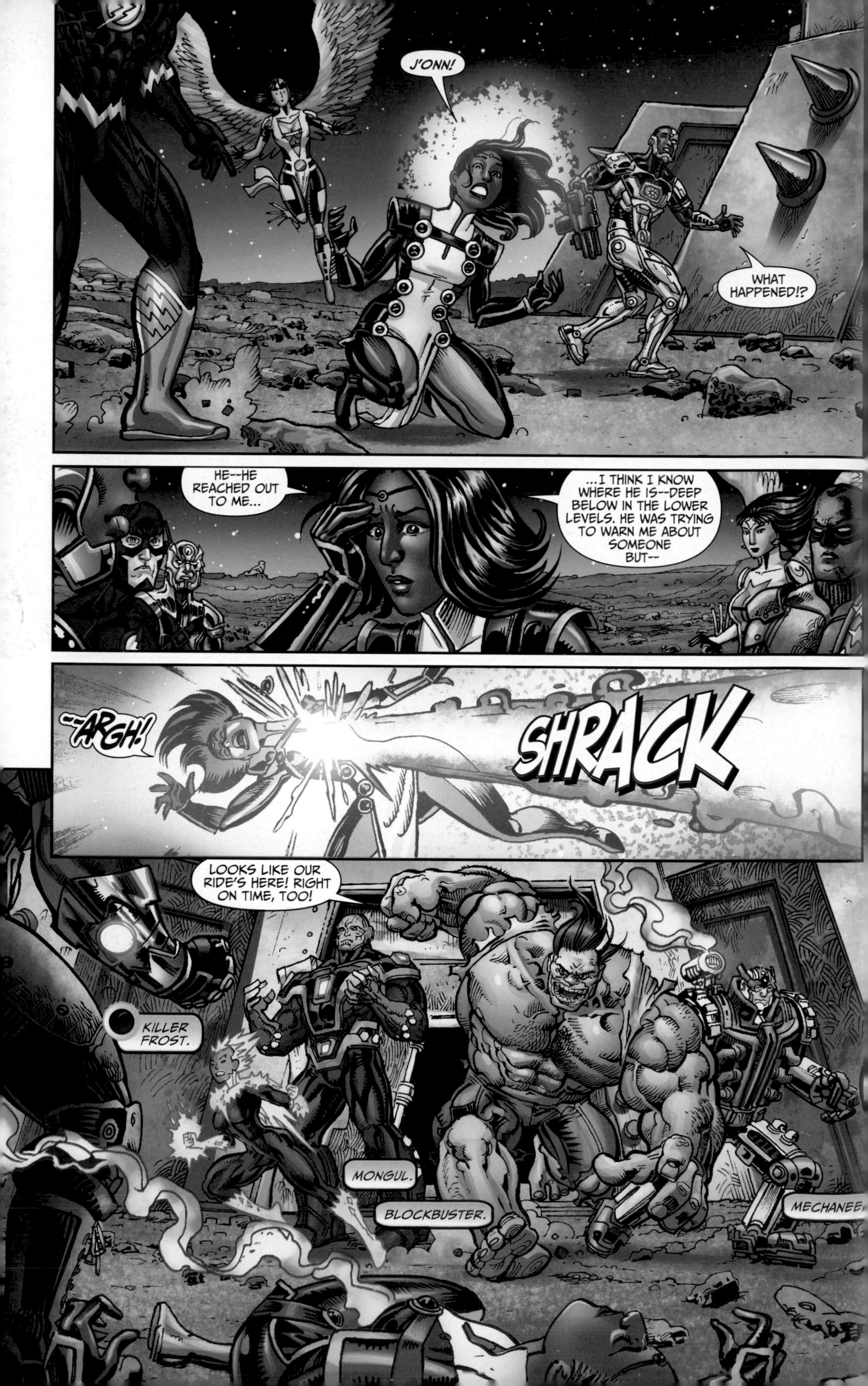
J'ONN!
WHAT HAPPENED!?
HE--HE REACHED OUT TO ME...
...I THINK I KNOW WHERE HE IS--DEEP BELOW IN THE LOWER LEVELS. HE WAS TRYING TO WARN ME ABOUT SOMEONE BUT--
--ARGH!
SHRACK
LOOKS LIKE OUR RIDE'S HERE! RIGHT ON TIME, TOO!
KILLER FROST.
MONGUL.
BLOCKBUSTER.
MECHANEER.

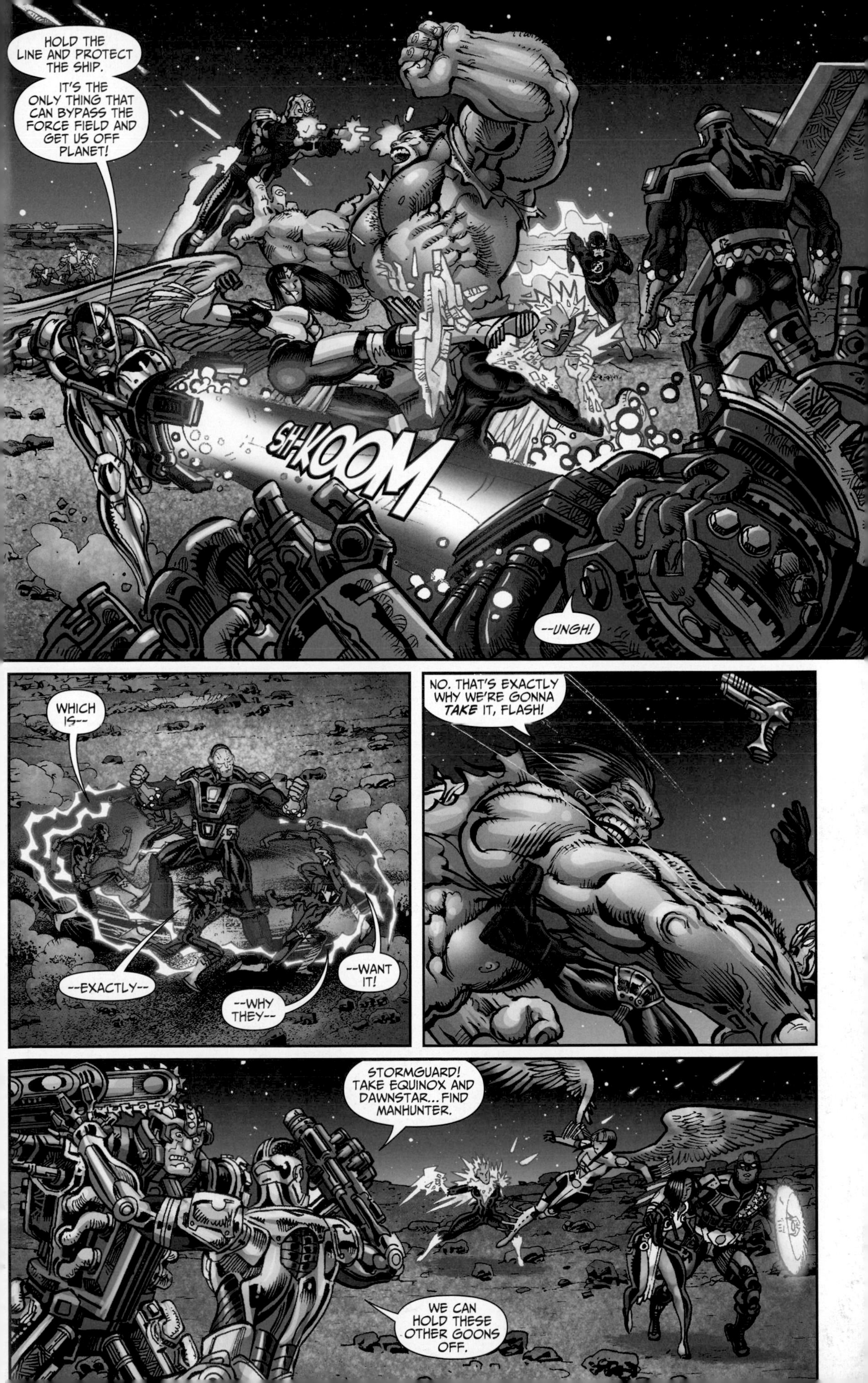
HOLD THE LINE AND PROTECT THE SHIP.
IT'S THE ONLY THING THAT CAN BYPASS THE FORCE FIELD AND GET US OFF PLANET!
SHKOOM
--UNGH!
WHICH IS--
--EXACTLY--
--WHY THEY--
--WANT IT!
NO. THAT'S EXACTLY WHY WE'RE GONNA *TAKE* IT, FLASH!
STORMGUARD! TAKE EQUINOX AND DAWNSTAR... FIND MANHUNTER.
WE CAN HOLD THESE OTHER GOONS OFF.

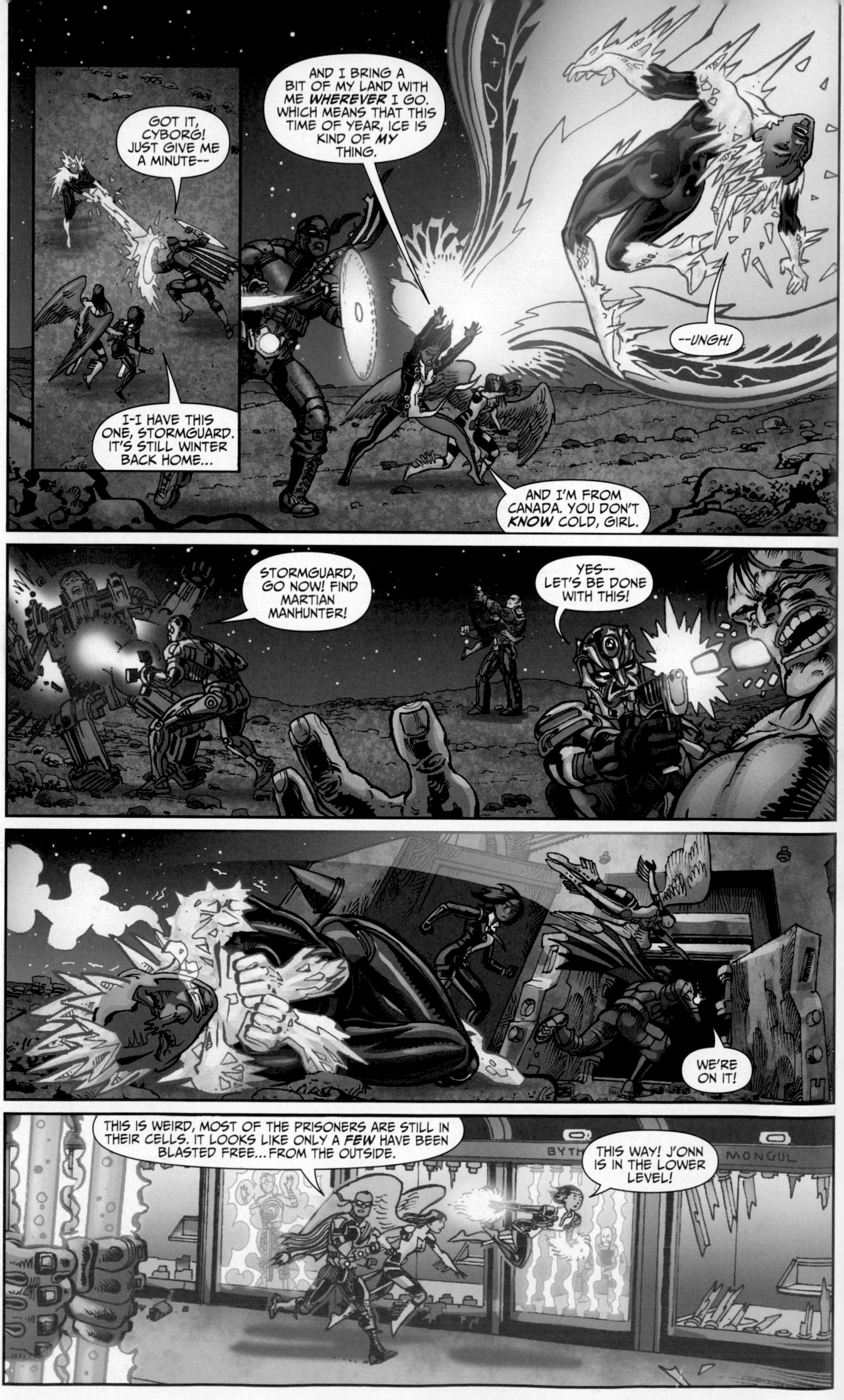
GOT IT, CYBORG! JUST GIVE ME A MINUTE--
I-I HAVE THIS ONE, STORMGUARD. IT'S STILL WINTER BACK HOME...
AND I BRING A BIT OF MY LAND WITH ME WHEREVER I GO. WHICH MEANS THAT THIS TIME OF YEAR, ICE IS KIND OF MY THING.
--UNGH!
AND I'M FROM CANADA. YOU DON'T KNOW COLD, GIRL.
STORMGUARD, GO NOW! FIND MARTIAN MANHUNTER!
YES-- LET'S BE DONE WITH THIS!
WE'RE ON IT!
THIS IS WEIRD, MOST OF THE PRISONERS ARE STILL IN THEIR CELLS. IT LOOKS LIKE ONLY A FEW HAVE BEEN BLASTED FREE...FROM THE OUTSIDE.
BYTH
THIS WAY! J'ONN IS IN THE LOWER LEVEL!
MONGUL

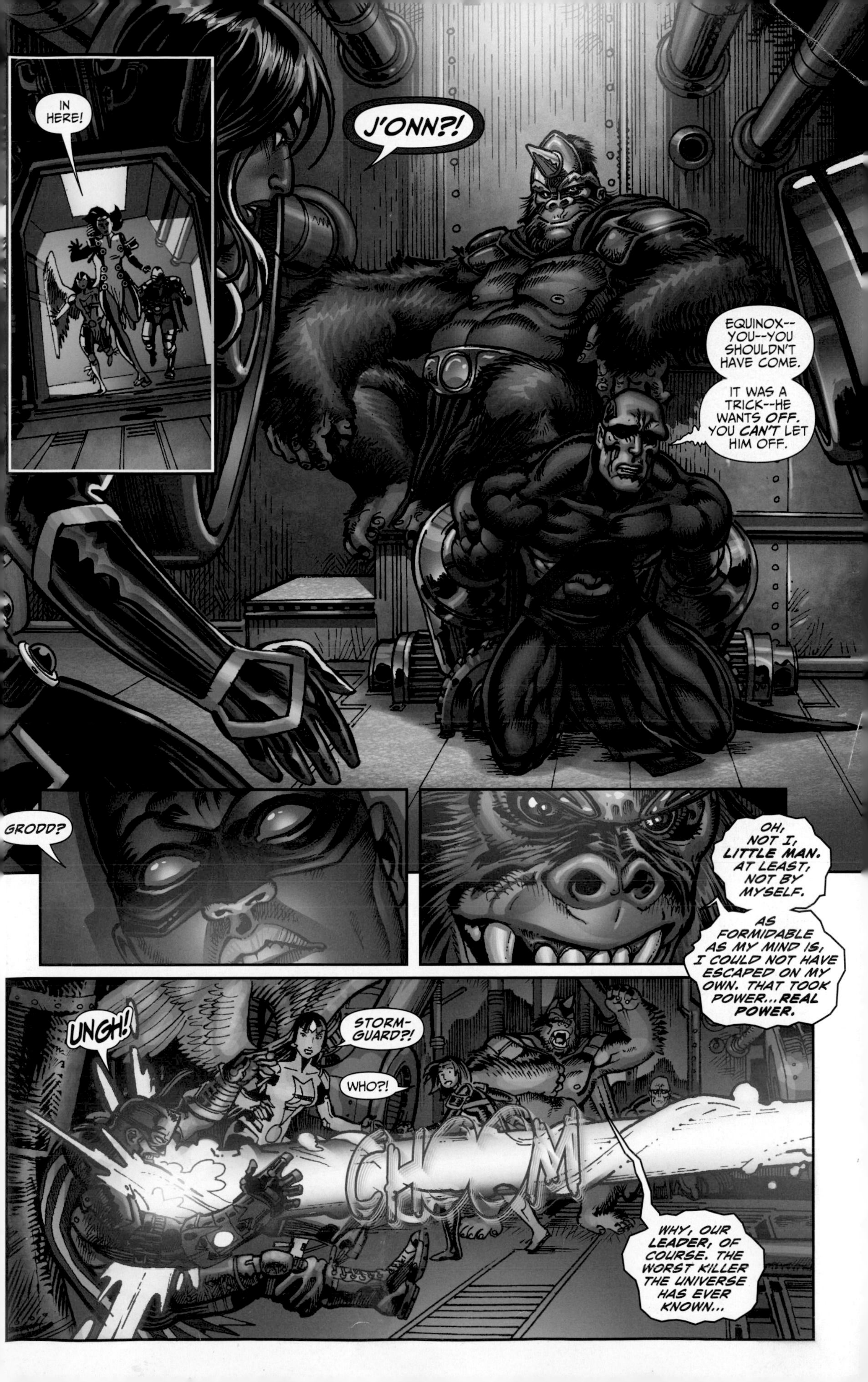
IN HERE!
J'ONN?!
EQUINOX--YOU--YOU SHOULDN'T HAVE COME.
IT WAS A TRICK--HE WANTS OFF. YOU CAN'T LET HIM OFF.
GRODD?
OH, NOT I, LITTLE MAN. AT LEAST, NOT BY MYSELF.
AS FORMIDABLE AS MY MIND IS, I COULD NOT HAVE ESCAPED ON MY OWN. THAT TOOK POWER...REAL POWER.
UNGH!
STORM-GUARD?!
WHO?!
CHOOM
WHY, OUR LEADER, OF COURSE. THE WORST KILLER THE UNIVERSE HAS EVER KNOWN...

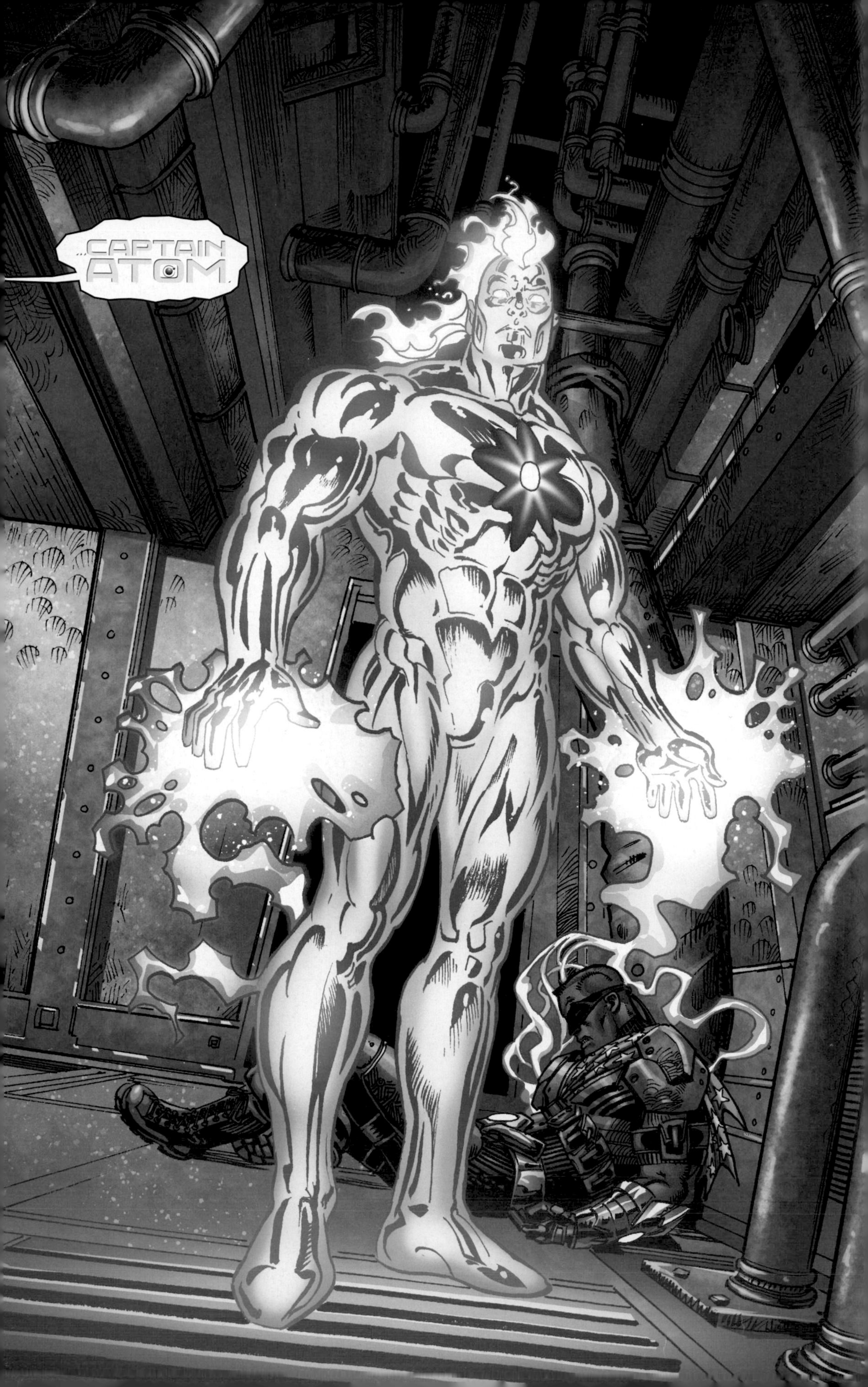
...CAPTAIN ATOM.

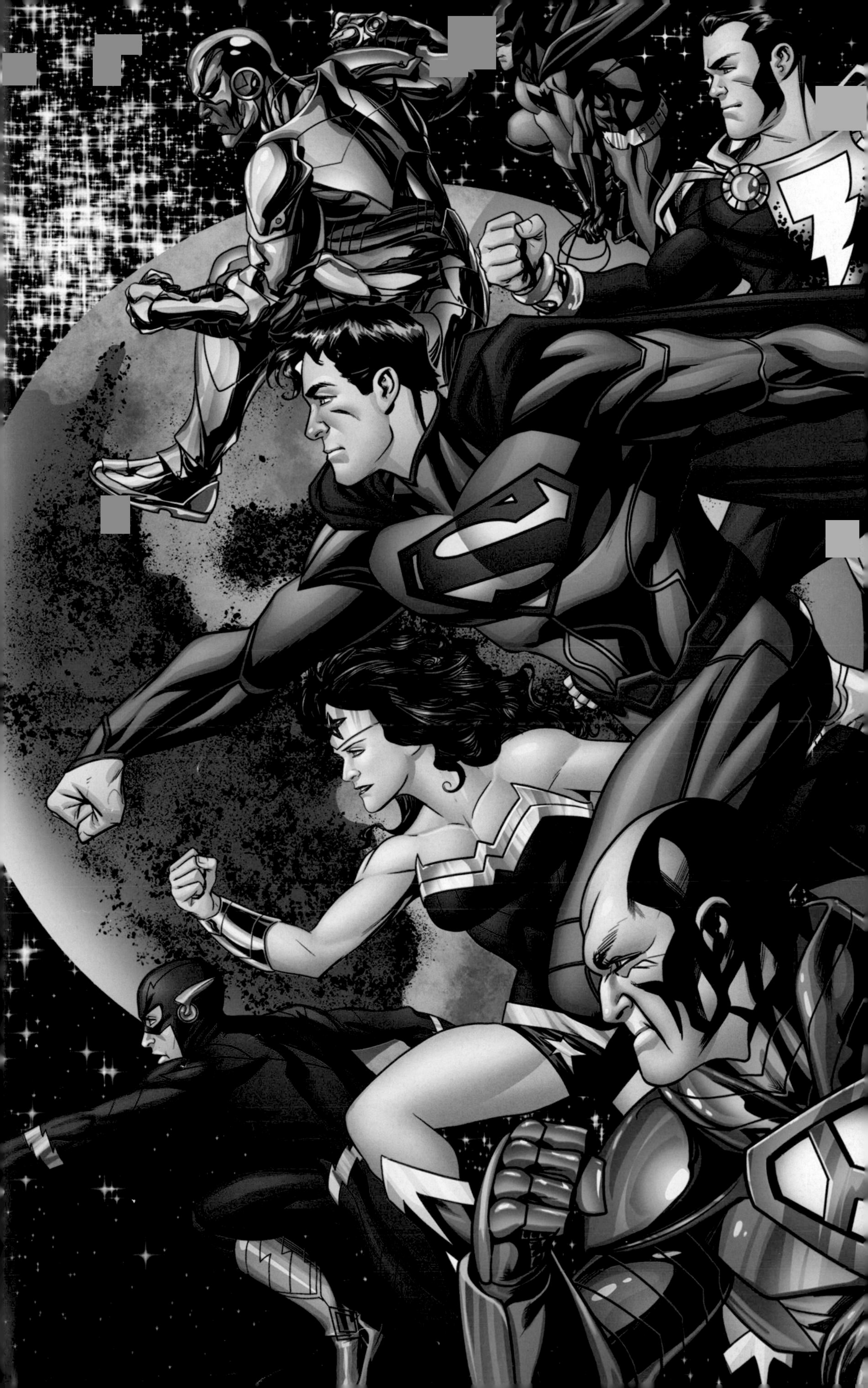

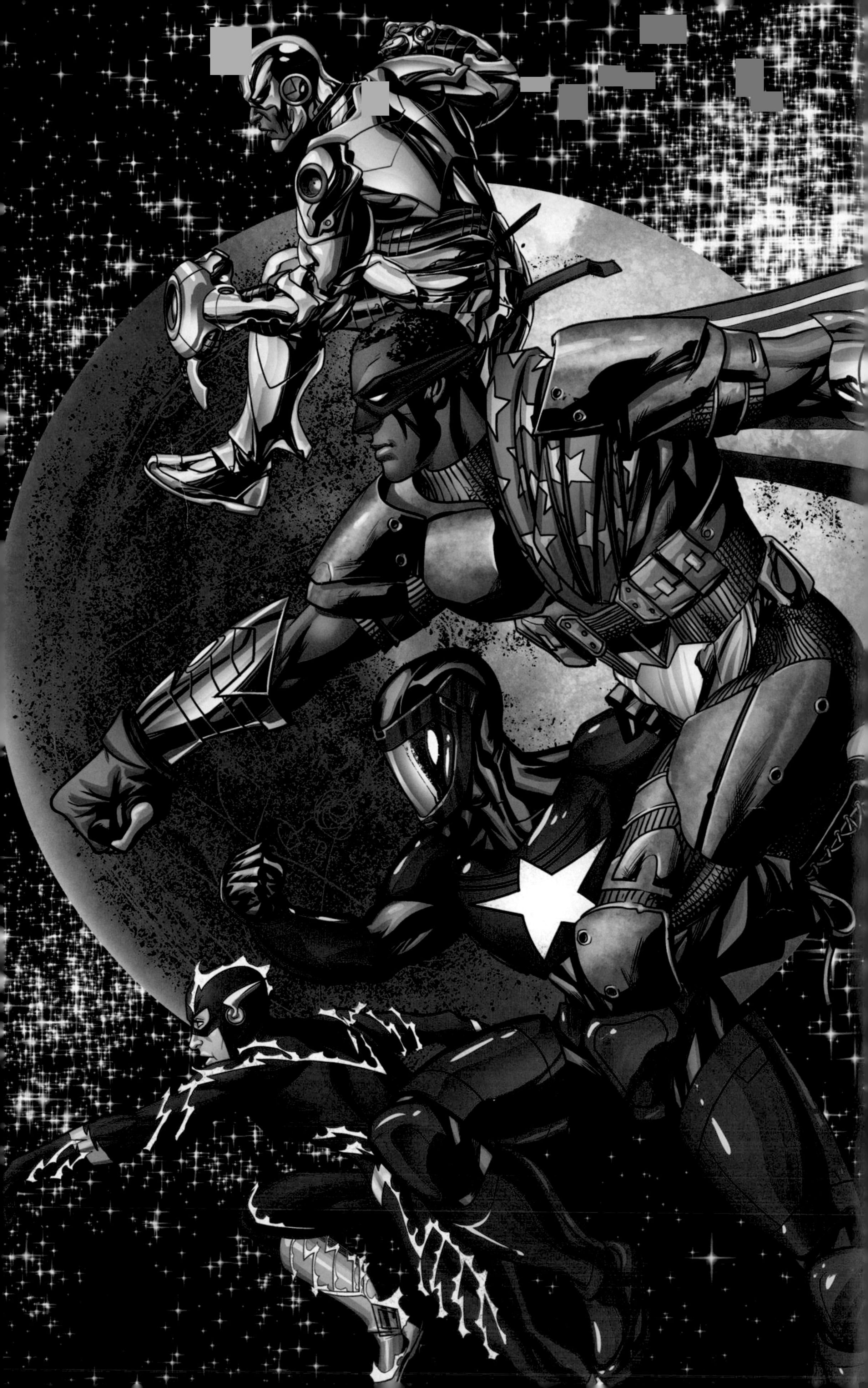

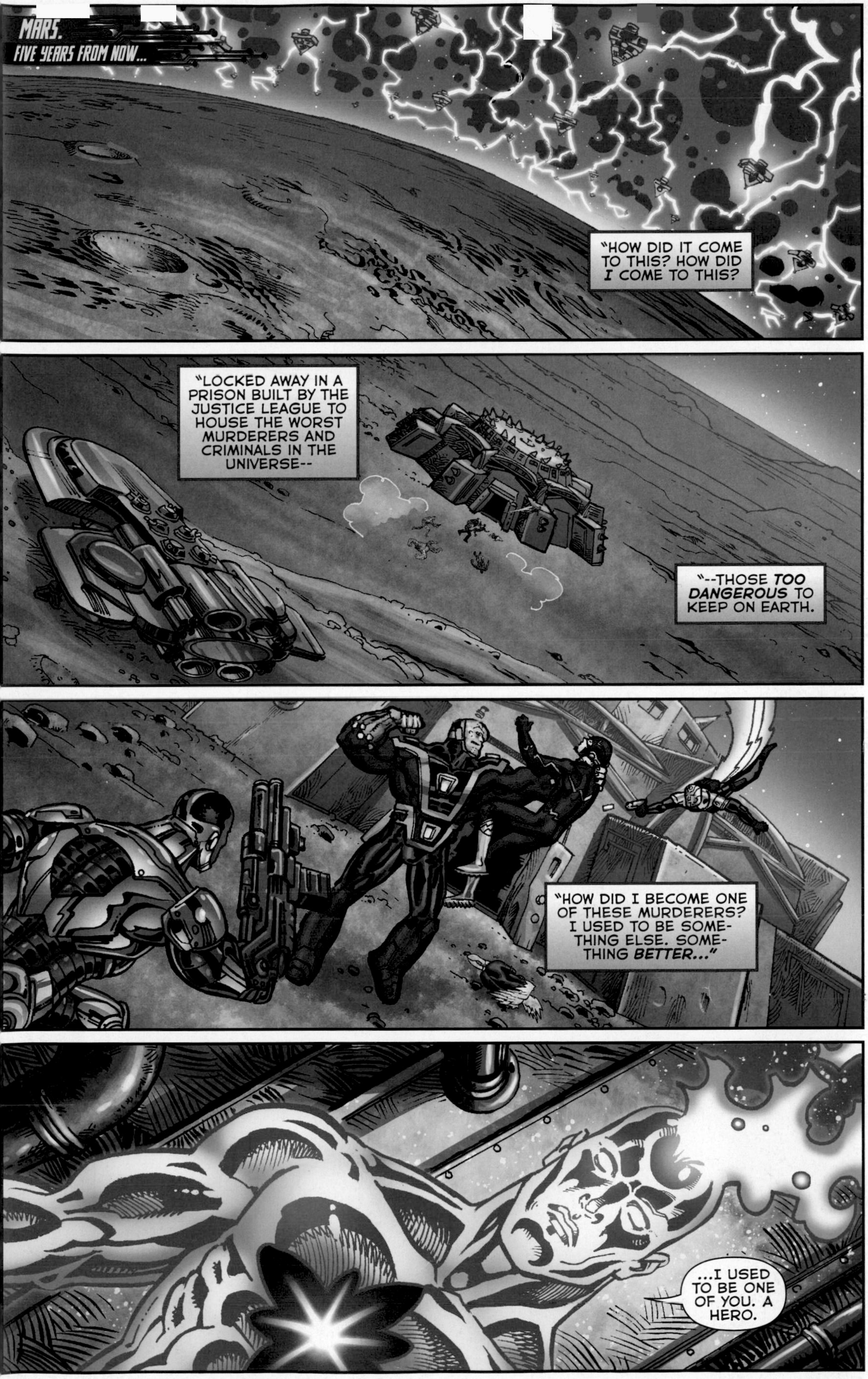
MARS.
FIVE YEARS FROM NOW...
"HOW DID IT COME TO THIS? HOW DID I COME TO THIS?
"LOCKED AWAY IN A PRISON BUILT BY THE JUSTICE LEAGUE TO HOUSE THE WORST MURDERERS AND CRIMINALS IN THE UNIVERSE--
"--THOSE TOO DANGEROUS TO KEEP ON EARTH.
"HOW DID I BECOME ONE OF THESE MURDERERS? I USED TO BE SOMETHING ELSE. SOMETHING BETTER..."
...I USED TO BE ONE OF YOU. A HERO.

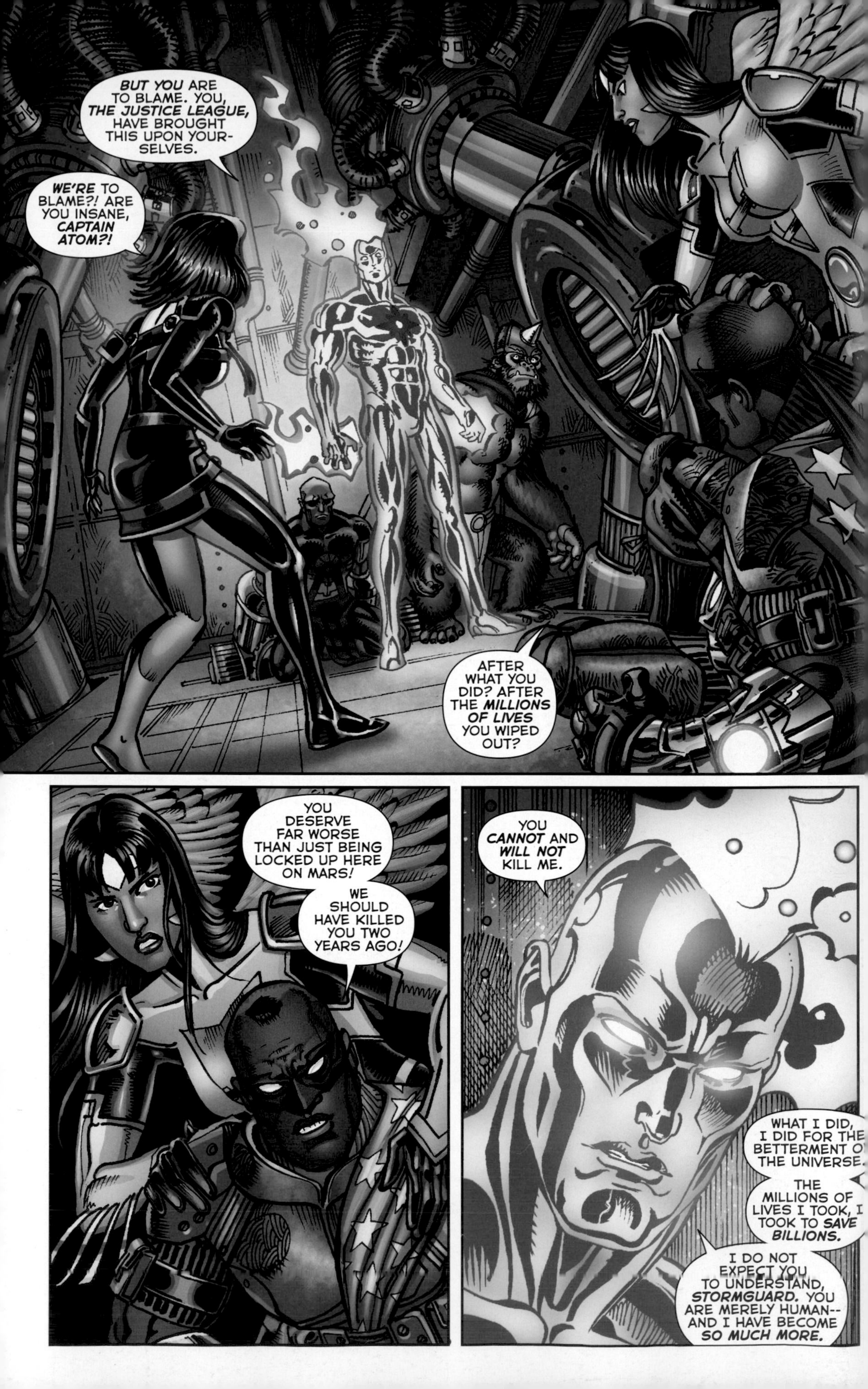
BUT YOU ARE TO BLAME. YOU, THE JUSTICE LEAGUE, HAVE BROUGHT THIS UPON YOURSELVES.
WE'RE TO BLAME?! ARE YOU INSANE, CAPTAIN ATOM?!
AFTER WHAT YOU DID? AFTER THE MILLIONS OF LIVES YOU WIPED OUT?
YOU DESERVE FAR WORSE THAN JUST BEING LOCKED UP HERE ON MARS!
WE SHOULD HAVE KILLED YOU TWO YEARS AGO!
YOU CANNOT AND WILL NOT KILL ME.
WHAT I DID, I DID FOR THE BETTERMENT O THE UNIVERSE.
THE MILLIONS OF LIVES I TOOK, I TOOK TO SAVE BILLIONS.
I DO NOT EXPECT YOU TO UNDERSTAND, STORMGUARD. YOU ARE MERELY HUMAN-- AND I HAVE BECOME SO MUCH MORE.

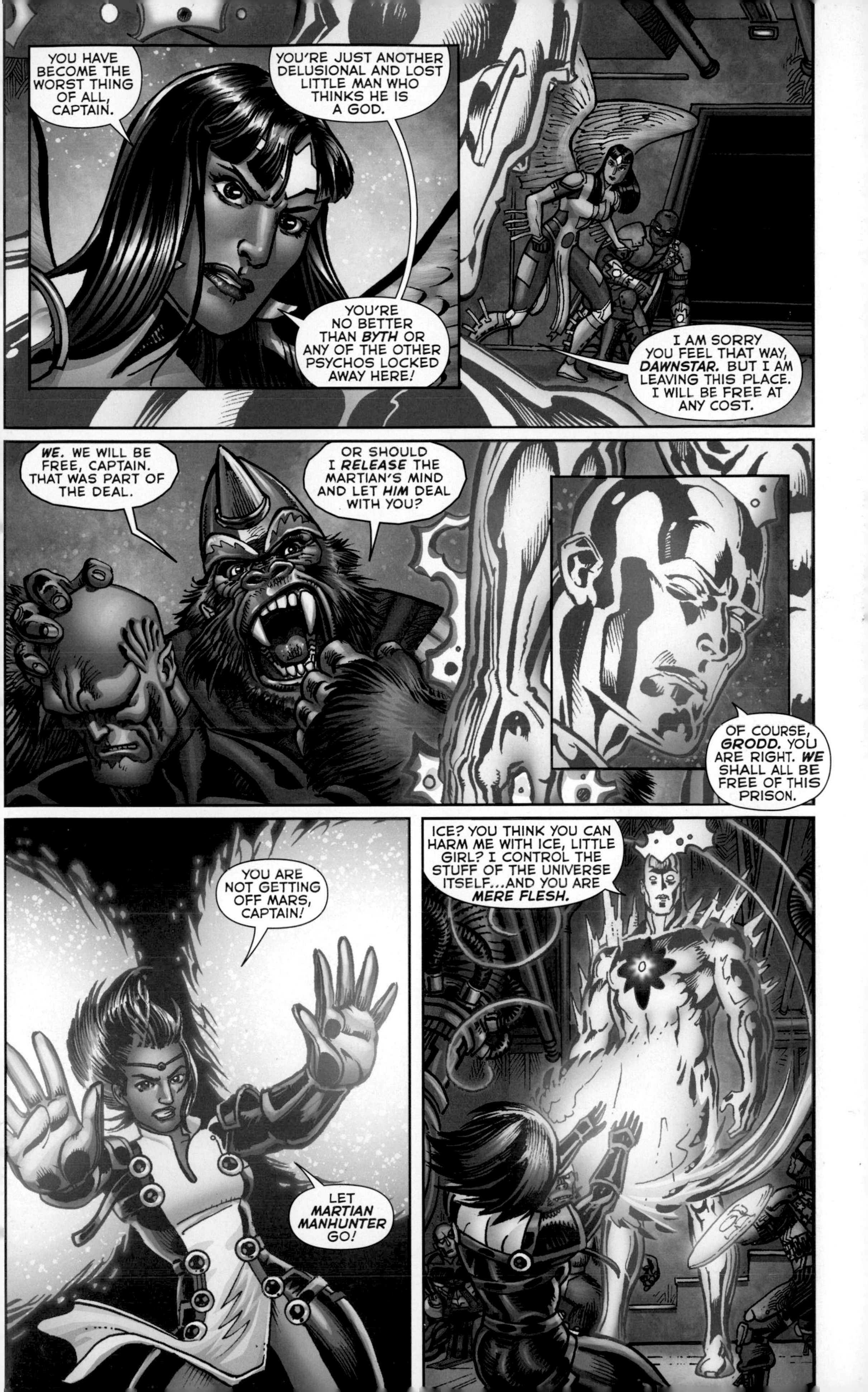
YOU HAVE BECOME THE WORST THING OF ALL, CAPTAIN.
YOU'RE JUST ANOTHER DELUSIONAL AND LOST LITTLE MAN WHO THINKS HE IS A GOD.
YOU'RE NO BETTER THAN BYTH OR ANY OF THE OTHER PSYCHOS LOCKED AWAY HERE!
I AM SORRY YOU FEEL THAT WAY, DAWNSTAR. BUT I AM LEAVING THIS PLACE. I WILL BE FREE AT ANY COST.
WE. WE WILL BE FREE, CAPTAIN. THAT WAS PART OF THE DEAL.
OR SHOULD I RELEASE THE MARTIAN'S MIND AND LET HIM DEAL WITH YOU?
OF COURSE, GRODD. YOU ARE RIGHT. WE SHALL ALL BE FREE OF THIS PRISON.
YOU ARE NOT GETTING OFF MARS, CAPTAIN!
LET MARTIAN MANHUNTER GO!
ICE? YOU THINK YOU CAN HARM ME WITH ICE, LITTLE GIRL? I CONTROL THE STUFF OF THE UNIVERSE ITSELF...AND YOU ARE MERE FLESH.

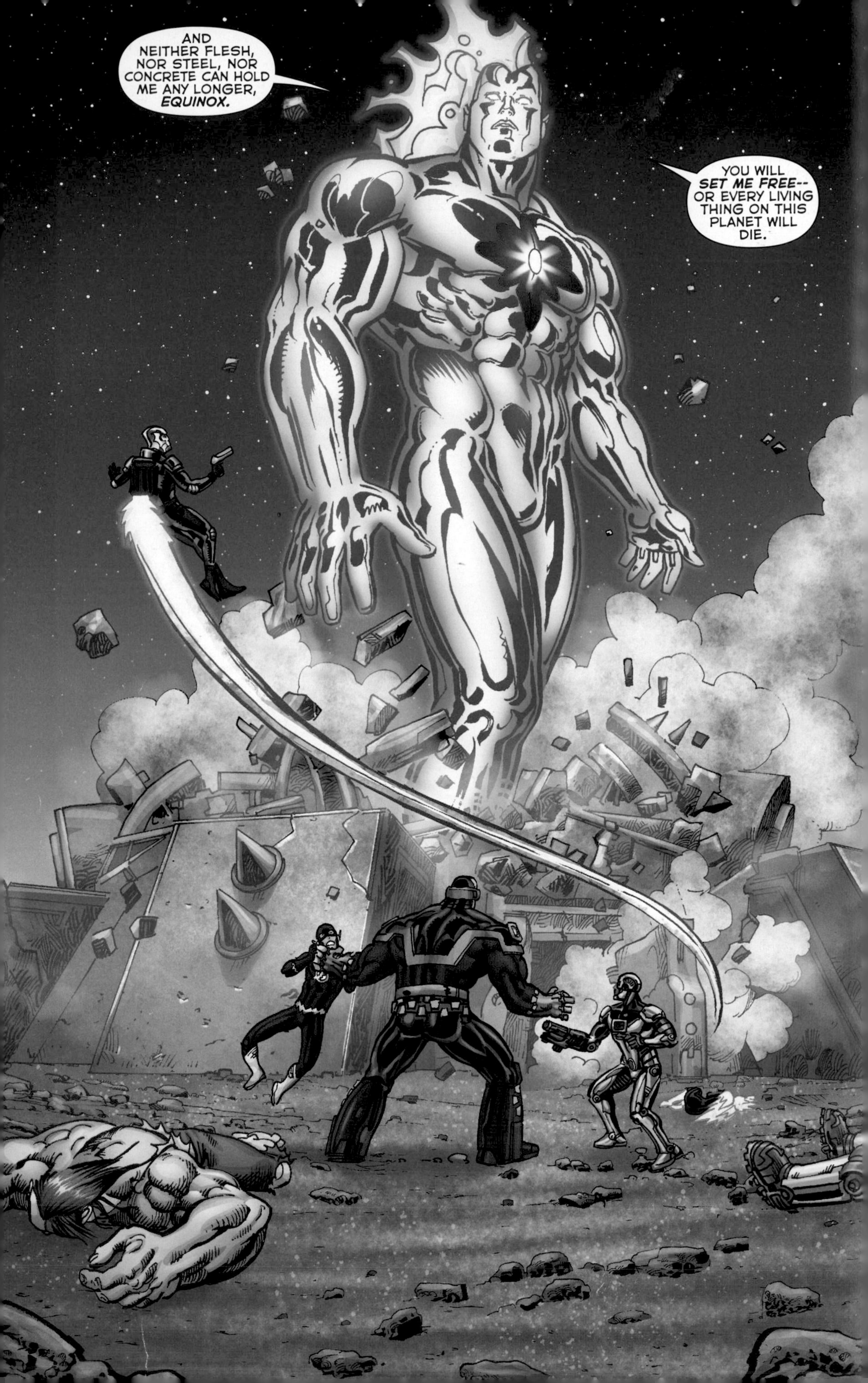
AND NEITHER FLESH, NOR STEEL, NOR CONCRETE CAN HOLD ME ANY LONGER, *EQUINOX.*
YOU WILL *SET ME FREE*-- OR EVERY LIVING THING ON THIS PLANET WILL DIE.

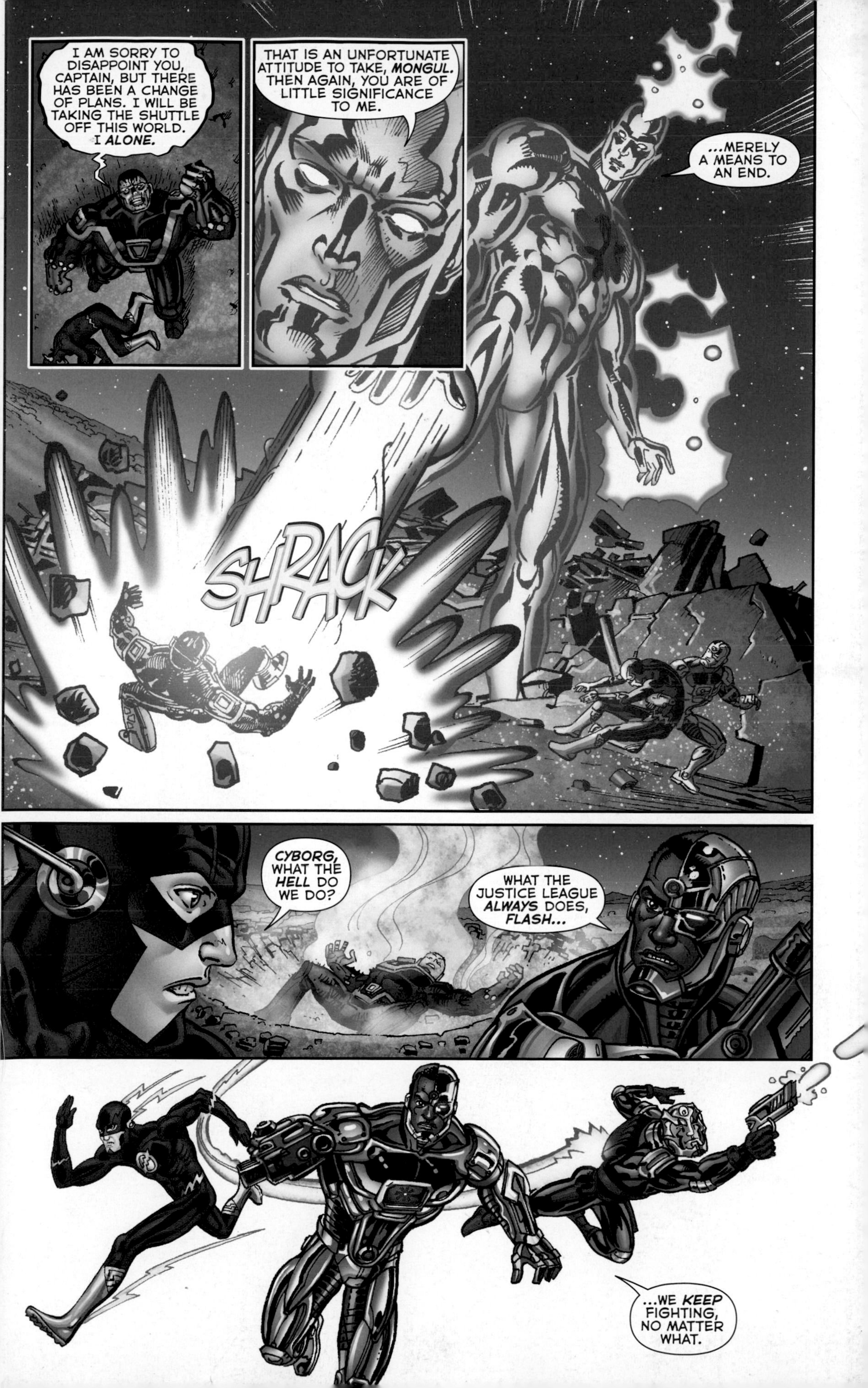
I AM SORRY TO DISAPPOINT YOU, CAPTAIN, BUT THERE HAS BEEN A CHANGE OF PLANS. I WILL BE TAKING THE SHUTTLE OFF THIS WORLD. I *ALONE.*
THAT IS AN UNFORTUNATE ATTITUDE TO TAKE, *MONGUL.* THEN AGAIN, YOU ARE OF LITTLE SIGNIFICANCE TO ME.
...MERELY A MEANS TO AN END.
SHRACK
CYBORG, WHAT THE *HELL* DO WE DO?
WHAT THE JUSTICE LEAGUE *ALWAYS* DOES, *FLASH...*
...WE *KEEP* FIGHTING, NO MATTER WHAT.

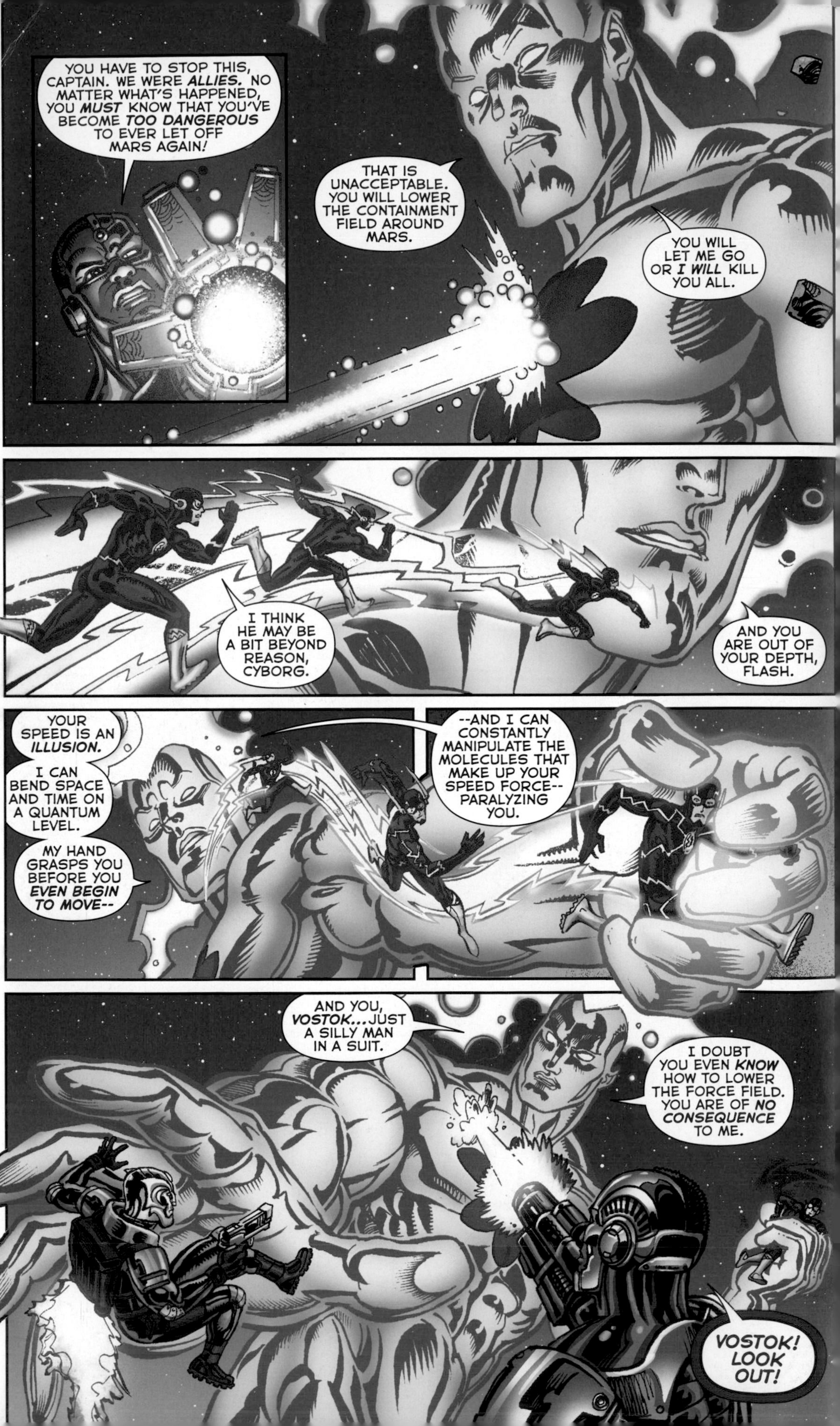
YOU HAVE TO STOP THIS, CAPTAIN. WE WERE ALLIES. NO MATTER WHAT'S HAPPENED, YOU MUST KNOW THAT YOU'VE BECOME TOO DANGEROUS TO EVER LET OFF MARS AGAIN!
THAT IS UNACCEPTABLE. YOU WILL LOWER THE CONTAINMENT FIELD AROUND MARS.
YOU WILL LET ME GO OR I WILL KILL YOU ALL.
I THINK HE MAY BE A BIT BEYOND REASON, CYBORG.
AND YOU ARE OUT OF YOUR DEPTH, FLASH.
YOUR SPEED IS AN ILLUSION.
I CAN BEND SPACE AND TIME ON A QUANTUM LEVEL.
MY HAND GRASPS YOU BEFORE YOU EVEN BEGIN TO MOVE--
--AND I CAN CONSTANTLY MANIPULATE THE MOLECULES THAT MAKE UP YOUR SPEED FORCE--PARALYZING YOU.
AND YOU, VOSTOK...JUST A SILLY MAN IN A SUIT.
I DOUBT YOU EVEN KNOW HOW TO LOWER THE FORCE FIELD. YOU ARE OF NO CONSEQUENCE TO ME.
VOSTOK! LOOK OUT!

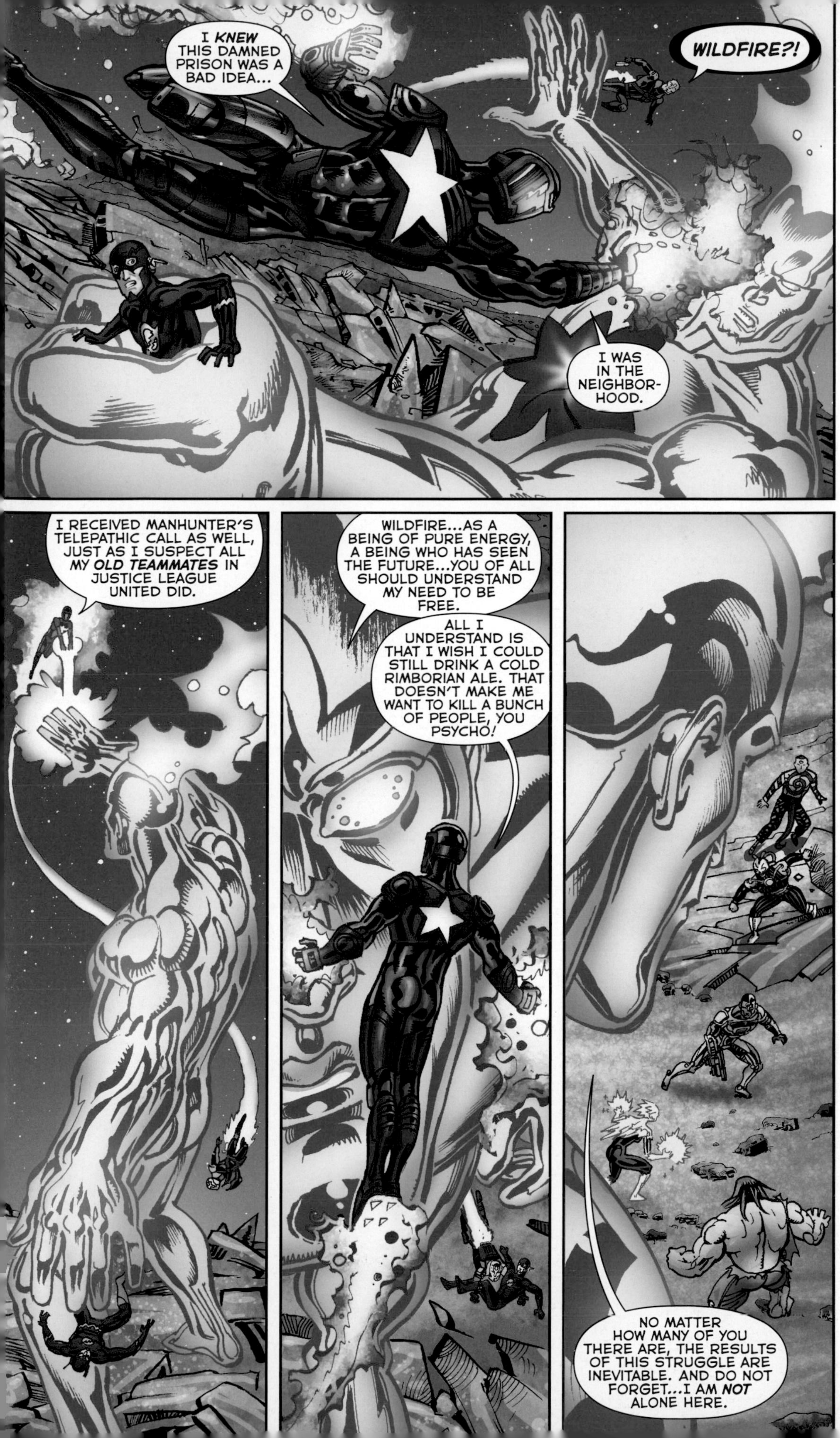
I KNEW THIS DAMNED PRISON WAS A BAD IDEA...
WILDFIRE?!
I WAS IN THE NEIGHBOR-HOOD.
I RECEIVED MANHUNTER'S TELEPATHIC CALL AS WELL, JUST AS I SUSPECT ALL MY OLD TEAMMATES IN JUSTICE LEAGUE UNITED DID.
WILDFIRE...AS A BEING OF PURE ENERGY, A BEING WHO HAS SEEN THE FUTURE...YOU OF ALL SHOULD UNDERSTAND MY NEED TO BE FREE.
ALL I UNDERSTAND IS THAT I WISH I COULD STILL DRINK A COLD RIMBORIAN ALE. THAT DOESN'T MAKE ME WANT TO KILL A BUNCH OF PEOPLE, YOU PSYCHO!
NO MATTER HOW MANY OF YOU THERE ARE, THE RESULTS OF THIS STRUGGLE ARE INEVITABLE. AND DO NOT FORGET...I AM NOT ALONE HERE.

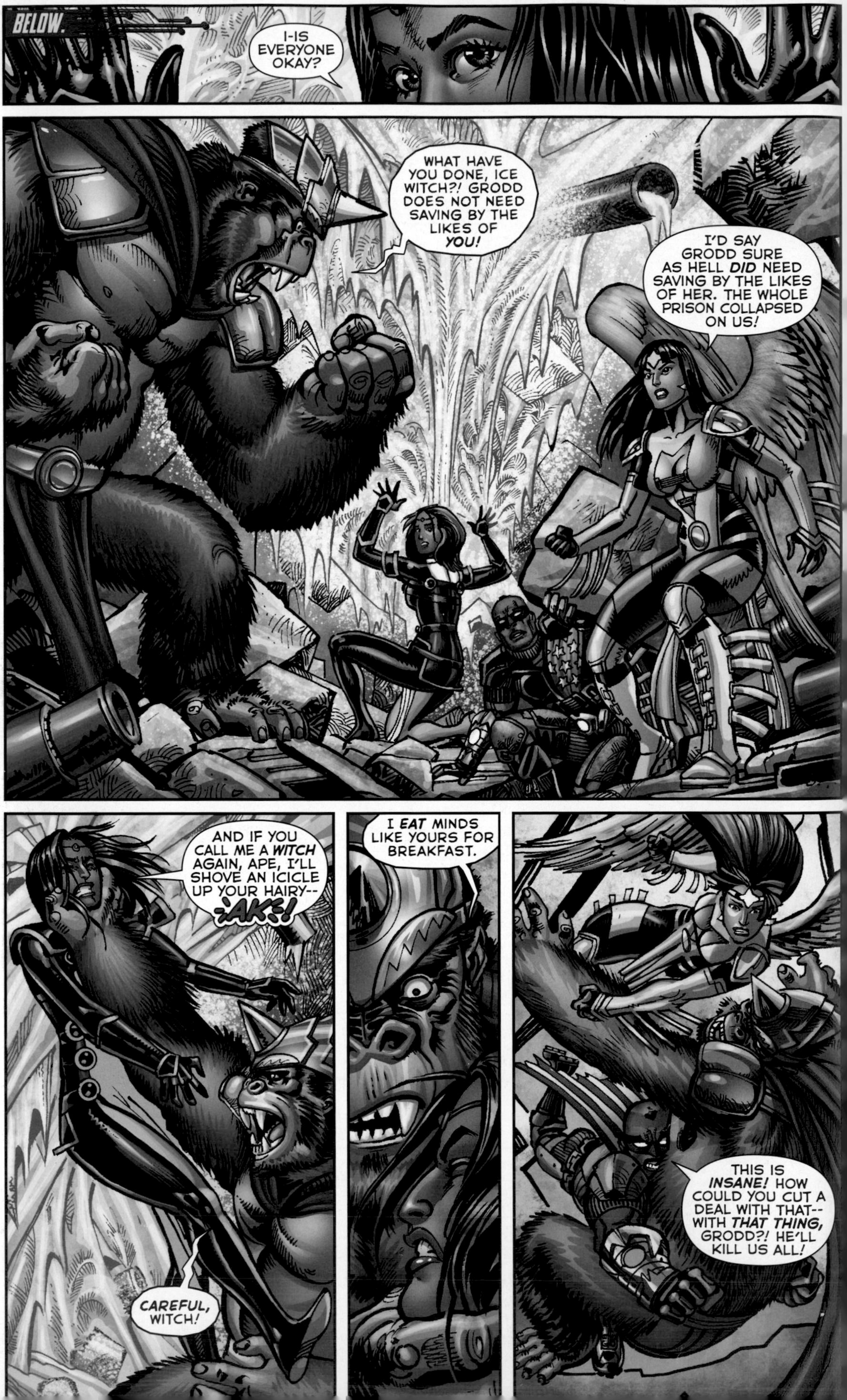
BELOW.
I-IS EVERYONE OKAY?
WHAT HAVE YOU DONE, ICE WITCH?! GRODD DOES NOT NEED SAVING BY THE LIKES OF YOU!
I'D SAY GRODD SURE AS HELL DID NEED SAVING BY THE LIKES OF HER. THE WHOLE PRISON COLLAPSED ON US!
AND IF YOU CALL ME A WITCH AGAIN, APE, I'LL SHOVE AN ICICLE UP YOUR HAIRY--
¡AK!
CAREFUL, WITCH!
I EAT MINDS LIKE YOURS FOR BREAKFAST.
THIS IS INSANE! HOW COULD YOU CUT A DEAL WITH THAT-- WITH THAT THING, GRODD?! HE'LL KILL US ALL!

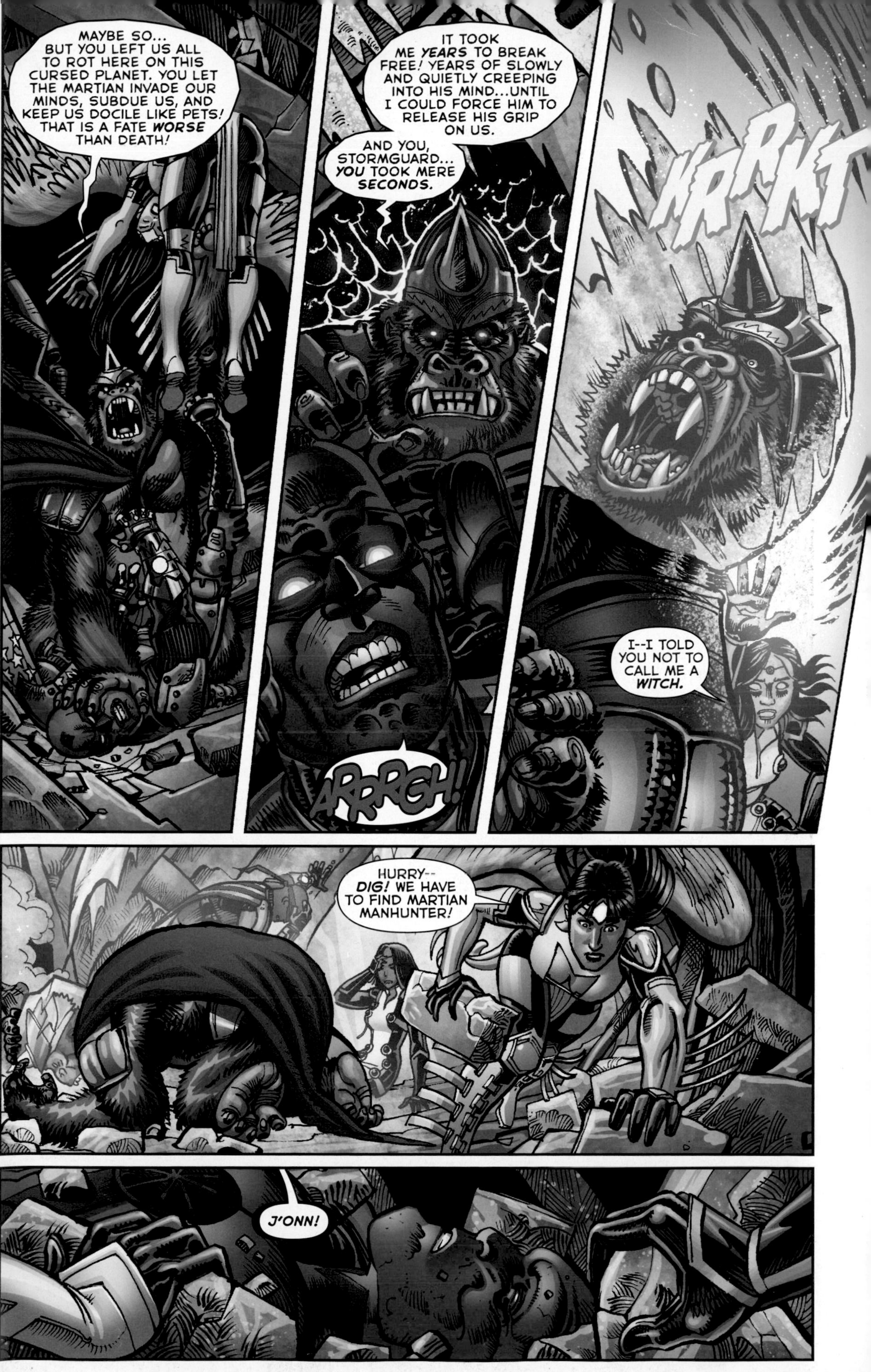
MAYBE SO... BUT YOU LEFT US ALL TO ROT HERE ON THIS CURSED PLANET. YOU LET THE MARTIAN INVADE OUR MINDS, SUBDUE US, AND KEEP US DOCILE LIKE PETS! THAT IS A FATE WORSE THAN DEATH!
IT TOOK ME YEARS TO BREAK FREE! YEARS OF SLOWLY AND QUIETLY CREEPING INTO HIS MIND...UNTIL I COULD FORCE HIM TO RELEASE HIS GRIP ON US.
AND YOU, STORMGUARD... YOU TOOK MERE SECONDS.
ARRRGH!
KRRKT
I--I TOLD YOU NOT TO CALL ME A WITCH.
HURRY-- DIG! WE HAVE TO FIND MARTIAN MANHUNTER!
J'ONN!

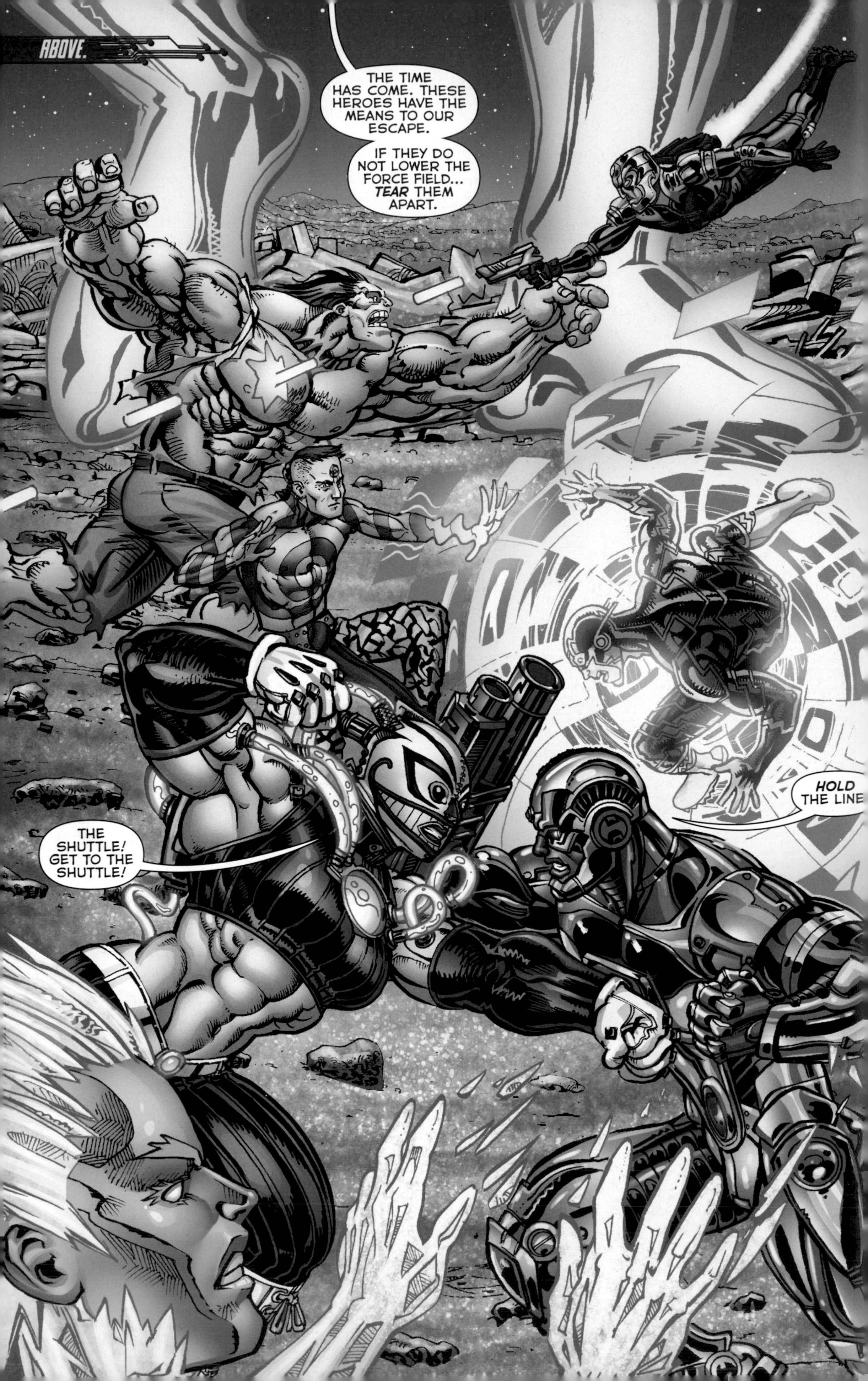
ABOVE.
THE TIME HAS COME. THESE HEROES HAVE THE MEANS TO OUR ESCAPE.
IF THEY DO NOT LOWER THE FORCE FIELD... TEAR THEM APART.
HOLD THE LINE
THE SHUTTLE! GET TO THE SHUTTLE!

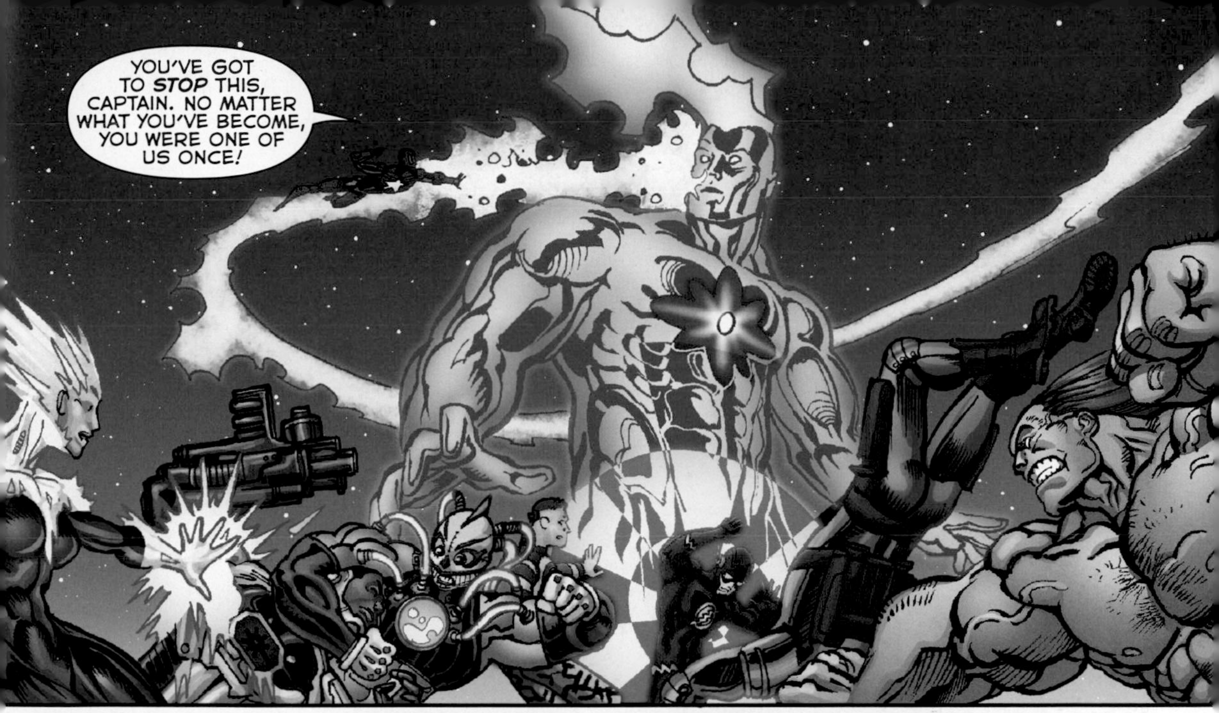
YOU'VE GOT TO STOP THIS, CAPTAIN. NO MATTER WHAT YOU'VE BECOME, YOU WERE ONE OF US ONCE!

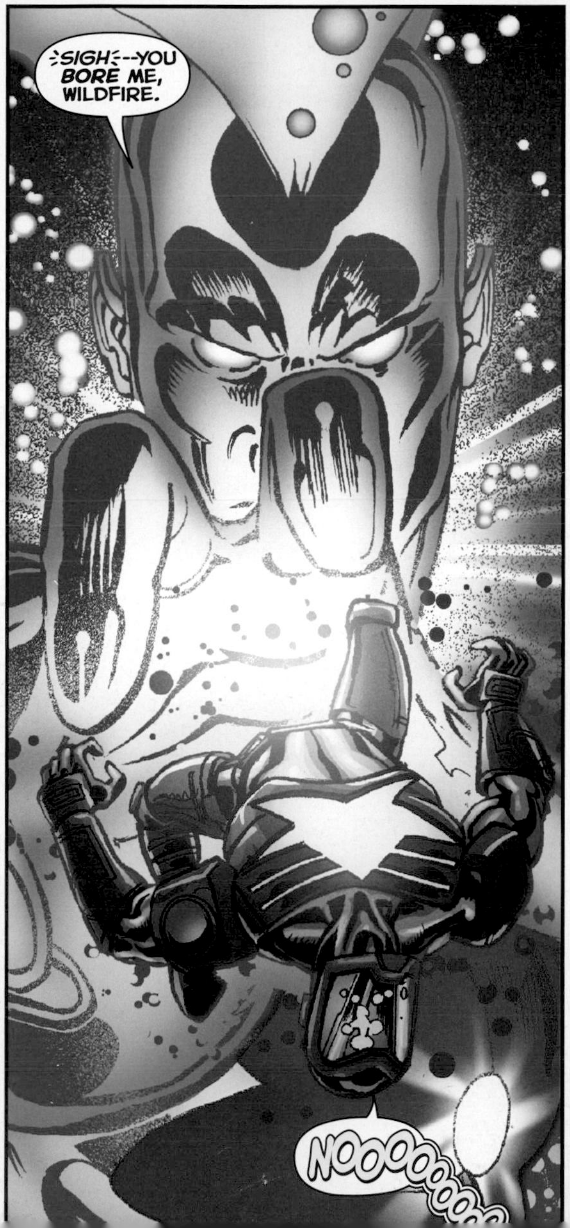
SIGH--YOU BORE ME, WILDFIRE.
NOOOOOOOO

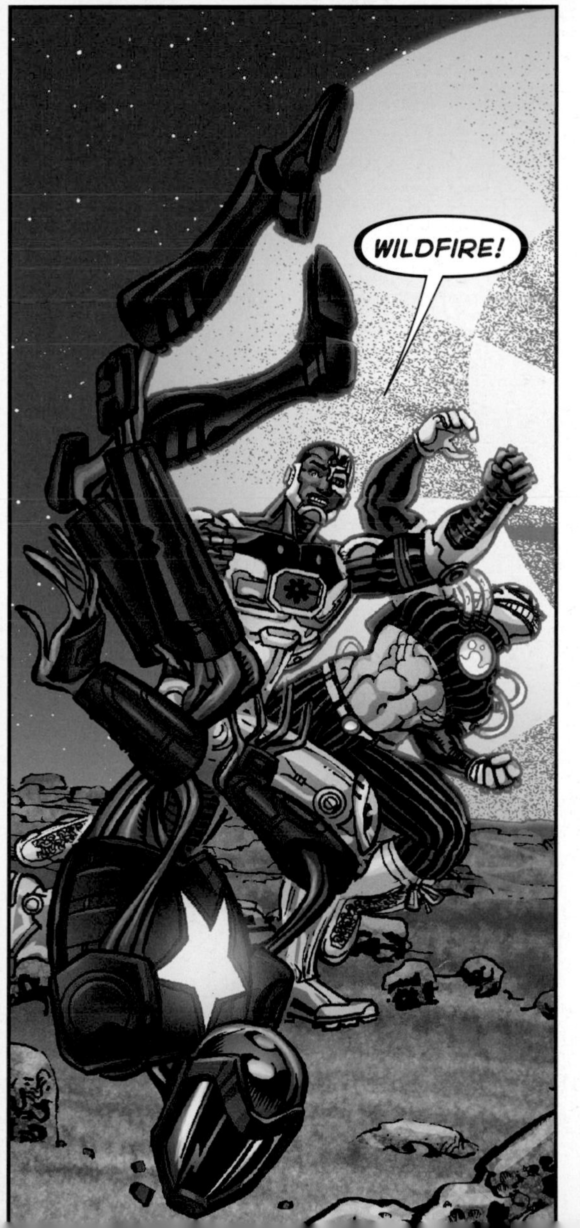
WILDFIRE!

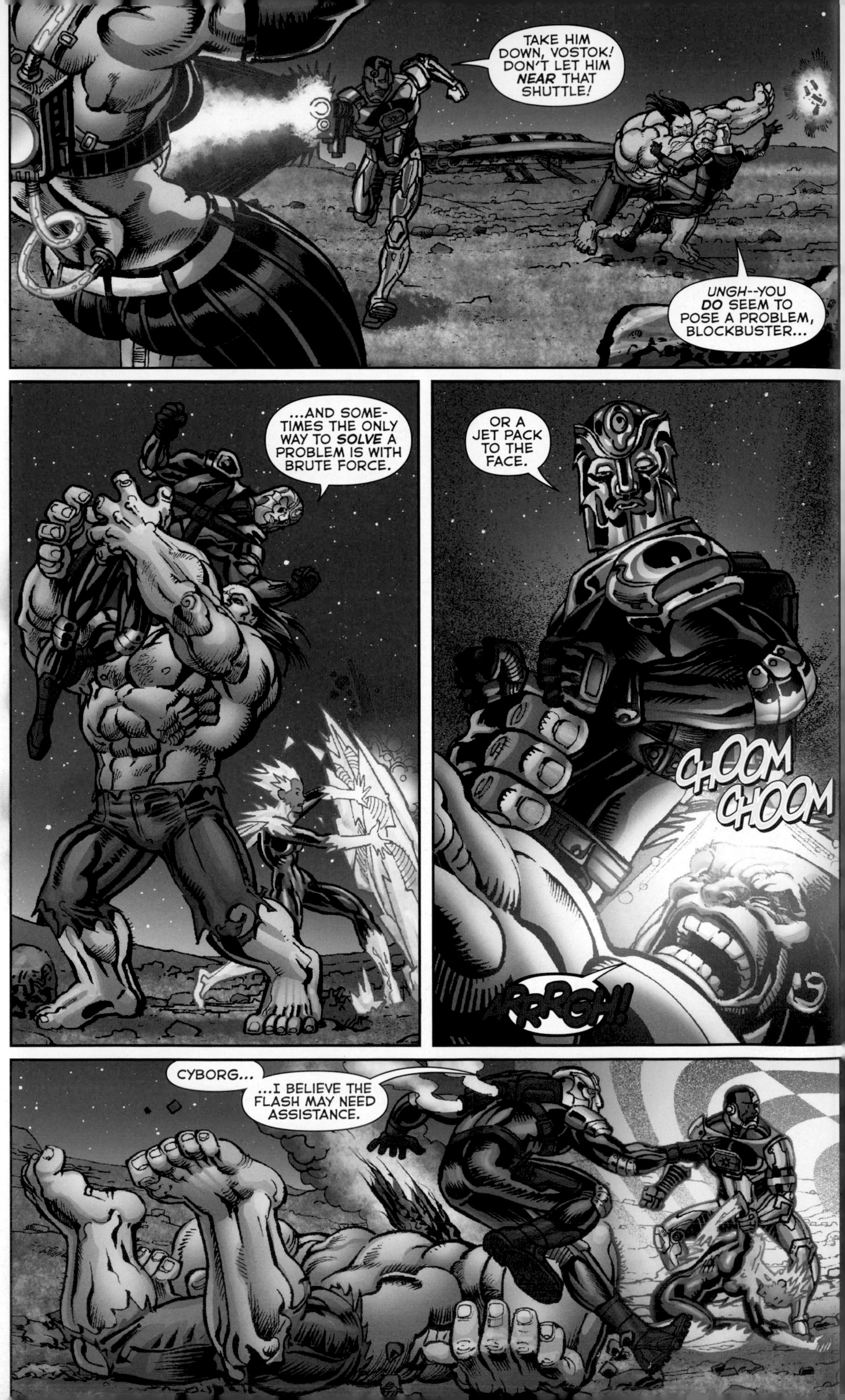
TAKE HIM DOWN, VOSTOK! DON'T LET HIM *NEAR* THAT SHUTTLE!
UNGH--YOU ***DO*** SEEM TO POSE A PROBLEM, BLOCKBUSTER...
...AND SOMETIMES THE ONLY WAY TO ***SOLVE*** A PROBLEM IS WITH BRUTE FORCE.
OR A JET PACK TO THE FACE.
CHOOM
CHOOM
RRRGH!!
CYBORG...
...I BELIEVE THE FLASH MAY NEED ASSISTANCE.

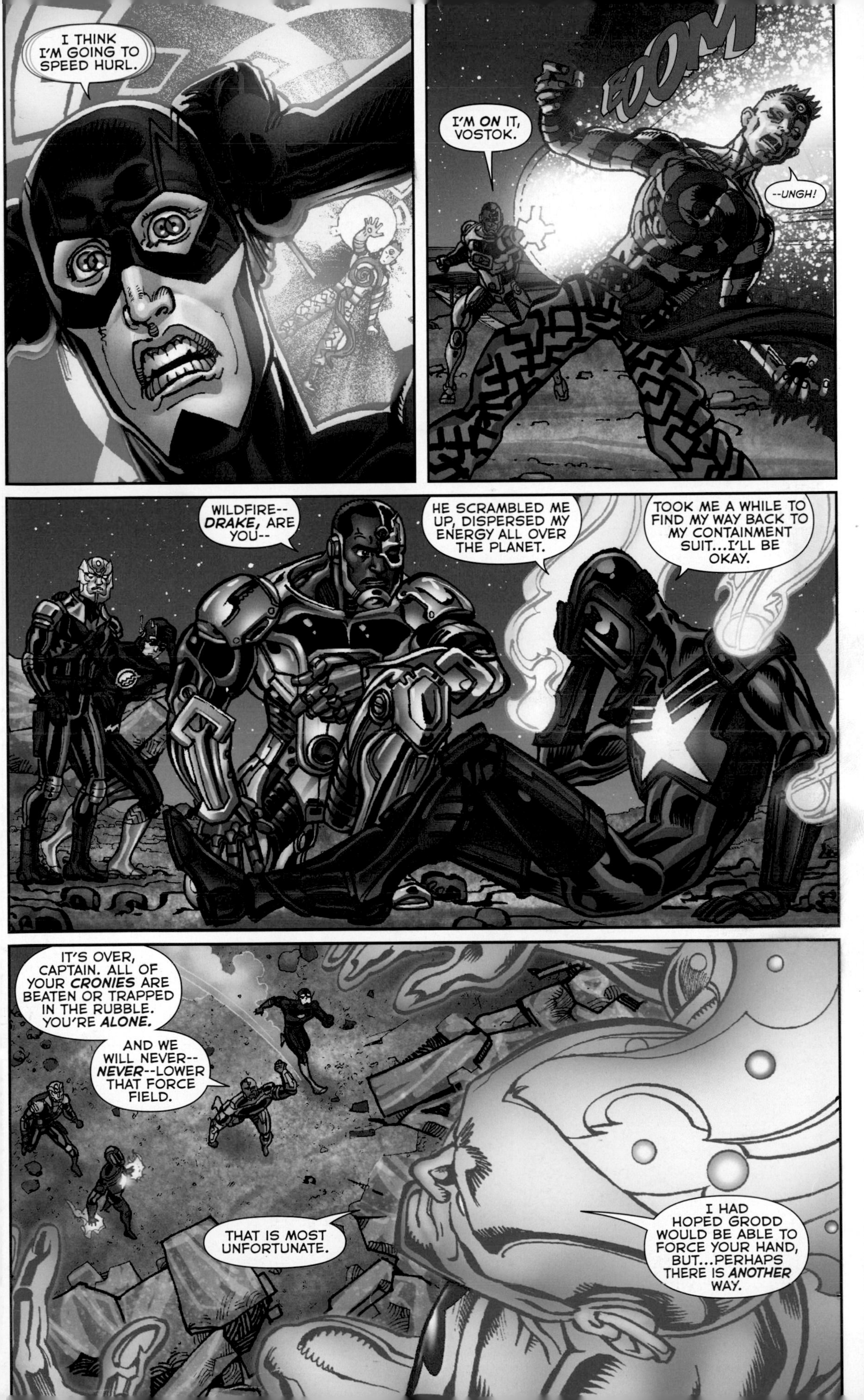
I THINK I'M GOING TO SPEED HURL.
BOOM
I'M ON IT, VOSTOK.
--UNGH!
WILDFIRE-- DRAKE, ARE YOU--
HE SCRAMBLED ME UP, DISPERSED MY ENERGY ALL OVER THE PLANET.
TOOK ME A WHILE TO FIND MY WAY BACK TO MY CONTAINMENT SUIT...I'LL BE OKAY.
IT'S OVER, CAPTAIN. ALL OF YOUR CRONIES ARE BEATEN OR TRAPPED IN THE RUBBLE. YOU'RE ALONE.
AND WE WILL NEVER-- NEVER--LOWER THAT FORCE FIELD.
THAT IS MOST UNFORTUNATE.
I HAD HOPED GRODD WOULD BE ABLE TO FORCE YOUR HAND, BUT...PERHAPS THERE IS ANOTHER WAY.

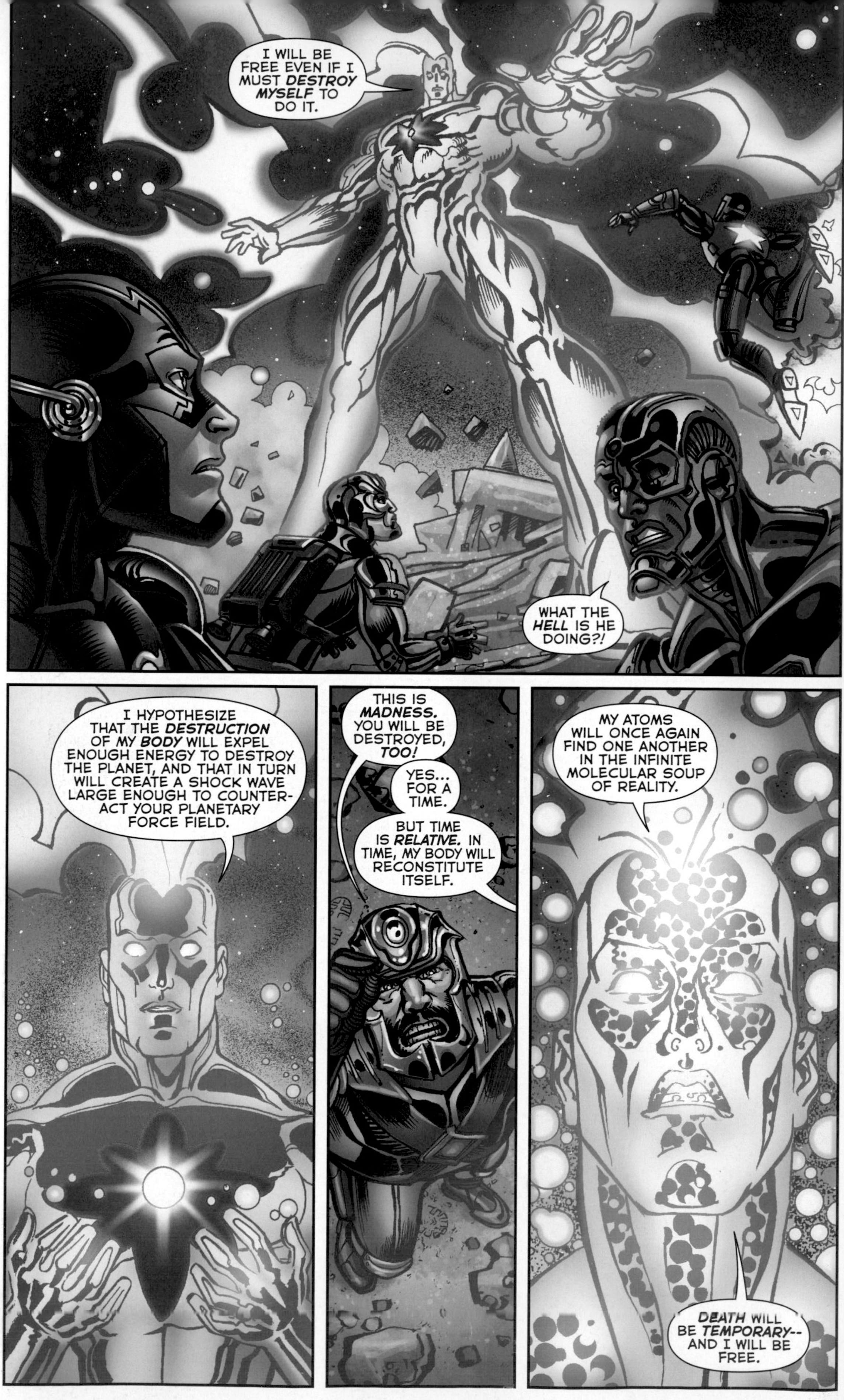
I WILL BE FREE EVEN IF I MUST *DESTROY MYSELF* TO DO IT.
WHAT THE *HELL* IS HE DOING?!
I HYPOTHESIZE THAT THE *DESTRUCTION* OF MY *BODY* WILL EXPEL ENOUGH ENERGY TO DESTROY THE PLANET, AND THAT IN TURN WILL CREATE A SHOCK WAVE LARGE ENOUGH TO COUNTER-ACT YOUR PLANETARY FORCE FIELD.
THIS IS *MADNESS.* YOU WILL BE DESTROYED, *TOO!*
YES... FOR A TIME.
BUT TIME IS *RELATIVE.* IN TIME, MY BODY WILL RECONSTITUTE ITSELF.
MY ATOMS WILL ONCE AGAIN FIND ONE ANOTHER IN THE INFINITE MOLECULAR SOUP OF REALITY.
DEATH WILL BE *TEMPORARY*-- AND I WILL BE FREE.

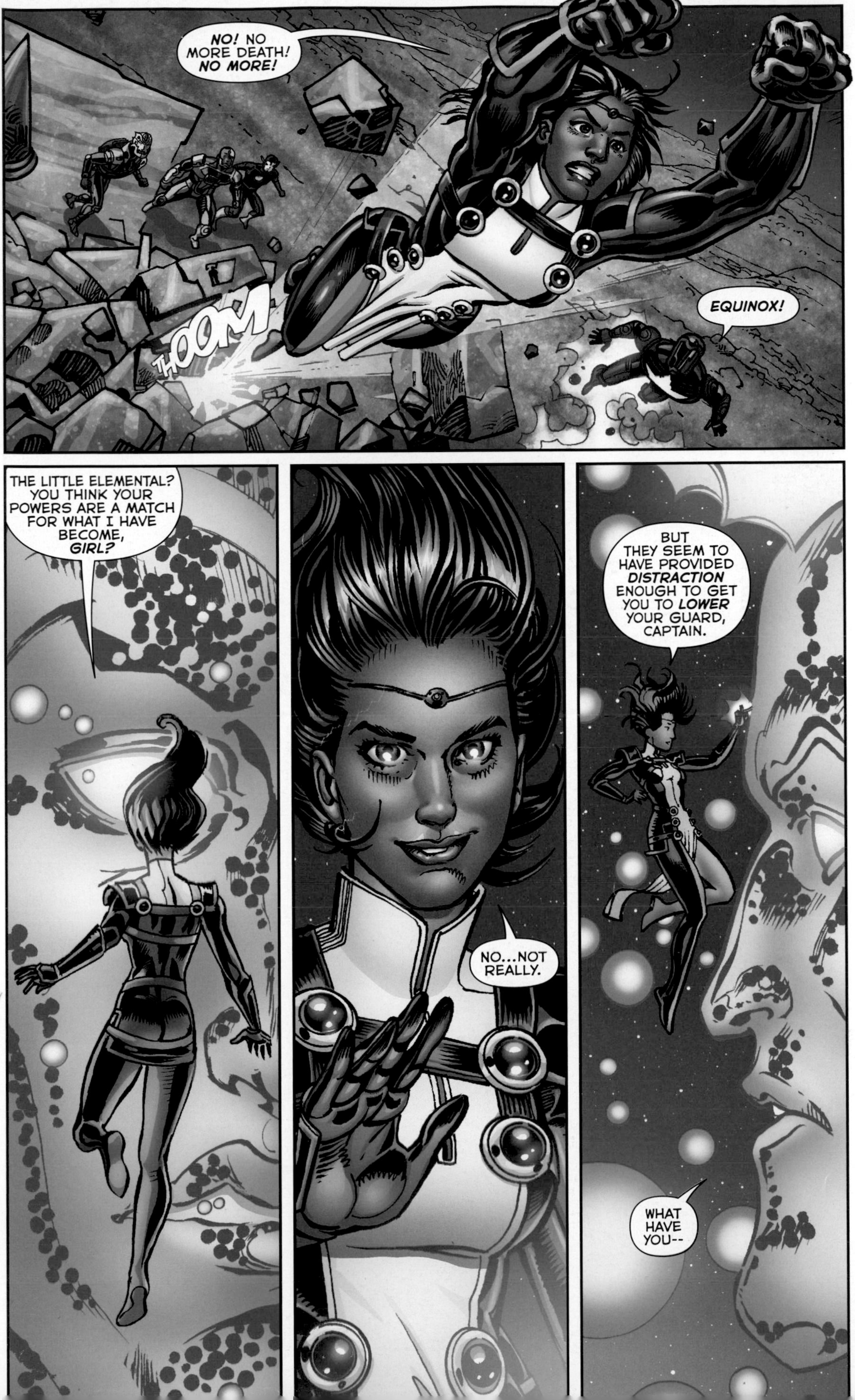
NO! NO MORE DEATH! NO MORE!
THOOM
EQUINOX!
THE LITTLE ELEMENTAL? YOU THINK YOUR POWERS ARE A MATCH FOR WHAT I HAVE BECOME, GIRL?
NO...NOT REALLY.
BUT THEY SEEM TO HAVE PROVIDED DISTRACTION ENOUGH TO GET YOU TO LOWER YOUR GUARD, CAPTAIN.
WHAT HAVE YOU--

--DONE?
H-HELLO?
DO NOT BE AFRAID, CAPTAIN. YOU ARE NOT ALONE. I AM HERE WITH YOU AGAIN.
YOU DO REMEMBER? YOU DO REMEMBER THIS PLACE?
YES...I REMEMBER.
IT WAS WHERE YOU WERE BORN. PORT CLYDE, MAINE.
I REMEMBER NOW!

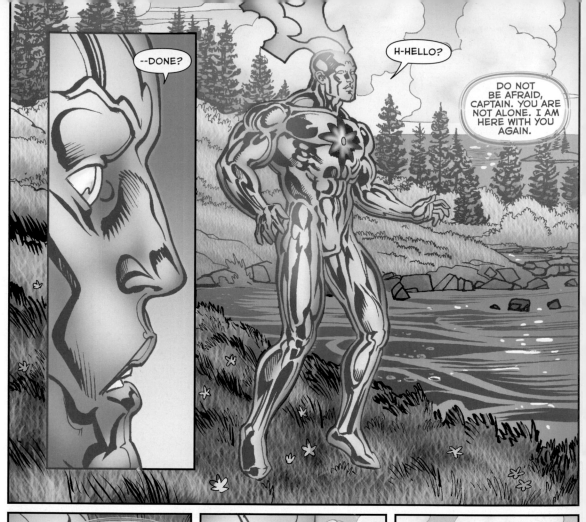

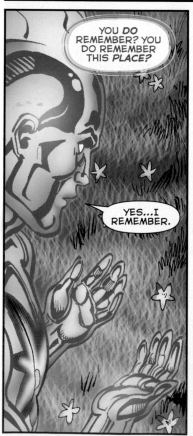

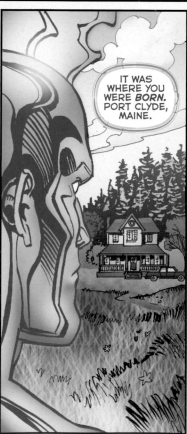

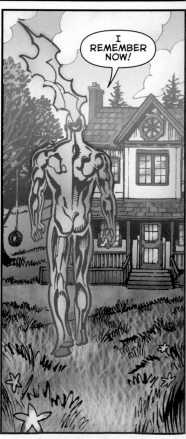

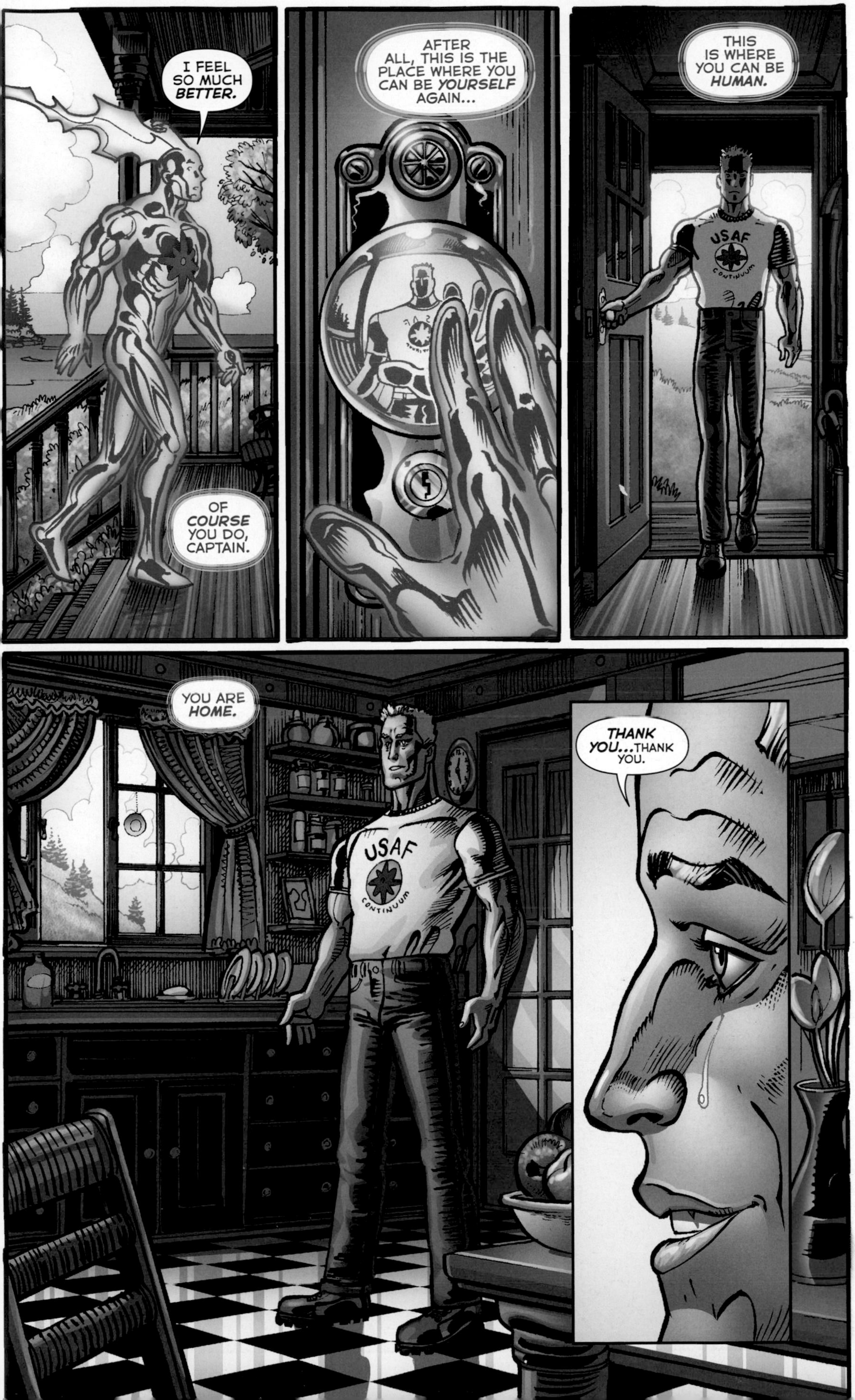
I FEEL SO MUCH BETTER.
OF COURSE YOU DO, CAPTAIN.
AFTER ALL, THIS IS THE PLACE WHERE YOU CAN BE YOURSELF AGAIN...
THIS IS WHERE YOU CAN BE HUMAN.
USAF CONTINUUM
YOU ARE HOME.
USAF CONTINUUM
THANK YOU... THANK YOU.

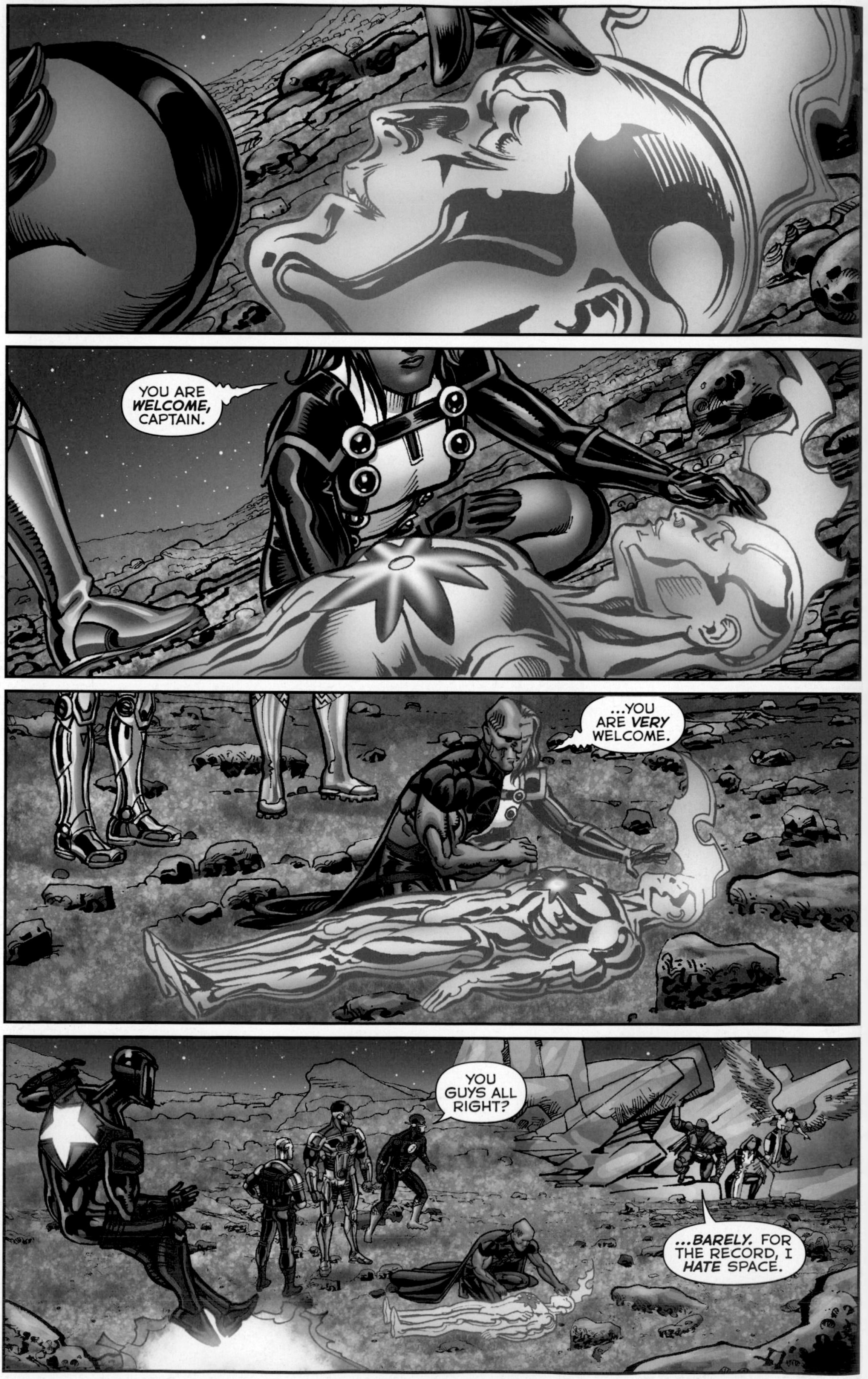
YOU ARE *WELCOME,* CAPTAIN.
...YOU ARE *VERY* WELCOME.
YOU GUYS ALL RIGHT?
...BARELY. FOR THE RECORD, I *HATE* SPACE.

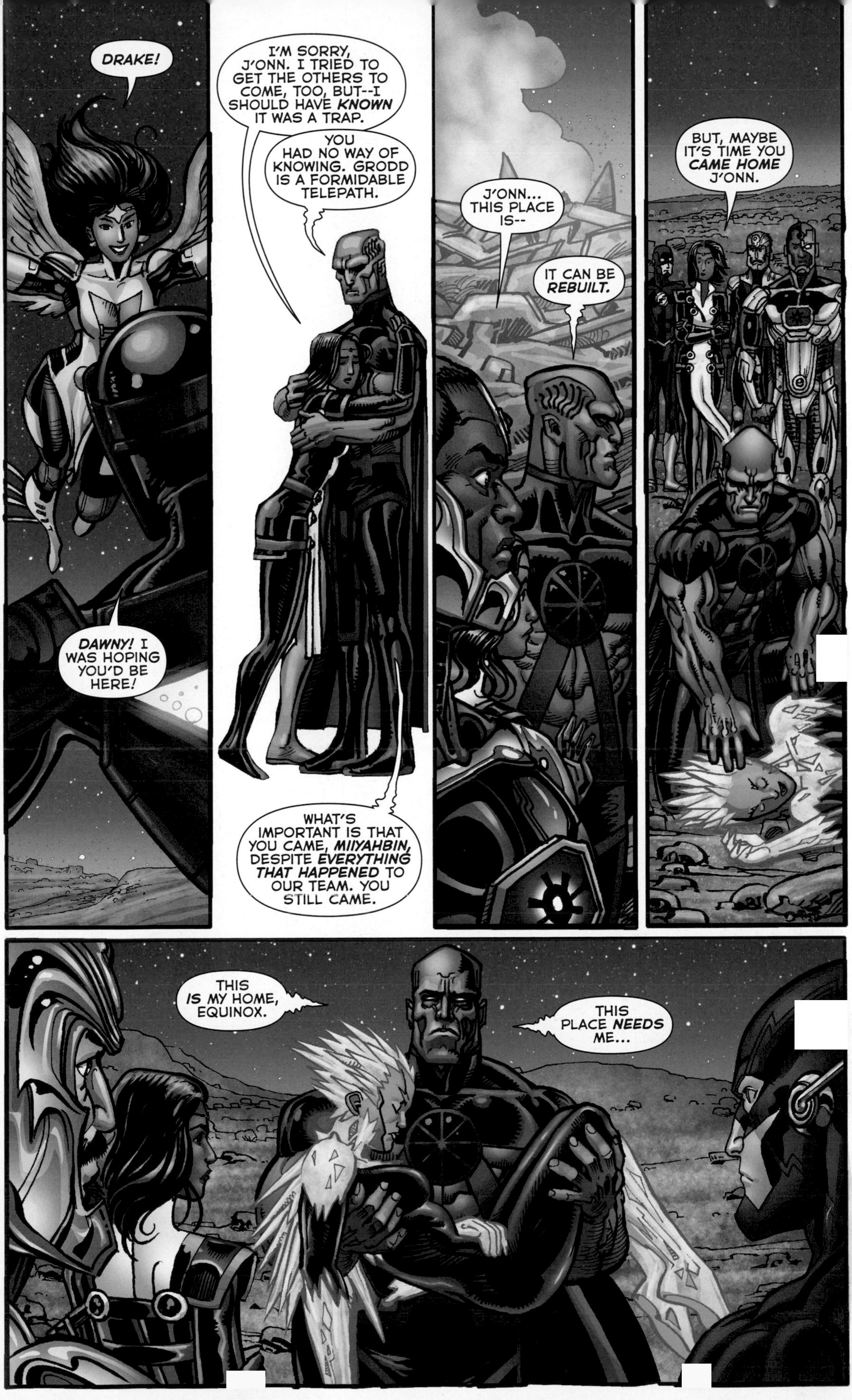
DRAKE!
DAWNY! I WAS HOPING YOU'D BE HERE!
I'M SORRY, J'ONN. I TRIED TO GET THE OTHERS TO COME, TOO, BUT--I SHOULD HAVE KNOWN IT WAS A TRAP.
YOU HAD NO WAY OF KNOWING. GRODD IS A FORMIDABLE TELEPATH.
WHAT'S IMPORTANT IS THAT YOU CAME, MIIYAHBIN, DESPITE EVERYTHING THAT HAPPENED TO OUR TEAM. YOU STILL CAME.
J'ONN... THIS PLACE IS--
IT CAN BE REBUILT.
BUT, MAYBE IT'S TIME YOU CAME HOME J'ONN.
THIS IS MY HOME, EQUINOX.
THIS PLACE NEEDS ME...

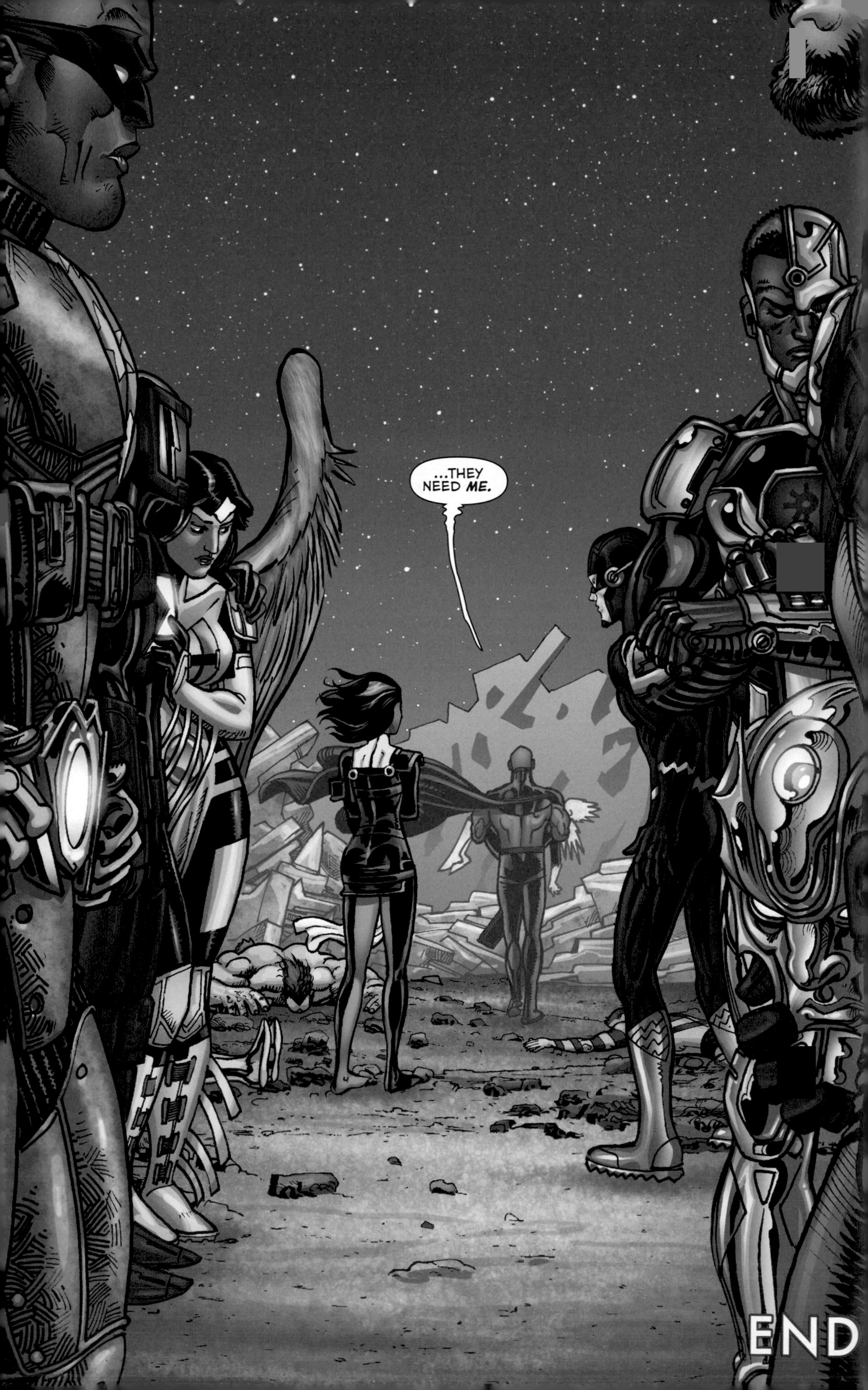
...THEY NEED ME.
END

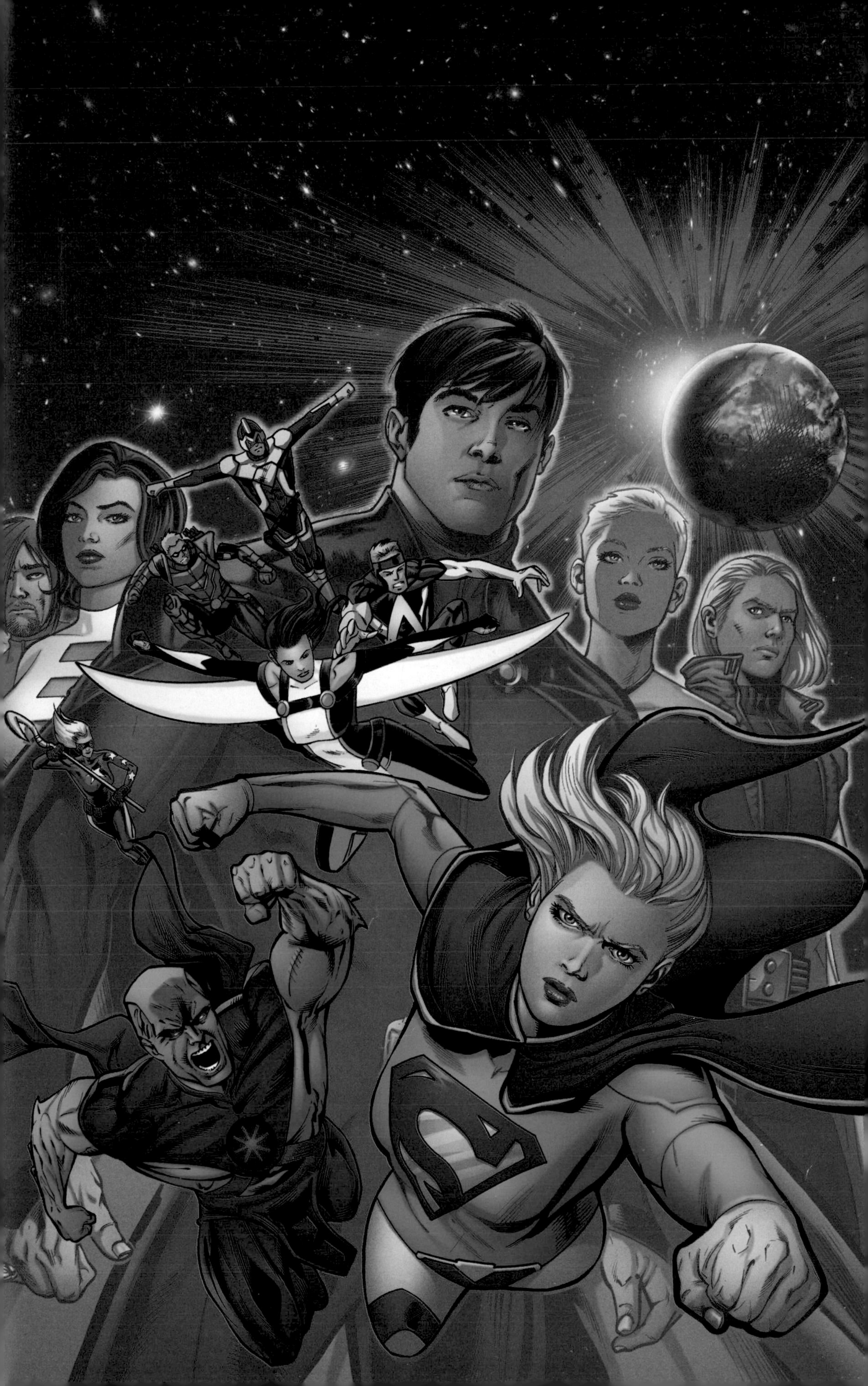

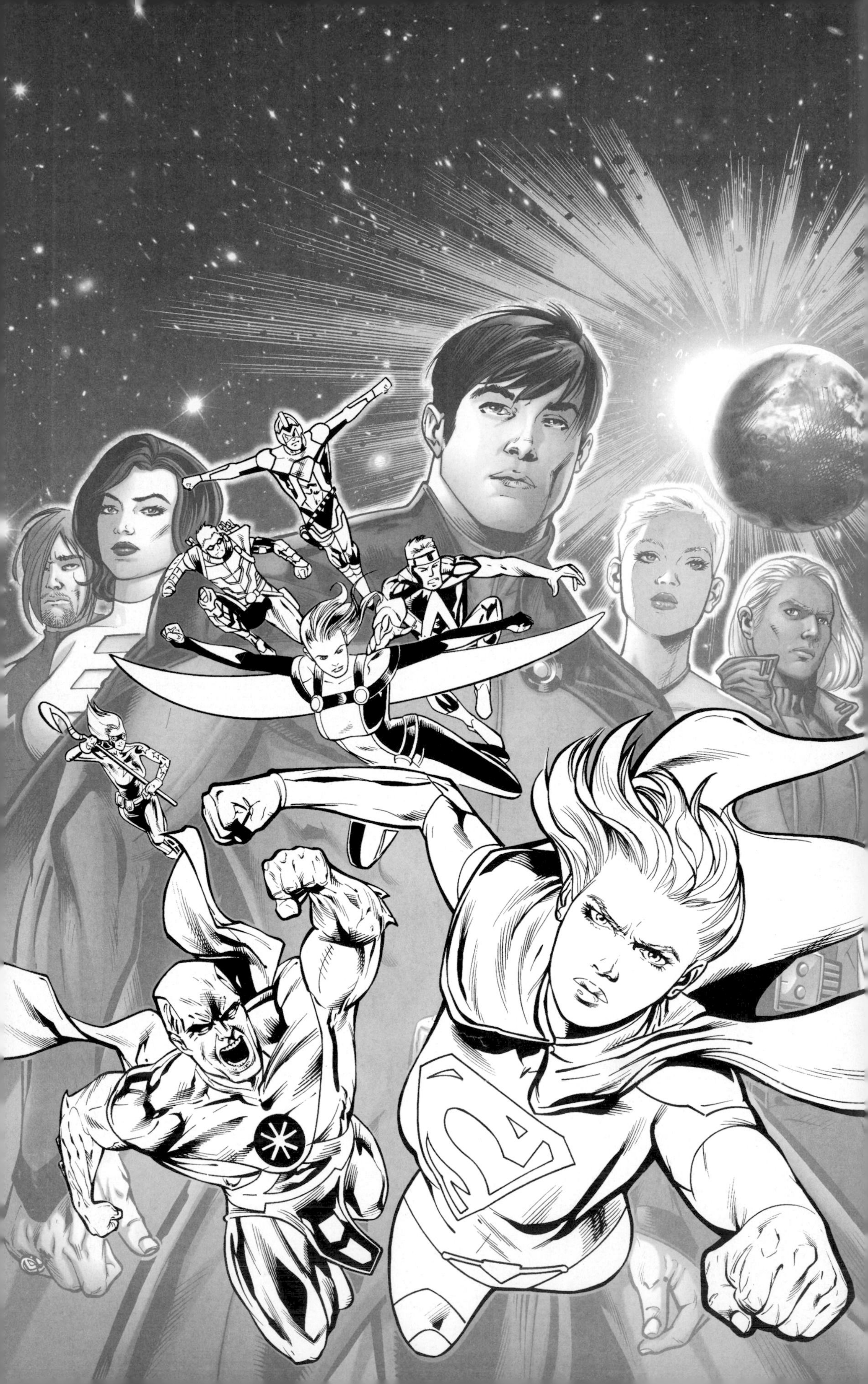

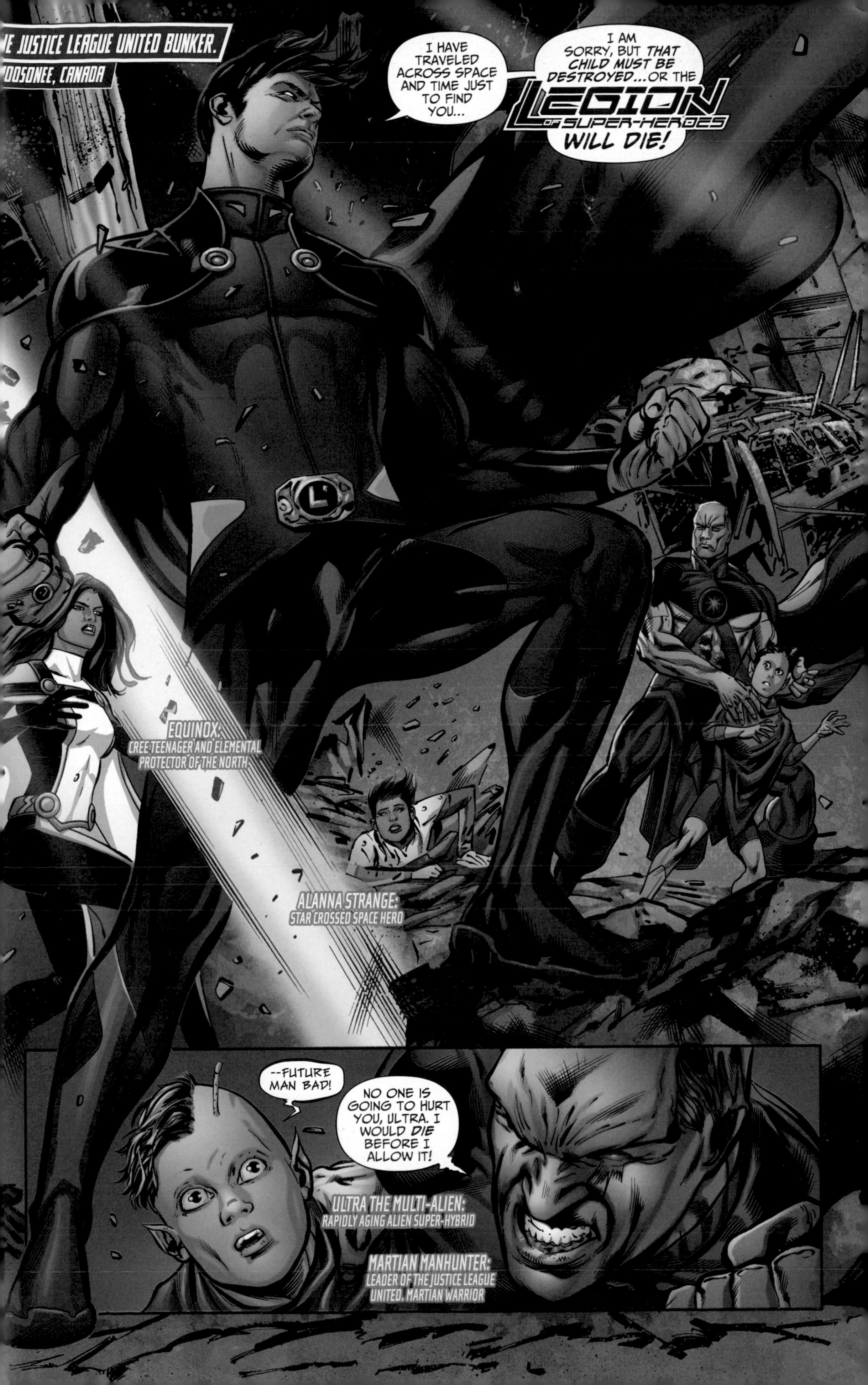

E JUSTICE LEAGUE UNITED BUNKER.
OOSONEE, CANADA
I HAVE TRAVELED ACROSS SPACE AND TIME JUST TO FIND YOU...
I AM SORRY, BUT THAT CHILD MUST BE DESTROYED...OR THE LEGION OF SUPER-HEROES WILL DIE!
EQUINOX: CREE TEENAGER AND ELEMENTAL PROTECTOR OF THE NORTH
ALANNA STRANGE: STAR CROSSED SPACE HERO
--FUTURE MAN BAD!
NO ONE IS GOING TO HURT YOU, ULTRA. I WOULD DIE BEFORE I ALLOW IT!
ULTRA THE MULTI-ALIEN: RAPIDLY AGING ALIEN SUPER-HYBRID
MARTIAN MANHUNTER: LEADER OF THE JUSTICE LEAGUE UNITED. MARTIAN WARRIOR

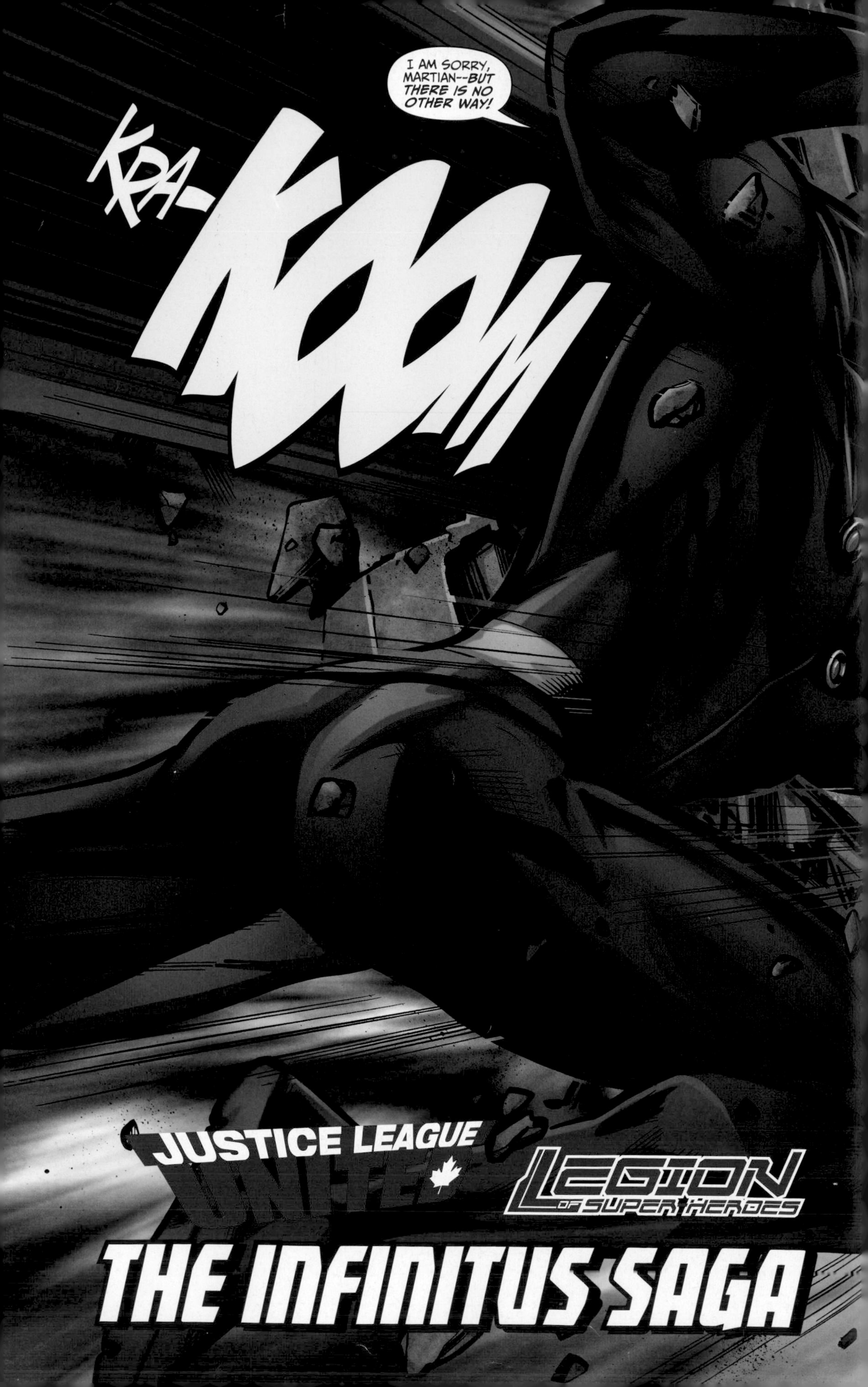
I AM SORRY, MARTIAN--BUT THERE IS NO OTHER WAY!
KRA-KOOM
JUSTICE LEAGUE UNITED
LEGION OF SUPER-HEROES
THE INFINITUS SAGA

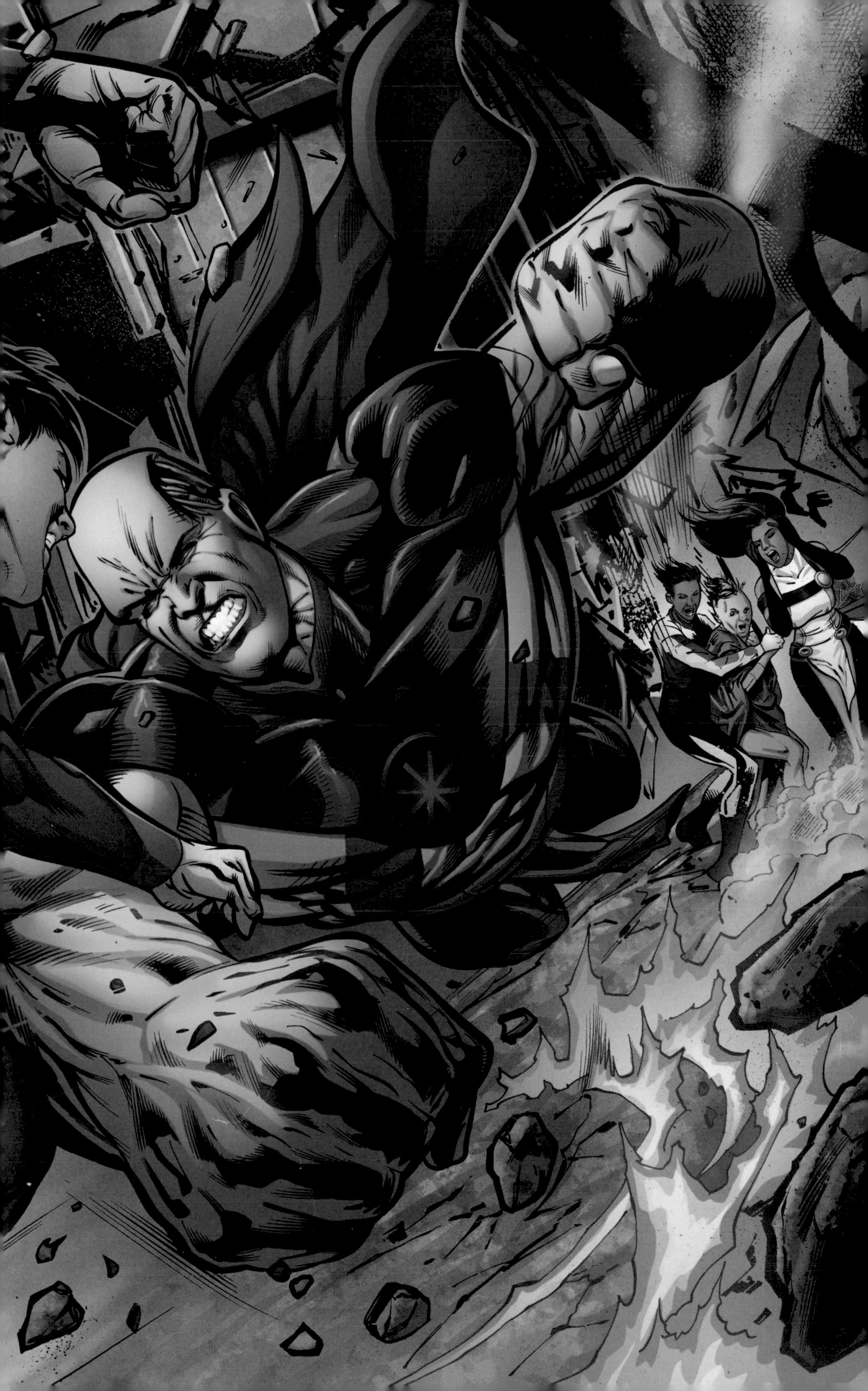

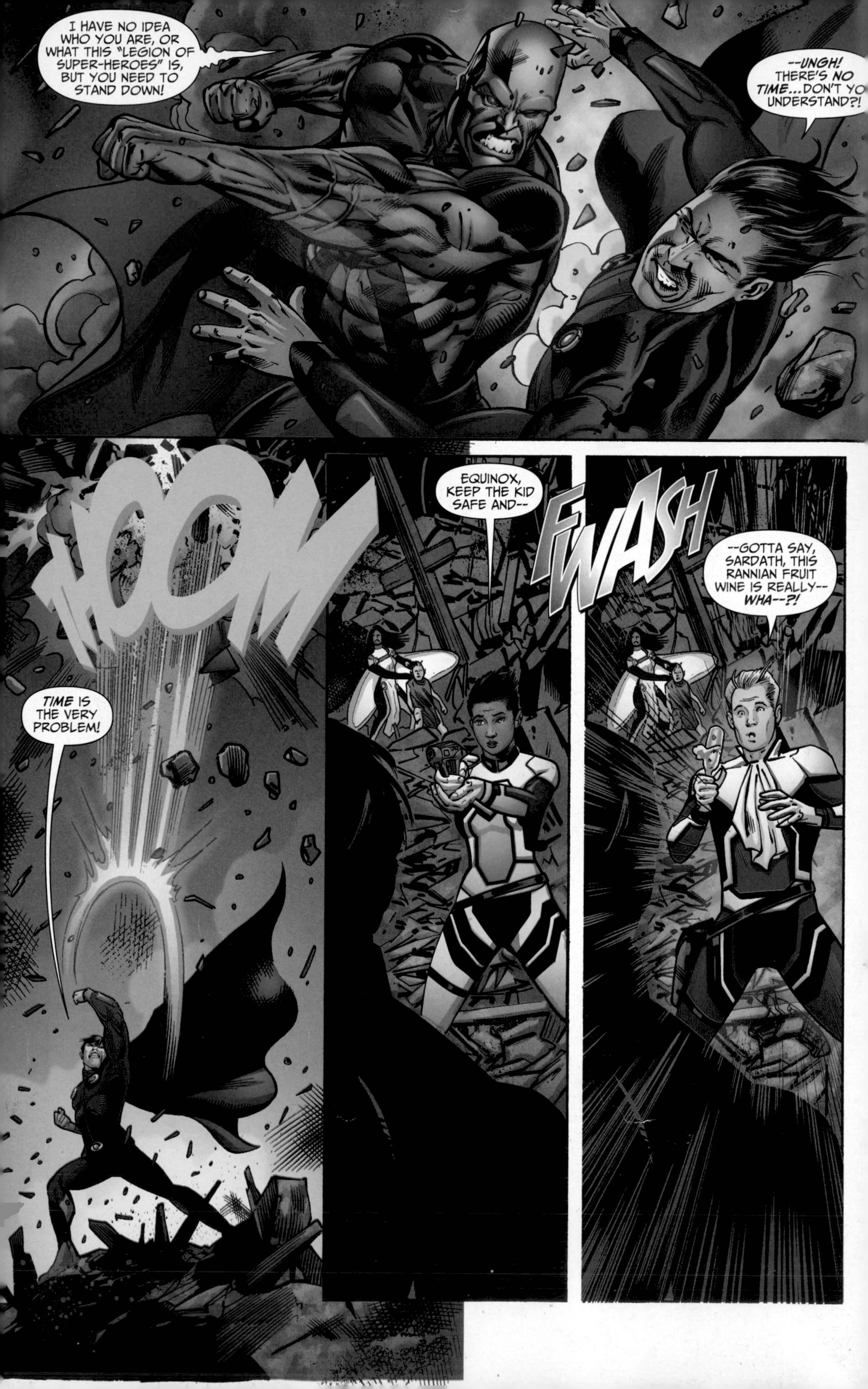

I HAVE NO IDEA WHO YOU ARE, OR WHAT THIS "LEGION OF SUPER-HEROES" IS, BUT YOU NEED TO STAND DOWN!
--UNGH! THERE'S NO TIME...DON'T YO UNDERSTAND?!
WOOM
TIME IS THE VERY PROBLEM!
EQUINOX, KEEP THE KID SAFE AND--
FWASH
--GOTTA SAY, SARDATH, THIS RANNIAN FRUIT WINE IS REALLY-- WHA--?!

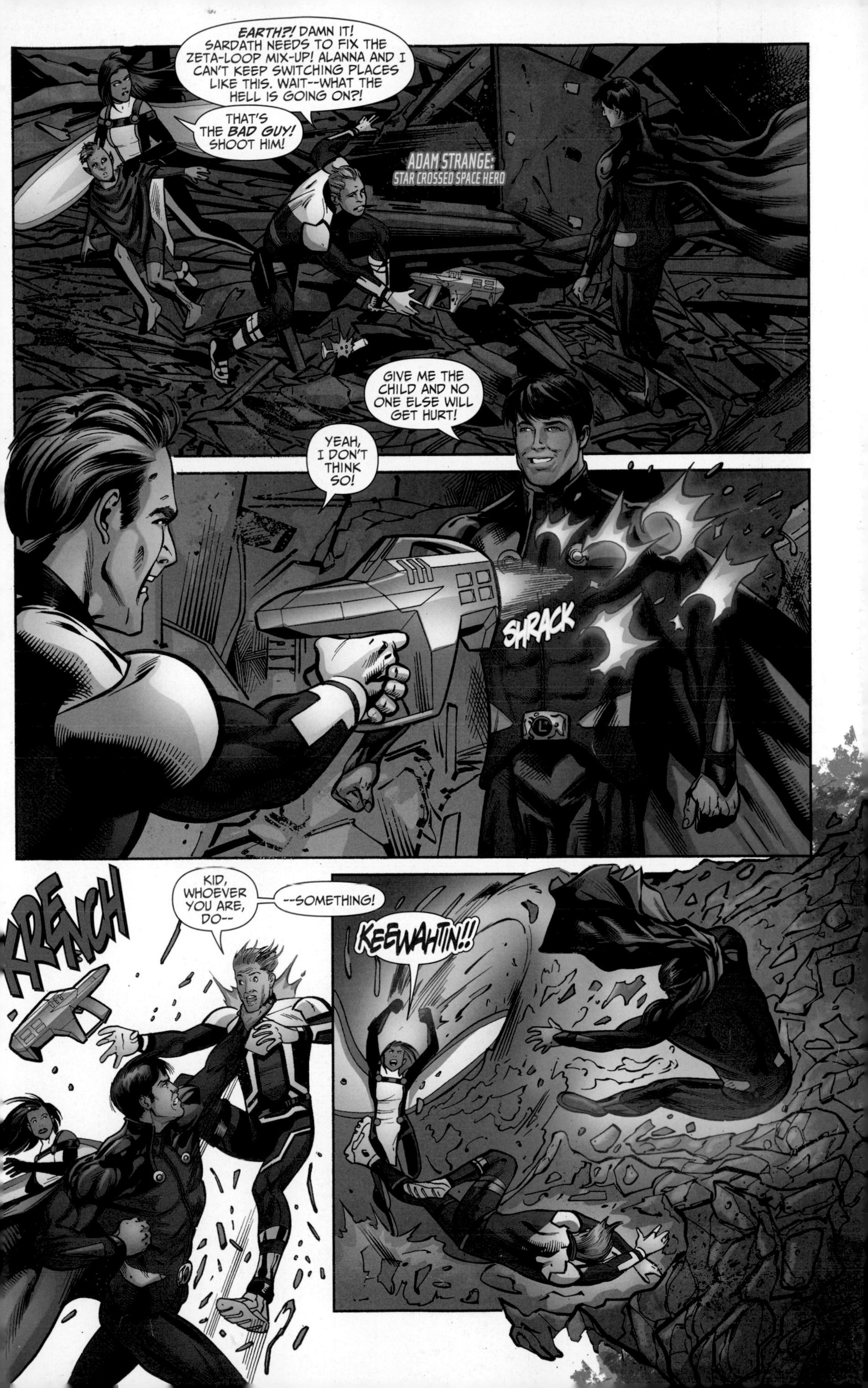
EARTH?! DAMN IT! SARDATH NEEDS TO FIX THE ZETA-LOOP MIX-UP! ALANNA AND I CAN'T KEEP SWITCHING PLACES LIKE THIS. WAIT--WHAT THE HELL IS GOING ON?!
THAT'S THE BAD GUY! SHOOT HIM!
ADAM STRANGE: STAR CROSSED SPACE HERO
GIVE ME THE CHILD AND NO ONE ELSE WILL GET HURT!
YEAH, I DON'T THINK SO!
SHRACK
KRENCH
KID, WHOEVER YOU ARE, DO--
--SOMETHING!
KEEWAHTIN!!

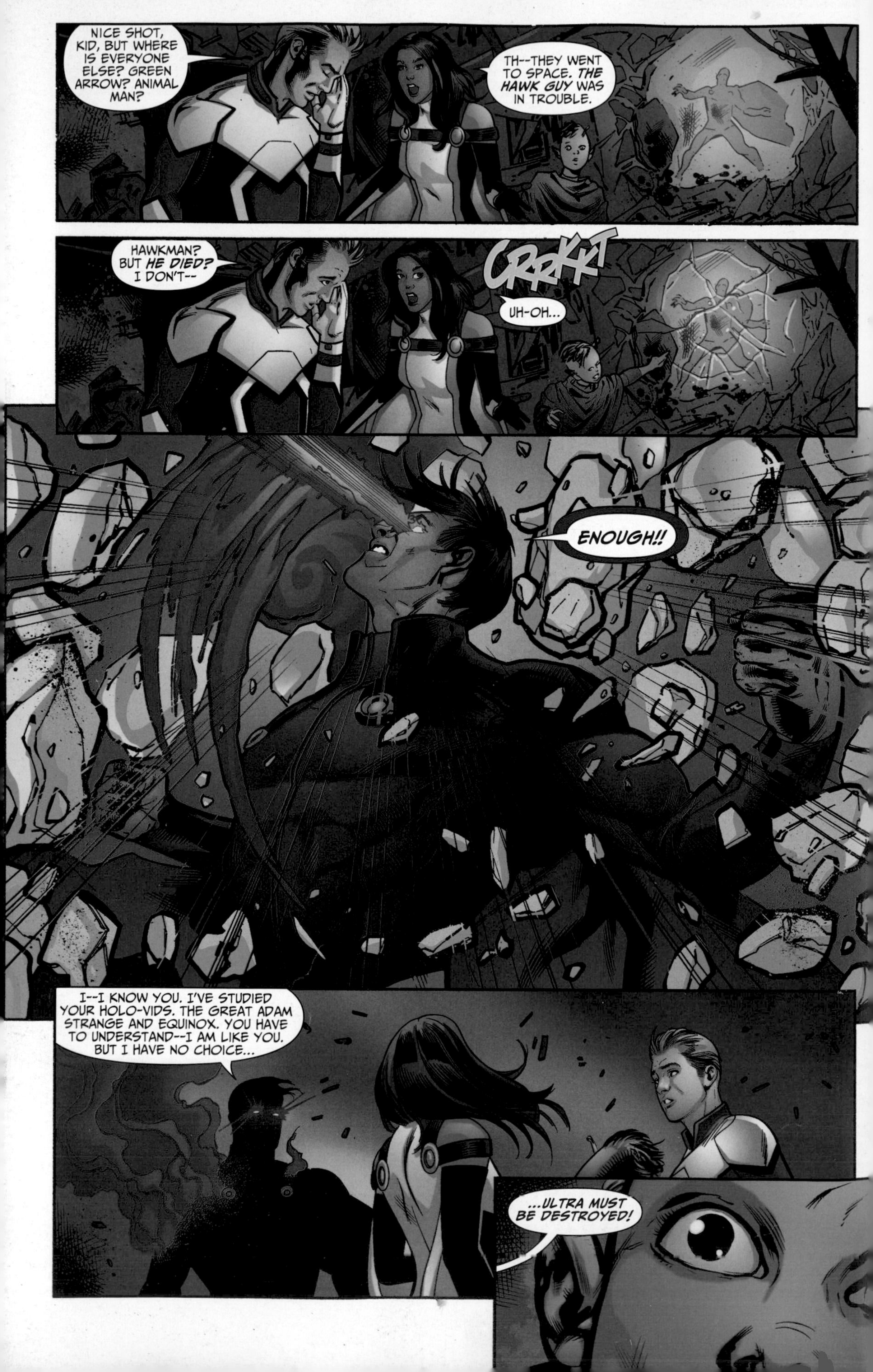
NICE SHOT, KID, BUT WHERE IS EVERYONE ELSE? GREEN ARROW? ANIMAL MAN?
TH--THEY WENT TO SPACE. THE HAWK GUY WAS IN TROUBLE.
HAWKMAN? BUT HE DIED? I DON'T--
CRRKKT
UH-OH...
ENOUGH!!
I--I KNOW YOU. I'VE STUDIED YOUR HOLO-VIDS. THE GREAT ADAM STRANGE AND EQUINOX. YOU HAVE TO UNDERSTAND--I AM LIKE YOU. BUT I HAVE NO CHOICE...
...ULTRA MUST BE DESTROYED!

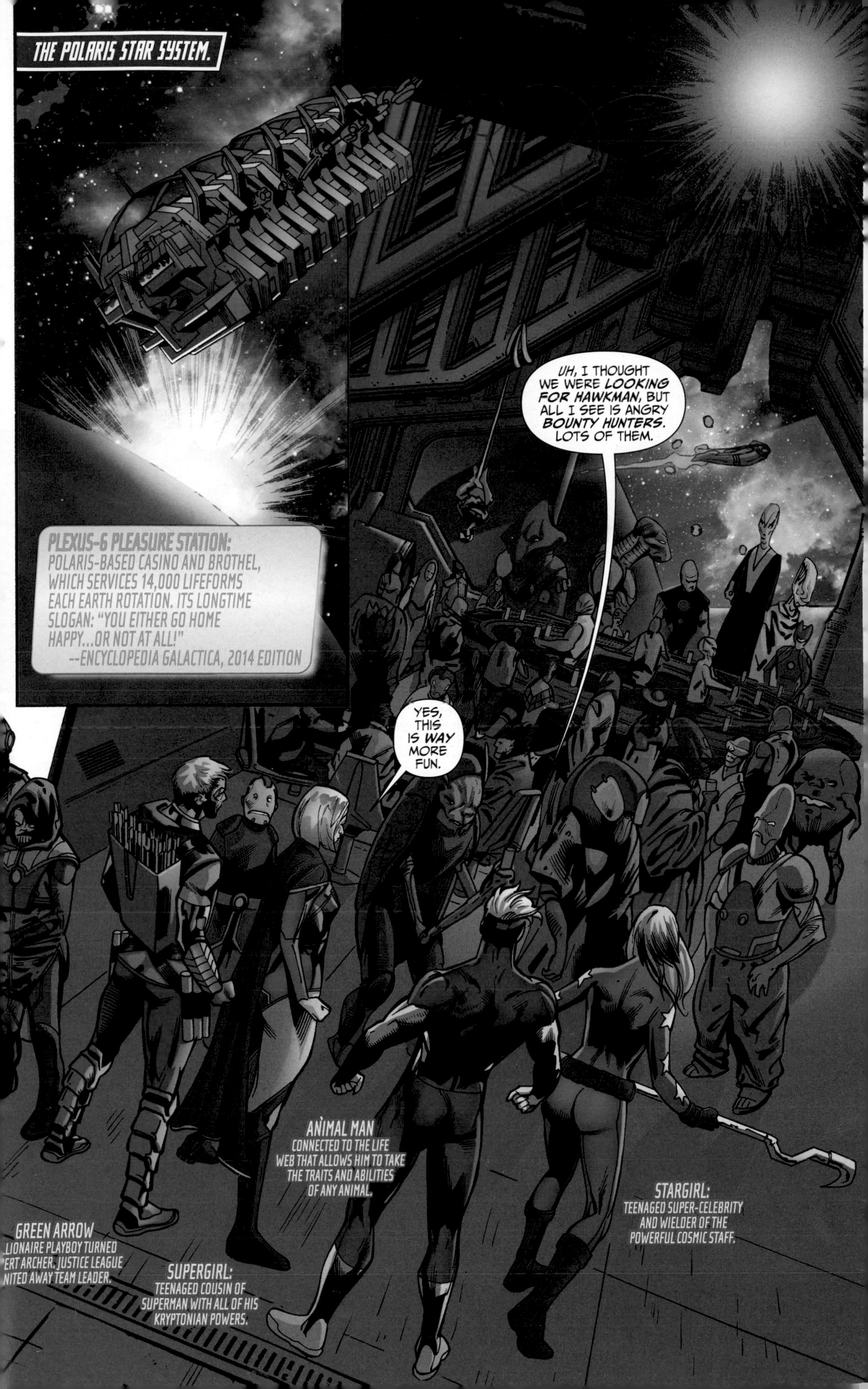
THE POLARIS STAR SYSTEM.
PLEXUS-6 PLEASURE STATION: POLARIS-BASED CASINO AND BROTHEL, WHICH SERVICES 14,000 LIFEFORMS EACH EARTH ROTATION. ITS LONGTIME SLOGAN: "YOU EITHER GO HOME HAPPY...OR NOT AT ALL!" --ENCYCLOPEDIA GALACTICA, 2014 EDITION
UH, I THOUGHT WE WERE LOOKING FOR HAWKMAN, BUT ALL I SEE IS ANGRY BOUNTY HUNTERS. LOTS OF THEM.
YES, THIS IS WAY MORE FUN.
ANIMAL MAN CONNECTED TO THE LIFE WEB THAT ALLOWS HIM TO TAKE THE TRAITS AND ABILITIES OF ANY ANIMAL.
STARGIRL: TEENAGED SUPER-CELEBRITY AND WIELDER OF THE POWERFUL COSMIC STAFF.
GREEN ARROW LIONAIRE PLAYBOY TURNED ERT ARCHER. JUSTICE LEAGUE NITED AWAY TEAM LEADER.
SUPERGIRL: TEENAGED COUSIN OF SUPERMAN WITH ALL OF HIS KRYPTONIAN POWERS.

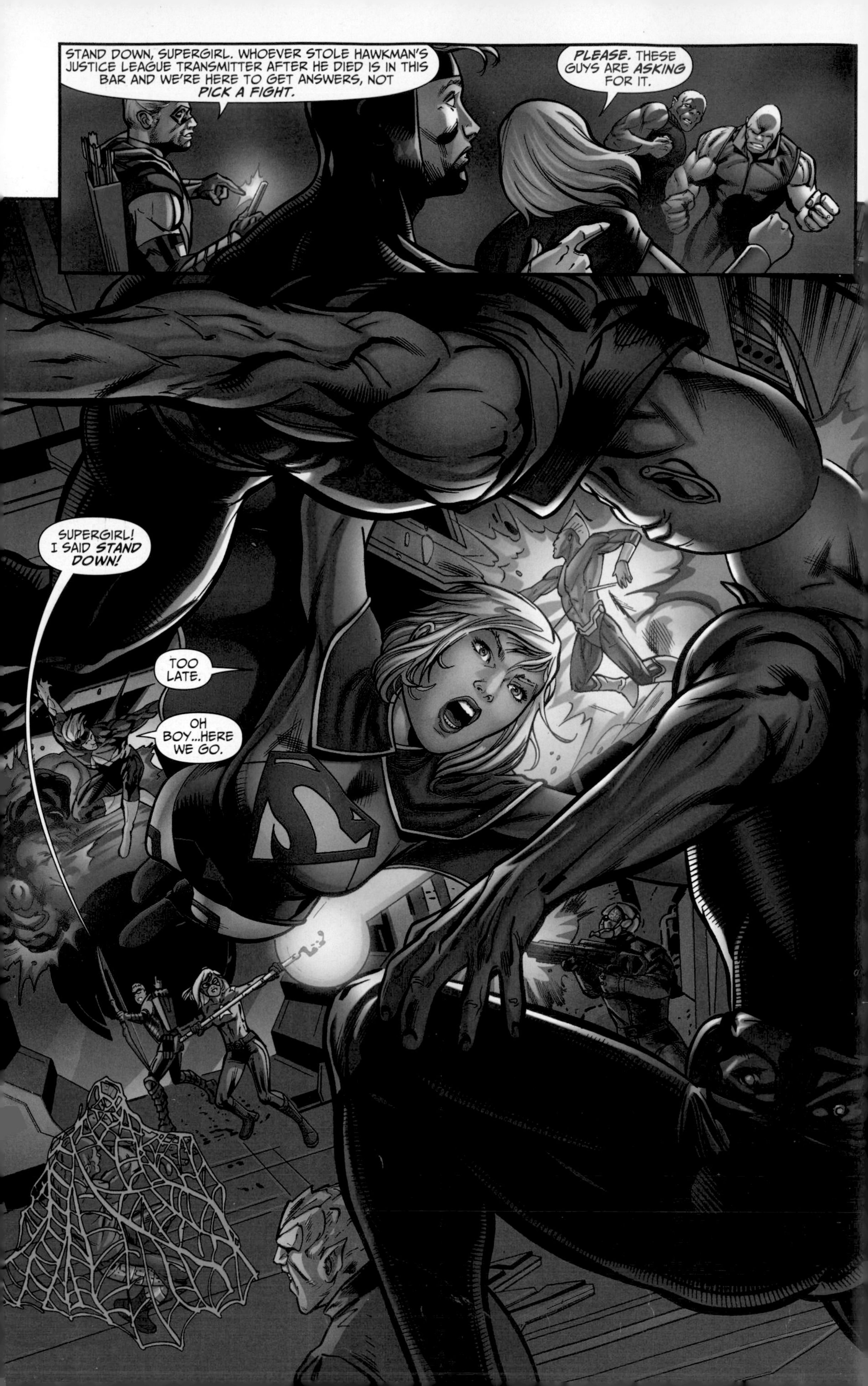
STAND DOWN, SUPERGIRL. WHOEVER STOLE HAWKMAN'S JUSTICE LEAGUE TRANSMITTER AFTER HE DIED IS IN THIS BAR AND WE'RE HERE TO GET ANSWERS, NOT *PICK A FIGHT.*
PLEASE. THESE GUYS ARE *ASKING* FOR IT.
SUPERGIRL! I SAID *STAND DOWN!*
TOO LATE.
OH BOY...HERE WE GO.

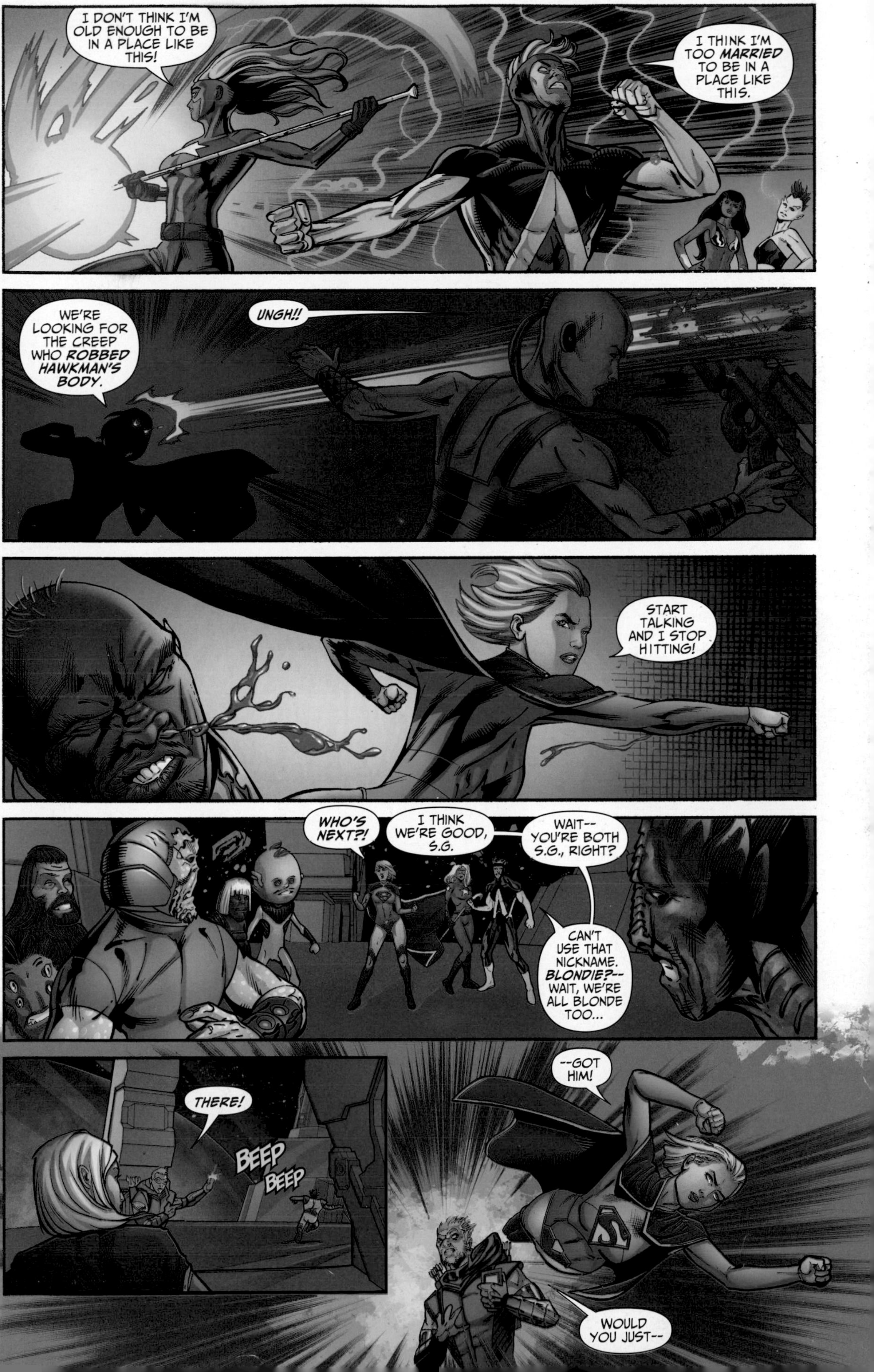
I DON'T THINK I'M OLD ENOUGH TO BE IN A PLACE LIKE THIS!
I THINK I'M TOO MARRIED TO BE IN A PLACE LIKE THIS.
WE'RE LOOKING FOR THE CREEP WHO ROBBED HAWKMAN'S BODY.
UNGH!!
START TALKING AND I STOP HITTING!
WHO'S NEXT?!
I THINK WE'RE GOOD, S.G.
WAIT-- YOU'RE BOTH S.G., RIGHT?
CAN'T USE THAT NICKNAME. BLONDIE?-- WAIT, WE'RE ALL BLONDE TOO...
THERE!
BEEP BEEP
--GOT HIM!
WOULD YOU JUST--

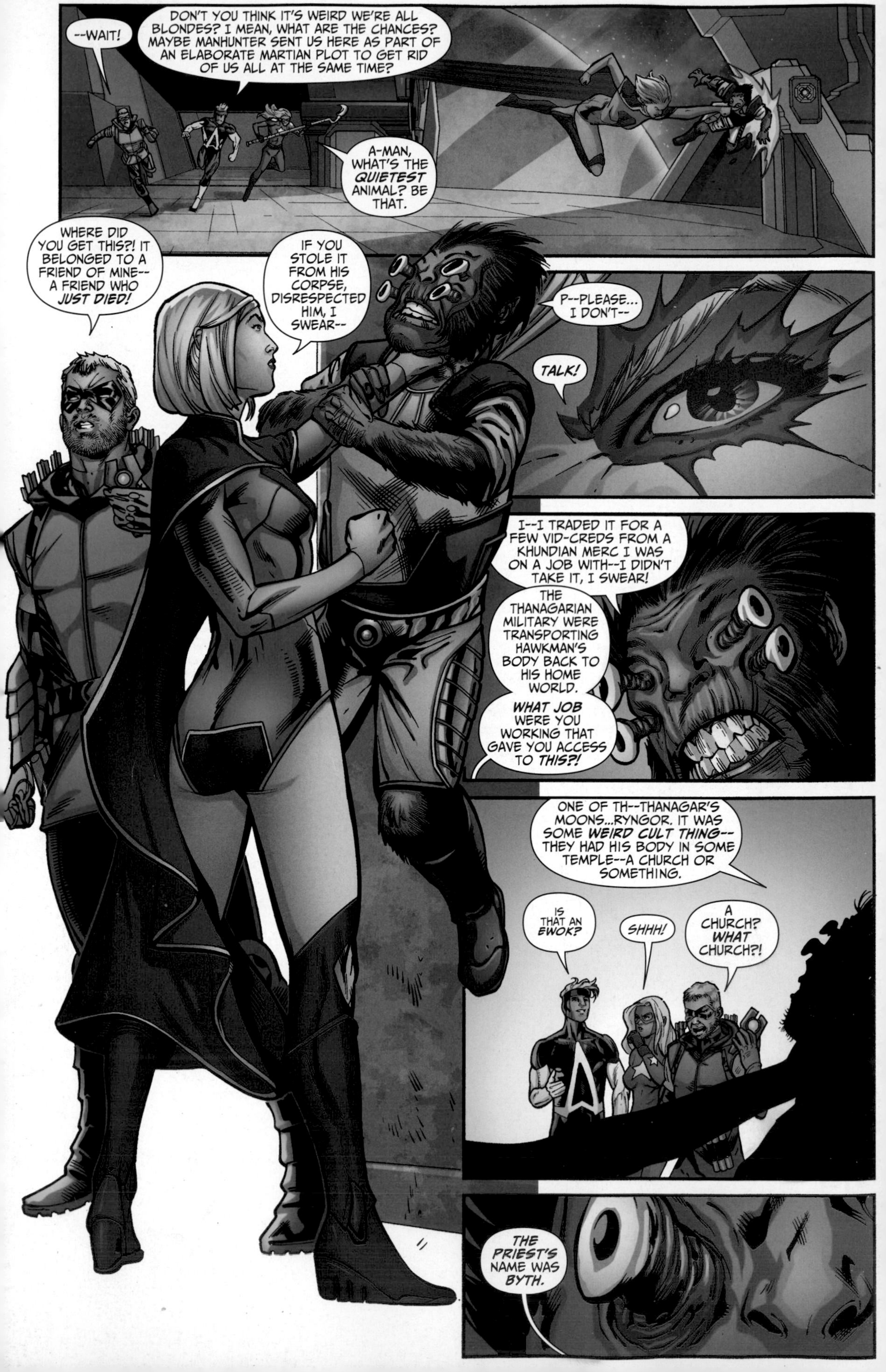
--WAIT!
DON'T YOU THINK IT'S WEIRD WE'RE ALL BLONDES? I MEAN, WHAT ARE THE CHANCES? MAYBE MANHUNTER SENT US HERE AS PART OF AN ELABORATE MARTIAN PLOT TO GET RID OF US ALL AT THE SAME TIME?
A-MAN, WHAT'S THE QUIETEST ANIMAL? BE THAT.
WHERE DID YOU GET THIS?! IT BELONGED TO A FRIEND OF MINE-- A FRIEND WHO JUST DIED!
IF YOU STOLE IT FROM HIS CORPSE, DISRESPECTED HIM, I SWEAR--
P--PLEASE... I DON'T--
TALK!
I--I TRADED IT FOR A FEW VID-CREDS FROM A KHUNDIAN MERC I WAS ON A JOB WITH--I DIDN'T TAKE IT, I SWEAR!
THE THANAGARIAN MILITARY WERE TRANSPORTING HAWKMAN'S BODY BACK TO HIS HOME WORLD.
WHAT JOB WERE YOU WORKING THAT GAVE YOU ACCESS TO THIS?!
ONE OF TH--THANAGAR'S MOONS...RYNGOR. IT WAS SOME WEIRD CULT THING-- THEY HAD HIS BODY IN SOME TEMPLE--A CHURCH OR SOMETHING.
IS THAT AN EWOK?
SHHH!
A CHURCH? WHAT CHURCH?!
THE PRIEST'S NAME WAS BYTH.

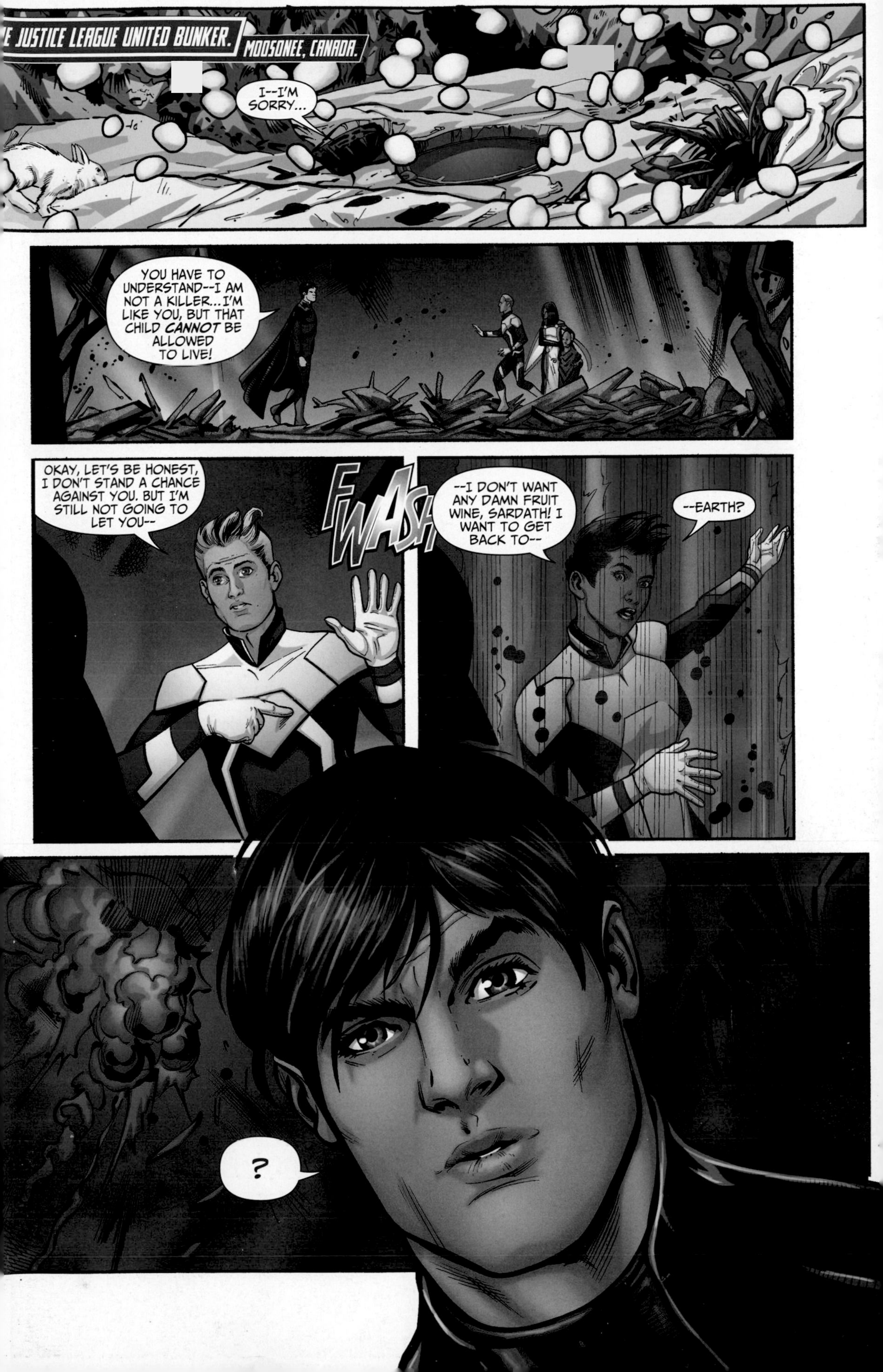
E JUSTICE LEAGUE UNITED BUNKER.
MOOSONEE, CANADA.
I--I'M SORRY...
YOU HAVE TO UNDERSTAND--I AM NOT A KILLER...I'M LIKE YOU, BUT THAT CHILD *CANNOT* BE ALLOWED TO LIVE!
OKAY, LET'S BE HONEST, I DON'T STAND A CHANCE AGAINST YOU. BUT I'M STILL NOT GOING TO LET YOU--
FWASH
--I DON'T WANT ANY DAMN FRUIT WINE, SARDATH! I WANT TO GET BACK TO--
--EARTH?
?

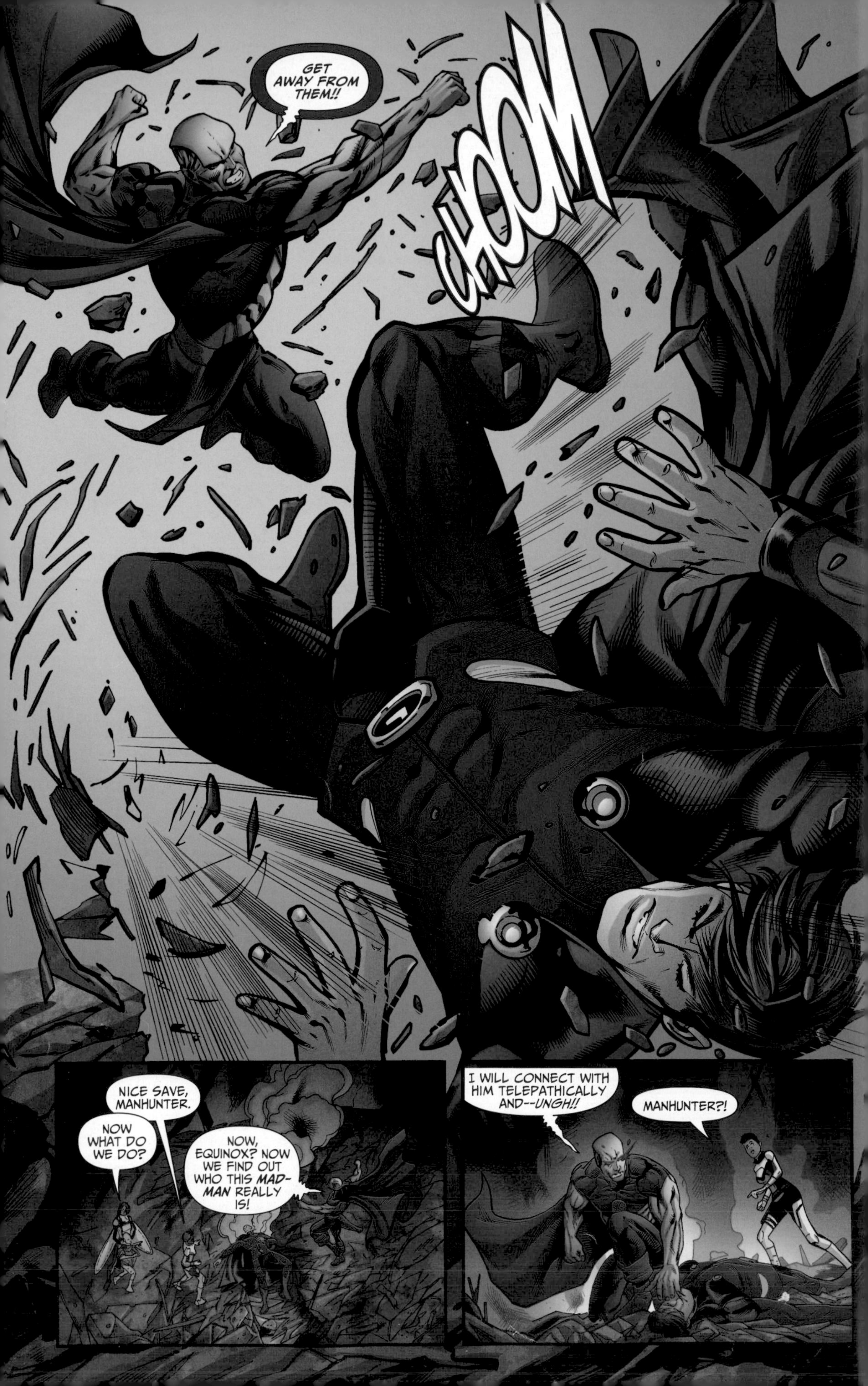
GET AWAY FROM THEM!!
CHOOM
NICE SAVE, MANHUNTER.
NOW WHAT DO WE DO?
NOW, EQUINOX? NOW WE FIND OUT WHO THIS MAD-MAN REALLY IS!
I WILL CONNECT WITH HIM TELEPATHICALLY AND--UNGH!!
MANHUNTER?!

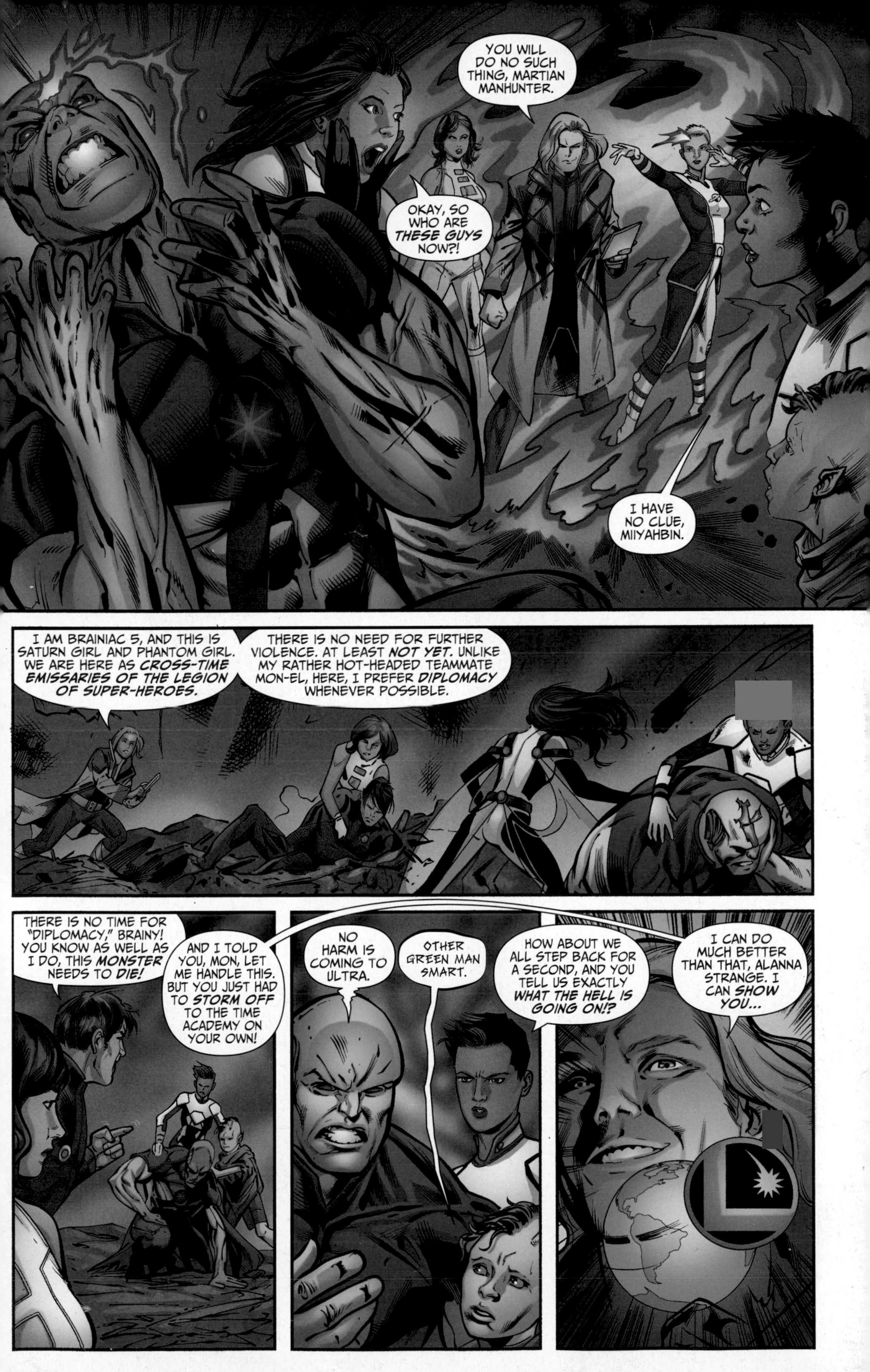
YOU WILL DO NO SUCH THING, MARTIAN MANHUNTER.
OKAY, SO WHO ARE THESE GUYS NOW?!
I HAVE NO CLUE, MIIYAHBIN.
I AM BRAINIAC 5, AND THIS IS SATURN GIRL AND PHANTOM GIRL. WE ARE HERE AS CROSS-TIME EMISSARIES OF THE LEGION OF SUPER-HEROES.
THERE IS NO NEED FOR FURTHER VIOLENCE. AT LEAST NOT YET. UNLIKE MY RATHER HOT-HEADED TEAMMATE MON-EL, HERE, I PREFER DIPLOMACY WHENEVER POSSIBLE.
THERE IS NO TIME FOR "DIPLOMACY," BRAINY! YOU KNOW AS WELL AS I DO, THIS MONSTER NEEDS TO DIE!
AND I TOLD YOU, MON, LET ME HANDLE THIS. BUT YOU JUST HAD TO STORM OFF TO THE TIME ACADEMY ON YOUR OWN!
NO HARM IS COMING TO ULTRA.
OTHER GREEN MAN SMART.
HOW ABOUT WE ALL STEP BACK FOR A SECOND, AND YOU TELL US EXACTLY WHAT THE HELL IS GOING ON!?
I CAN DO MUCH BETTER THAN THAT, ALANNA STRANGE. I CAN SHOW YOU...

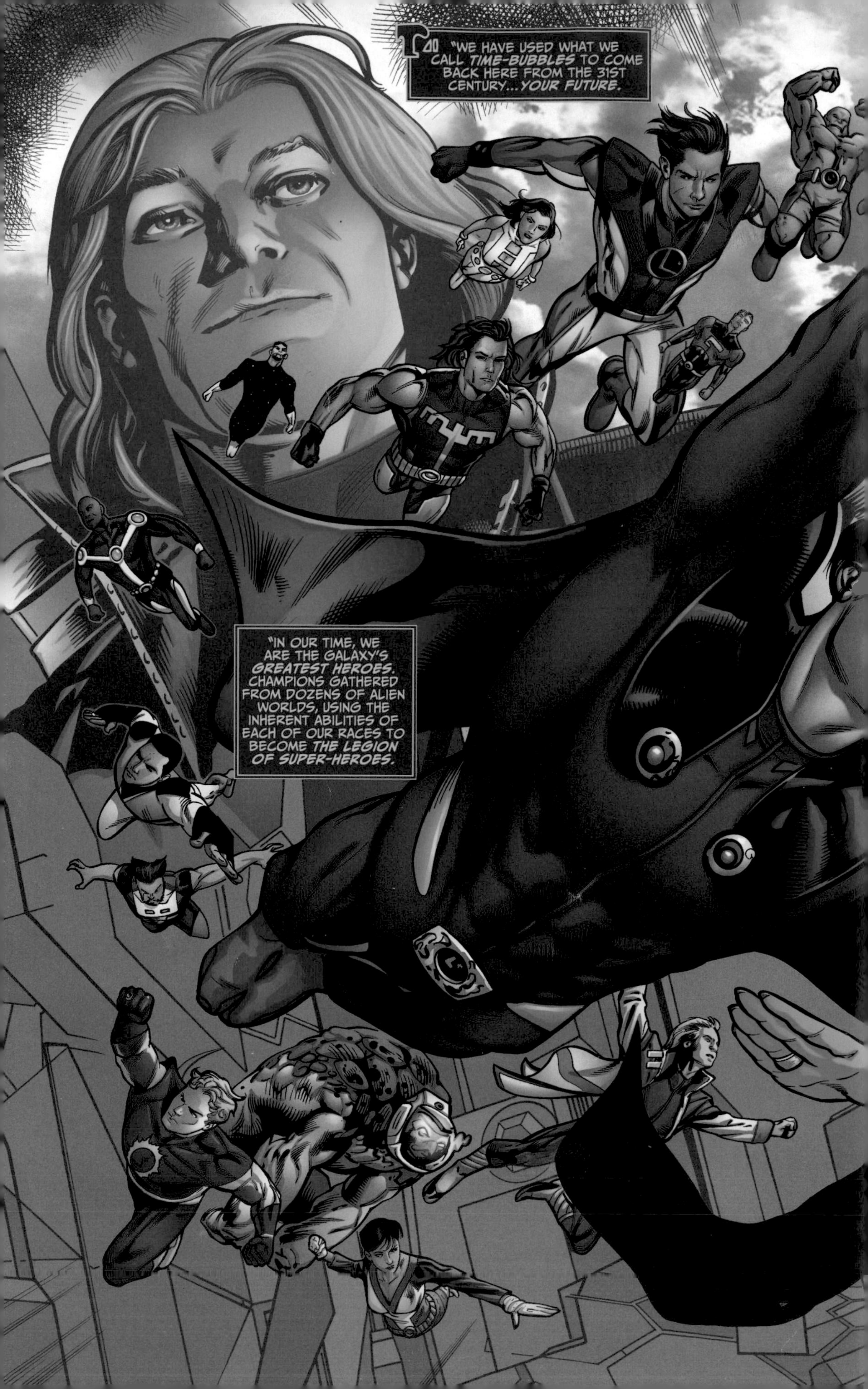
"WE HAVE USED WHAT WE CALL *TIME-BUBBLES* TO COME BACK HERE FROM THE 31ST CENTURY... *YOUR FUTURE*.
"IN OUR TIME, WE ARE THE GALAXY'S *GREATEST HEROES*. CHAMPIONS GATHERED FROM DOZENS OF ALIEN WORLDS, USING THE INHERENT ABILITIES OF EACH OF OUR RACES TO BECOME *THE LEGION OF SUPER-HEROES*.

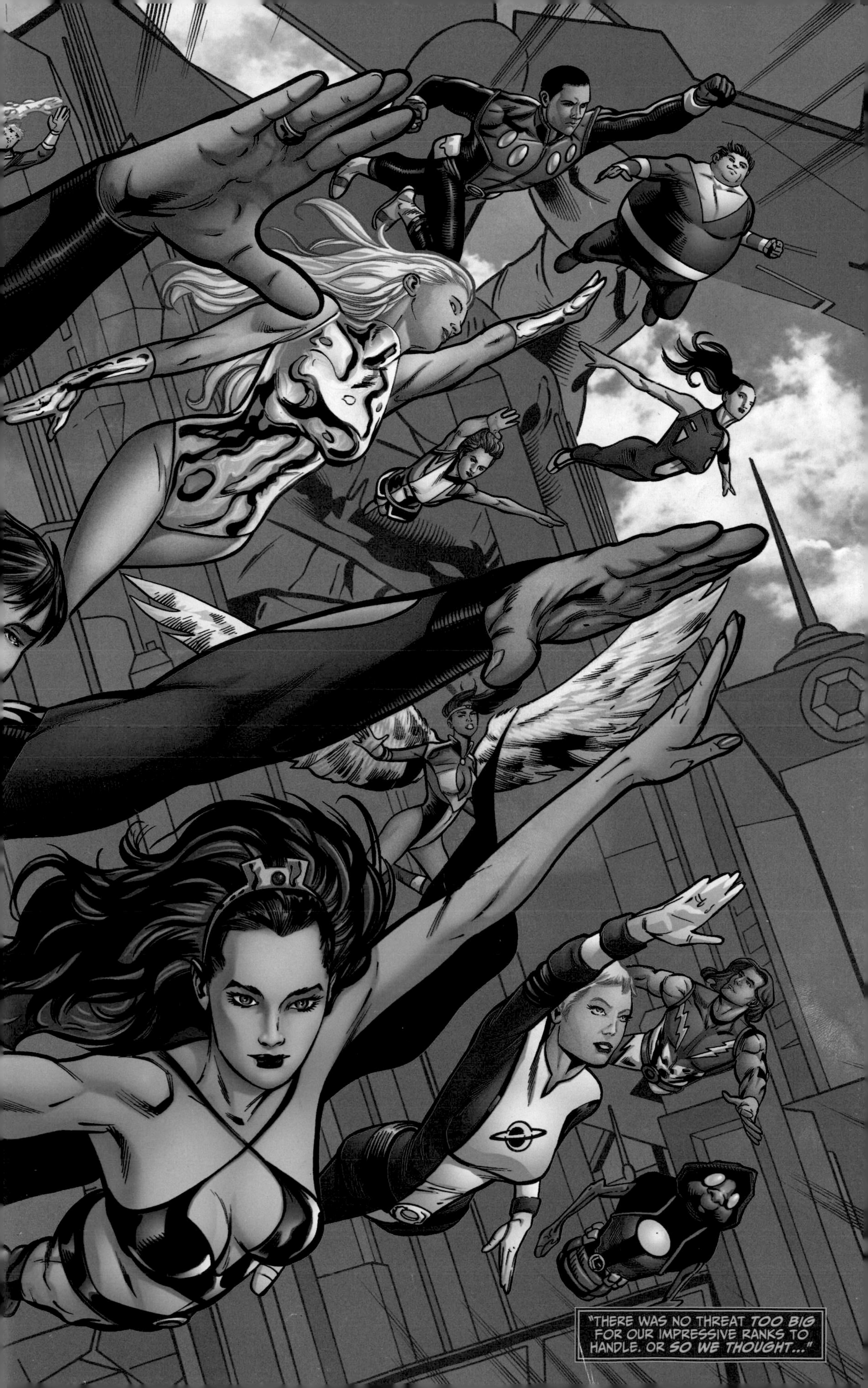
"THERE WAS NO THREAT *TOO BIG* FOR OUR IMPRESSIVE RANKS TO HANDLE. OR *SO WE THOUGHT...*"

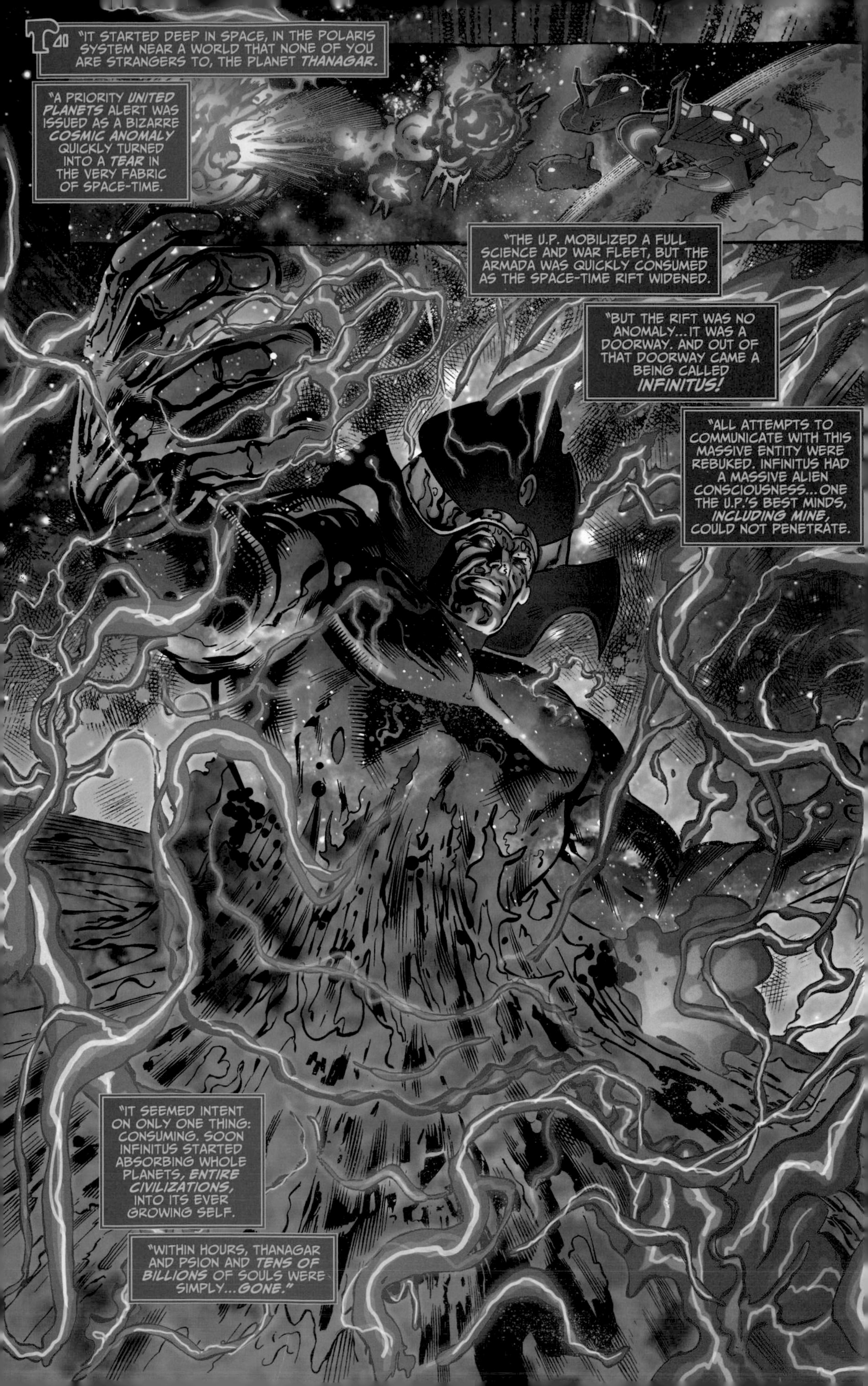
"IT STARTED DEEP IN SPACE, IN THE POLARIS SYSTEM NEAR A WORLD THAT NONE OF YOU ARE STRANGERS TO, THE PLANET THANAGAR.
"A PRIORITY UNITED PLANETS ALERT WAS ISSUED AS A BIZARRE COSMIC ANOMALY QUICKLY TURNED INTO A TEAR IN THE VERY FABRIC OF SPACE-TIME.
"THE U.P. MOBILIZED A FULL SCIENCE AND WAR FLEET, BUT THE ARMADA WAS QUICKLY CONSUMED AS THE SPACE-TIME RIFT WIDENED.
"BUT THE RIFT WAS NO ANOMALY...IT WAS A DOORWAY. AND OUT OF THAT DOORWAY CAME A BEING CALLED INFINITUS!
"ALL ATTEMPTS TO COMMUNICATE WITH THIS MASSIVE ENTITY WERE REBUKED. INFINITUS HAD A MASSIVE ALIEN CONSCIOUSNESS...ONE THE U.P.'S BEST MINDS, INCLUDING MINE, COULD NOT PENETRATE.
"IT SEEMED INTENT ON ONLY ONE THING: CONSUMING. SOON INFINITUS STARTED ABSORBING WHOLE PLANETS, ENTIRE CIVILIZATIONS, INTO ITS EVER GROWING SELF.
"WITHIN HOURS, THANAGAR AND PSION AND TENS OF BILLIONS OF SOULS WERE SIMPLY...GONE."

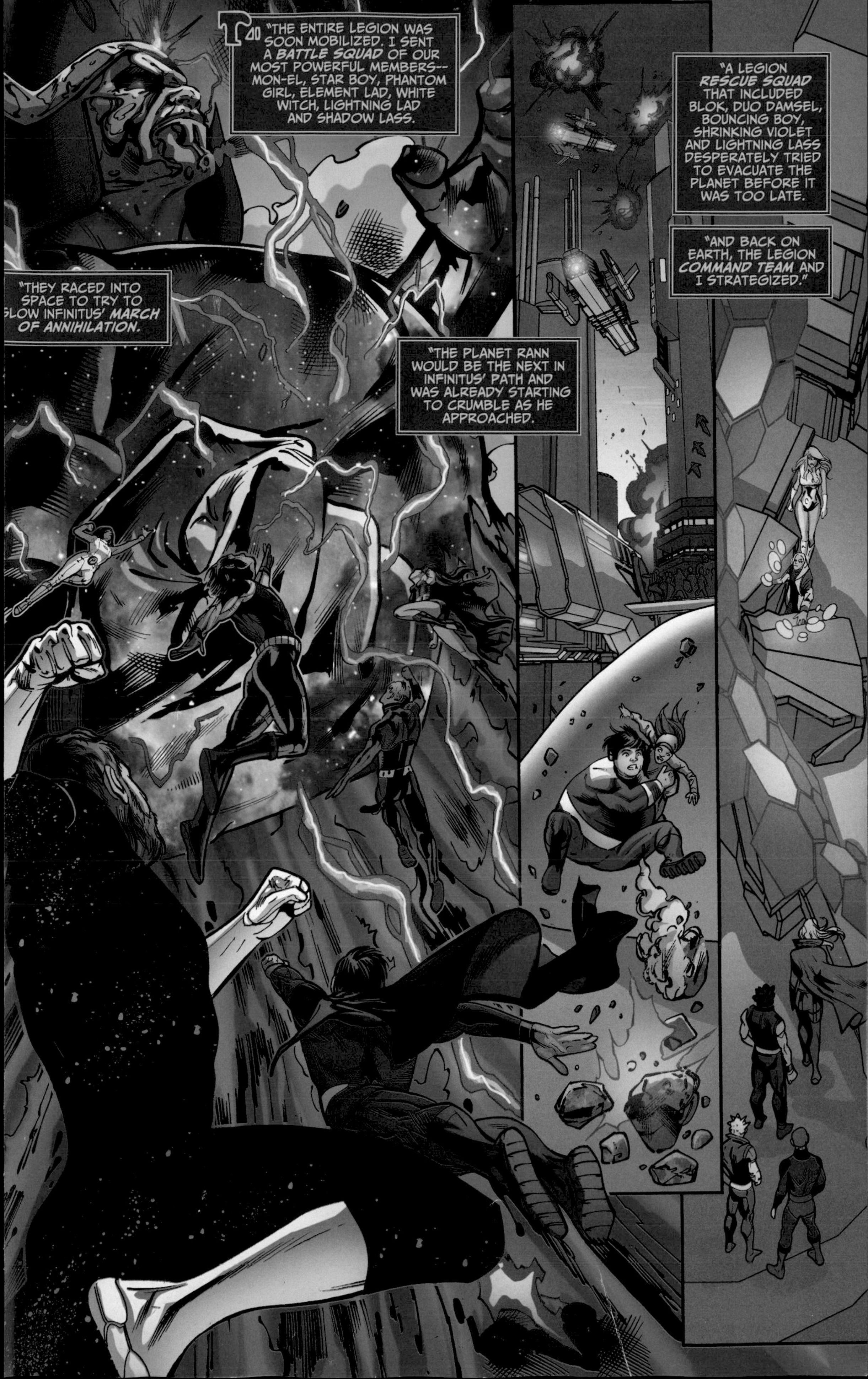
"THE ENTIRE LEGION WAS SOON MOBILIZED. I SENT A BATTLE SQUAD OF OUR MOST POWERFUL MEMBERS-- MON-EL, STAR BOY, PHANTOM GIRL, ELEMENT LAD, WHITE WITCH, LIGHTNING LAD AND SHADOW LASS.
"THEY RACED INTO SPACE TO TRY TO SLOW INFINITUS' MARCH OF ANNIHILATION.
"THE PLANET RANN WOULD BE THE NEXT IN INFINITUS' PATH AND WAS ALREADY STARTING TO CRUMBLE AS HE APPROACHED.
"A LEGION RESCUE SQUAD THAT INCLUDED BLOK, DUO DAMSEL, BOUNCING BOY, SHRINKING VIOLET AND LIGHTNING LASS DESPERATELY TRIED TO EVACUATE THE PLANET BEFORE IT WAS TOO LATE.
"AND BACK ON EARTH, THE LEGION COMMAND TEAM AND I STRATEGIZED."

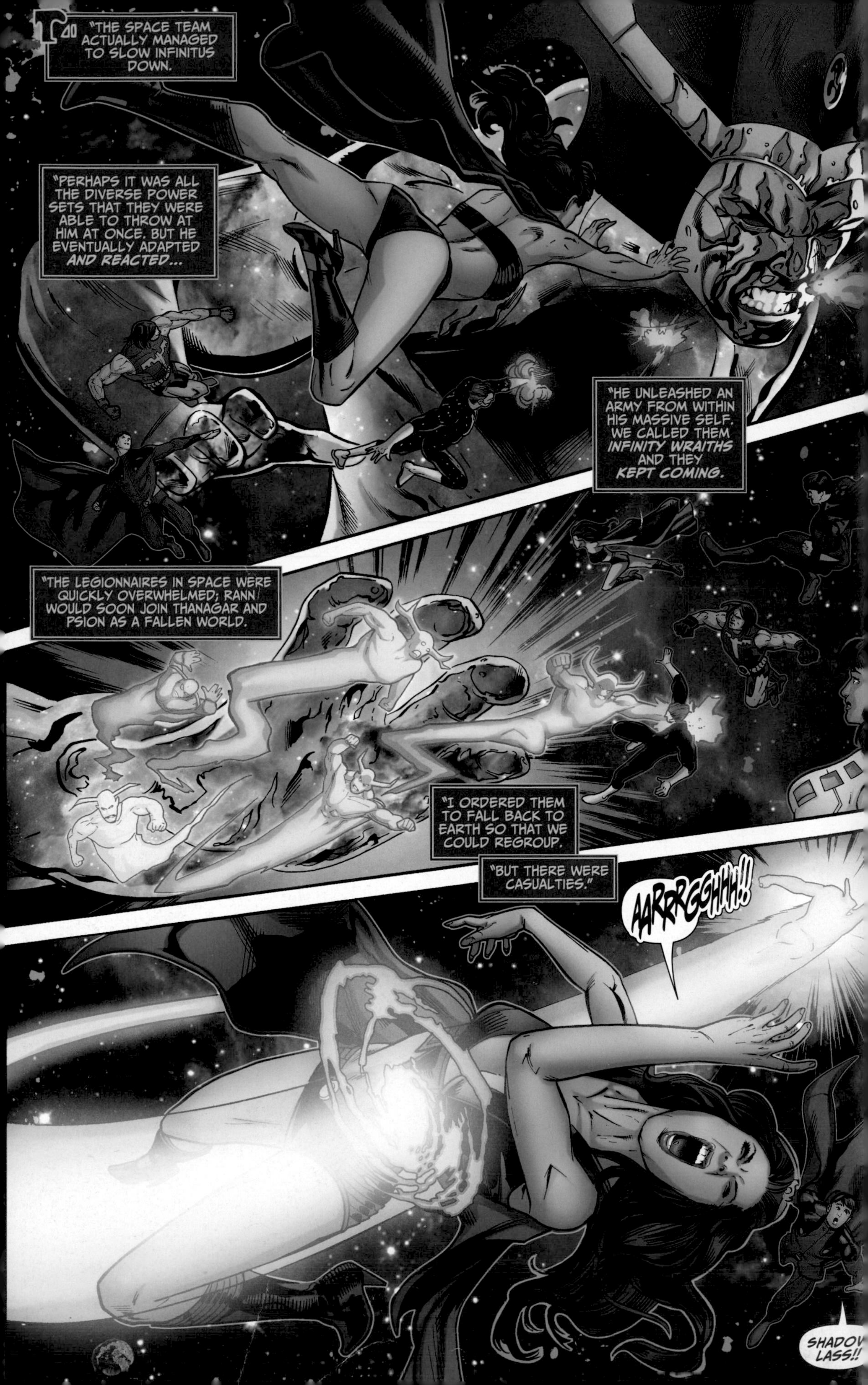
"THE SPACE TEAM ACTUALLY MANAGED TO SLOW INFINITUS DOWN.
"PERHAPS IT WAS ALL THE DIVERSE POWER SETS THAT THEY WERE ABLE TO THROW AT HIM AT ONCE. BUT HE EVENTUALLY ADAPTED AND REACTED...
"HE UNLEASHED AN ARMY FROM WITHIN HIS MASSIVE SELF. WE CALLED THEM INFINITY WRAITHS AND THEY KEPT COMING.
"THE LEGIONNAIRES IN SPACE WERE QUICKLY OVERWHELMED; RANN WOULD SOON JOIN THANAGAR AND PSION AS A FALLEN WORLD.
"I ORDERED THEM TO FALL BACK TO EARTH SO THAT WE COULD REGROUP.
"BUT THERE WERE CASUALTIES."
AARRRGGHHH!!
SHADOW LASS!!

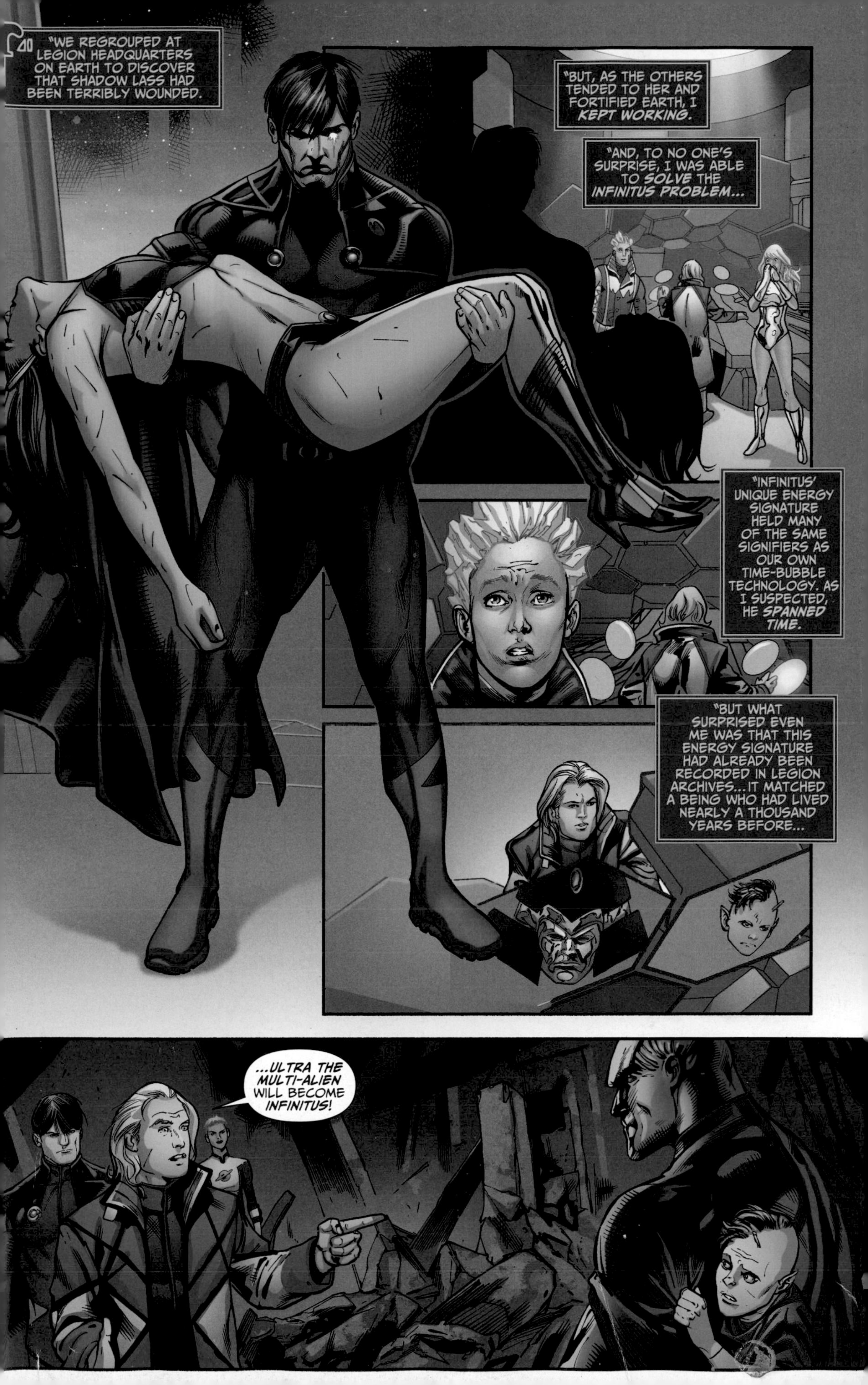
"WE REGROUPED AT LEGION HEADQUARTERS ON EARTH TO DISCOVER THAT SHADOW LASS HAD BEEN TERRIBLY WOUNDED.
"BUT, AS THE OTHERS TENDED TO HER AND FORTIFIED EARTH, I KEPT WORKING.
"AND, TO NO ONE'S SURPRISE, I WAS ABLE TO SOLVE THE INFINITUS PROBLEM...
"INFINITUS' UNIQUE ENERGY SIGNATURE HELD MANY OF THE SAME SIGNIFIERS AS OUR OWN TIME-BUBBLE TECHNOLOGY. AS I SUSPECTED, HE SPANNED TIME.
"BUT WHAT SURPRISED EVEN ME WAS THAT THIS ENERGY SIGNATURE HAD ALREADY BEEN RECORDED IN LEGION ARCHIVES...IT MATCHED A BEING WHO HAD LIVED NEARLY A THOUSAND YEARS BEFORE...
...ULTRA THE MULTI-ALIEN WILL BECOME INFINITUS!

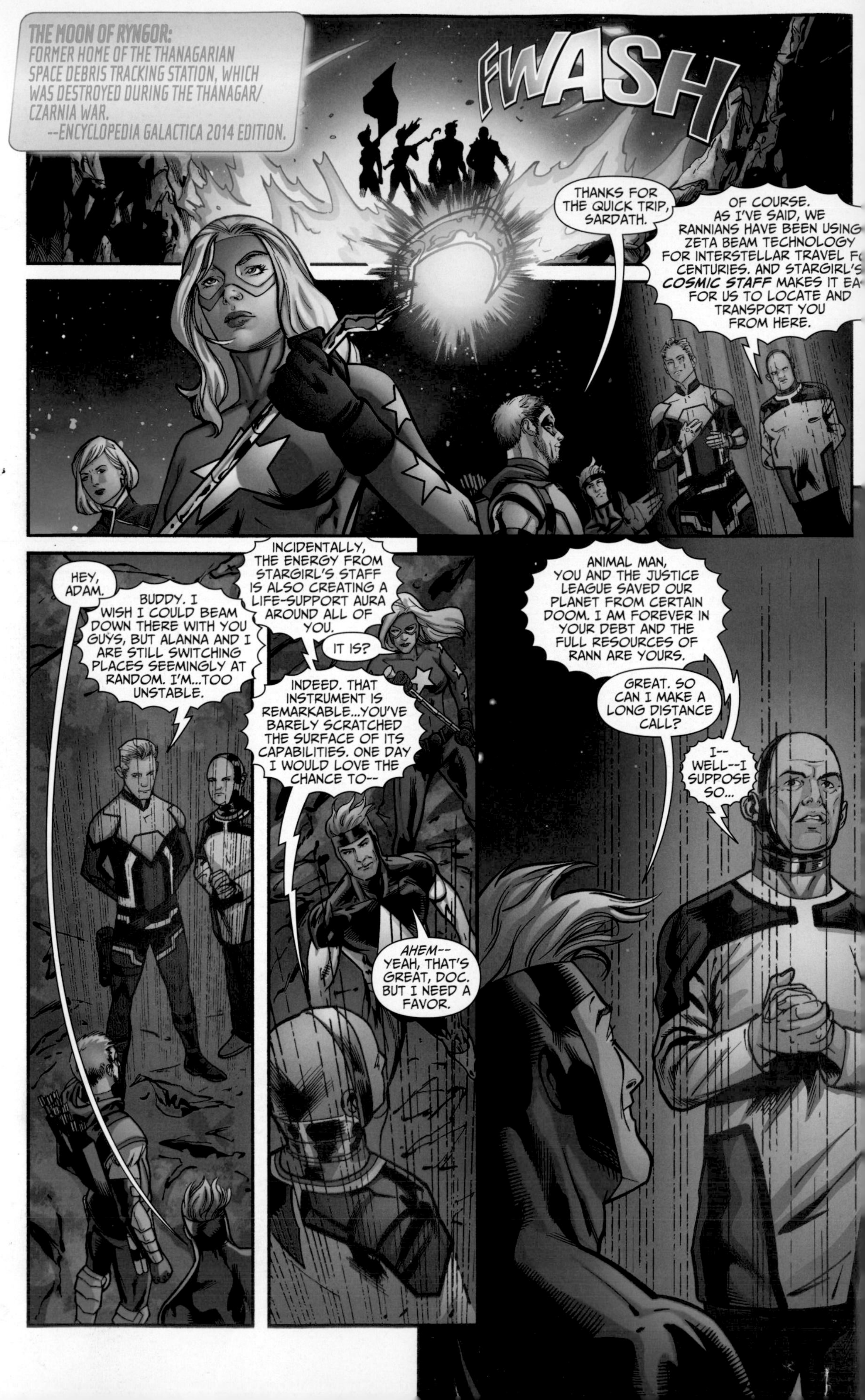
THE MOON OF RYNGOR: FORMER HOME OF THE THANAGARIAN SPACE DEBRIS TRACKING STATION, WHICH WAS DESTROYED DURING THE THANAGAR/CZARNIA WAR. --ENCYCLOPEDIA GALACTICA 2014 EDITION.
FWASH
THANKS FOR THE QUICK TRIP, SARDATH.
OF COURSE. AS I'VE SAID, WE RANNIANS HAVE BEEN USING ZETA BEAM TECHNOLOGY FOR INTERSTELLAR TRAVEL F CENTURIES. AND STARGIRL'S COSMIC STAFF MAKES IT EA FOR US TO LOCATE AND TRANSPORT YOU FROM HERE.
HEY, ADAM.
BUDDY. I WISH I COULD BEAM DOWN THERE WITH YOU GUYS, BUT ALANNA AND I ARE STILL SWITCHING PLACES SEEMINGLY AT RANDOM. I'M...TOO UNSTABLE.
INCIDENTALLY, THE ENERGY FROM STARGIRL'S STAFF IS ALSO CREATING A LIFE-SUPPORT AURA AROUND ALL OF YOU.
IT IS?
INDEED. THAT INSTRUMENT IS REMARKABLE...YOU'VE BARELY SCRATCHED THE SURFACE OF ITS CAPABILITIES. ONE DAY I WOULD LOVE THE CHANCE TO--
AHEM-- YEAH, THAT'S GREAT, DOC. BUT I NEED A FAVOR.
ANIMAL MAN, YOU AND THE JUSTICE LEAGUE SAVED OUR PLANET FROM CERTAIN DOOM. I AM FOREVER IN YOUR DEBT AND THE FULL RESOURCES OF RANN ARE YOURS.
GREAT. SO CAN I MAKE A LONG DISTANCE CALL?
I-- WELL--I SUPPOSE SO...

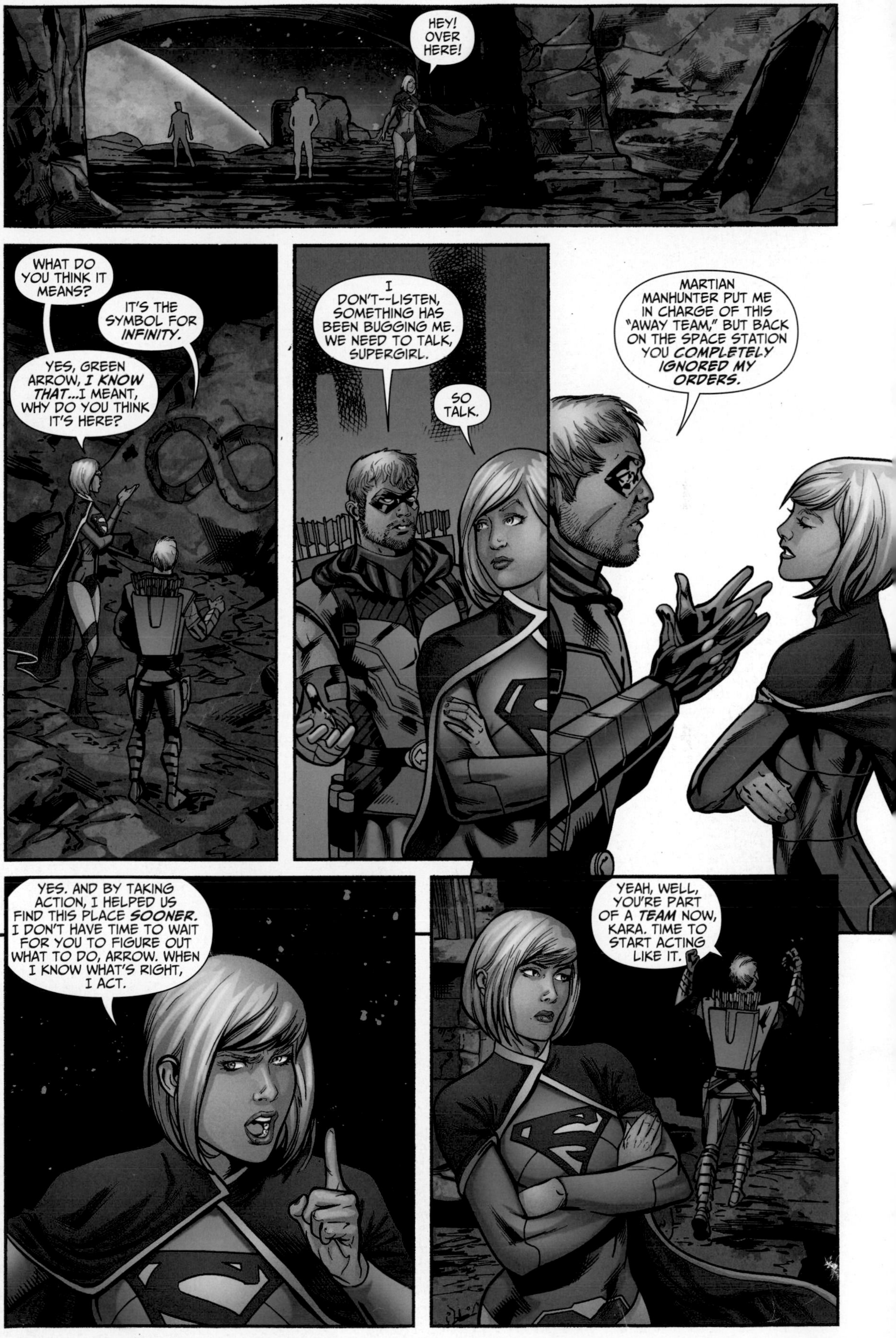
HEY! OVER HERE!
WHAT DO YOU THINK IT MEANS?
IT'S THE SYMBOL FOR *INFINITY.*
YES, GREEN ARROW, *I KNOW THAT...*I MEANT, WHY DO YOU THINK IT'S HERE?
I DON'T--LISTEN, SOMETHING HAS BEEN BUGGING ME. WE NEED TO TALK, SUPERGIRL.
SO TALK.
MARTIAN MANHUNTER PUT ME IN CHARGE OF THIS "AWAY TEAM," BUT BACK ON THE SPACE STATION YOU *COMPLETELY IGNORED MY ORDERS.*
YES. AND BY TAKING ACTION, I HELPED US FIND THIS PLACE *SOONER.* I DON'T HAVE TIME TO WAIT FOR YOU TO FIGURE OUT WHAT TO DO, ARROW. WHEN I KNOW WHAT'S RIGHT, I ACT.
YEAH, WELL, YOU'RE PART OF A *TEAM* NOW, KARA. TIME TO START ACTING LIKE IT.

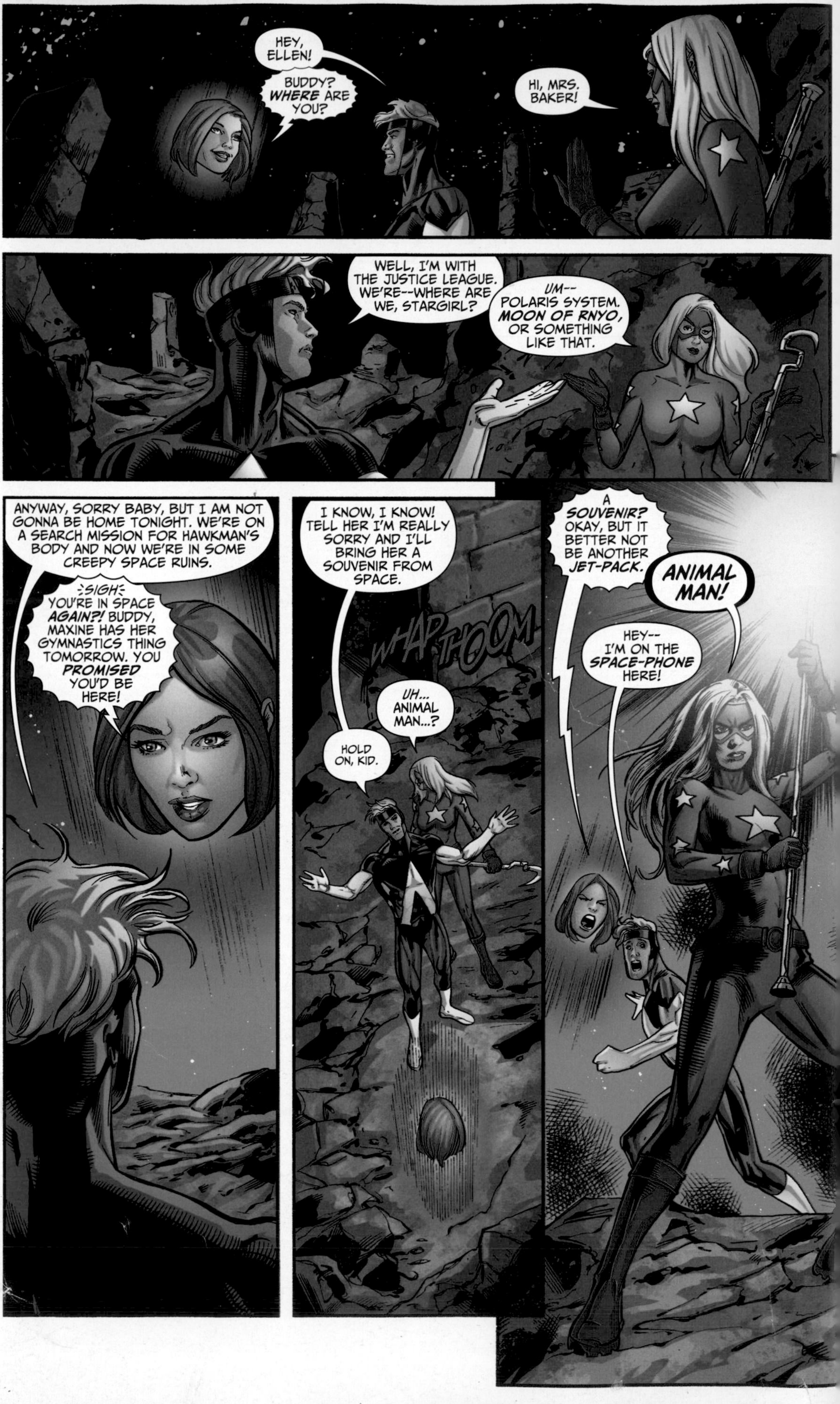
HEY, ELLEN!
BUDDY? WHERE ARE YOU?
HI, MRS. BAKER!
WELL, I'M WITH THE JUSTICE LEAGUE. WE'RE--WHERE ARE WE, STARGIRL?
UM-- POLARIS SYSTEM. MOON OF RNYO, OR SOMETHING LIKE THAT.
ANYWAY, SORRY BABY, BUT I AM NOT GONNA BE HOME TONIGHT. WE'RE ON A SEARCH MISSION FOR HAWKMAN'S BODY AND NOW WE'RE IN SOME CREEPY SPACE RUINS.
SIGH YOU'RE IN SPACE AGAIN?! BUDDY, MAXINE HAS HER GYMNASTICS THING TOMORROW. YOU PROMISED YOU'D BE HERE!
I KNOW, I KNOW! TELL HER I'M REALLY SORRY AND I'LL BRING HER A SOUVENIR FROM SPACE.
WHAP THOOM
UH... ANIMAL MAN...?
HOLD ON, KID.
A SOUVENIR? OKAY, BUT IT BETTER NOT BE ANOTHER JET-PACK.
ANIMAL MAN!
HEY-- I'M ON THE SPACE-PHONE HERE!

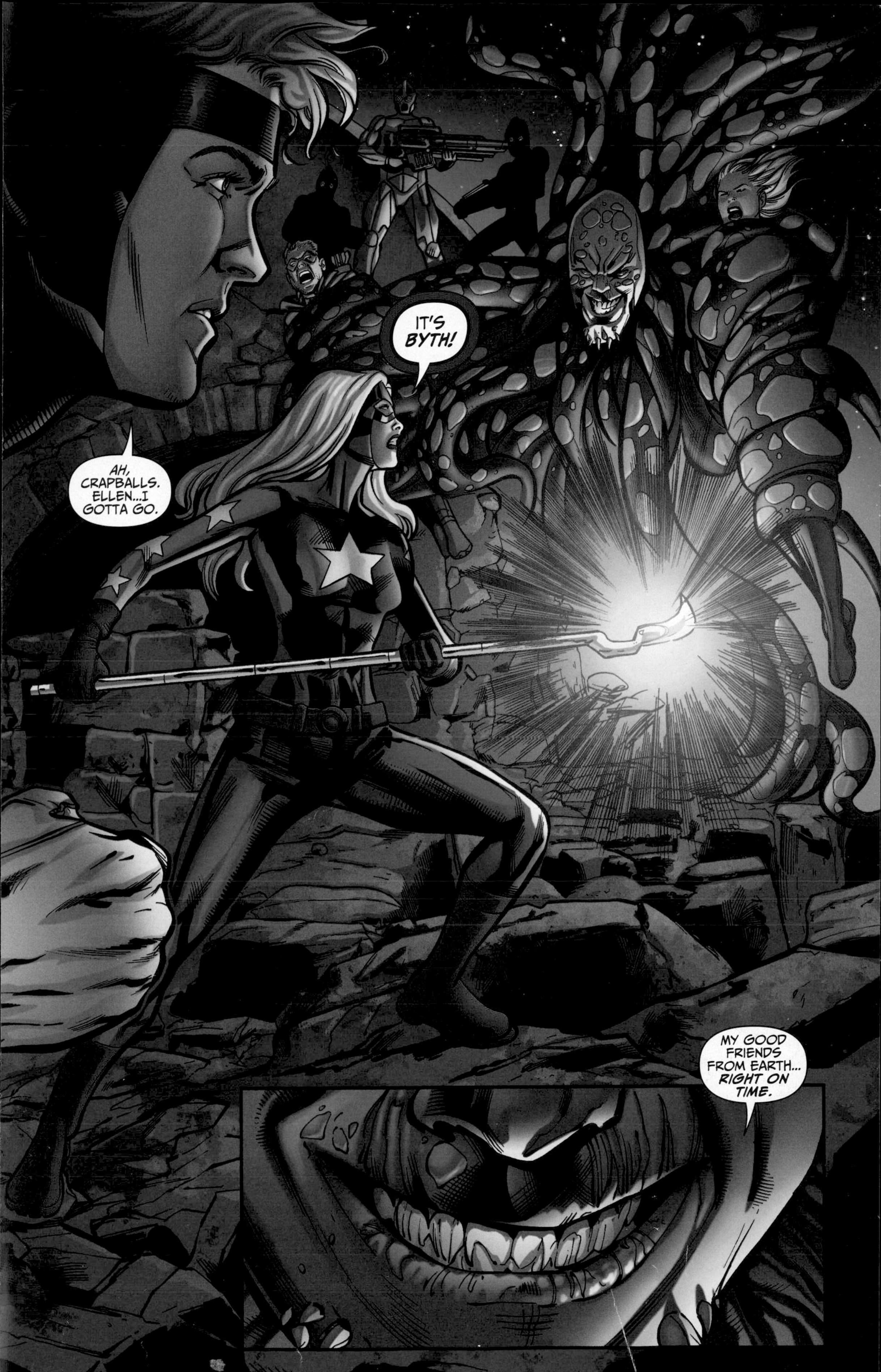
IT'S *BYTH!*
AH, CRAPBALLS. ELLEN...I GOTTA GO.
MY GOOD FRIENDS FROM EARTH... *RIGHT ON TIME.*

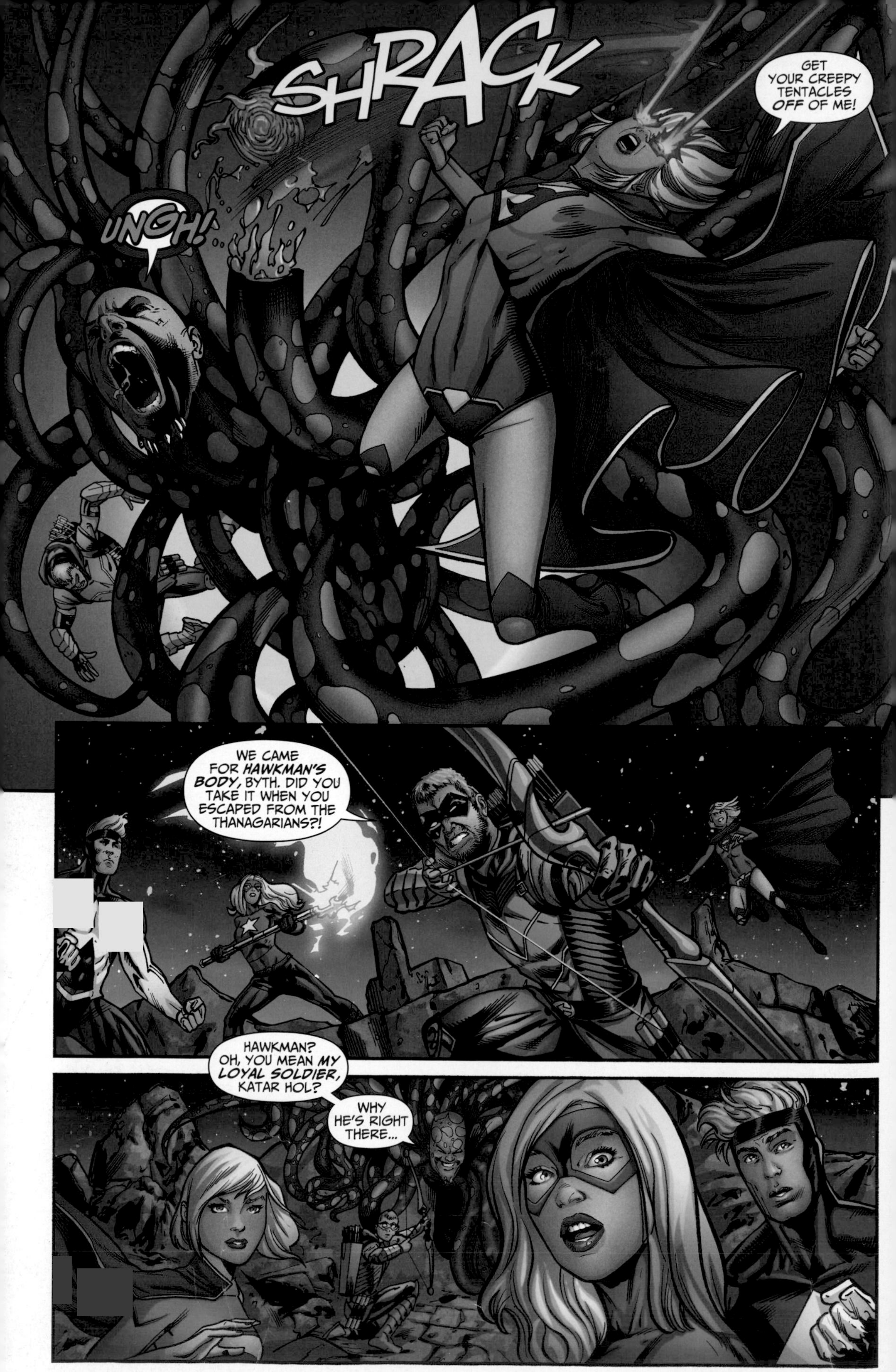
SHRACK
GET YOUR CREEPY TENTACLES OFF OF ME!
UNGH!
WE CAME FOR HAWKMAN'S BODY, BYTH. DID YOU TAKE IT WHEN YOU ESCAPED FROM THE THANAGARIANS?!
HAWKMAN? OH, YOU MEAN MY LOYAL SOLDIER, KATAR HOL?
WHY HE'S RIGHT THERE...

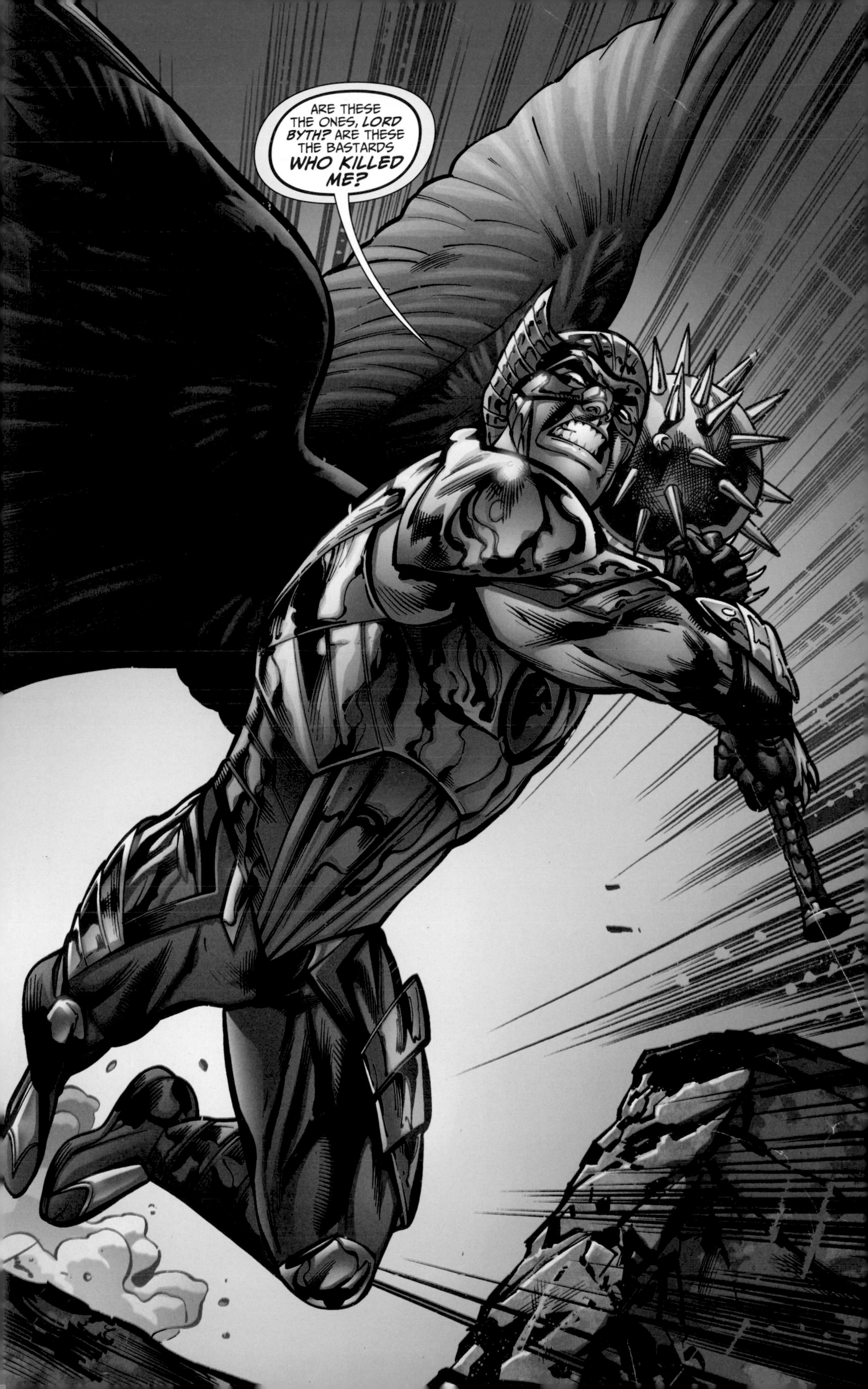
ARE THESE THE ONES, LORD BYTH? ARE THESE THE BASTARDS WHO KILLED ME?

EARTH.

WAIT--HOW IS THIS *CHILD* GOING TO BECOME THIS INFINTUS THING? I'M TOTALLY LOST.

YOU'RE LOST?!

THE HOW ISN'T IMPORTANT! THAT THING IS GOING TO *KILL SHADOW LASS!* I WILL *NOT* ALLOW THAT TO HAPPEN!

MON-EL, STOP! SHADOW LASS IS *NOT* DEAD!

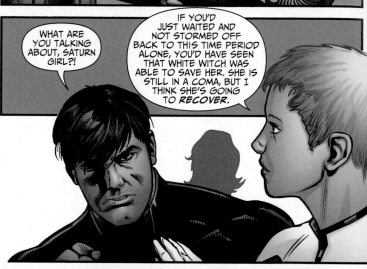

WHAT ARE YOU TALKING ABOUT, SATURN GIRL?!

IF YOU'D JUST WAITED AND NOT STORMED OFF BACK TO THIS TIME PERIOD ALONE, YOU'D HAVE SEEN THAT WHITE WITCH WAS ABLE TO SAVE HER. SHE IS STILL IN A COMA, BUT I THINK SHE'S GOING TO *RECOVER.*

IT'S TRUE, MON. SHE'S GOING TO BE OKAY.

THIS SHADOW LASS...IS SHE YOUR...?

YES. I--I THOUGHT I'D LOST HER.

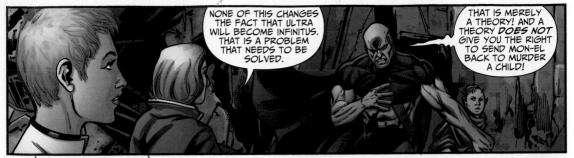

NONE OF THIS CHANGES THE FACT THAT ULTRA WILL BECOME INFINITUS. THAT IS A PROBLEM THAT NEEDS TO BE SOLVED.

THAT IS MERELY A THEORY! AND A THEORY *DOES NOT* GIVE YOU THE RIGHT TO SEND MON-EL BACK TO MURDER A CHILD!

IT IS NO THEORY...IT IS *FACT*. THAT CHILD WILL BECOME INFINITUS AND *HE WILL* MURDER BILLIONS OF ALIEN LIVES.

MANHUNTER, I COULD GO OVER ALL OF MY CALCULATIONS AND DATA, BUT I HAVE A *LEVEL-TWELVE INTELLIGENCE*, AND QUITE FRANKLY I'M AFRAID IT WOULD BE *LOST ON YOU*.

NOW...AS I SAID, MON-EL ACTED RASHLY.

HE RACED OFF AND TOOK MATTERS INTO HIS OWN HANDS, BUT I PREFER MEDIATION WHEN-EVER POSSIBLE. SO, HERE IS MY OFFER...

WHEN WE LEFT THE 31ST CENTURY INFINITUS WAS STILL *THIRTY-SIX HOURS* FROM EARTH. SO I WILL ALLOW US *TWENTY-FOUR HOURS* TO WORK TOGETHER TO DETERMINE EXACTLY HOW ULTRA BECOMES INFINITUS AND *PREVENT* IT.

TWENTY-FOUR HOURS? OR WHAT, BRAINIAC-5?

OR, MANHUNTER, THE REST OF THE LEGION, NEARLY TWENTY *OTHER* SUPER HUMANS-- MANY AS POWERFUL AS MON-EL--WILL FOLLOW US BACK HERE...

AND TOGETHER WE WILL DESTROY THE CHILD *AT ANY COST*.

--ANHUNTER, COME IN!

GREEN ARROW?! THIS IS *NOT* A GOOD TIME.

YEAH, WELL, *MAKE IT A GOOD TIME*--WE GOT TROUBLE! WE FOUND HAWKMAN *AND* BYTH--

AH, THE *FIRST* GREEN ARROW... FASCINATING.

BYTH? HOW IS HE INVOLVED IN THIS?!

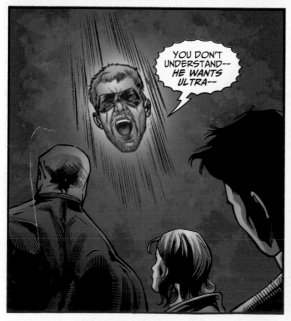

YOU DON'T UNDERSTAND-- *HE WANTS ULTRA*--

AND THAT'S NOT ALL. HAWKMAN IS ALI--

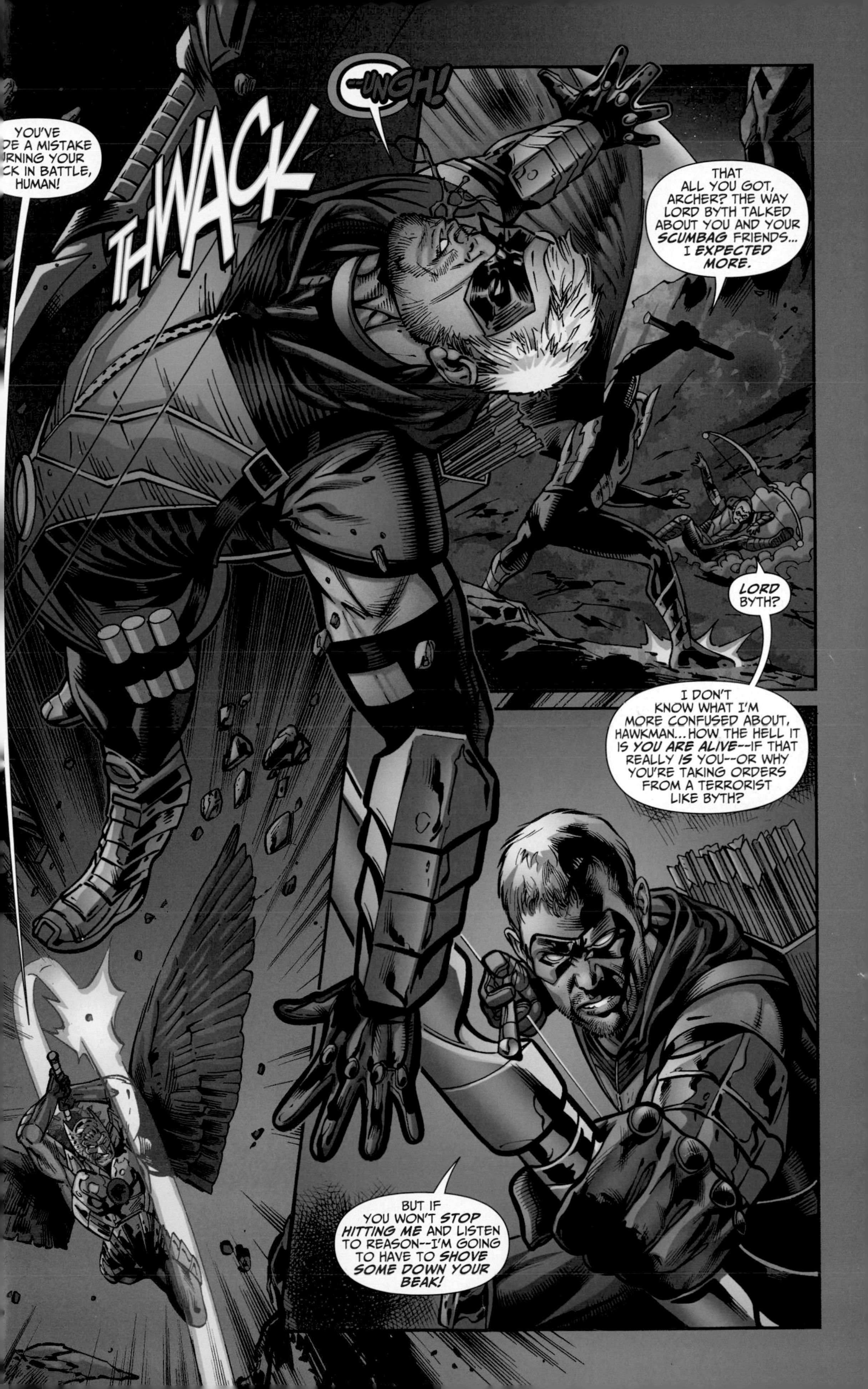
YOU'VE DE A MISTAKE URNING YOUR CK IN BATTLE, HUMAN!
THWACK
--UNGH!
THAT ALL YOU GOT, ARCHER? THE WAY LORD BYTH TALKED ABOUT YOU AND YOUR SCUMBAG FRIENDS... I EXPECTED MORE.
LORD BYTH?
I DON'T KNOW WHAT I'M MORE CONFUSED ABOUT, HAWKMAN...HOW THE HELL IT IS YOU ARE ALIVE--IF THAT REALLY IS YOU--OR WHY YOU'RE TAKING ORDERS FROM A TERRORIST LIKE BYTH?
BUT IF YOU WON'T STOP HITTING ME AND LISTEN TO REASON--I'M GOING TO HAVE TO SHOVE SOME DOWN YOUR BEAK!

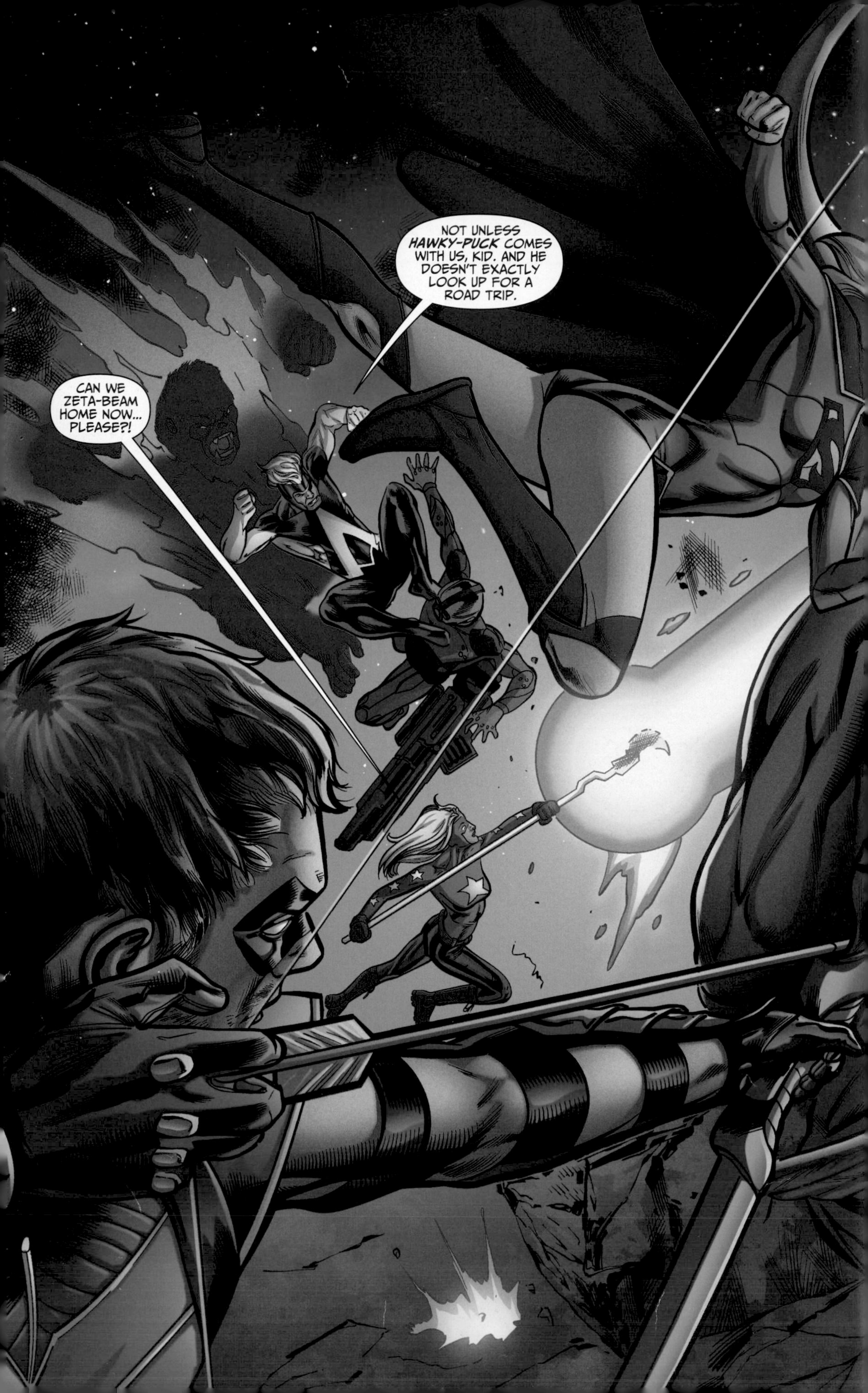
NOT UNLESS HAWKY-PUCK COMES WITH US, KID. AND HE DOESN'T EXACTLY LOOK UP FOR A ROAD TRIP.
CAN WE ZETA-BEAM HOME NOW... PLEASE?!

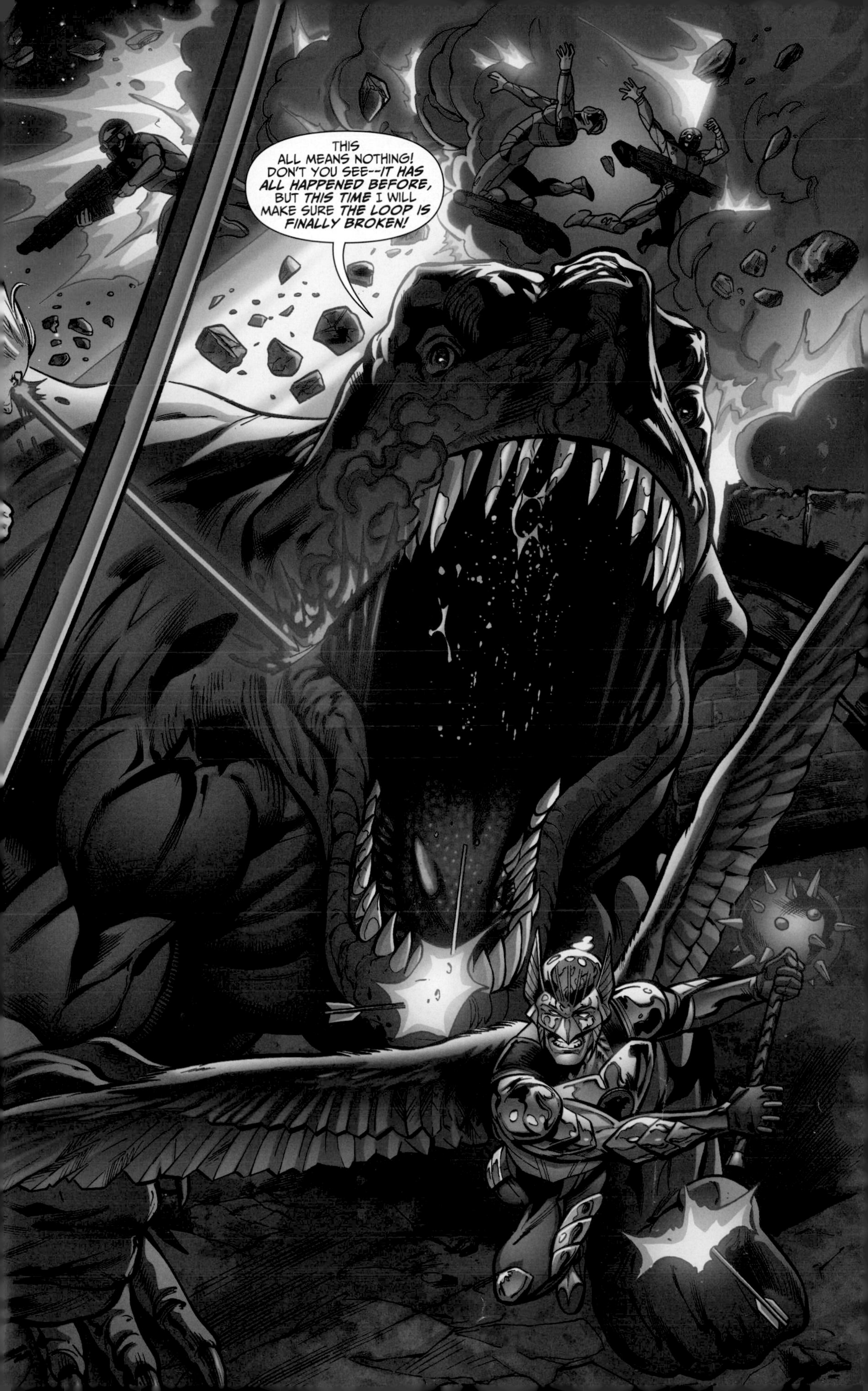
THIS ALL MEANS NOTHING! DON'T YOU SEE--IT HAS ALL HAPPENED BEFORE, BUT THIS TIME I WILL MAKE SURE THE LOOP IS FINALLY BROKEN!

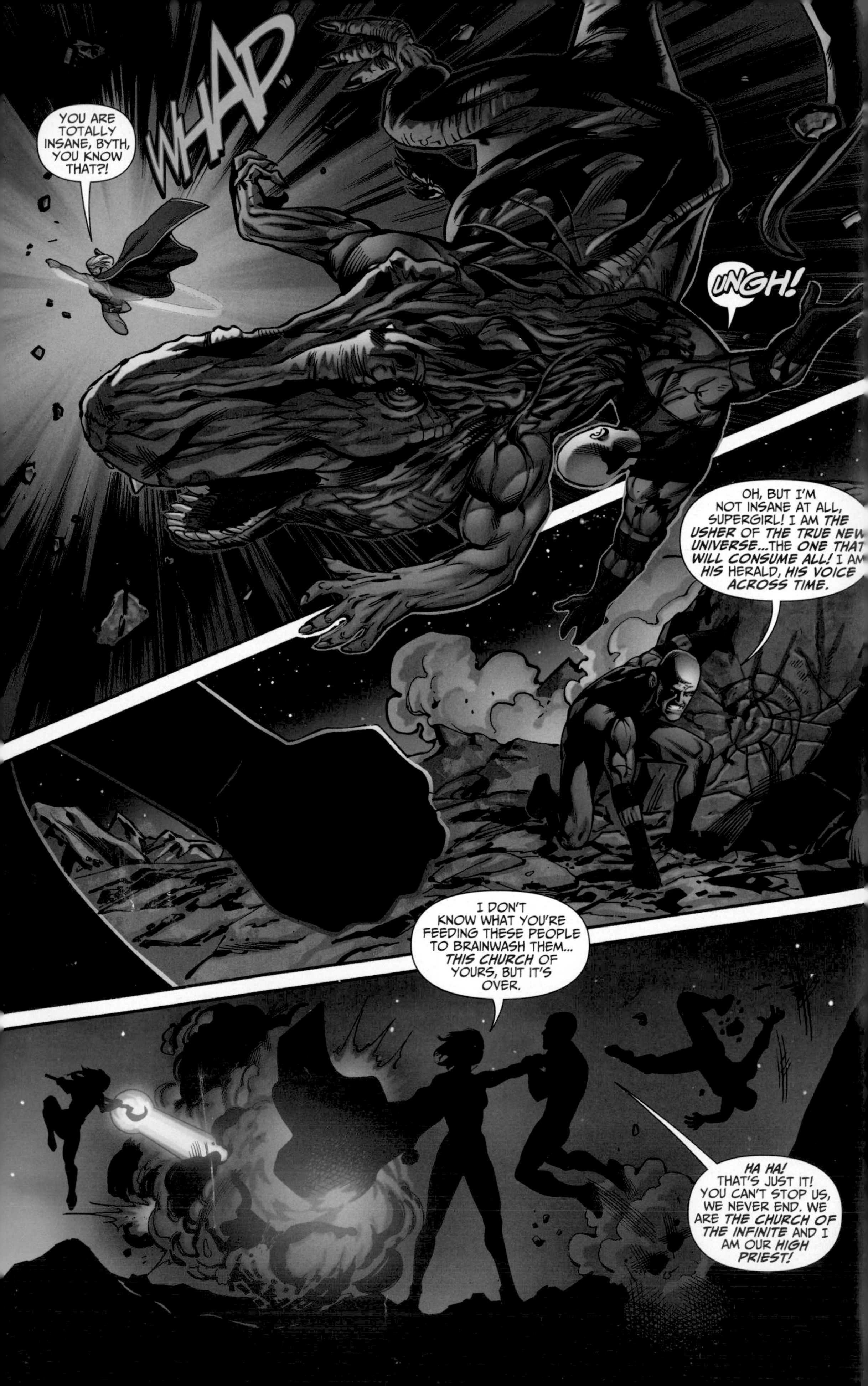
WHAP
YOU ARE TOTALLY INSANE, BYTH, YOU KNOW THAT?!
UNGH!
OH, BUT I'M NOT INSANE AT ALL, SUPERGIRL! I AM THE USHER OF THE TRUE NEW UNIVERSE...THE ONE THAT WILL CONSUME ALL! I AM HIS HERALD, HIS VOICE ACROSS TIME.
I DON'T KNOW WHAT YOU'RE FEEDING THESE PEOPLE TO BRAINWASH THEM... THIS CHURCH OF YOURS, BUT IT'S OVER.
HA HA! THAT'S JUST IT! YOU CAN'T STOP US, WE NEVER END. WE ARE THE CHURCH OF THE INFINITE AND I AM OUR HIGH PRIEST!

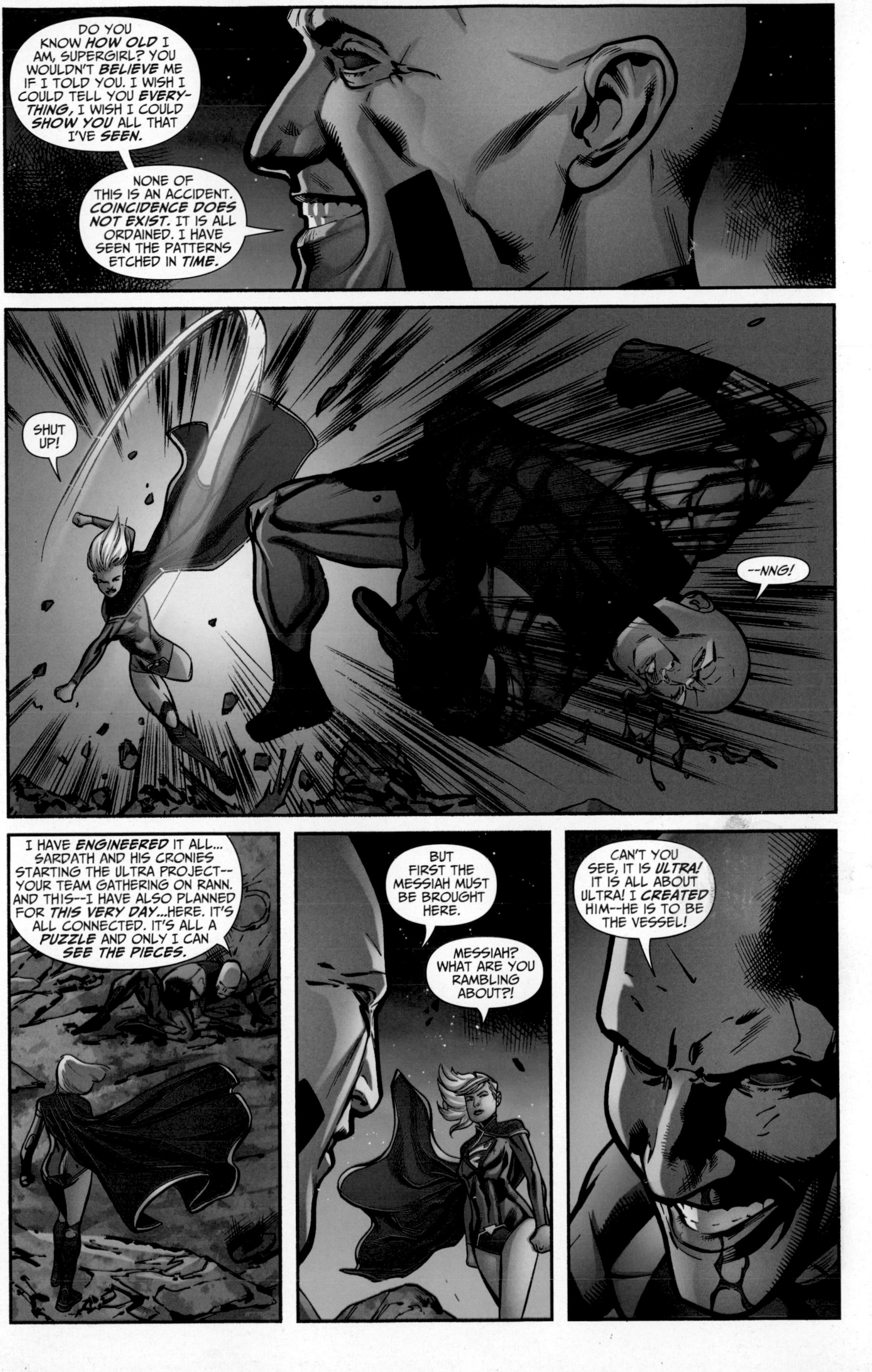
DO YOU KNOW HOW OLD I AM, SUPERGIRL? YOU WOULDN'T BELIEVE ME IF I TOLD YOU. I WISH I COULD TELL YOU EVERY-THING, I WISH I COULD SHOW YOU ALL THAT I'VE SEEN.
NONE OF THIS IS AN ACCIDENT. COINCIDENCE DOES NOT EXIST. IT IS ALL ORDAINED. I HAVE SEEN THE PATTERNS ETCHED IN TIME.
SHUT UP!
--NNG!
I HAVE ENGINEERED IT ALL... SARDATH AND HIS CRONIES STARTING THE ULTRA PROJECT--YOUR TEAM GATHERING ON RANN. AND THIS--I HAVE ALSO PLANNED FOR THIS VERY DAY...HERE. IT'S ALL CONNECTED. IT'S ALL A PUZZLE AND ONLY I CAN SEE THE PIECES.
BUT FIRST THE MESSIAH MUST BE BROUGHT HERE.
MESSIAH? WHAT ARE YOU RAMBLING ABOUT?!
CAN'T YOU SEE, IT IS ULTRA! IT IS ALL ABOUT ULTRA! I CREATED HIM--HE IS TO BE THE VESSEL!

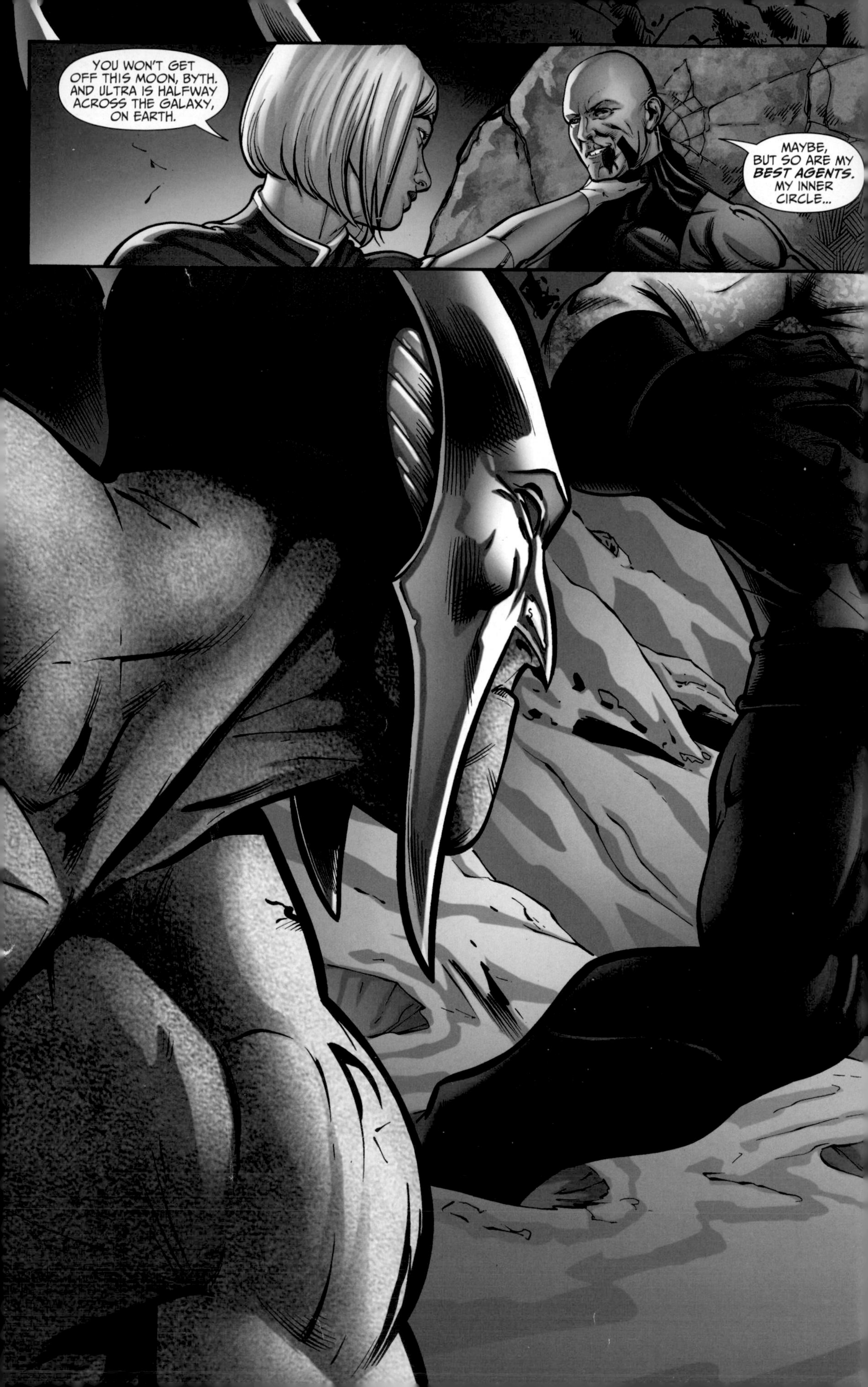
YOU WON'T GET OFF THIS MOON, BYTH. AND ULTRA IS HALFWAY ACROSS THE GALAXY, ON EARTH.
MAYBE, BUT SO ARE MY BEST AGENTS. MY INNER CIRCLE...

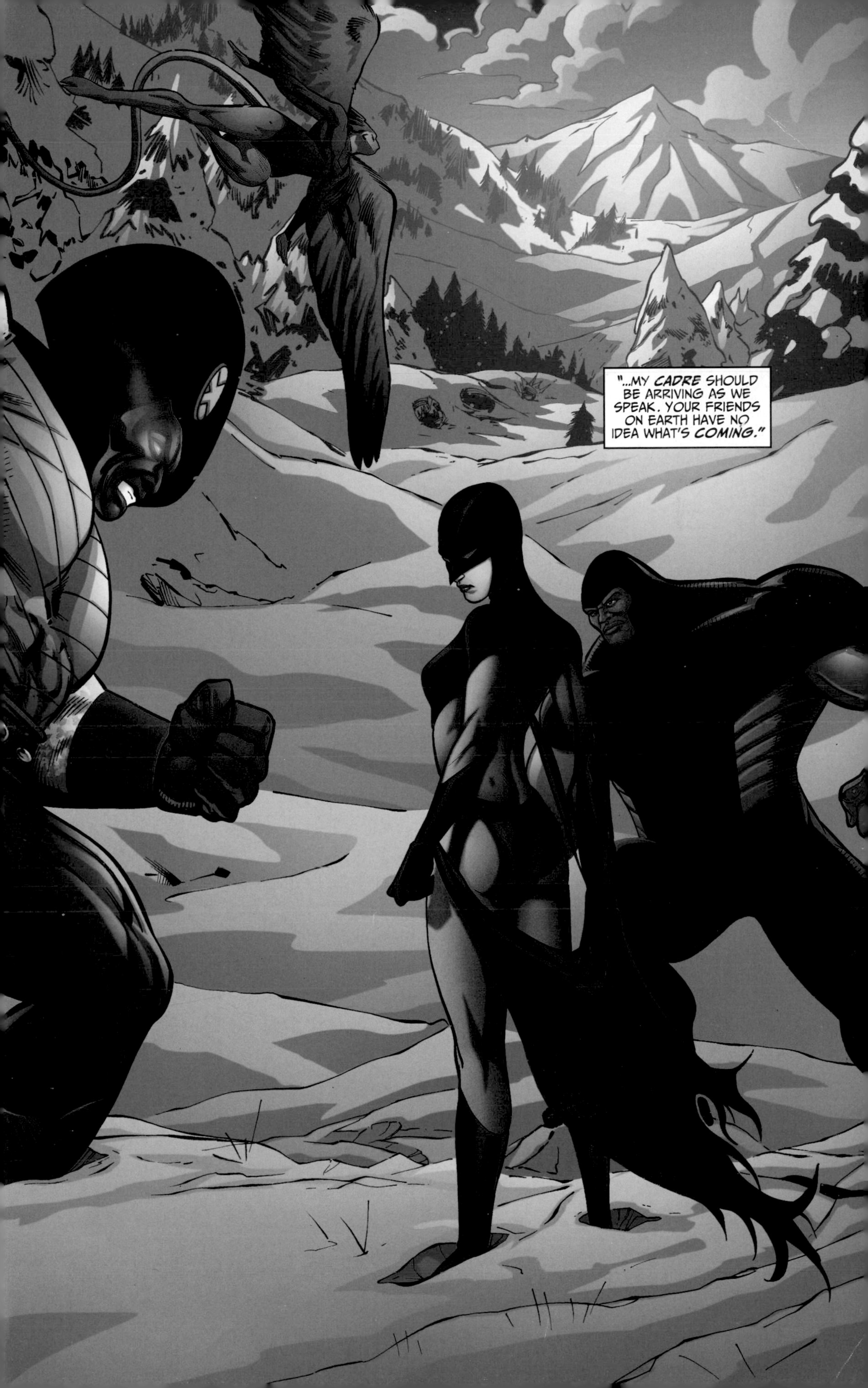
"...MY CADRE SHOULD BE ARRIVING AS WE SPEAK. YOUR FRIENDS ON EARTH HAVE NO IDEA WHAT'S COMING."

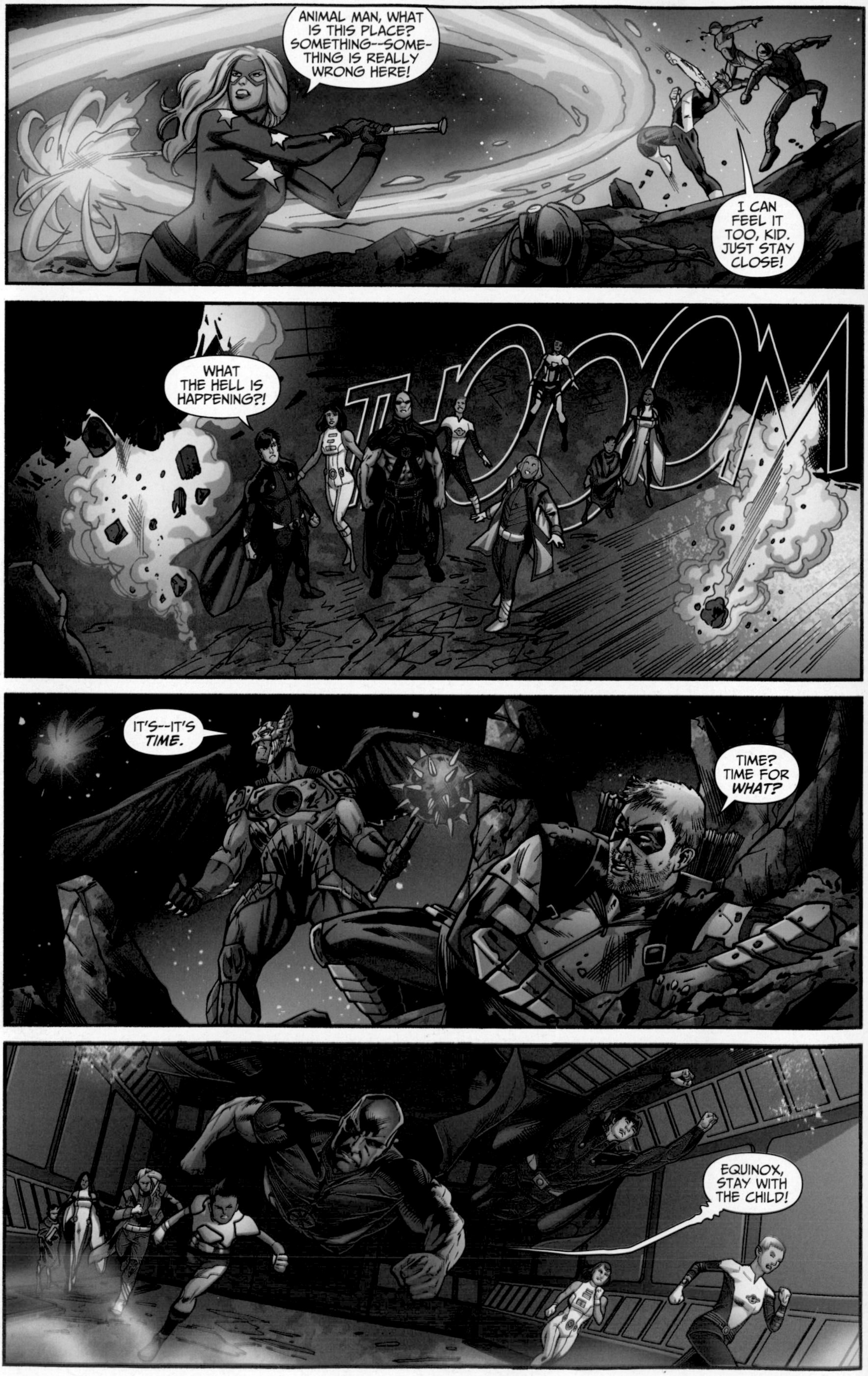
ANIMAL MAN, WHAT IS THIS PLACE? SOMETHING--SOME-THING IS REALLY WRONG HERE!
I CAN FEEL IT TOO, KID. JUST STAY CLOSE!
WHAT THE HELL IS HAPPENING?!
THOOOM
IT'S--IT'S TIME.
TIME? TIME FOR WHAT?
EQUINOX, STAY WITH THE CHILD!

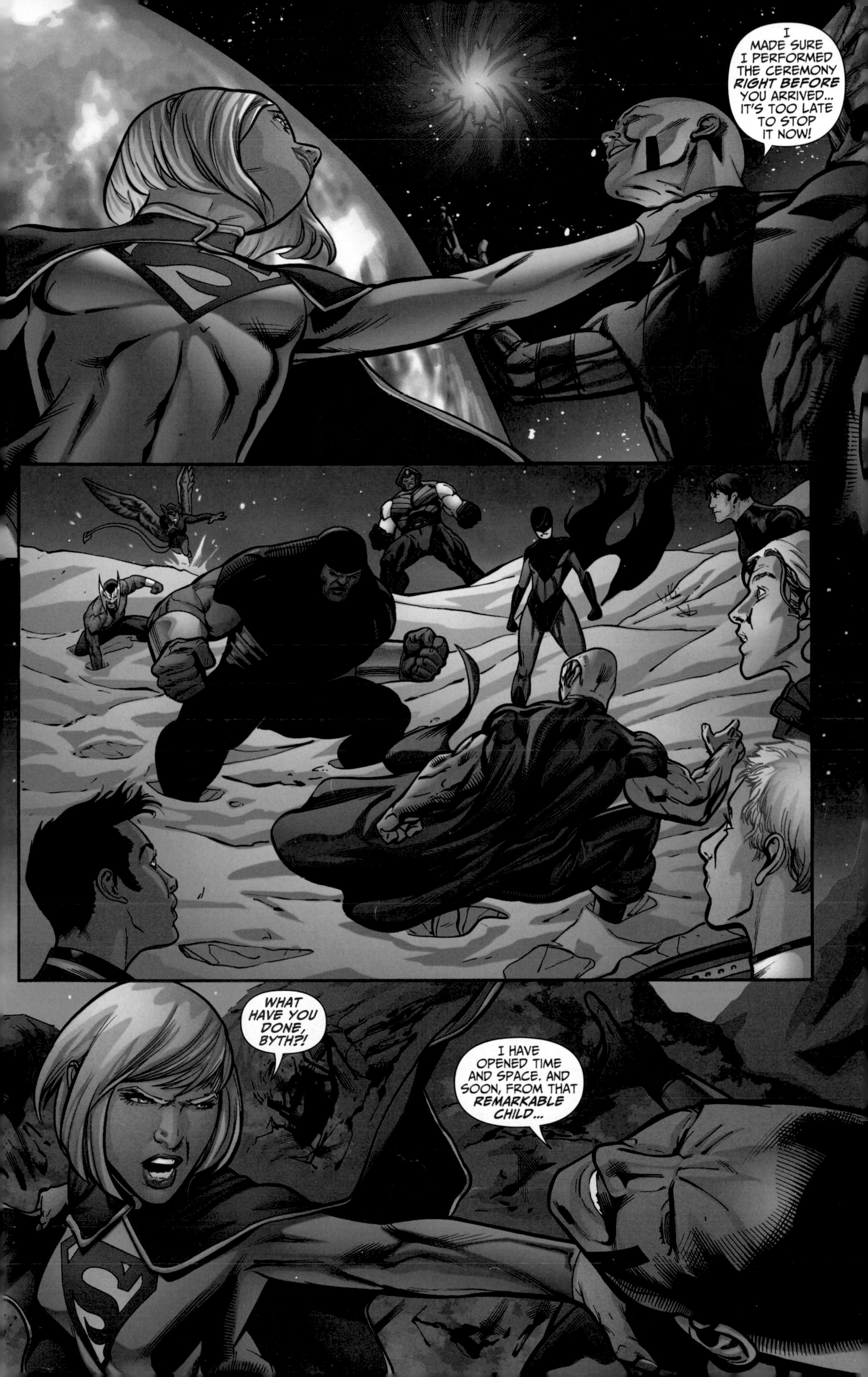

I MADE SURE I PERFORMED THE CEREMONY *RIGHT BEFORE* YOU ARRIVED... IT'S TOO LATE TO STOP IT NOW!
WHAT HAVE YOU DONE, BYTH?!
I HAVE OPENED TIME AND SPACE. AND SOON, FROM THAT *REMARKABLE CHILD...*

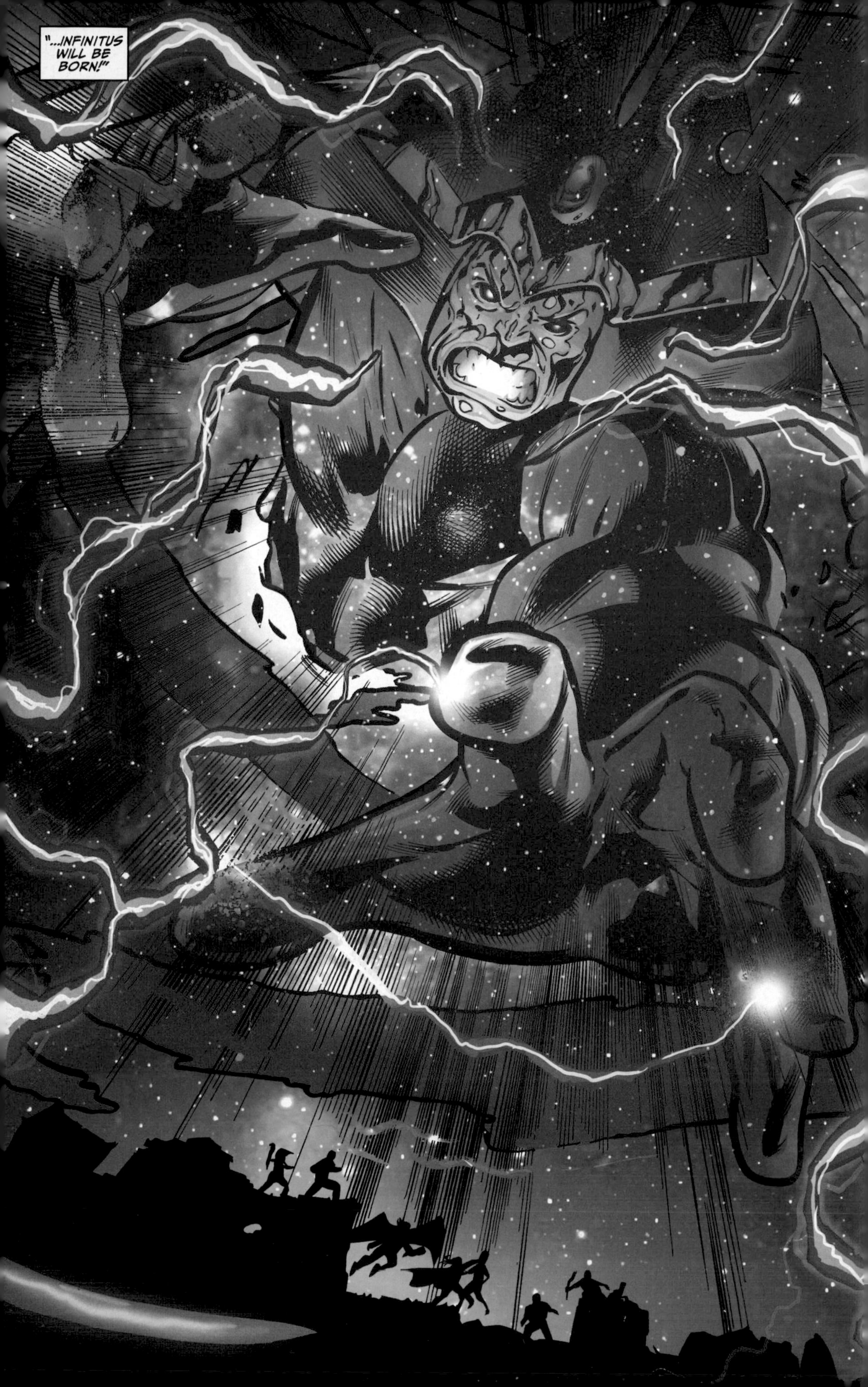
"...INFINITUS WILL BE BORN!"

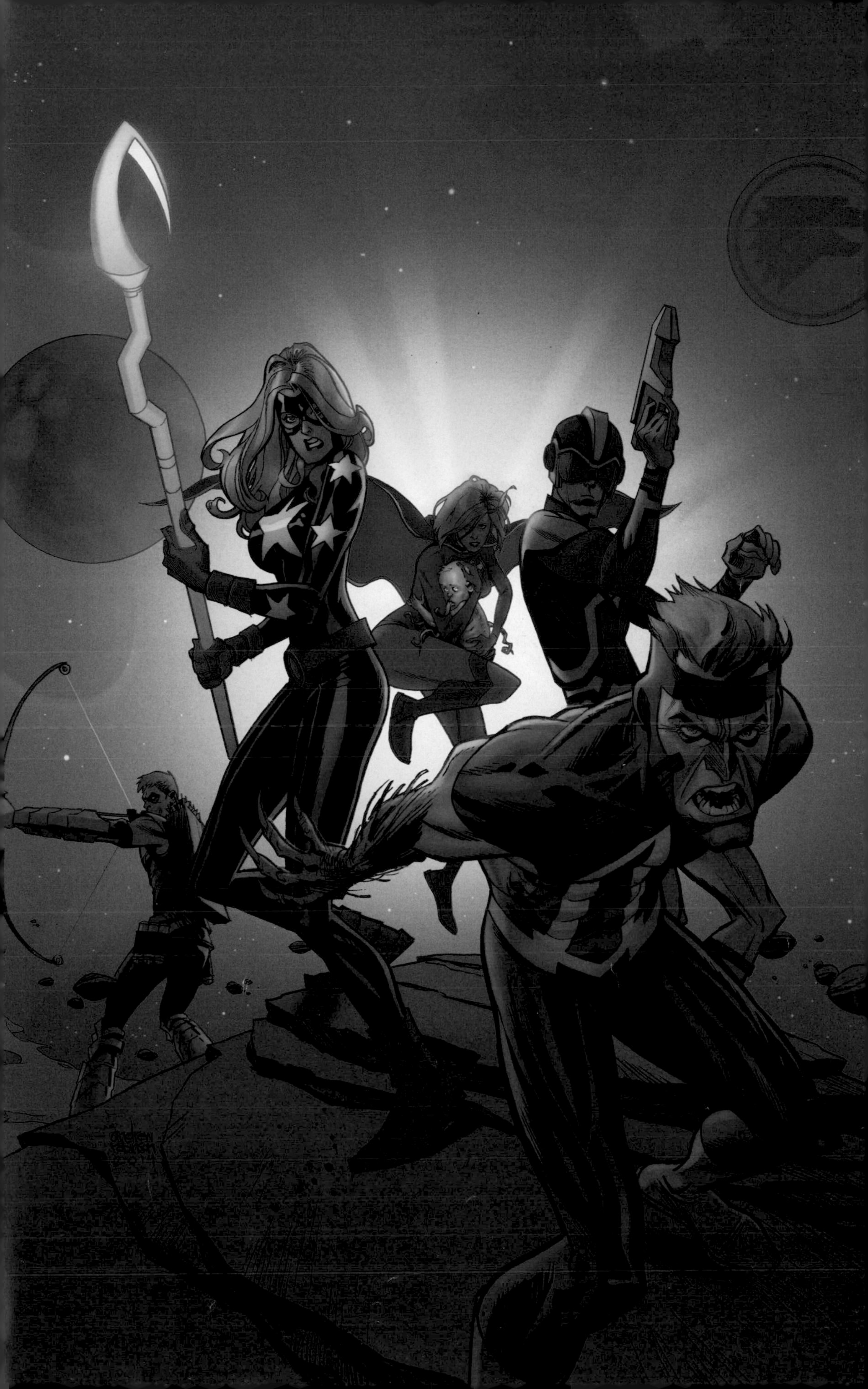

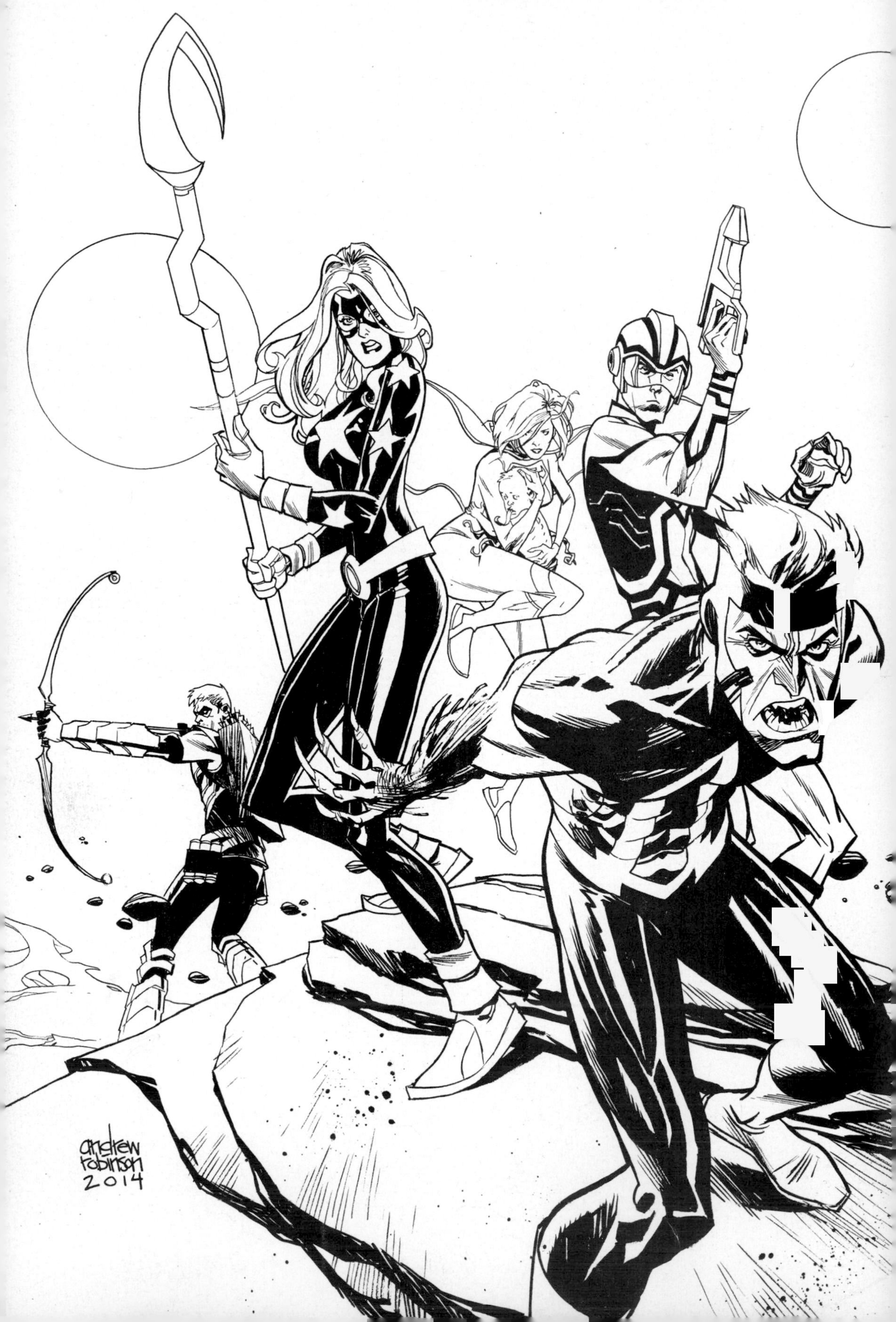
andrew robinson 2014

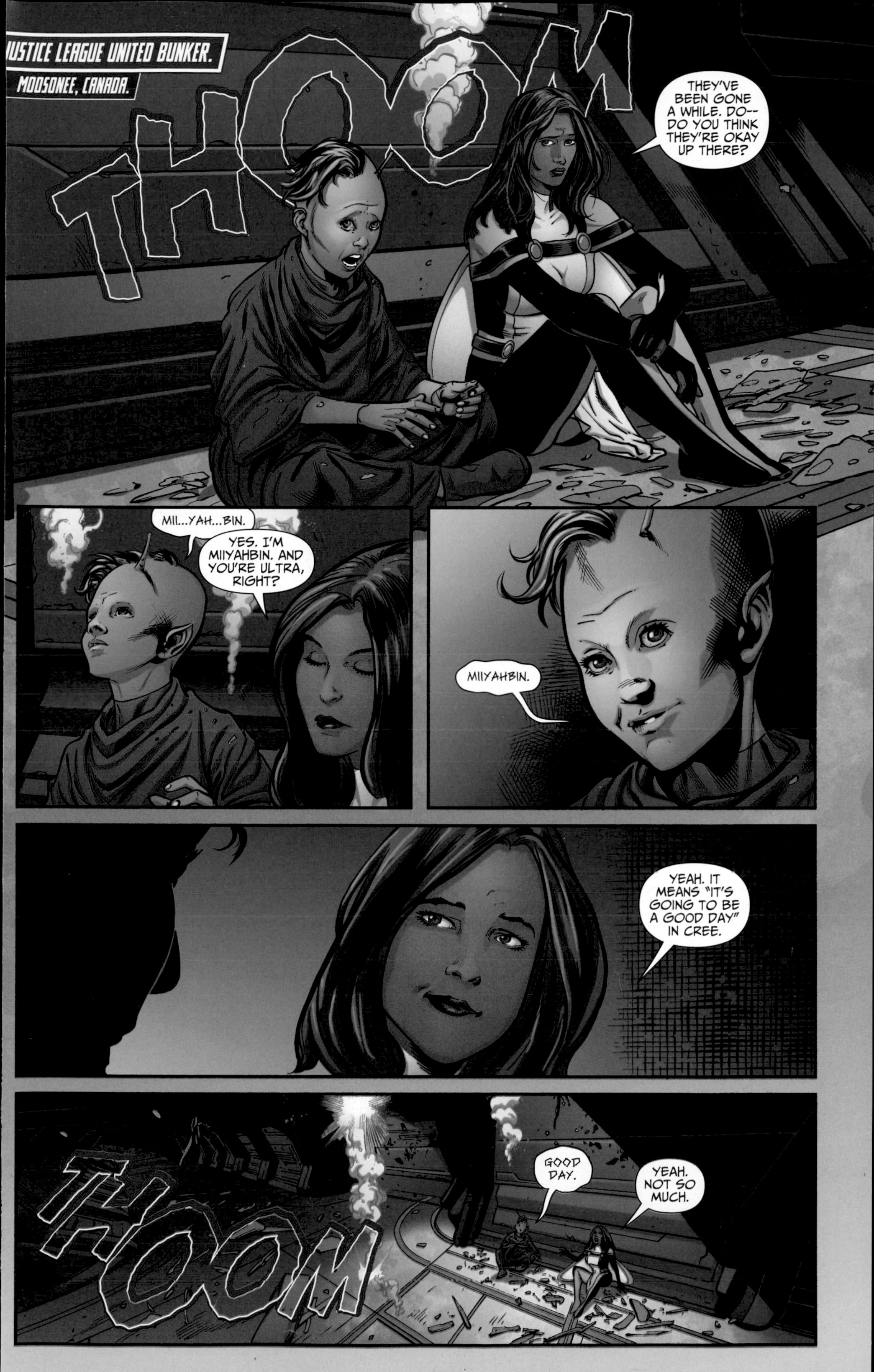
JUSTICE LEAGUE UNITED BUNKER.
MOOSONEE, CANADA.
THOOOM
THEY'VE BEEN GONE A WHILE. DO-- DO YOU THINK THEY'RE OKAY UP THERE?
MII...YAH...BIN.
YES. I'M MIIYAHBIN. AND YOU'RE ULTRA, RIGHT?
MIIYAHBIN.
YEAH. IT MEANS "IT'S GOING TO BE A GOOD DAY" IN CREE.
THOOM
GOOD DAY.
YEAH. NOT SO MUCH.

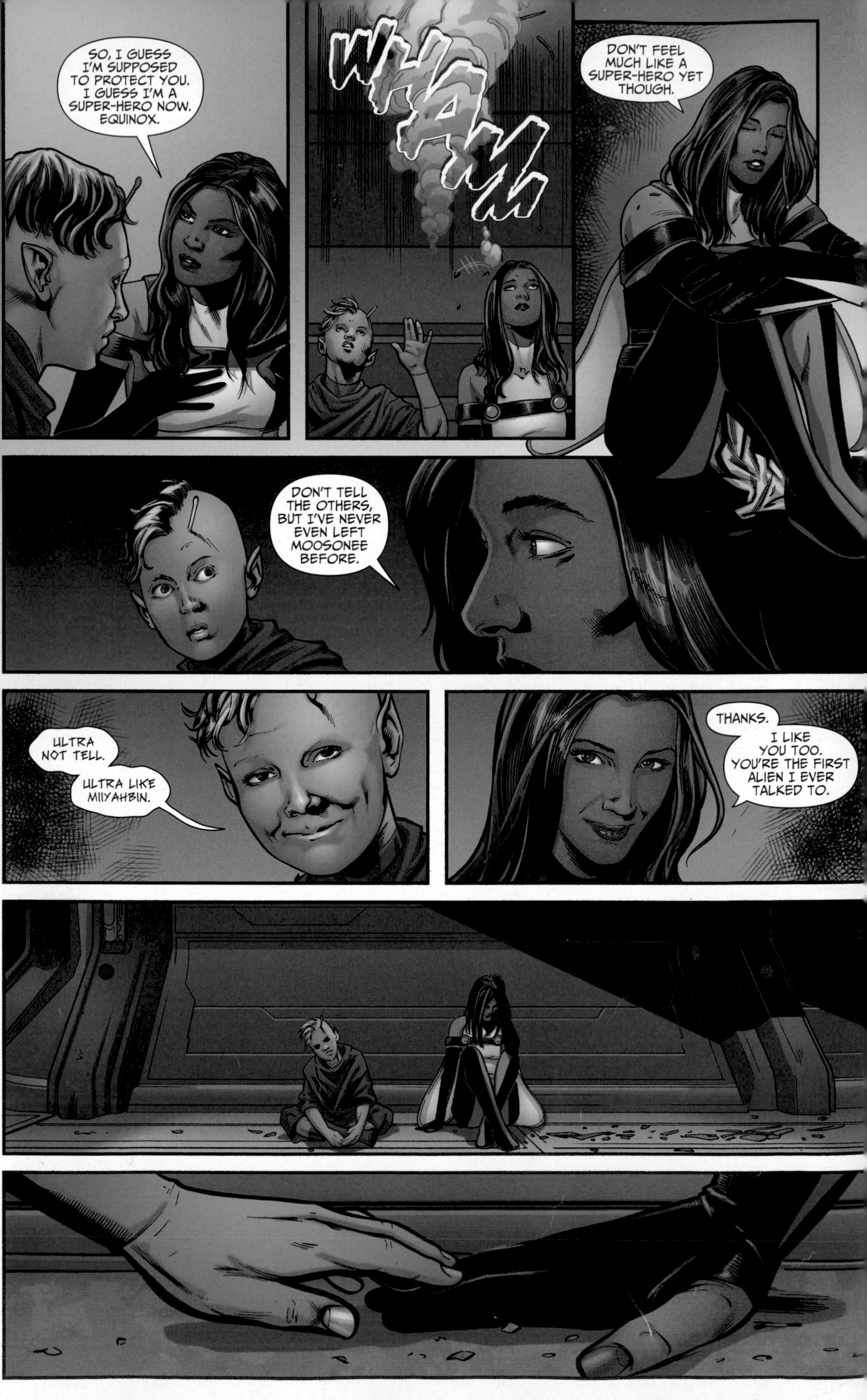
SO, I GUESS I'M SUPPOSED TO PROTECT YOU. I GUESS I'M A SUPER-HERO NOW. EQUINOX.
WHAM
DON'T FEEL MUCH LIKE A SUPER-HERO YET THOUGH.
DON'T TELL THE OTHERS, BUT I'VE NEVER EVEN LEFT MOOSONEE BEFORE.
ULTRA NOT TELL.
ULTRA LIKE MIIYAHBIN.
THANKS.
I LIKE YOU TOO. YOU'RE THE FIRST ALIEN I EVER TALKED TO.

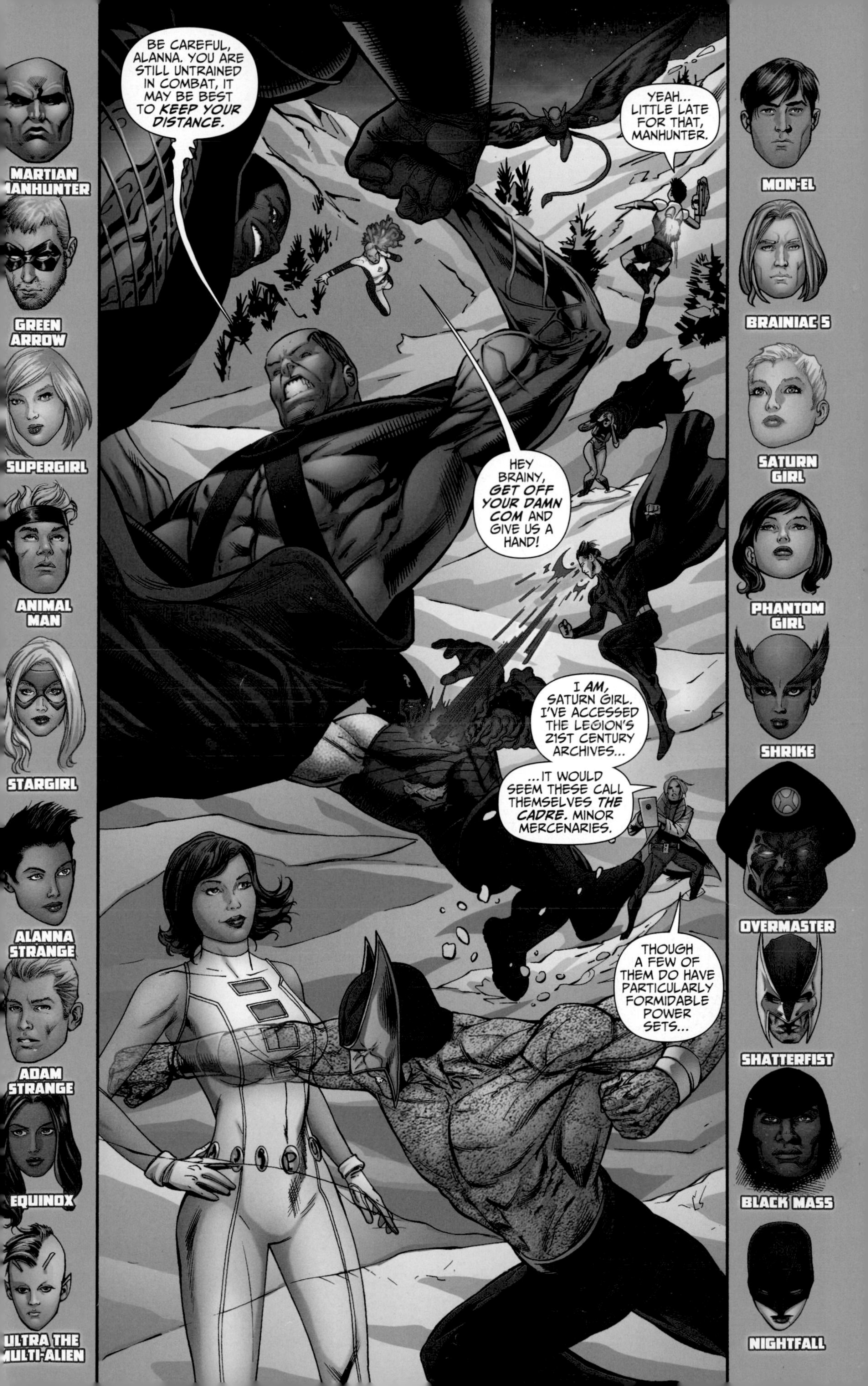
MARTIAN MANHUNTER
GREEN ARROW
SUPERGIRL
ANIMAL MAN
STARGIRL
ALANNA STRANGE
ADAM STRANGE
EQUINOX
ULTRA THE MULTI-ALIEN
BE CAREFUL, ALANNA. YOU ARE STILL UNTRAINED IN COMBAT, IT MAY BE BEST TO KEEP YOUR DISTANCE.
YEAH... LITTLE LATE FOR THAT, MANHUNTER.
HEY BRAINY, GET OFF YOUR DAMN COM AND GIVE US A HAND!
I AM, SATURN GIRL. I'VE ACCESSED THE LEGION'S 21ST CENTURY ARCHIVES...
...IT WOULD SEEM THESE CALL THEMSELVES THE CADRE. MINOR MERCENARIES.
THOUGH A FEW OF THEM DO HAVE PARTICULARLY FORMIDABLE POWER SETS...
MON-EL
BRAINIAC 5
SATURN GIRL
PHANTOM GIRL
SHRIKE
OVERMASTER
SHATTERFIST
BLACK MASS
NIGHTFALL

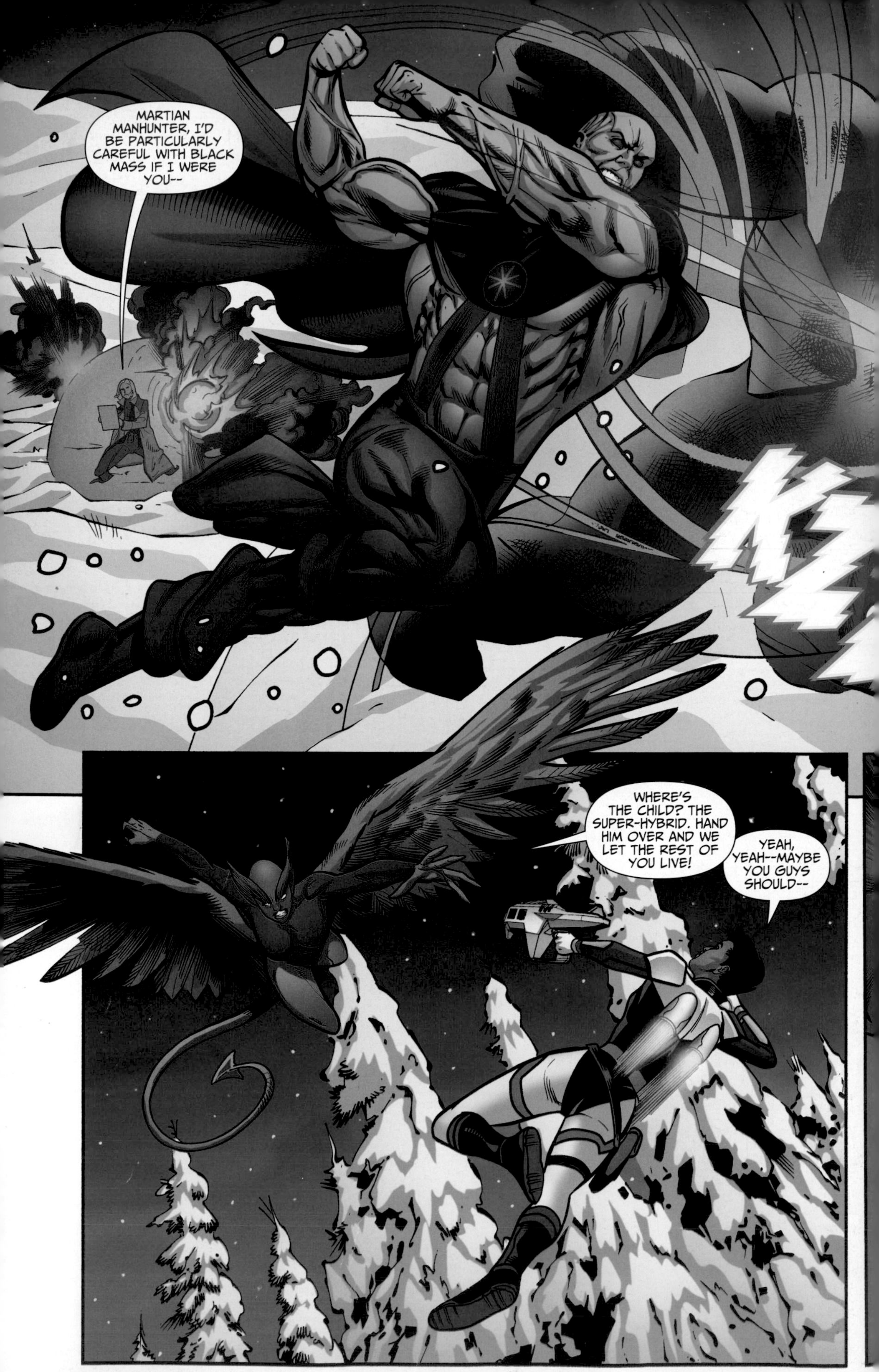

MARTIAN MANHUNTER, I'D BE PARTICULARLY CAREFUL WITH BLACK MASS IF I WERE YOU--
WHERE'S THE CHILD? THE SUPER-HYBRID. HAND HIM OVER AND WE LET THE REST OF YOU LIVE!
YEAH, YEAH--MAYBE YOU GUYS SHOULD--

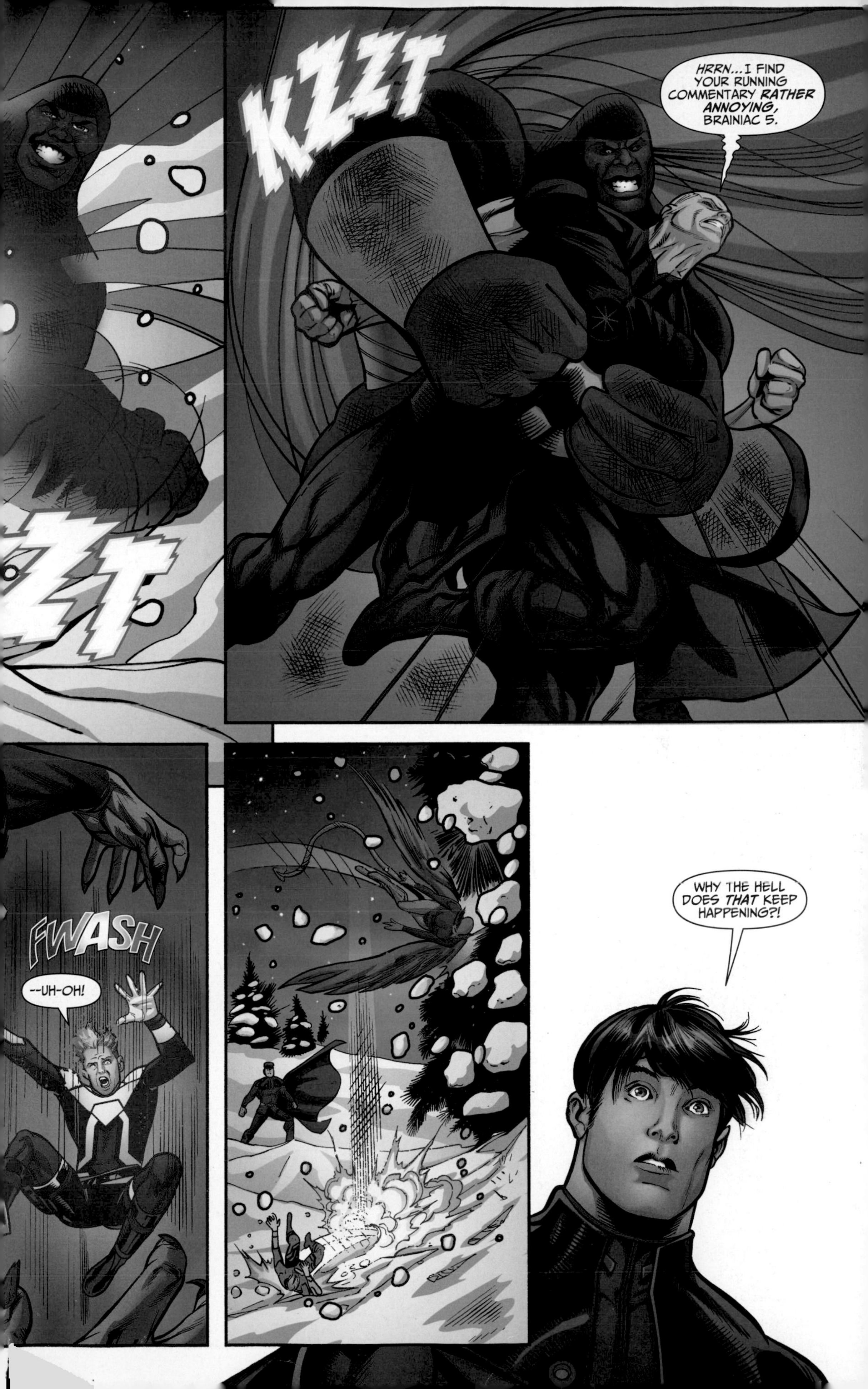
KZZT
KZZT
HRRN...I FIND YOUR RUNNING COMMENTARY RATHER ANNOYING, BRAINIAC 5.
FWASH
--UH-OH!
WHY THE HELL DOES THAT KEEP HAPPENING?!

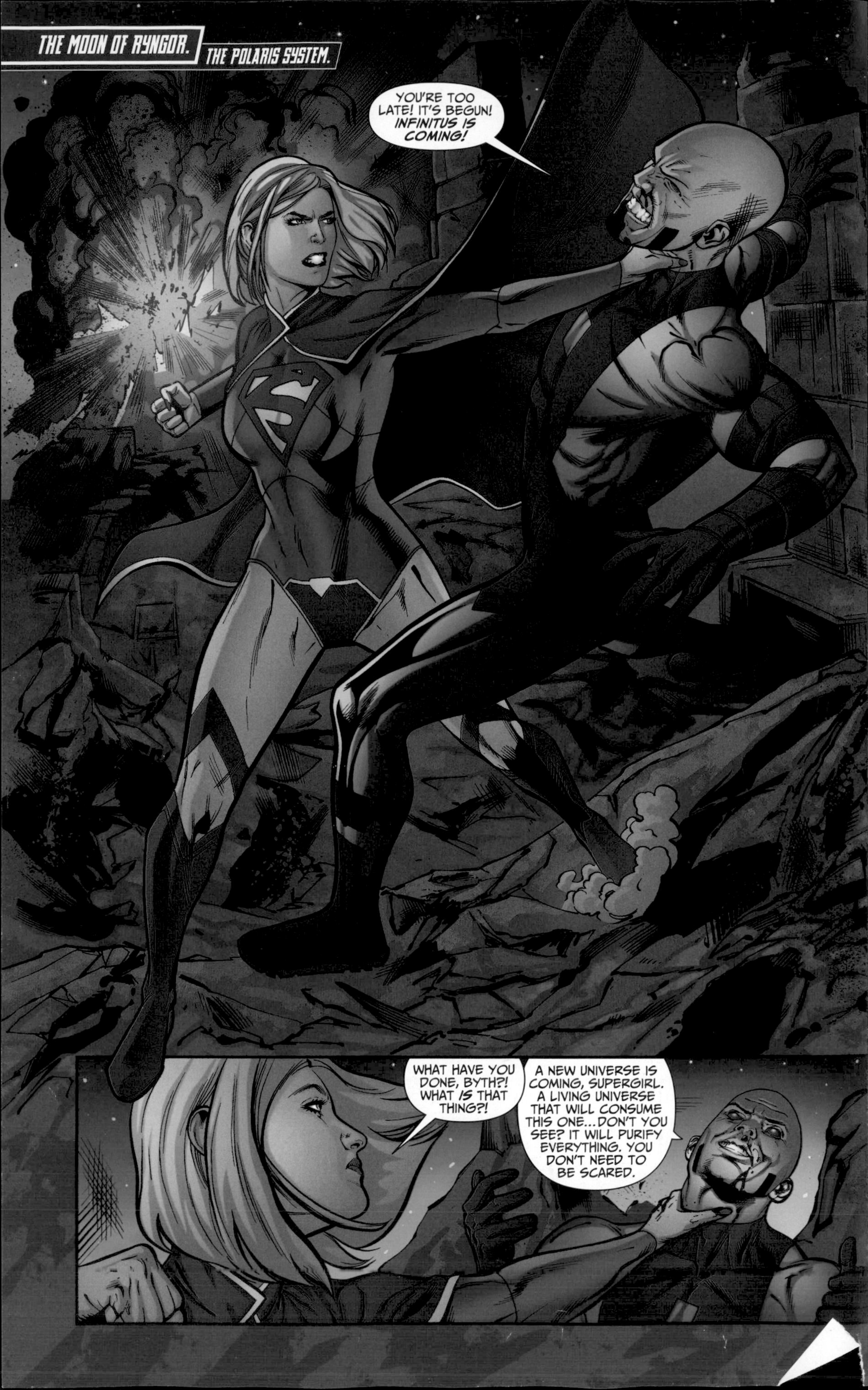
THE MOON OF RYNGOR.
THE POLARIS SYSTEM.
YOU'RE TOO LATE! IT'S BEGUN! INFINITUS IS COMING!
WHAT HAVE YOU DONE, BYTH?! WHAT IS THAT THING?!
A NEW UNIVERSE IS COMING, SUPERGIRL. A LIVING UNIVERSE THAT WILL CONSUME THIS ONE...DON'T YOU SEE? IT WILL PURIFY EVERYTHING. YOU DON'T NEED TO BE SCARED.

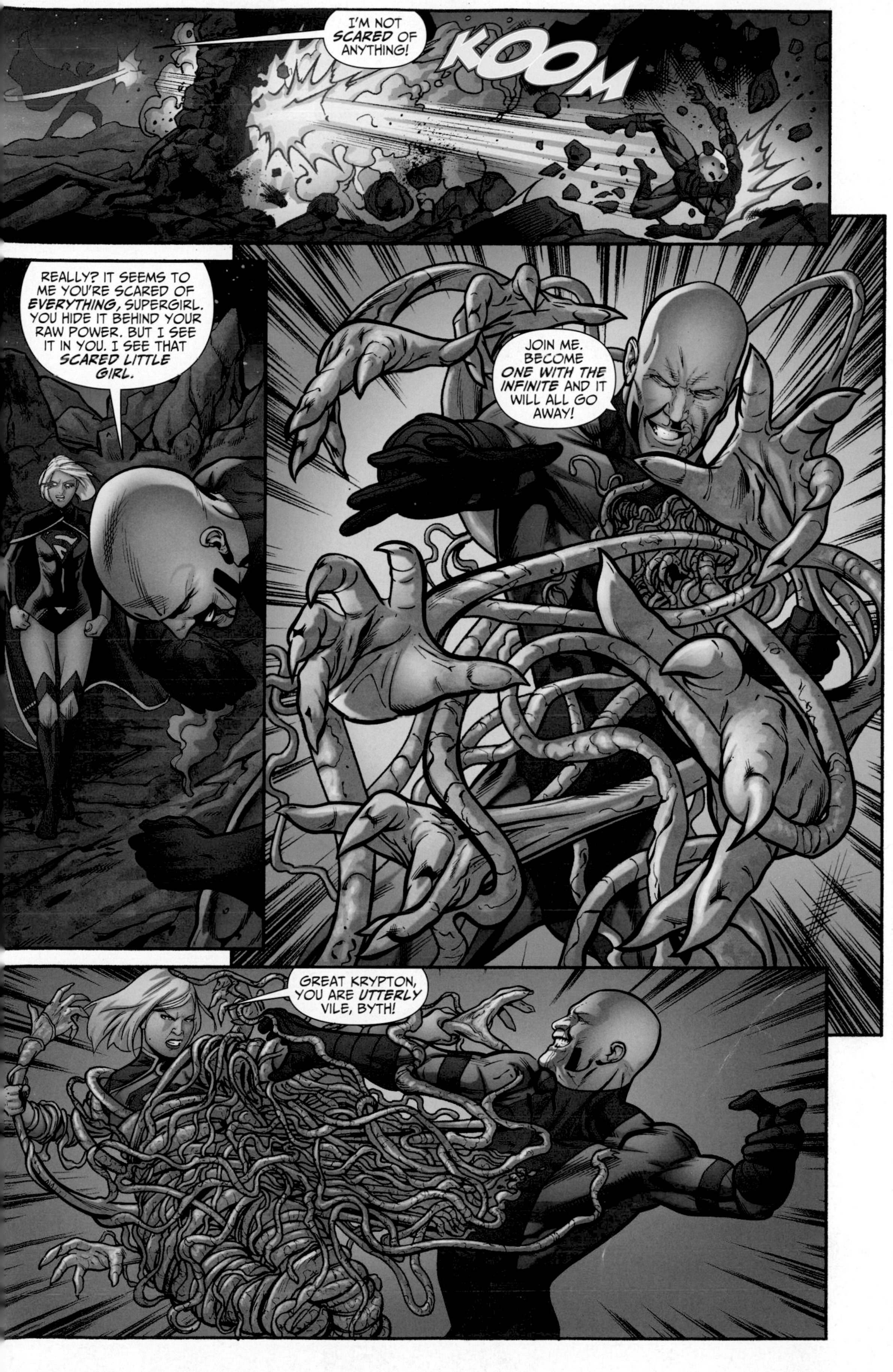
I'M NOT SCARED OF ANYTHING!
KOOM
REALLY? IT SEEMS TO ME YOU'RE SCARED OF EVERYTHING, SUPERGIRL. YOU HIDE IT BEHIND YOUR RAW POWER. BUT I SEE IT IN YOU. I SEE THAT SCARED LITTLE GIRL.
JOIN ME. BECOME ONE WITH THE INFINITE AND IT WILL ALL GO AWAY!
GREAT KRYPTON, YOU ARE UTTERLY VILE, BYTH!

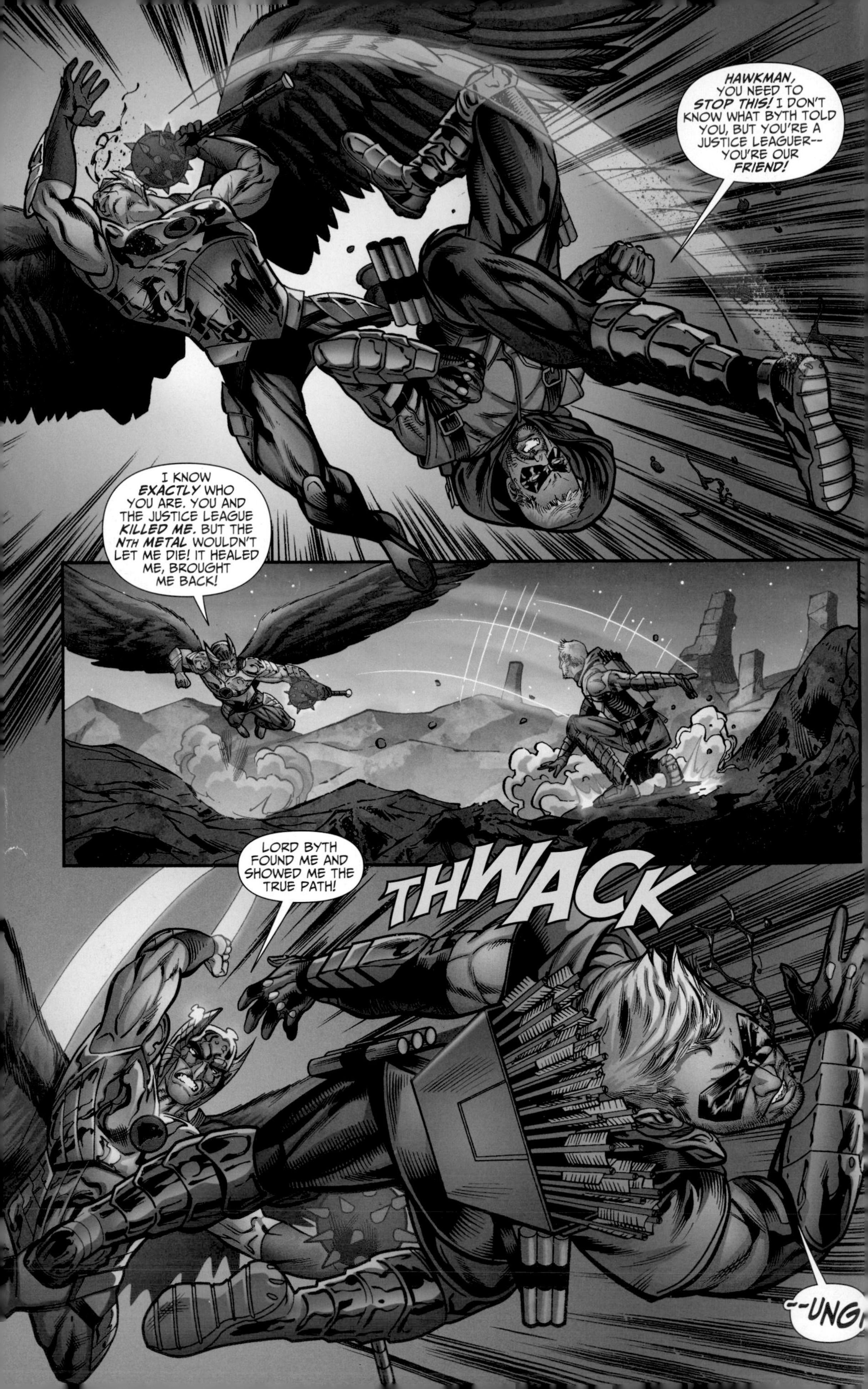
HAWKMAN, YOU NEED TO STOP THIS! I DON'T KNOW WHAT BYTH TOLD YOU, BUT YOU'RE A JUSTICE LEAGUER-- YOU'RE OUR FRIEND!
I KNOW EXACTLY WHO YOU ARE. YOU AND THE JUSTICE LEAGUE KILLED ME. BUT THE NTH METAL WOULDN'T LET ME DIE! IT HEALED ME, BROUGHT ME BACK!
LORD BYTH FOUND ME AND SHOWED ME THE TRUE PATH!
THWACK
--UNG!

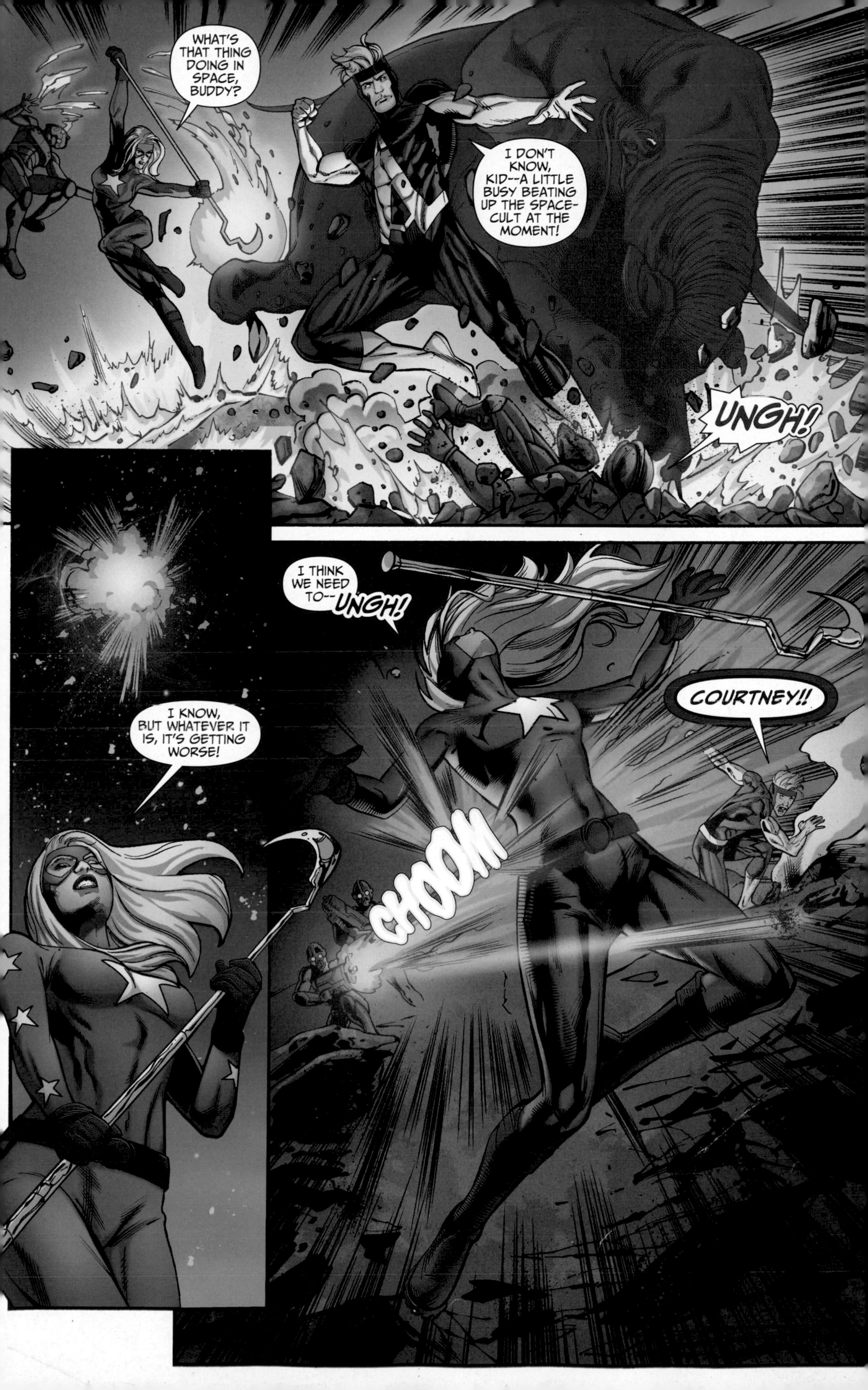
WHAT'S THAT THING DOING IN SPACE, BUDDY?
I DON'T KNOW, KID--A LITTLE BUSY BEATING UP THE SPACE-CULT AT THE MOMENT!
UNGH!
I KNOW, BUT WHATEVER IT IS, IT'S GETTING WORSE!
I THINK WE NEED TO--UNGH!
COURTNEY!!
CHOOM

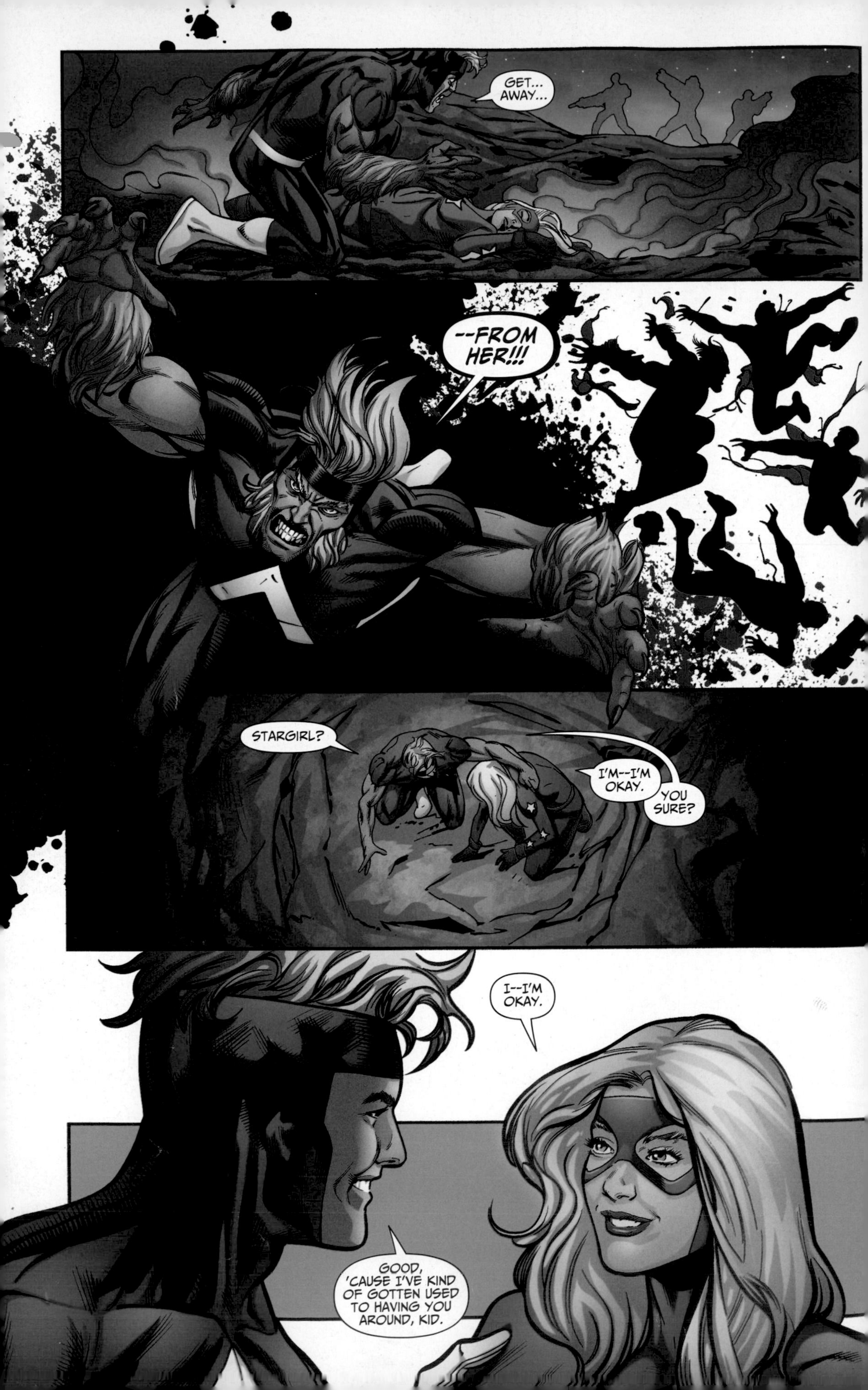

GET... AWAY...
--FROM HER!!!
STARGIRL?
I'M--I'M OKAY.
YOU SURE?
I--I'M OKAY.
GOOD, 'CAUSE I'VE KIND OF GOTTEN USED TO HAVING YOU AROUND, KID.

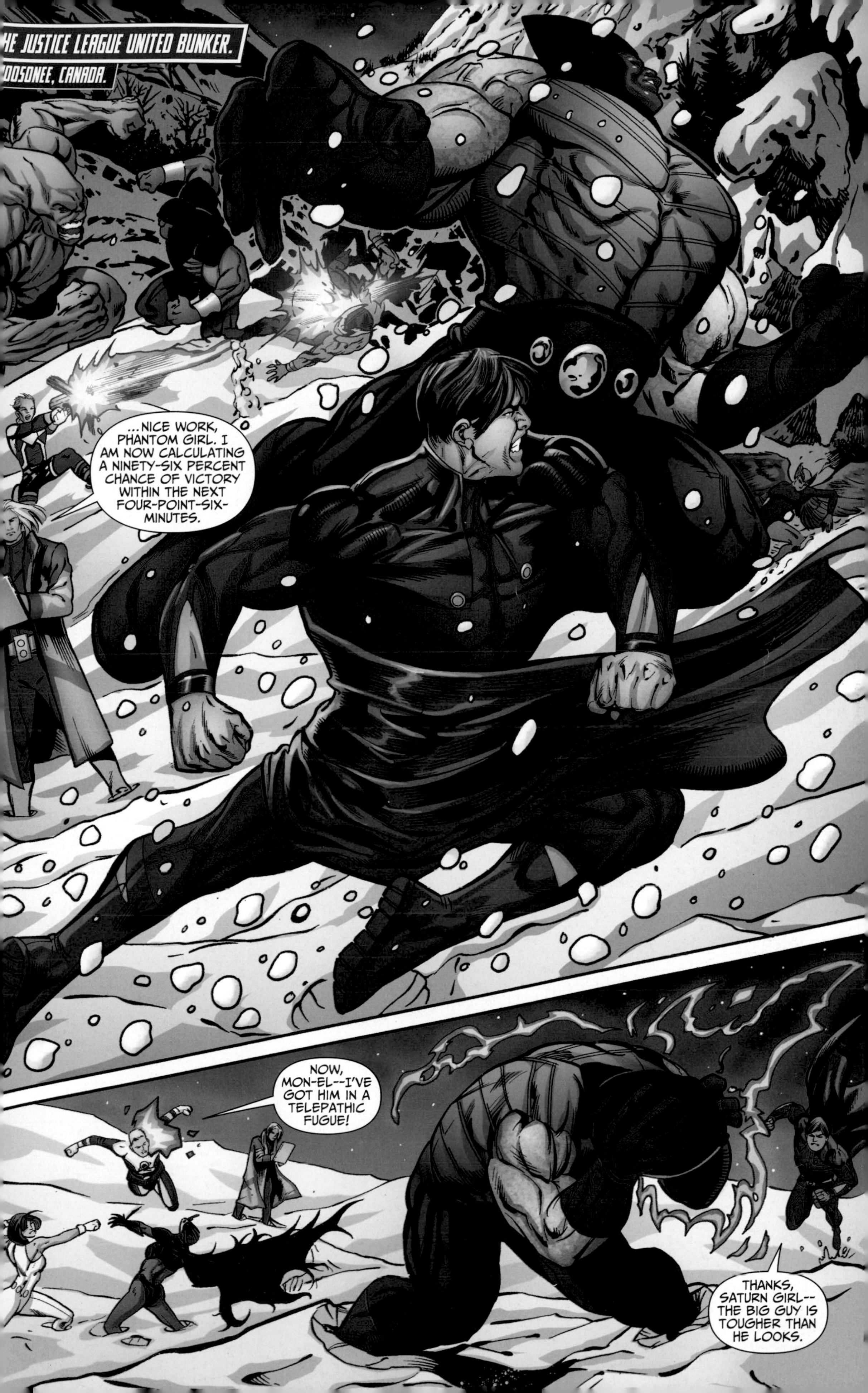
HE JUSTICE LEAGUE UNITED BUNKER.
OOSONEE, CANADA.
...NICE WORK, PHANTOM GIRL. I AM NOW CALCULATING A NINETY-SIX PERCENT CHANCE OF VICTORY WITHIN THE NEXT FOUR-POINT-SIX-MINUTES.
NOW, MON-EL--I'VE GOT HIM IN A TELEPATHIC FUGUE!
THANKS, SATURN GIRL-- THE BIG GUY IS TOUGHER THAN HE LOOKS.

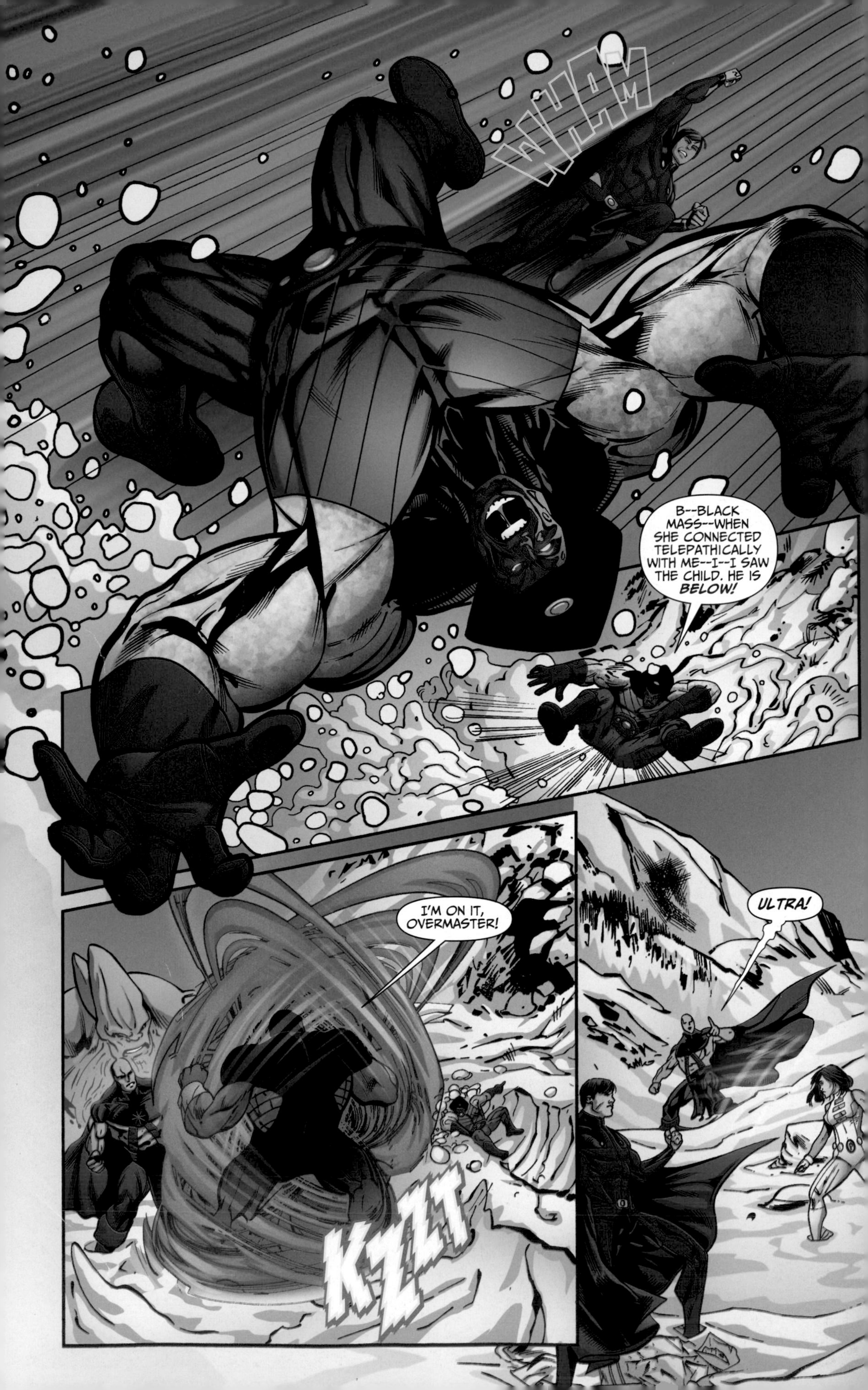
WHAM
B--BLACK MASS--WHEN SHE CONNECTED TELEPATHICALLY WITH ME--I--I SAW THE CHILD. HE IS BELOW!
I'M ON IT, OVERMASTER!
KZZZT
ULTRA!

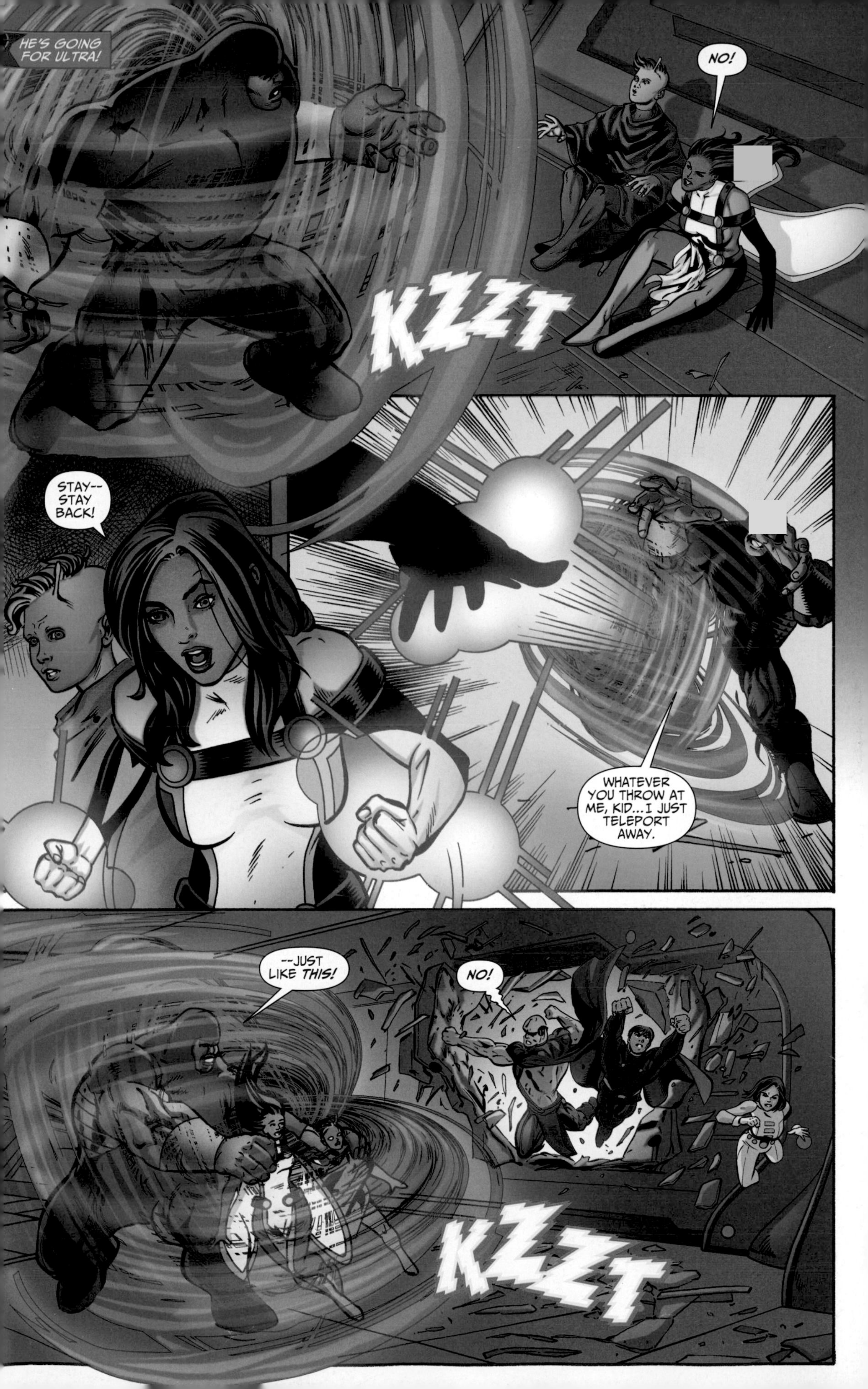
HE'S GOING FOR ULTRA!
NO!
KZZZT
STAY-- STAY BACK!
WHATEVER YOU THROW AT ME, KID... I JUST TELEPORT AWAY.
--JUST LIKE *THIS!*
NO!
KZZZT

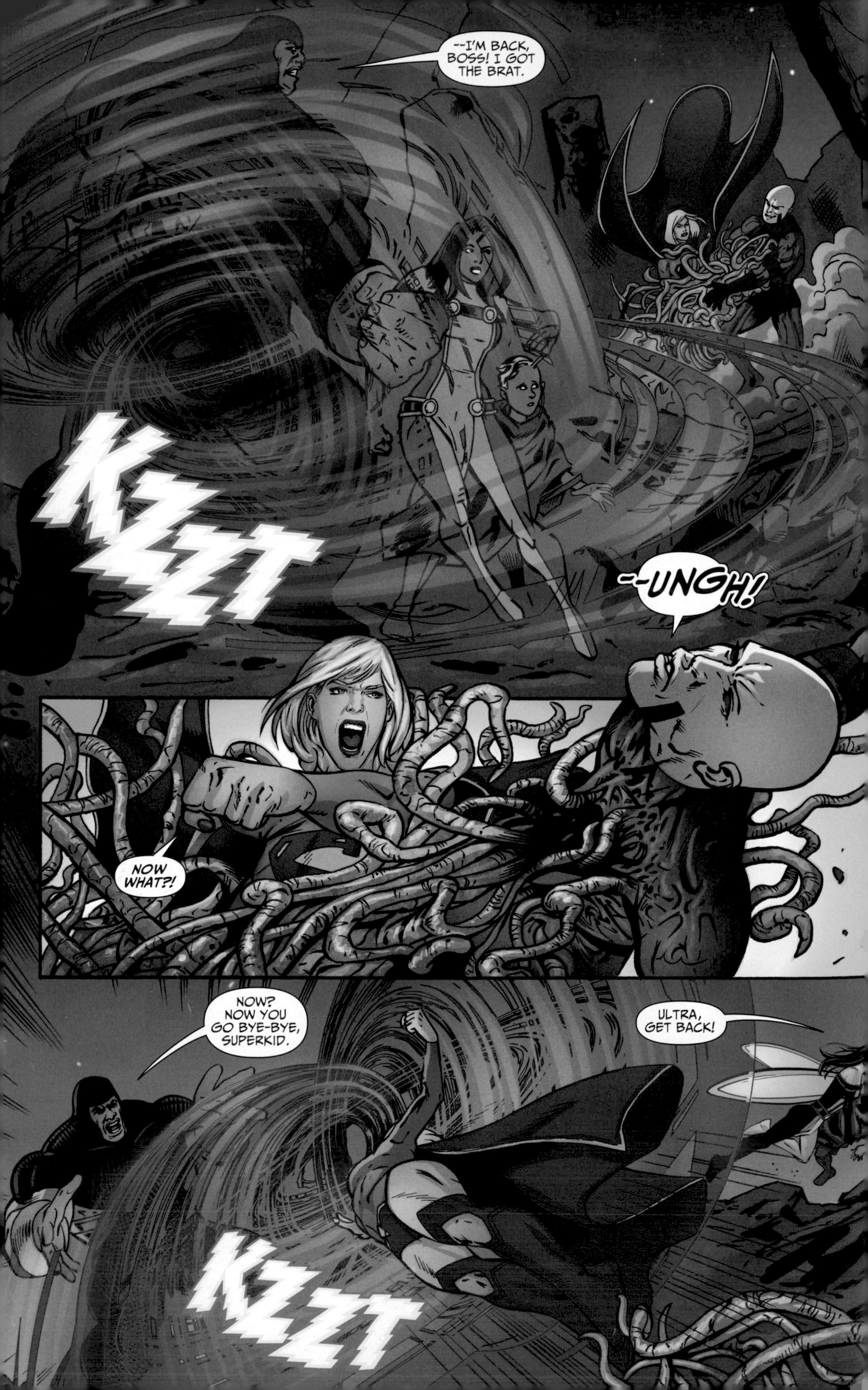
--I'M BACK, BOSS! I GOT THE BRAT.
KZZZT
--UNGH!
NOW WHAT?!
NOW? NOW YOU GO BYE-BYE, SUPERKID.
ULTRA, GET BACK!
KZZZT

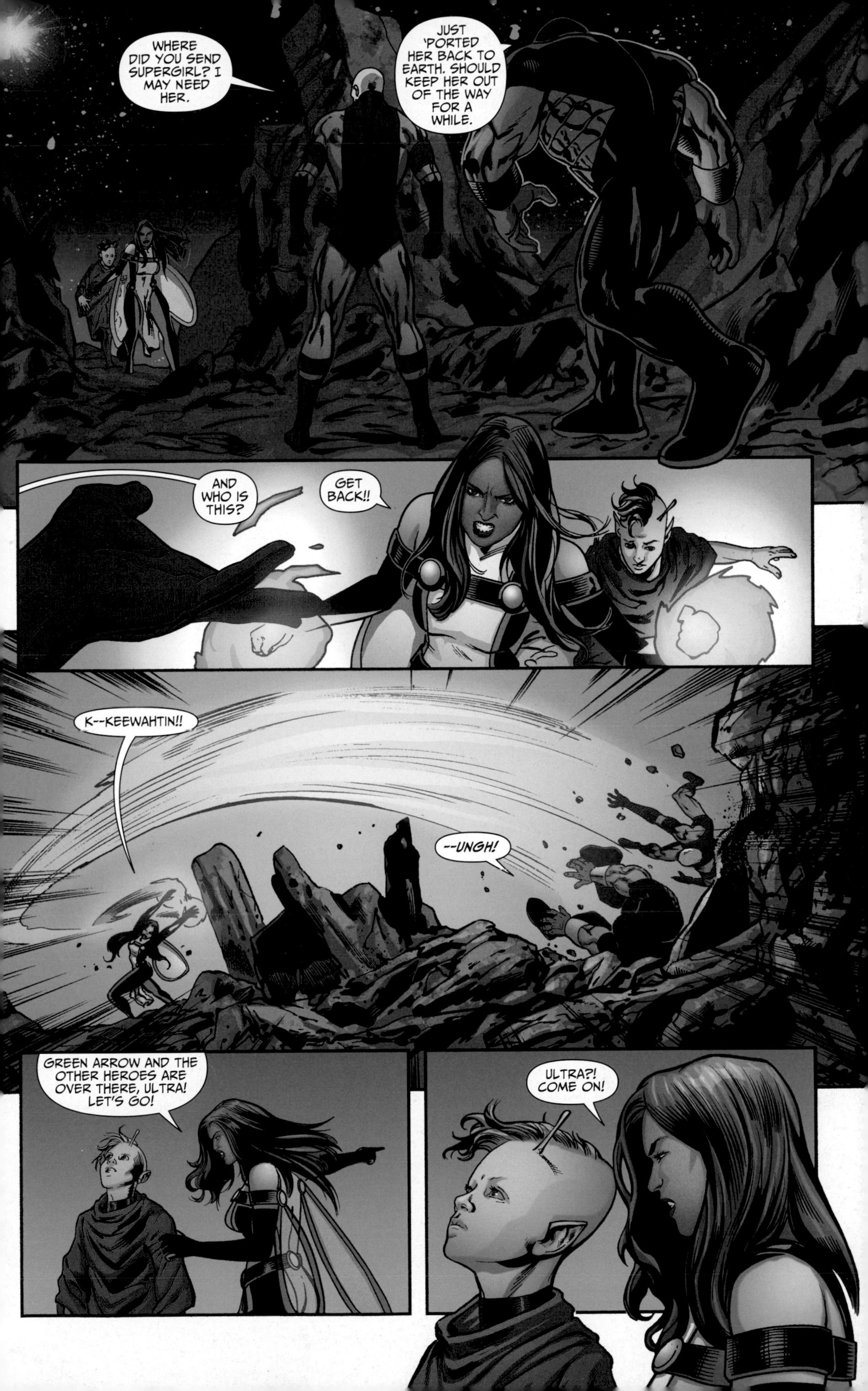
WHERE DID YOU SEND SUPERGIRL? I MAY NEED HER.
JUST 'PORTED HER BACK TO EARTH. SHOULD KEEP HER OUT OF THE WAY FOR A WHILE.
AND WHO IS THIS?
GET BACK!!
K--KEEWAHTIN!!
--UNGH!
GREEN ARROW AND THE OTHER HEROES ARE OVER THERE, ULTRA! LET'S GO!
ULTRA?! COME ON!

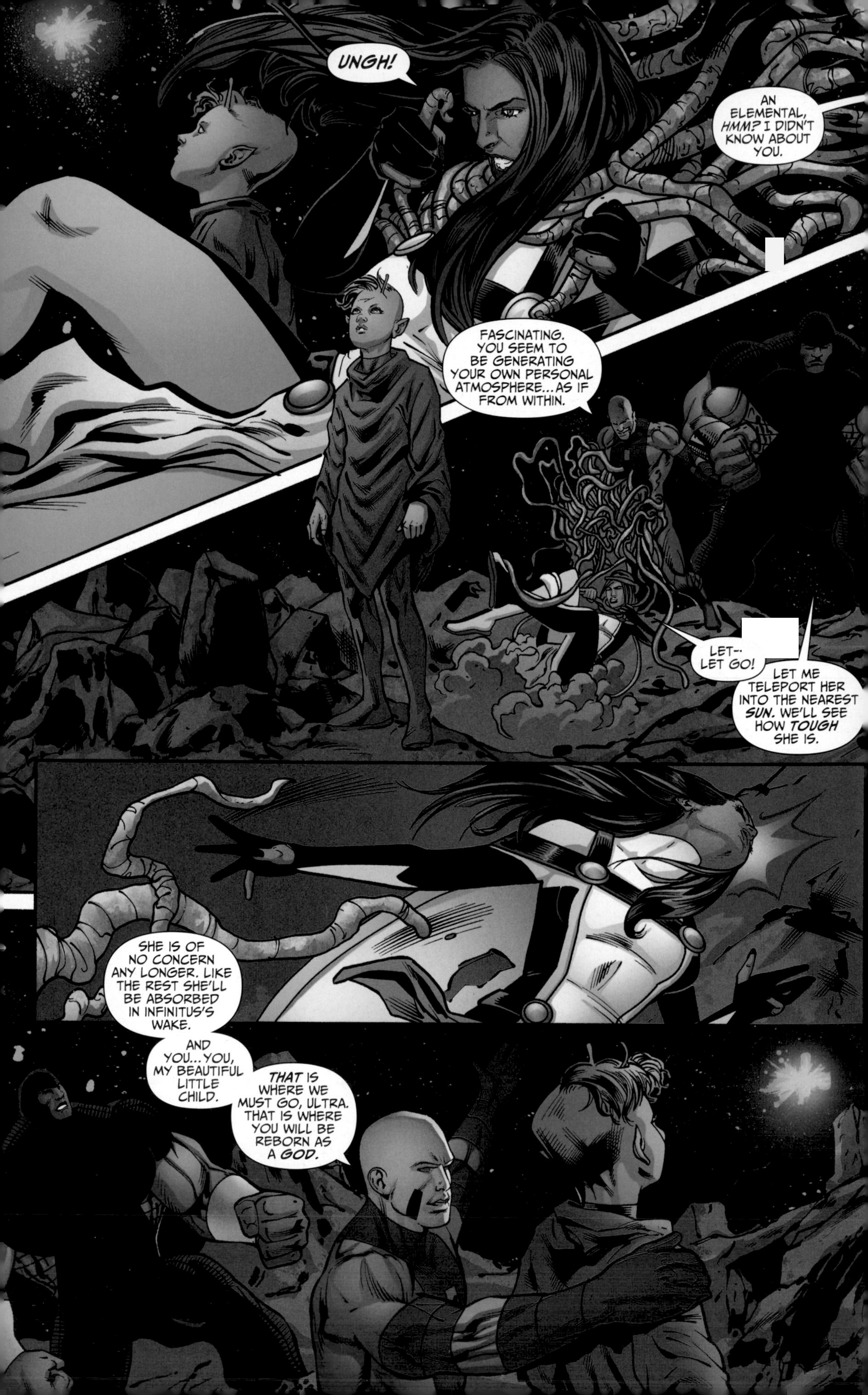
UNGH!
AN ELEMENTAL, *HMM?* I DIDN'T KNOW ABOUT YOU.
FASCINATING. YOU SEEM TO BE GENERATING YOUR OWN PERSONAL ATMOSPHERE...AS IF FROM WITHIN.
LET-- LET GO!
LET ME TELEPORT HER INTO THE NEAREST *SUN.* WE'LL SEE HOW *TOUGH* SHE IS.
SHE IS OF NO CONCERN ANY LONGER. LIKE THE REST SHE'LL BE ABSORBED IN INFINITUS'S WAKE.
AND YOU...YOU, MY BEAUTIFUL LITTLE CHILD.
THAT IS WHERE WE MUST GO, ULTRA. THAT IS WHERE YOU WILL BE REBORN AS A *GOD.*

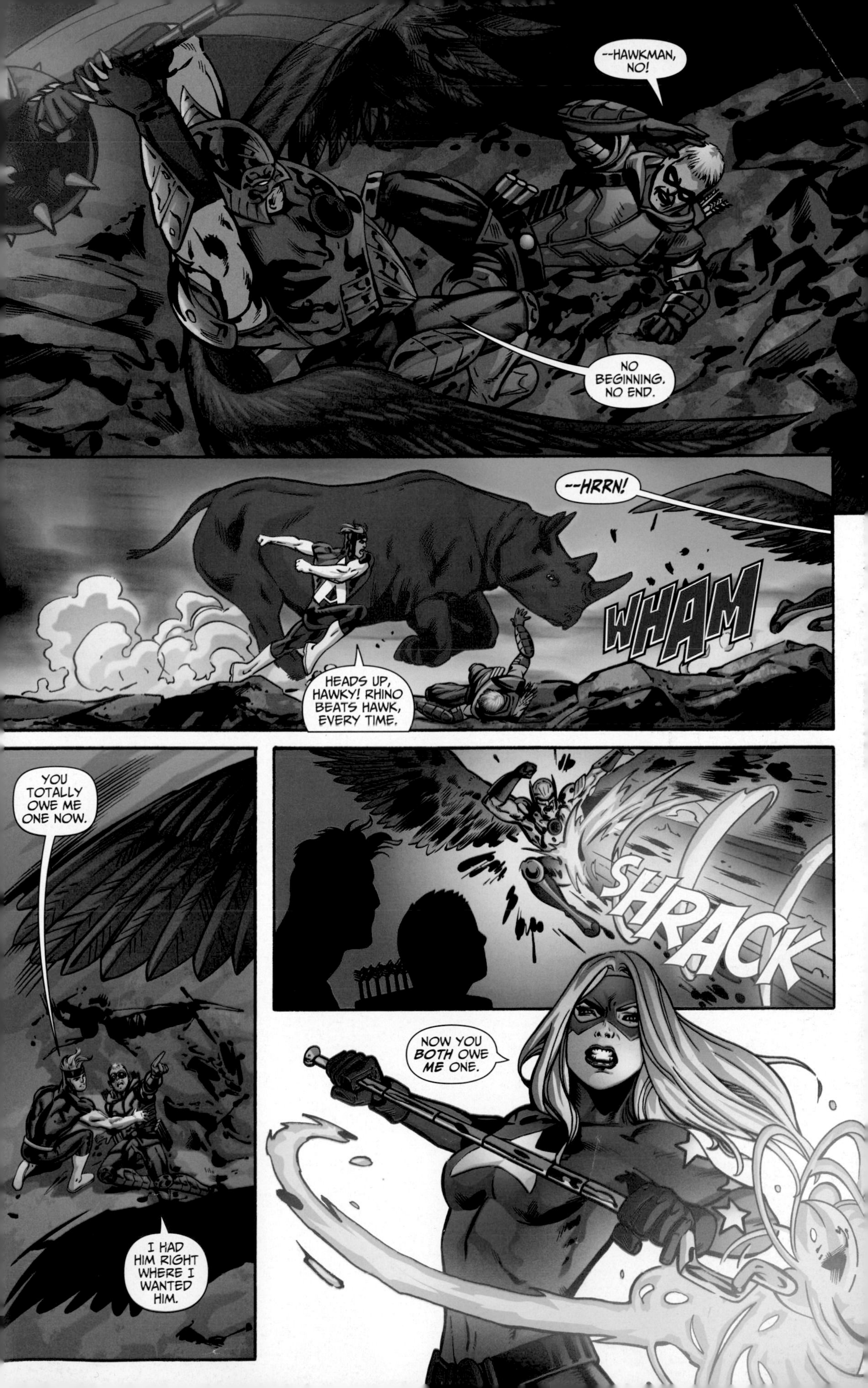
--HAWKMAN, NO!
NO BEGINNING. NO END.
--HRRN!
WHAM
HEADS UP, HAWKY! RHINO BEATS HAWK, EVERY TIME.
YOU TOTALLY OWE ME ONE NOW.
I HAD HIM RIGHT WHERE I WANTED HIM.
SHRACK
NOW YOU BOTH OWE ME ONE.

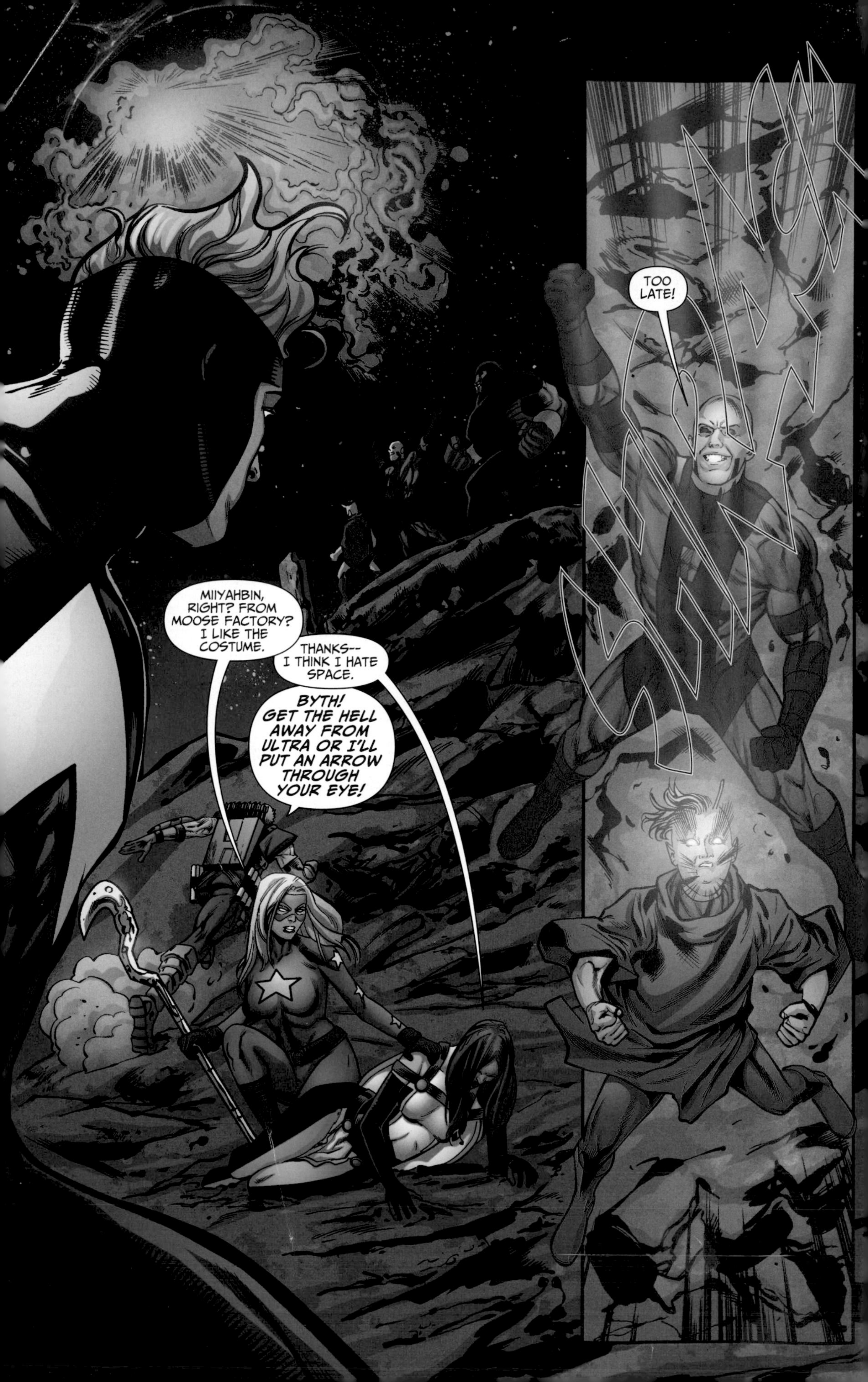
MIIYAHBIN, RIGHT? FROM MOOSE FACTORY? I LIKE THE COSTUME.
THANKS-- I THINK I HATE SPACE.
BYTH! GET THE HELL AWAY FROM ULTRA OR I'LL PUT AN ARROW THROUGH YOUR EYE!
TOO LATE!

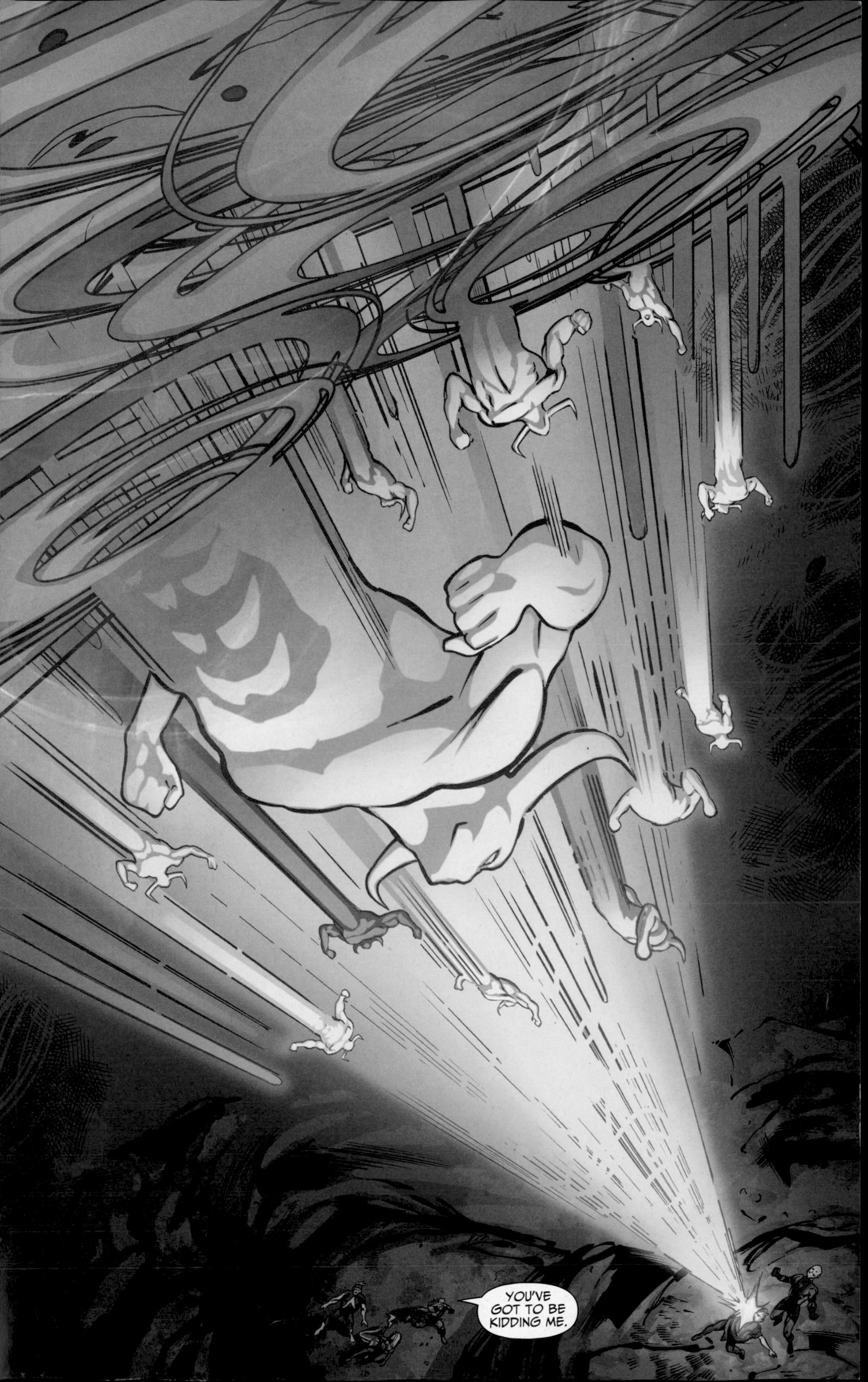
YOU'VE GOT TO BE KIDDING ME.

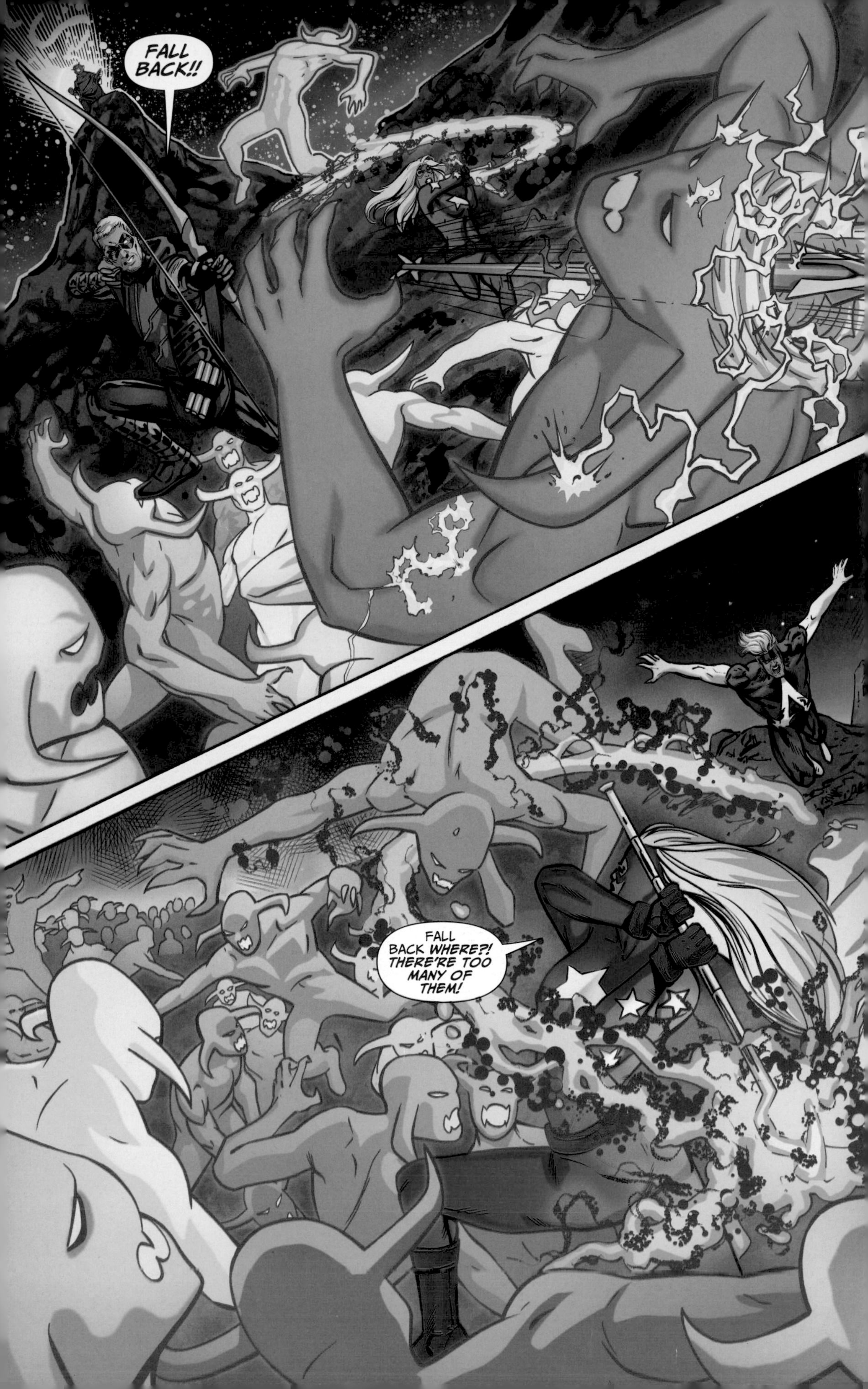
FALL BACK!!
FALL BACK WHERE?! THERE'RE TOO MANY OF THEM!

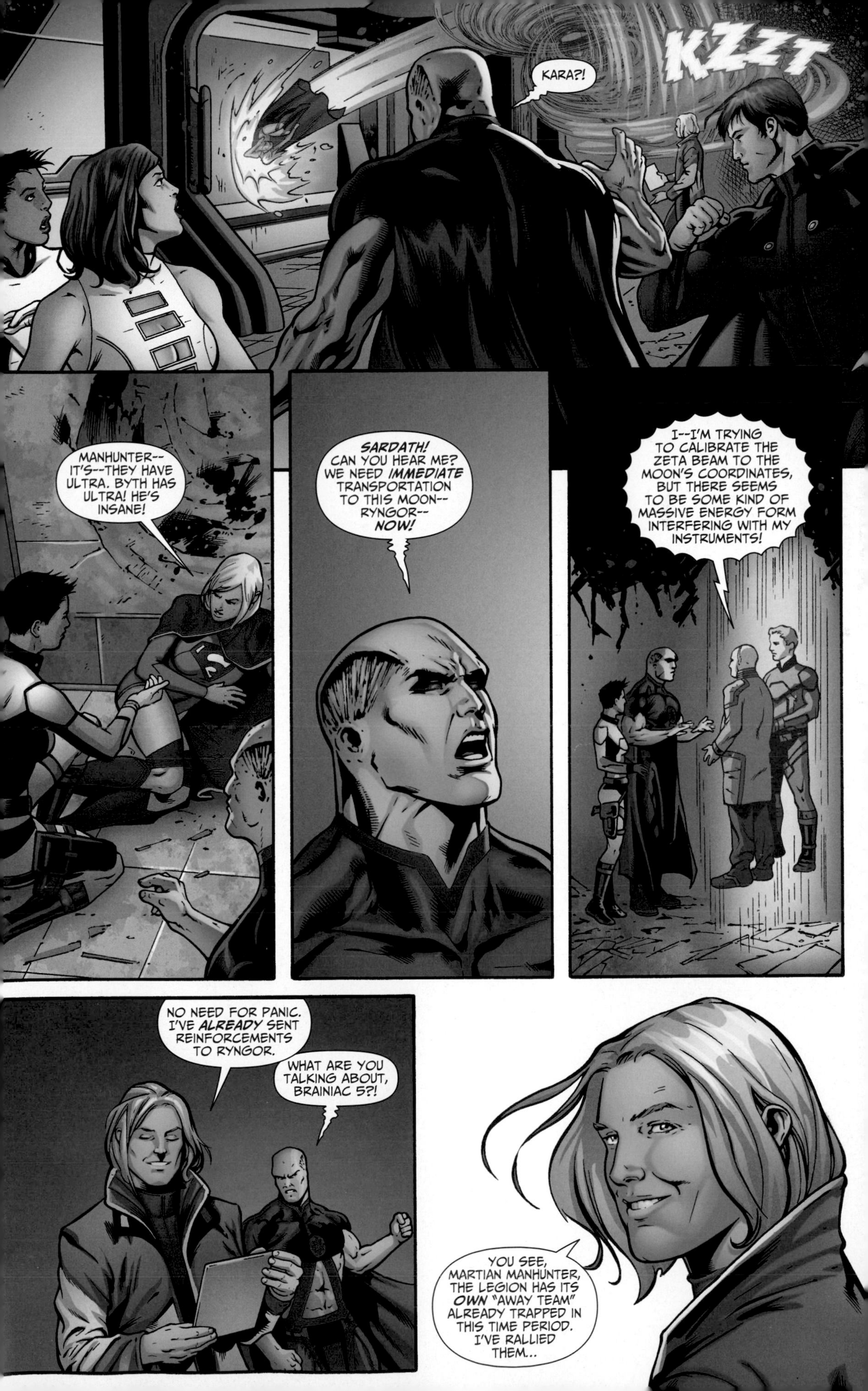

KZZT
KARA?!
MANHUNTER--IT'S--THEY HAVE ULTRA. BYTH HAS ULTRA! HE'S INSANE!
SARDATH! CAN YOU HEAR ME? WE NEED IMMEDIATE TRANSPORTATION TO THIS MOON--RYNGOR--NOW!
I--I'M TRYING TO CALIBRATE THE ZETA BEAM TO THE MOON'S COORDINATES, BUT THERE SEEMS TO BE SOME KIND OF MASSIVE ENERGY FORM INTERFERING WITH MY INSTRUMENTS!
NO NEED FOR PANIC. I'VE ALREADY SENT REINFORCEMENTS TO RYNGOR.
WHAT ARE YOU TALKING ABOUT, BRAINIAC 5?!
YOU SEE, MARTIAN MANHUNTER, THE LEGION HAS ITS OWN "AWAY TEAM" ALREADY TRAPPED IN THIS TIME PERIOD. I'VE RALLIED THEM...

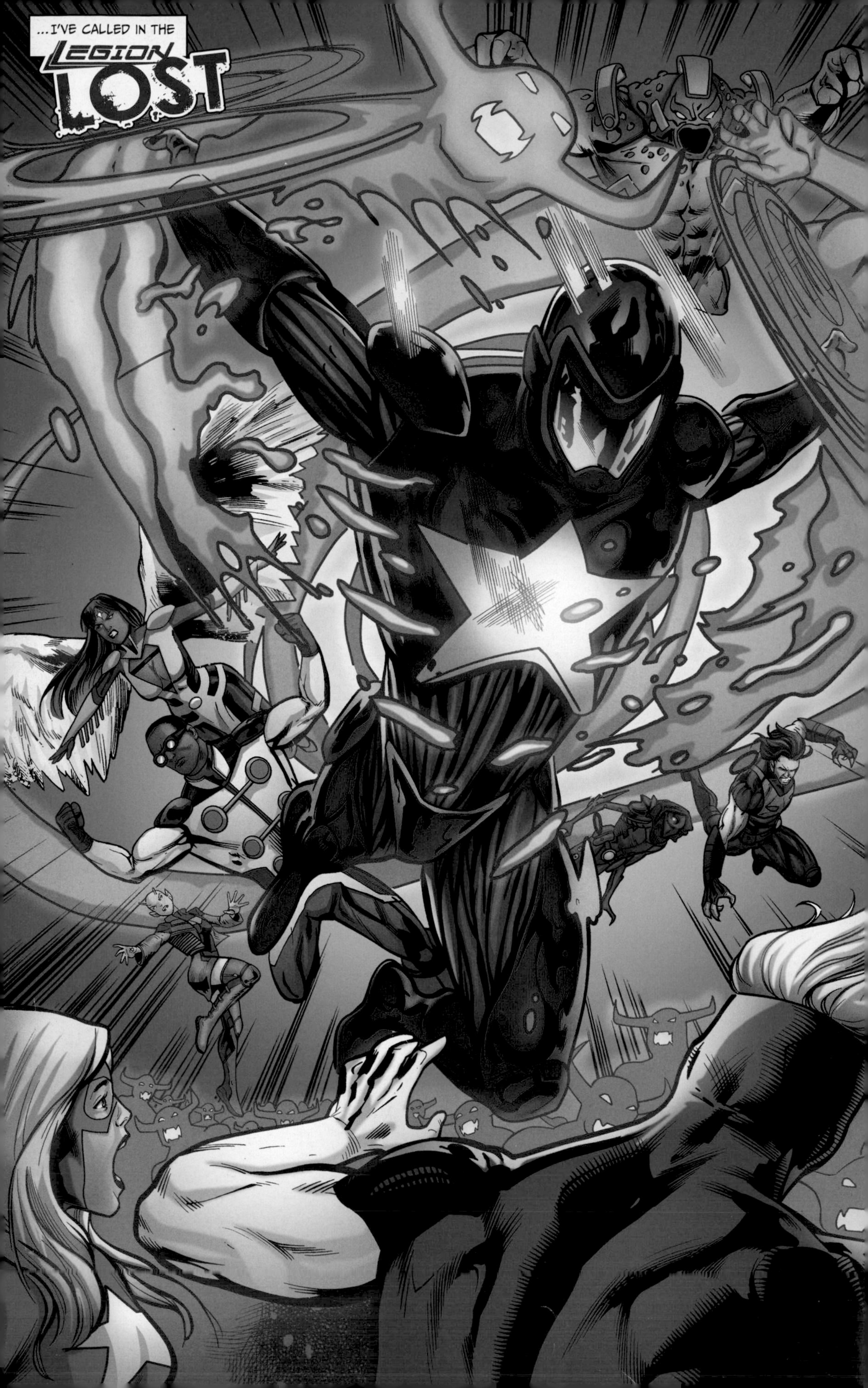
...I'VE CALLED IN THE
LEGION LOST

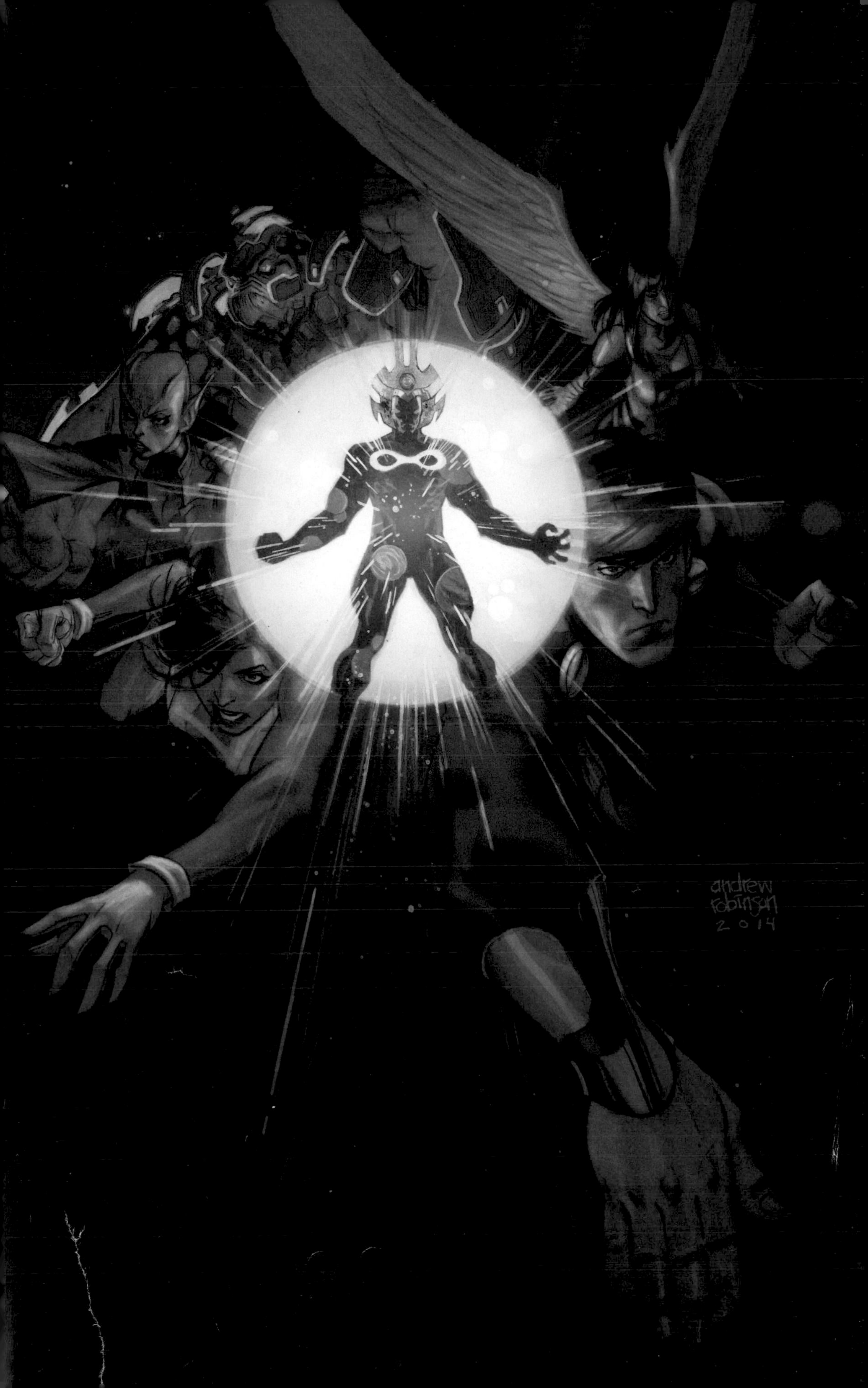
andrew
robinson
2014

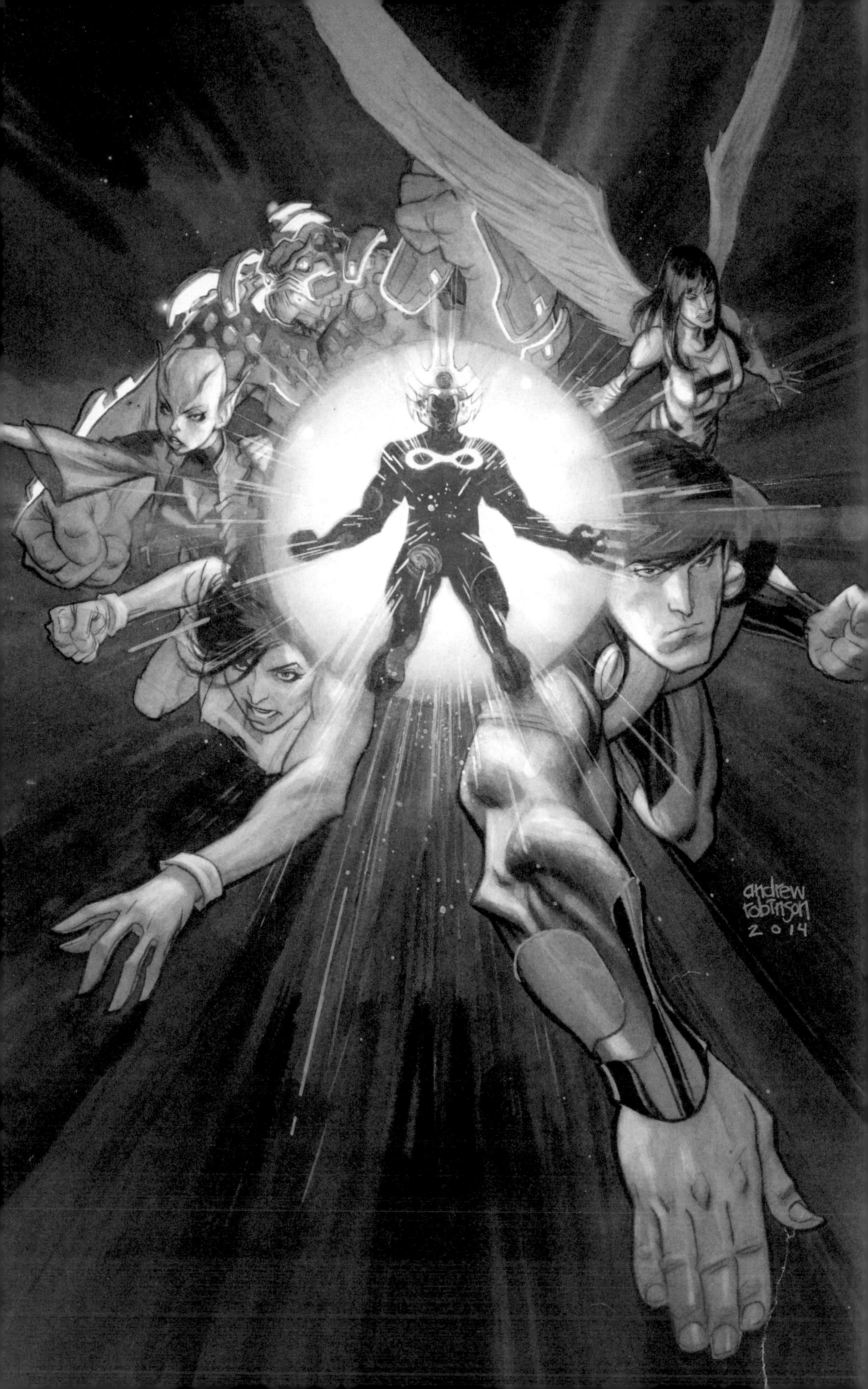
andrew robinson 2014

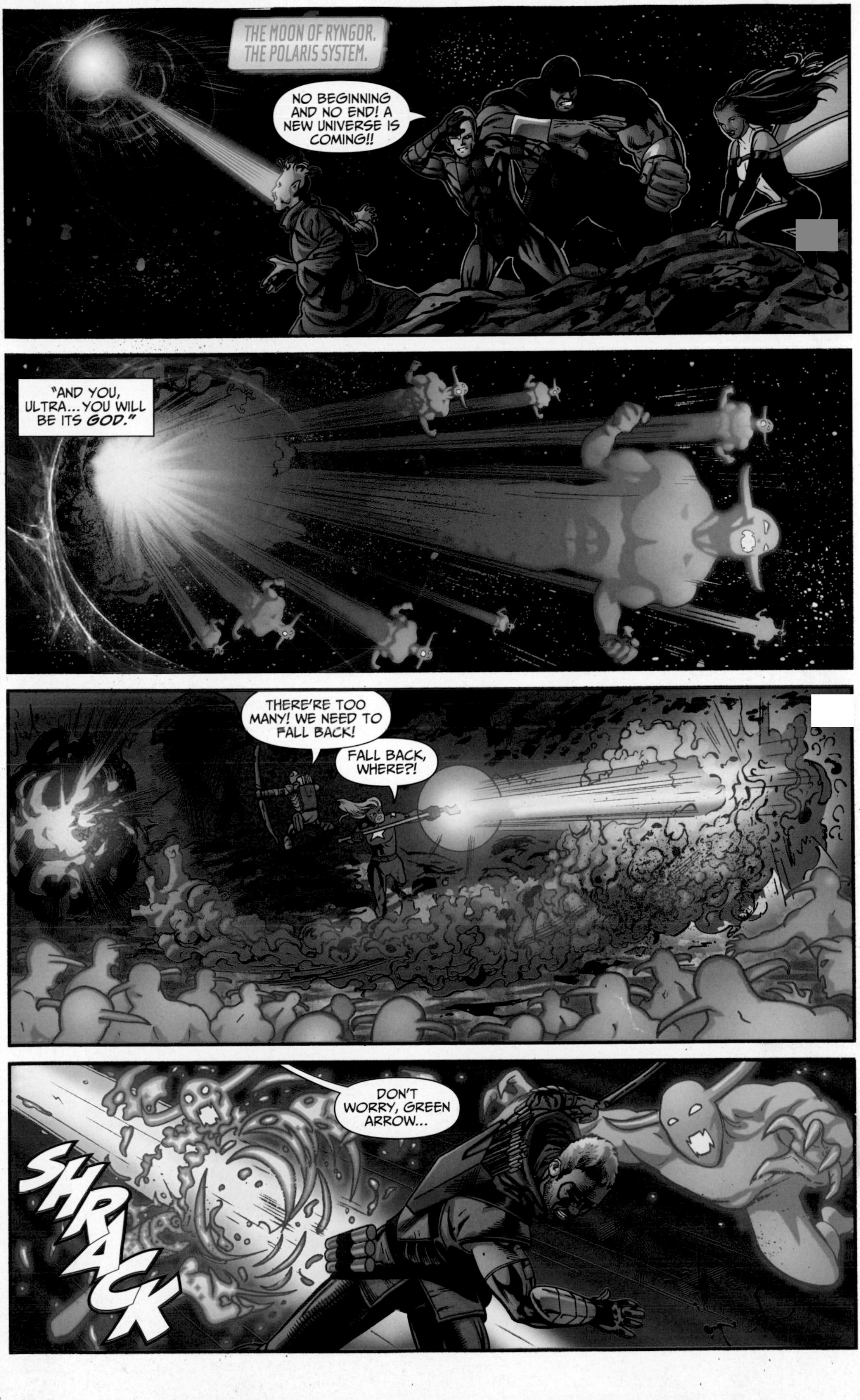
THE MOON OF RYNGOR. THE POLARIS SYSTEM.
NO BEGINNING AND NO END! A NEW UNIVERSE IS COMING!!
"AND YOU, ULTRA...YOU WILL BE ITS GOD."
THERE'RE TOO MANY! WE NEED TO FALL BACK!
FALL BACK, WHERE?!
DON'T WORRY, GREEN ARROW...
SHRACK

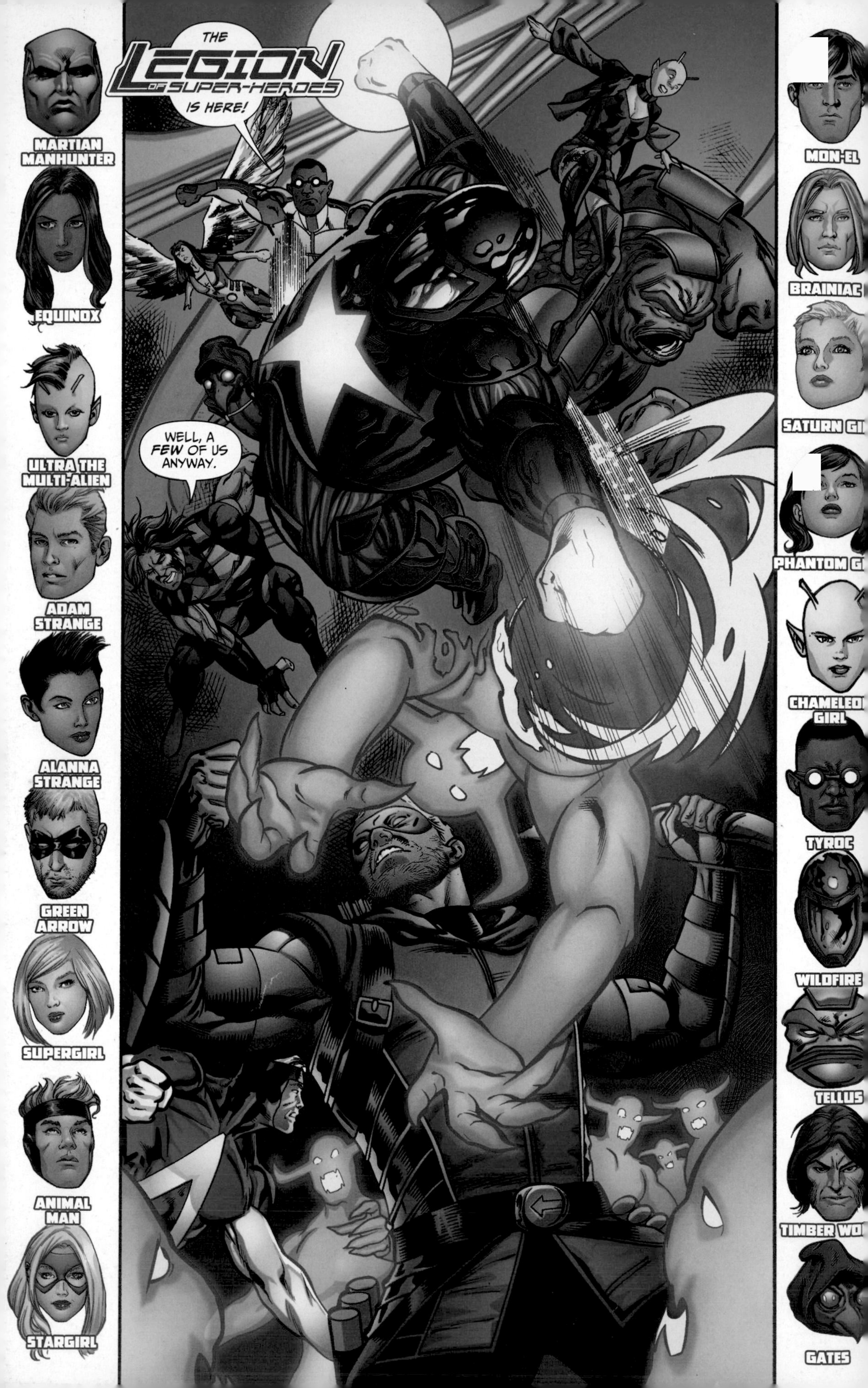
THE LEGION OF SUPER-HEROES IS HERE!
WELL, A FEW OF US ANYWAY.
MARTIAN MANHUNTER
EQUINOX
ULTRA THE MULTI-ALIEN
ADAM STRANGE
ALANNA STRANGE
GREEN ARROW
SUPERGIRL
ANIMAL MAN
STARGIRL
MON-EL
BRAINIAC
SATURN GI
PHANTOM GI
CHAMELEO GIRL
TYROC
WILDFIRE
TELLUS
TIMBER WO
GATES

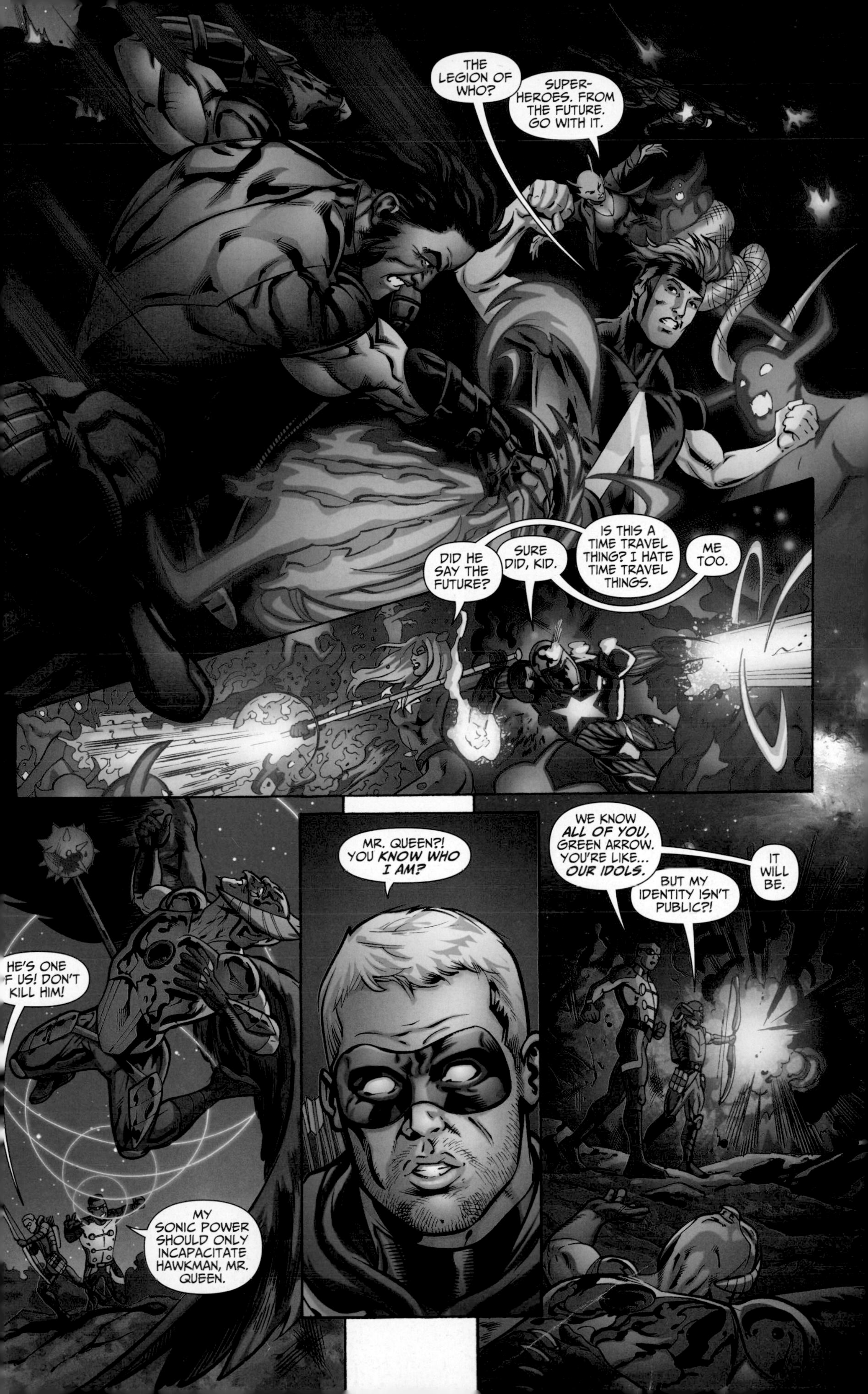
THE LEGION OF WHO?
SUPER-HEROES. FROM THE FUTURE. GO WITH IT.
DID HE SAY THE FUTURE?
SURE DID, KID.
IS THIS A TIME TRAVEL THING? I HATE TIME TRAVEL THINGS.
ME TOO.
HE'S ONE OF US! DON'T KILL HIM!
MY SONIC POWER SHOULD ONLY INCAPACITATE HAWKMAN, MR. QUEEN.
MR. QUEEN?! YOU KNOW WHO I AM?
WE KNOW ALL OF YOU, GREEN ARROW. YOU'RE LIKE... OUR IDOLS.
BUT MY IDENTITY ISN'T PUBLIC?!
IT WILL BE.

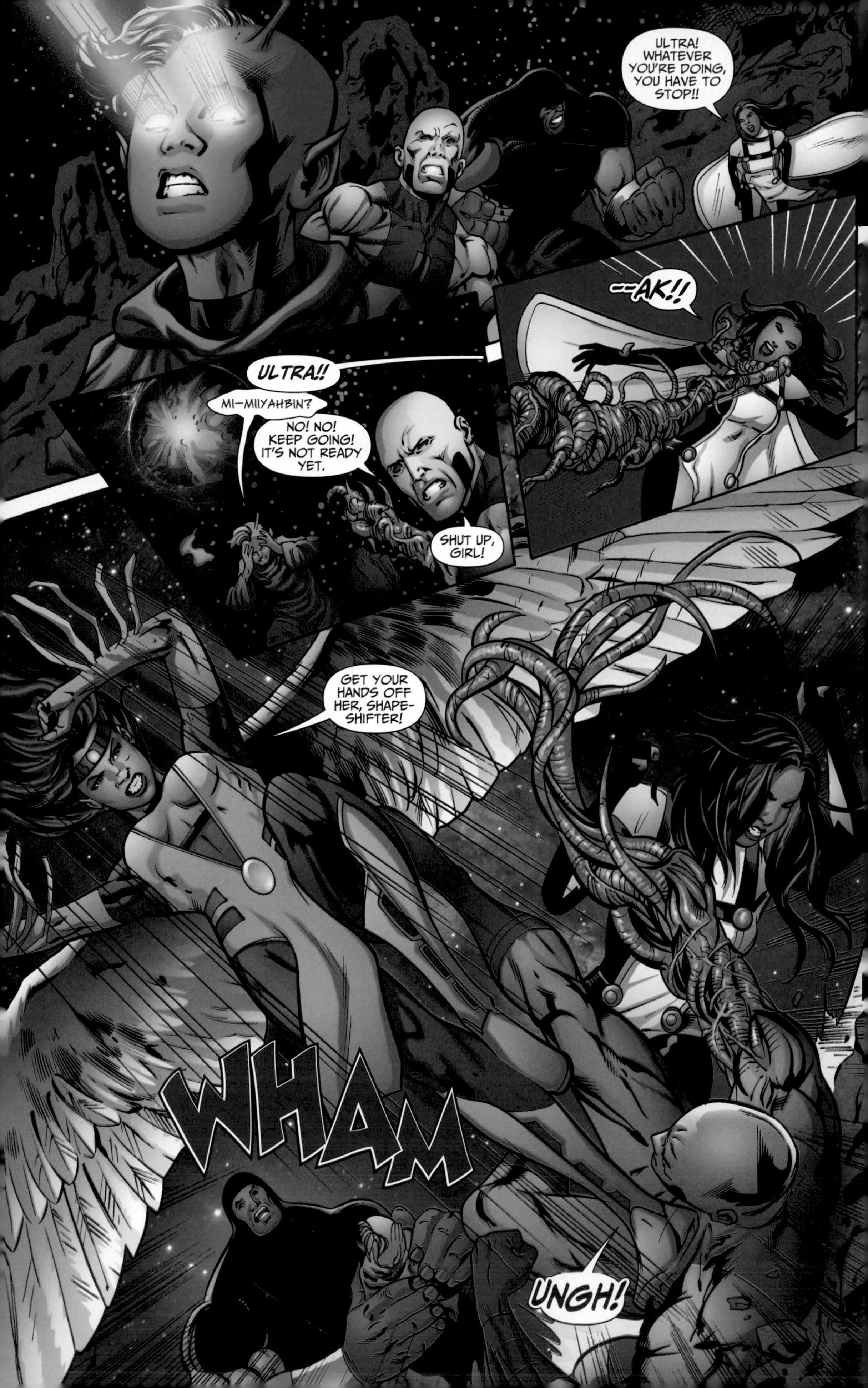
ULTRA! WHATEVER YOU'RE DOING, YOU HAVE TO STOP!!
--AK!!
ULTRA!!
MI-MIIYAHBIN?
NO! NO! KEEP GOING! IT'S NOT READY YET.
SHUT UP, GIRL!
GET YOUR HANDS OFF HER, SHAPE-SHIFTER!
WHAM
UNGH!

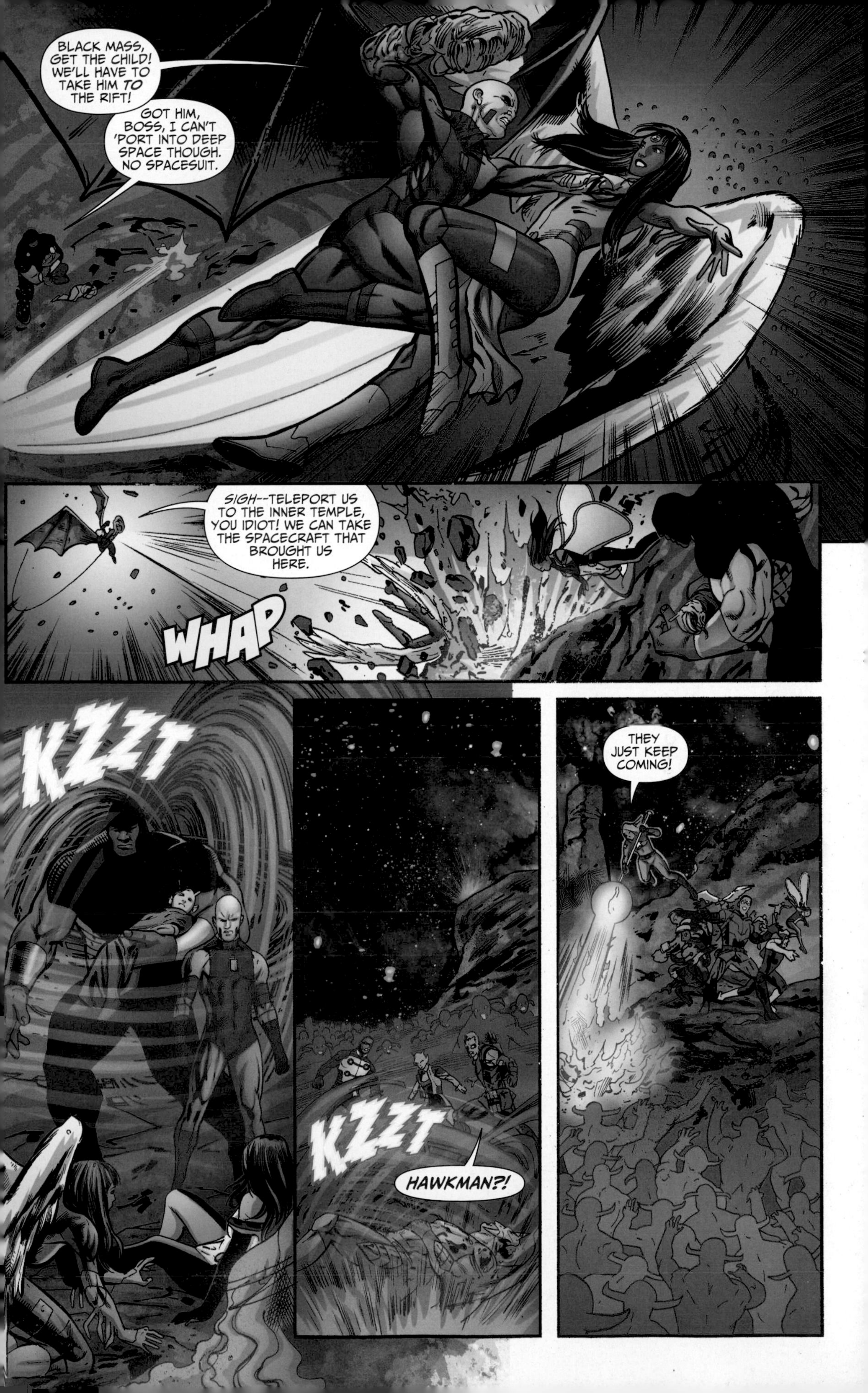
BLACK MASS, GET THE CHILD! WE'LL HAVE TO TAKE HIM *TO* THE RIFT!
GOT HIM, BOSS, I CAN'T 'PORT INTO DEEP SPACE THOUGH. NO SPACESUIT.
SIGH--TELEPORT US TO THE INNER TEMPLE, YOU IDIOT! WE CAN TAKE THE SPACECRAFT THAT BROUGHT US HERE.
WHAP
KZZT
KZZT
HAWKMAN?!
THEY JUST KEEP COMING!

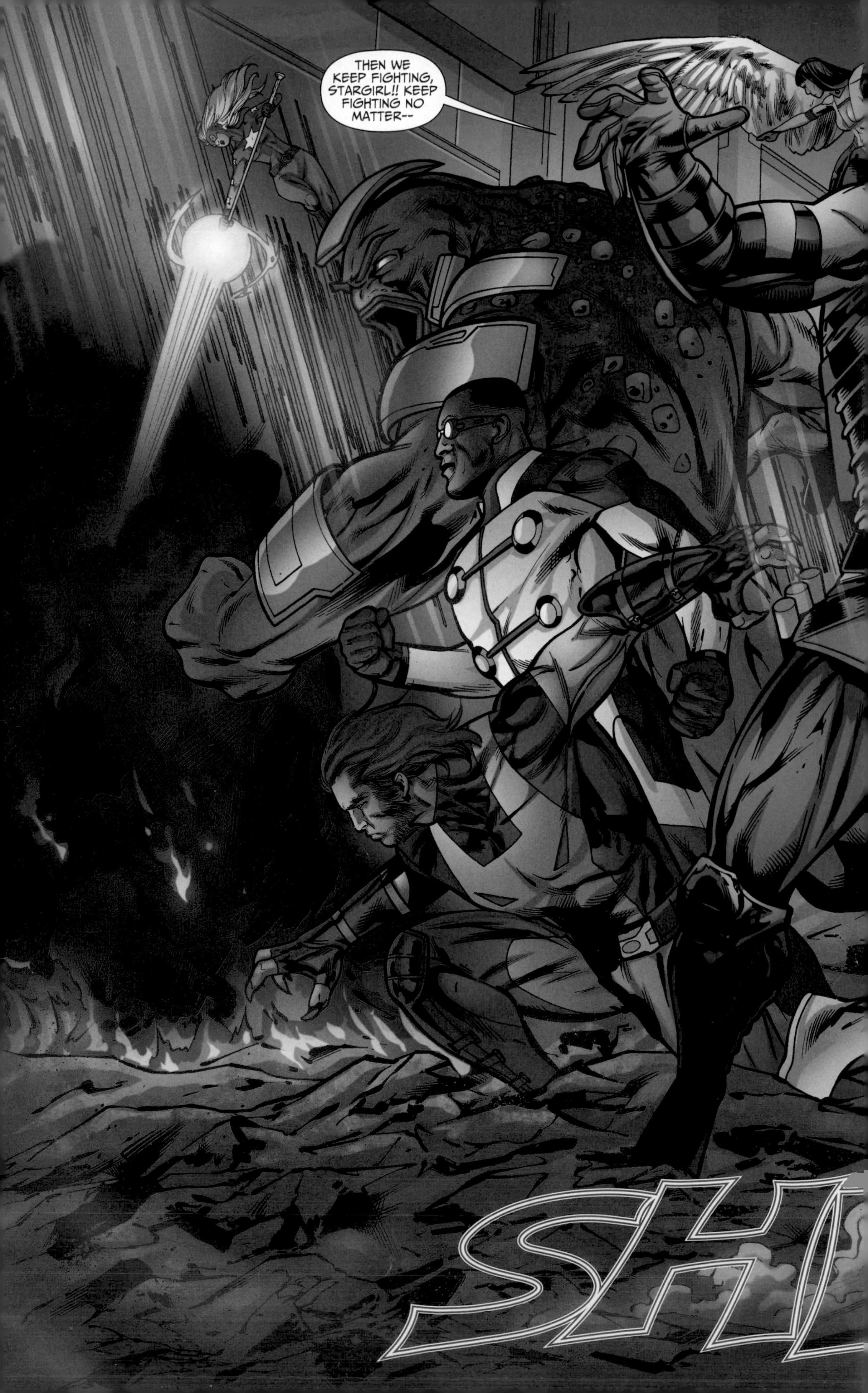
THEN WE KEEP FIGHTING, STARGIRL!! KEEP FIGHTING NO MATTER--
SHI

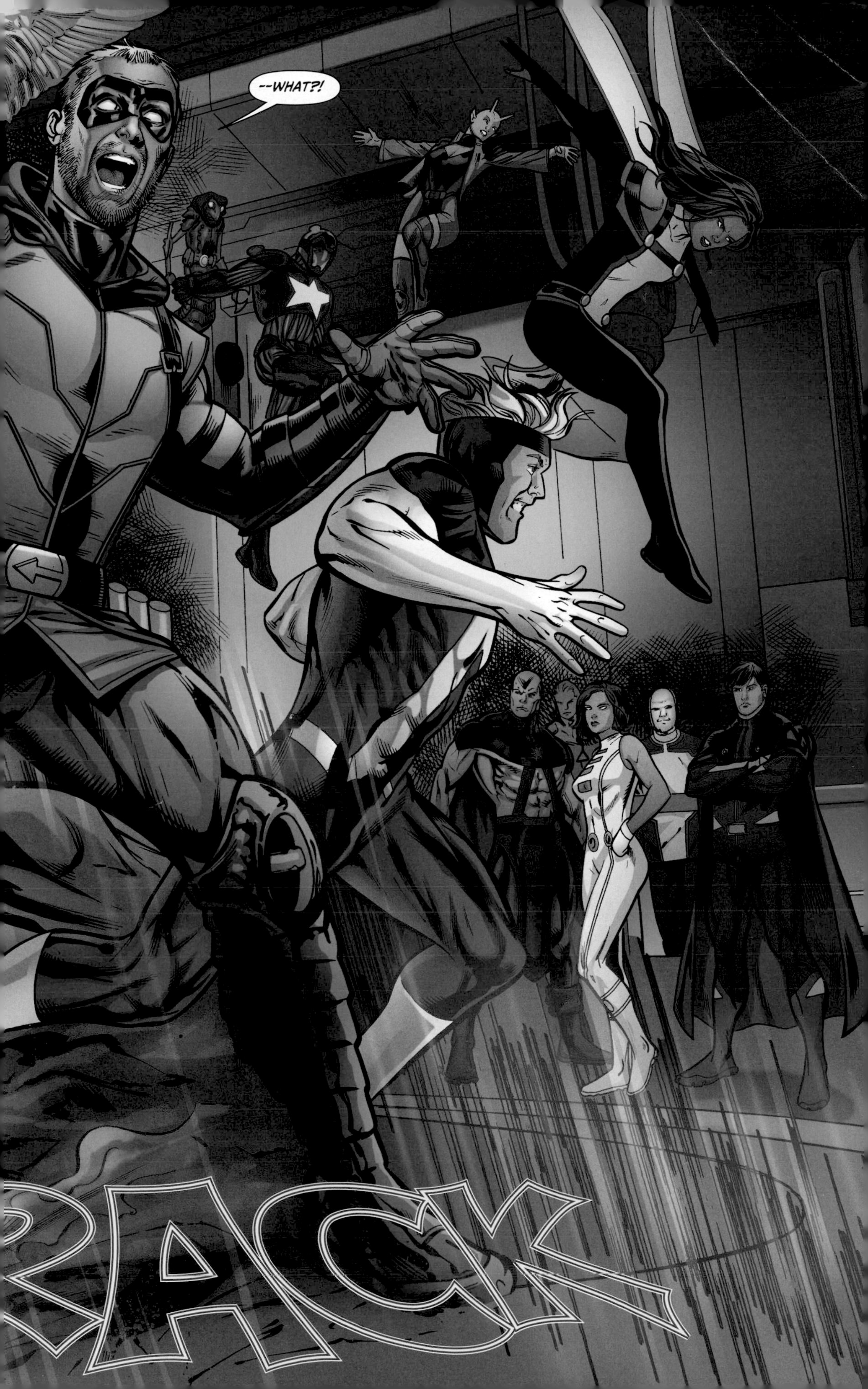
--WHAT?!
RACK

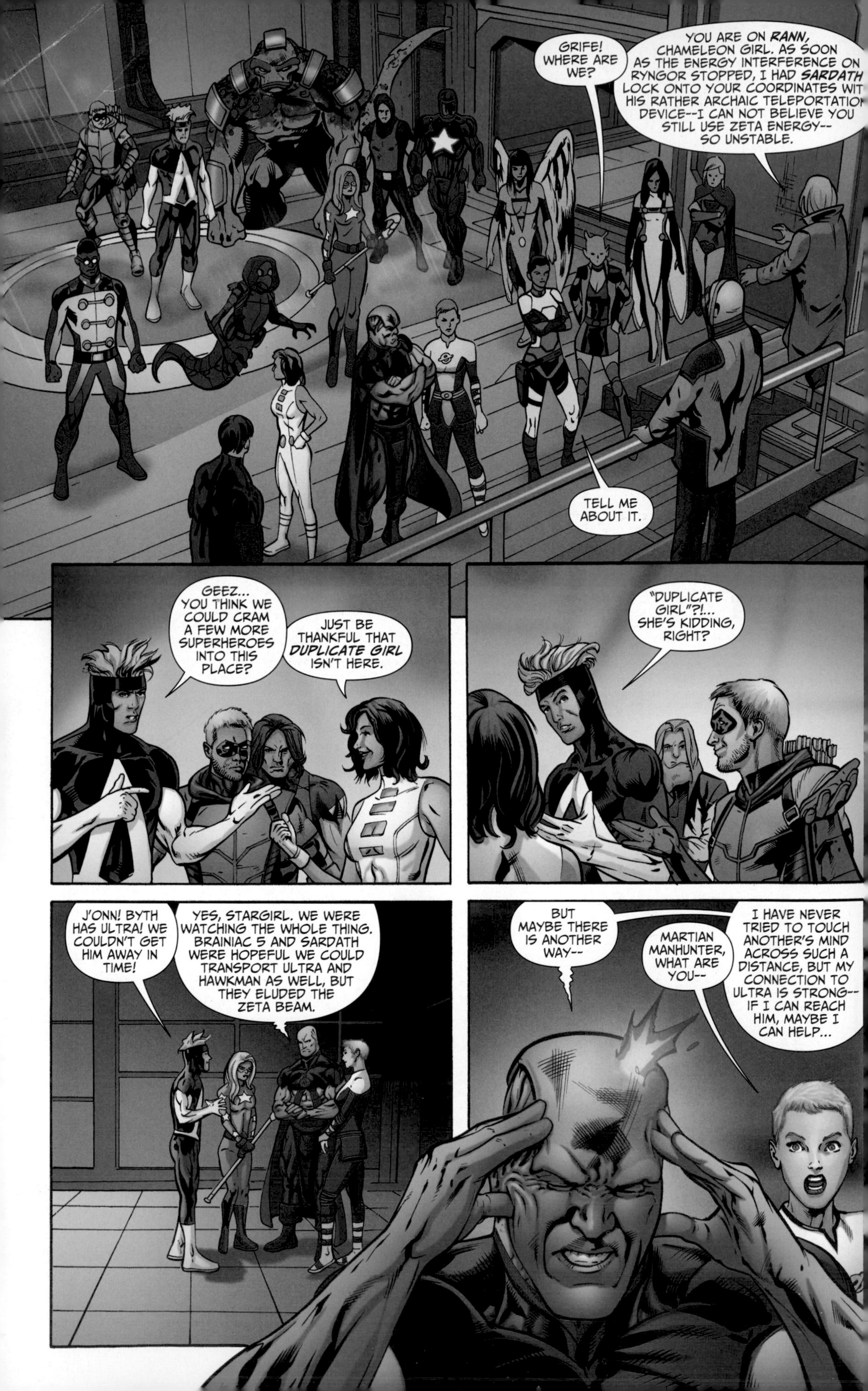
GRIFE! WHERE ARE WE?
YOU ARE ON RANN, CHAMELEON GIRL. AS SOON AS THE ENERGY INTERFERENCE ON RYNGOR STOPPED, I HAD SARDATH LOCK ONTO YOUR COORDINATES WIT HIS RATHER ARCHAIC TELEPORTATIO DEVICE--I CAN NOT BELIEVE YOU STILL USE ZETA ENERGY-- SO UNSTABLE.
TELL ME ABOUT IT.
GEEZ... YOU THINK WE COULD CRAM A FEW MORE SUPERHEROES INTO THIS PLACE?
JUST BE THANKFUL THAT DUPLICATE GIRL ISN'T HERE.
"DUPLICATE GIRL"?!... SHE'S KIDDING, RIGHT?
J'ONN! BYTH HAS ULTRA! WE COULDN'T GET HIM AWAY IN TIME!
YES, STARGIRL. WE WERE WATCHING THE WHOLE THING. BRAINIAC 5 AND SARDATH WERE HOPEFUL WE COULD TRANSPORT ULTRA AND HAWKMAN AS WELL, BUT THEY ELUDED THE ZETA BEAM.
BUT MAYBE THERE IS ANOTHER WAY--
MARTIAN MANHUNTER, WHAT ARE YOU--
I HAVE NEVER TRIED TO TOUCH ANOTHER'S MIND ACROSS SUCH A DISTANCE, BUT MY CONNECTION TO ULTRA IS STRONG-- IF I CAN REACH HIM, MAYBE I CAN HELP...

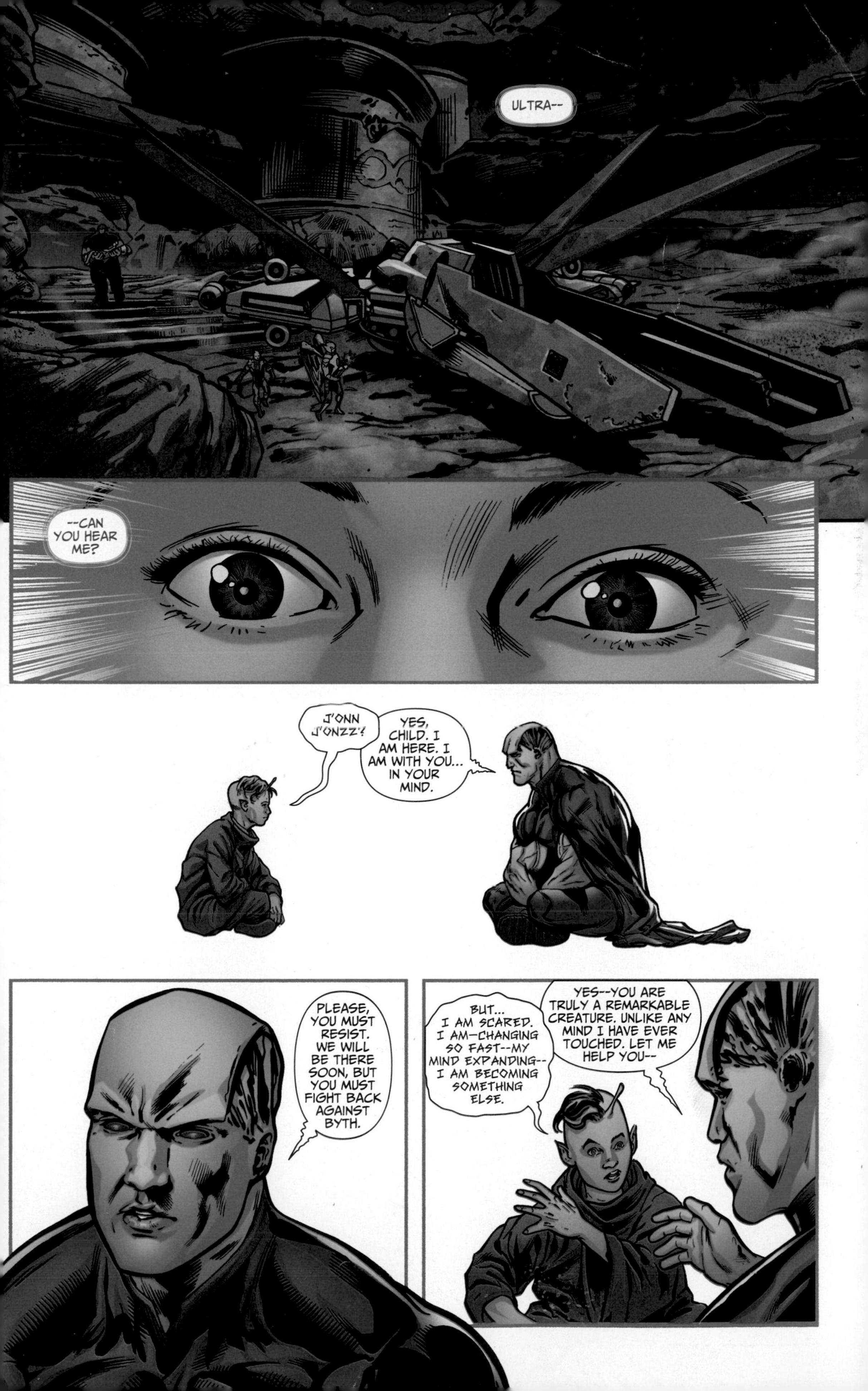
ULTRA--
--CAN YOU HEAR ME?
J'ONN J'ONZZ?
YES, CHILD. I AM HERE. I AM WITH YOU... IN YOUR MIND.
PLEASE, YOU MUST RESIST. WE WILL BE THERE SOON, BUT YOU MUST FIGHT BACK AGAINST BYTH.
BUT... I AM SCARED. I AM--CHANGING SO FAST--MY MIND EXPANDING-- I AM BECOMING SOMETHING ELSE.
YES--YOU ARE TRULY A REMARKABLE CREATURE. UNLIKE ANY MIND I HAVE EVER TOUCHED. LET ME HELP YOU--

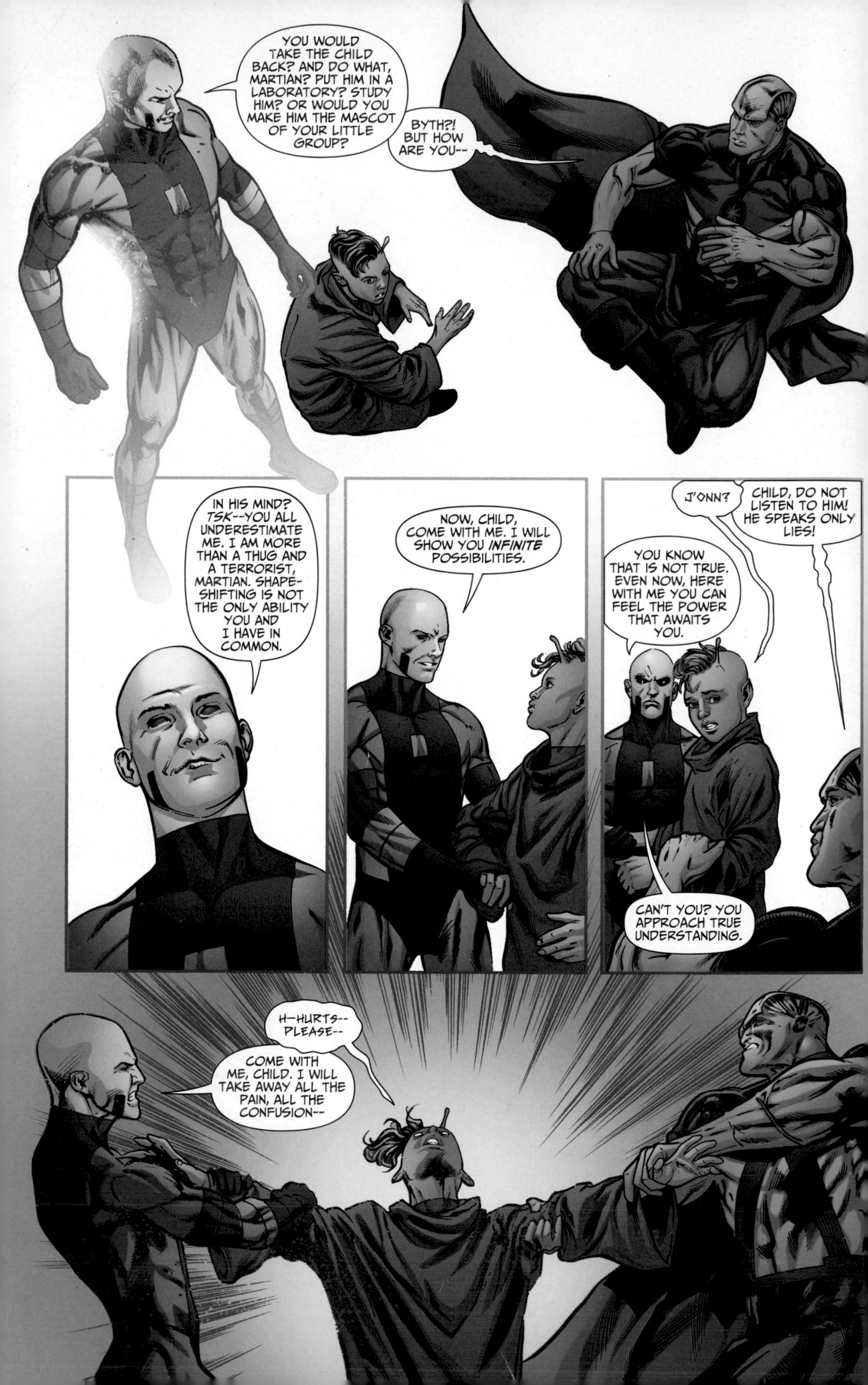

YOU WOULD TAKE THE CHILD BACK? AND DO WHAT, MARTIAN? PUT HIM IN A LABORATORY? STUDY HIM? OR WOULD YOU MAKE HIM THE MASCOT OF YOUR LITTLE GROUP?
BYTH?! BUT HOW ARE YOU--
IN HIS MIND? *TSK*--YOU ALL UNDERESTIMATE ME. I AM MORE THAN A THUG AND A TERRORIST, MARTIAN. SHAPE-SHIFTING IS NOT THE ONLY ABILITY YOU AND I HAVE IN COMMON.
NOW, CHILD, COME WITH ME. I WILL SHOW YOU *INFINITE* POSSIBILITIES.
J'ONN?
CHILD, DO NOT LISTEN TO HIM! HE SPEAKS ONLY LIES!
YOU KNOW THAT IS NOT TRUE. EVEN NOW, HERE WITH ME YOU CAN FEEL THE POWER THAT AWAITS YOU.
CAN'T YOU? YOU APPROACH TRUE UNDERSTANDING.
H-HURTS-- PLEASE--
COME WITH ME, CHILD. I WILL TAKE AWAY ALL THE PAIN, ALL THE CONFUSION--

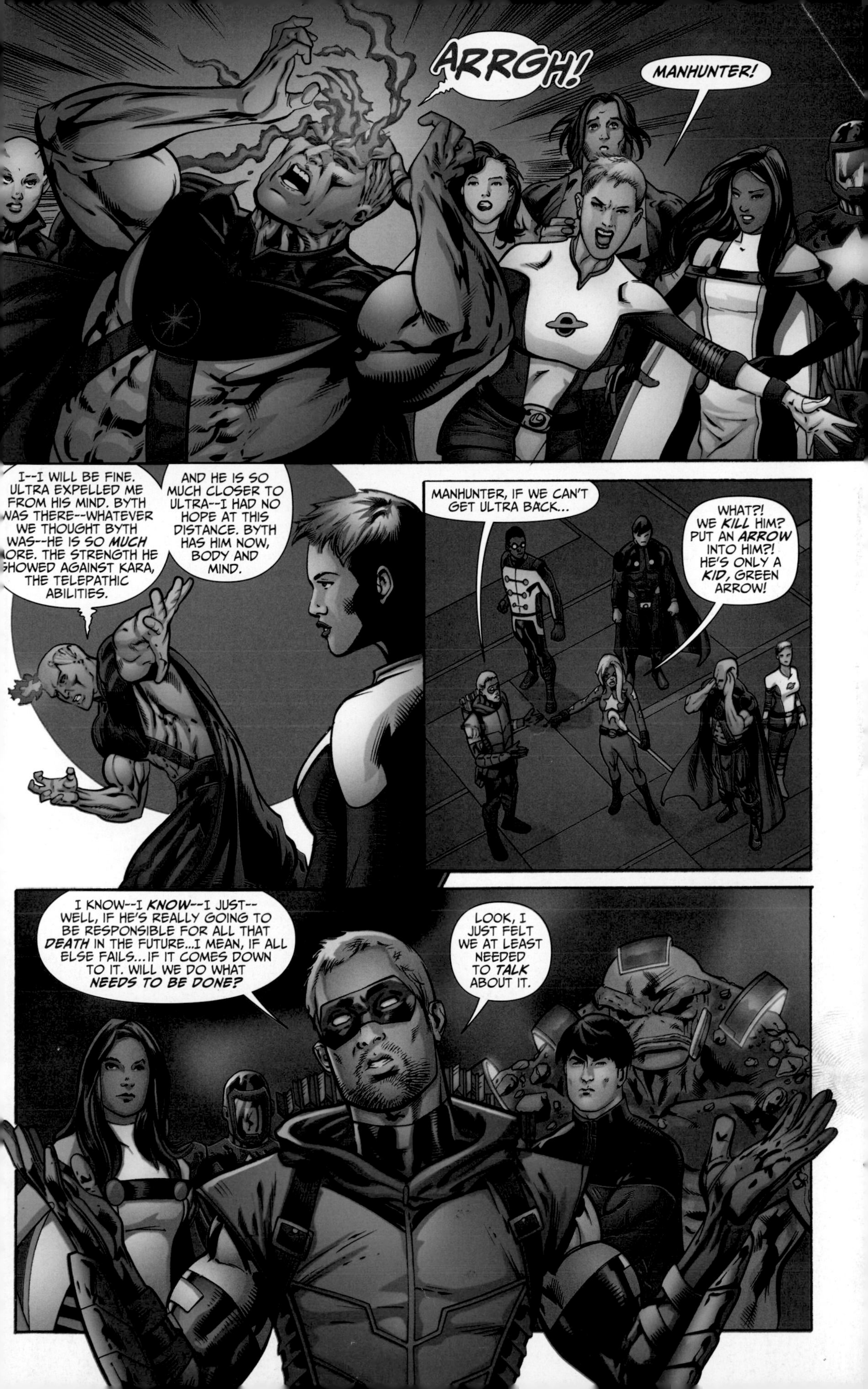
ARRGH!
MANHUNTER!
I--I WILL BE FINE. ULTRA EXPELLED ME FROM HIS MIND. BYTH WAS THERE--WHATEVER WE THOUGHT BYTH WAS--HE IS SO MUCH MORE. THE STRENGTH HE SHOWED AGAINST KARA, THE TELEPATHIC ABILITIES.
AND HE IS SO MUCH CLOSER TO ULTRA--I HAD NO HOPE AT THIS DISTANCE. BYTH HAS HIM NOW, BODY AND MIND.
MANHUNTER, IF WE CAN'T GET ULTRA BACK...
WHAT?! WE KILL HIM? PUT AN ARROW INTO HIM?! HE'S ONLY A KID, GREEN ARROW!
I KNOW--I KNOW--I JUST--WELL, IF HE'S REALLY GOING TO BE RESPONSIBLE FOR ALL THAT DEATH IN THE FUTURE...I MEAN, IF ALL ELSE FAILS...IF IT COMES DOWN TO IT. WILL WE DO WHAT NEEDS TO BE DONE?
LOOK, I JUST FELT WE AT LEAST NEEDED TO TALK ABOUT IT.

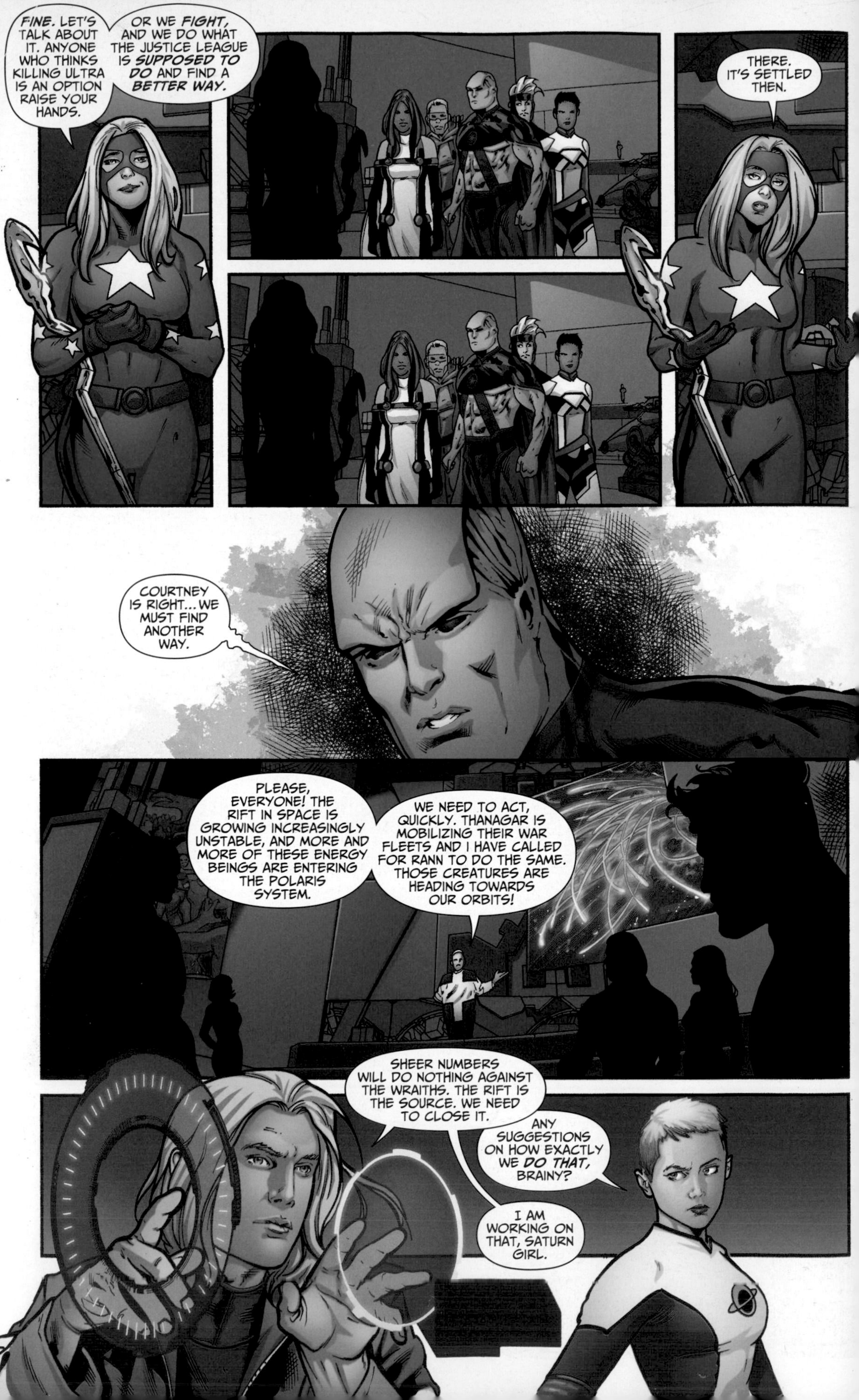
FINE. LET'S TALK ABOUT IT. ANYONE WHO THINKS KILLING ULTRA IS AN OPTION RAISE YOUR HANDS.
OR WE FIGHT, AND WE DO WHAT THE JUSTICE LEAGUE IS SUPPOSED TO DO AND FIND A BETTER WAY.
THERE. IT'S SETTLED THEN.
COURTNEY IS RIGHT... WE MUST FIND ANOTHER WAY.
PLEASE, EVERYONE! THE RIFT IN SPACE IS GROWING INCREASINGLY UNSTABLE, AND MORE AND MORE OF THESE ENERGY BEINGS ARE ENTERING THE POLARIS SYSTEM.
WE NEED TO ACT, QUICKLY. THANAGAR IS MOBILIZING THEIR WAR FLEETS AND I HAVE CALLED FOR RANN TO DO THE SAME. THOSE CREATURES ARE HEADING TOWARDS OUR ORBITS!
SHEER NUMBERS WILL DO NOTHING AGAINST THE WRAITHS. THE RIFT IS THE SOURCE. WE NEED TO CLOSE IT.
ANY SUGGESTIONS ON HOW EXACTLY WE DO THAT, BRAINY?
I AM WORKING ON THAT, SATURN GIRL.

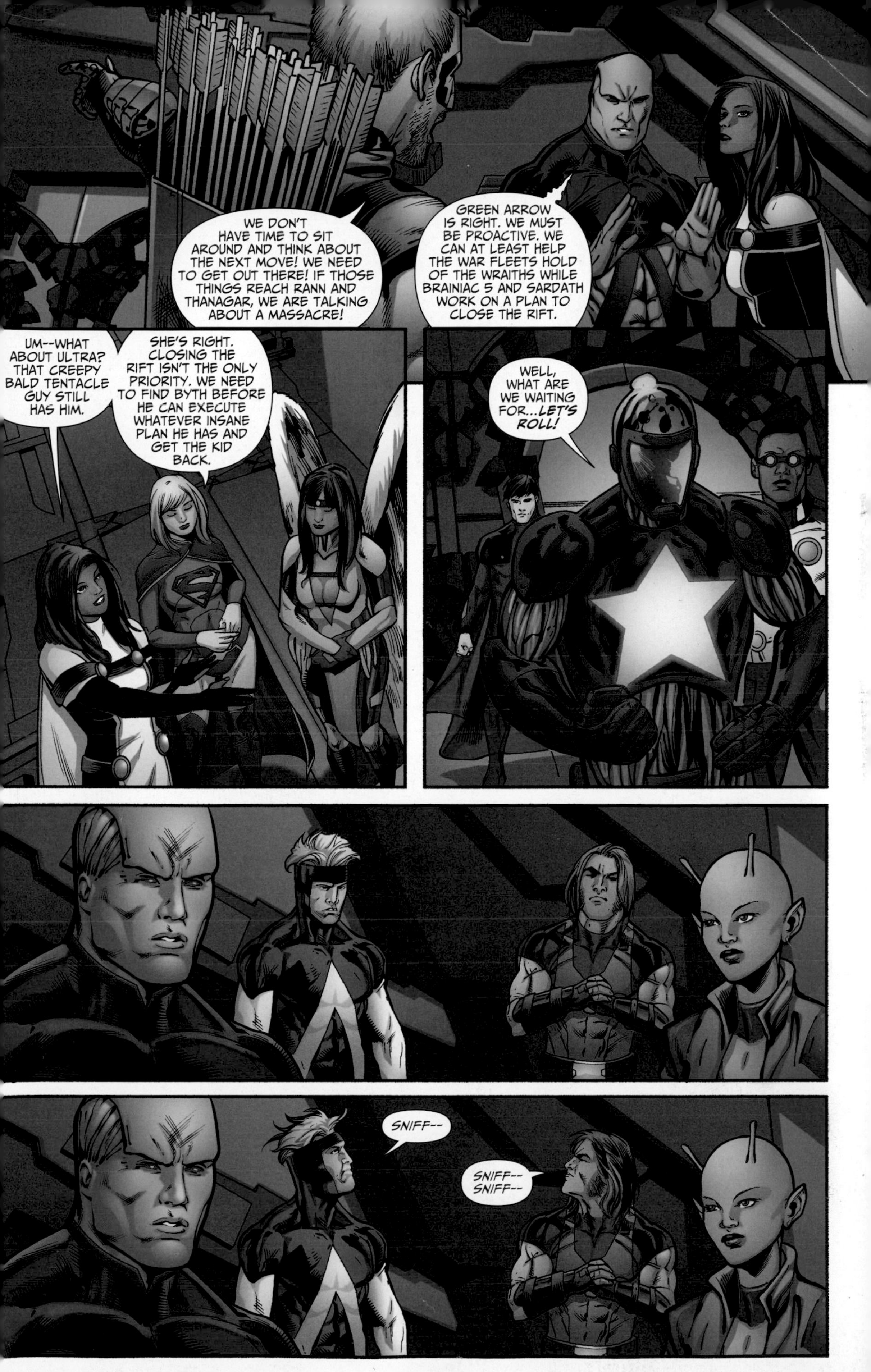
WE DON'T HAVE TIME TO SIT AROUND AND THINK ABOUT THE NEXT MOVE! WE NEED TO GET OUT THERE! IF THOSE THINGS REACH RANN AND THANAGAR, WE ARE TALKING ABOUT A MASSACRE!
GREEN ARROW IS RIGHT. WE MUST BE PROACTIVE. WE CAN AT LEAST HELP THE WAR FLEETS HOLD OF THE WRAITHS WHILE BRAINIAC 5 AND SARDATH WORK ON A PLAN TO CLOSE THE RIFT.
UM--WHAT ABOUT ULTRA? THAT CREEPY BALD TENTACLE GUY STILL HAS HIM.
SHE'S RIGHT. CLOSING THE RIFT ISN'T THE ONLY PRIORITY. WE NEED TO FIND BYTH BEFORE HE CAN EXECUTE WHATEVER INSANE PLAN HE HAS AND GET THE KID BACK.
WELL, WHAT ARE WE WAITING FOR...LET'S ROLL!
SNIFF--
SNIFF-- SNIFF--

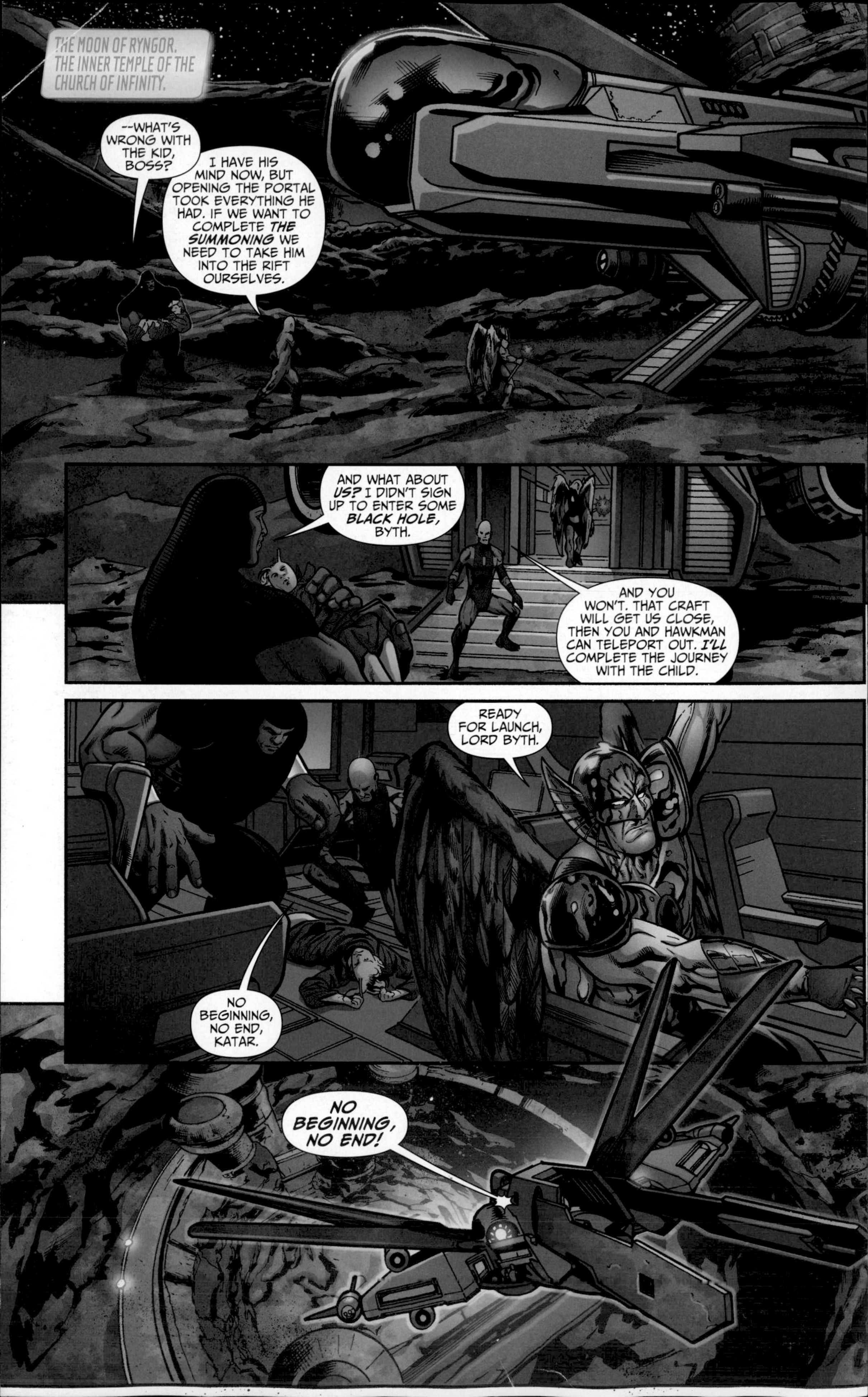
THE MOON OF RYNGOR. THE INNER TEMPLE OF THE CHURCH OF INFINITY.
--WHAT'S WRONG WITH THE KID, BOSS?
I HAVE HIS MIND NOW, BUT OPENING THE PORTAL TOOK EVERYTHING HE HAD. IF WE WANT TO COMPLETE THE SUMMONING WE NEED TO TAKE HIM INTO THE RIFT OURSELVES.
AND WHAT ABOUT US? I DIDN'T SIGN UP TO ENTER SOME BLACK HOLE, BYTH.
AND YOU WON'T. THAT CRAFT WILL GET US CLOSE, THEN YOU AND HAWKMAN CAN TELEPORT OUT. I'LL COMPLETE THE JOURNEY WITH THE CHILD.
READY FOR LAUNCH, LORD BYTH.
NO BEGINNING, NO END, KATAR.
NO BEGINNING, NO END!

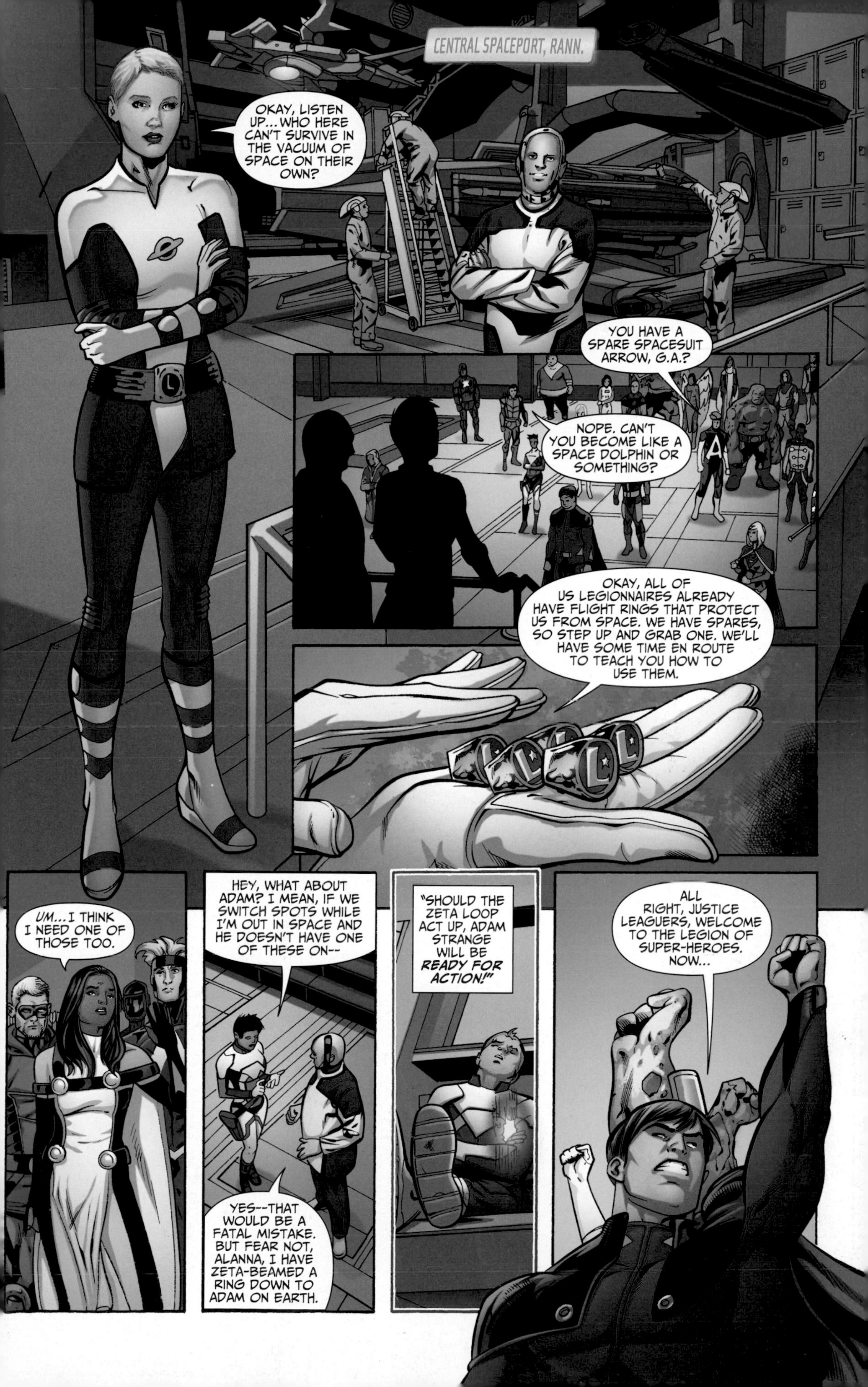
CENTRAL SPACEPORT, RANN.
OKAY, LISTEN UP... WHO HERE CAN'T SURVIVE IN THE VACUUM OF SPACE ON THEIR OWN?
YOU HAVE A SPARE SPACESUIT ARROW, G.A.?
NOPE. CAN'T YOU BECOME LIKE A SPACE DOLPHIN OR SOMETHING?
OKAY, ALL OF US LEGIONNAIRES ALREADY HAVE FLIGHT RINGS THAT PROTECT US FROM SPACE. WE HAVE SPARES, SO STEP UP AND GRAB ONE. WE'LL HAVE SOME TIME EN ROUTE TO TEACH YOU HOW TO USE THEM.
UM... I THINK I NEED ONE OF THOSE TOO.
HEY, WHAT ABOUT ADAM? I MEAN, IF WE SWITCH SPOTS WHILE I'M OUT IN SPACE AND HE DOESN'T HAVE ONE OF THESE ON--
YES--THAT WOULD BE A FATAL MISTAKE. BUT FEAR NOT, ALANNA, I HAVE ZETA-BEAMED A RING DOWN TO ADAM ON EARTH.
"SHOULD THE ZETA LOOP ACT UP, ADAM STRANGE WILL BE READY FOR ACTION!"
ALL RIGHT, JUSTICE LEAGUERS, WELCOME TO THE LEGION OF SUPER-HEROES. NOW...

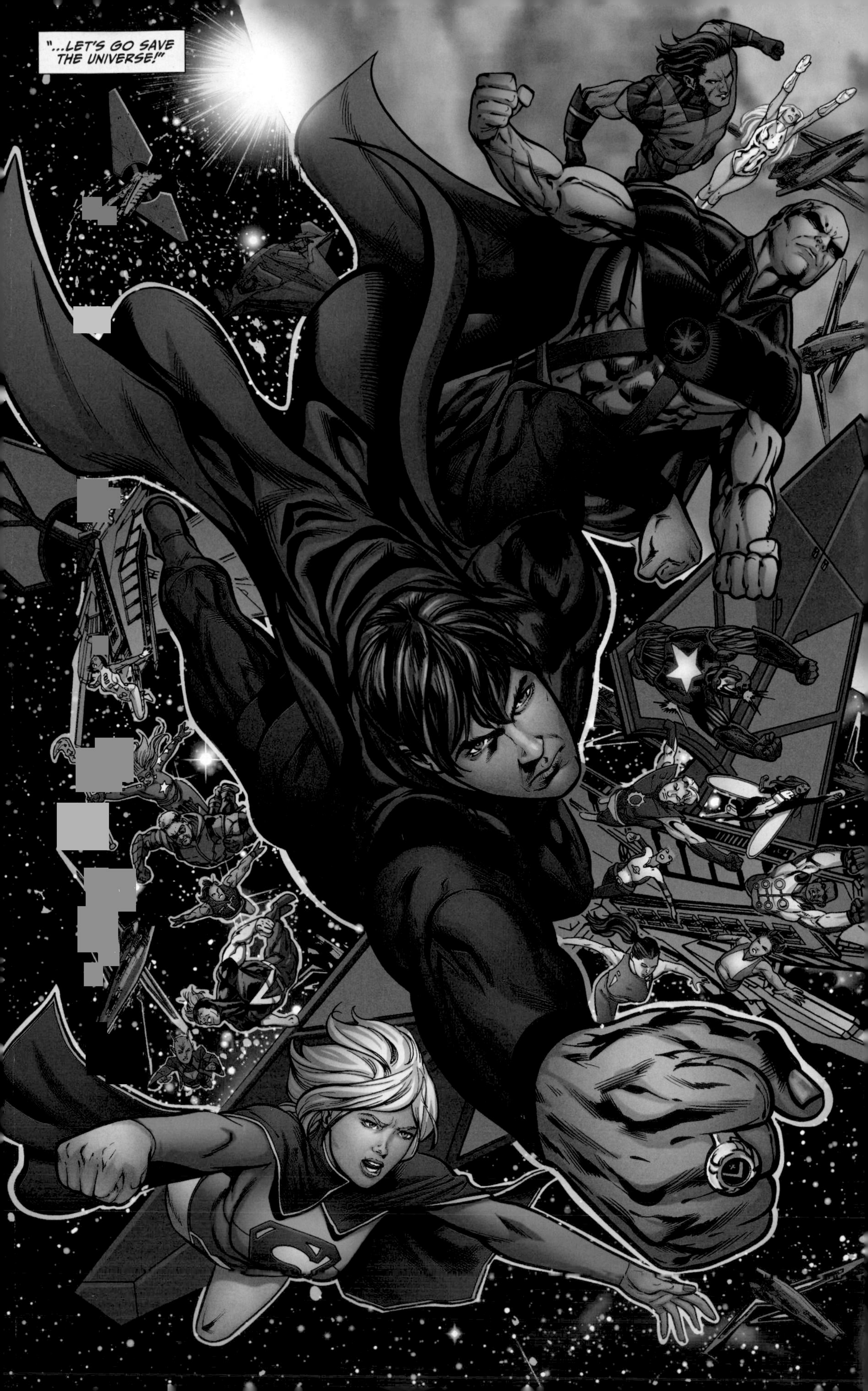
"...LET'S GO SAVE THE UNIVERSE!"

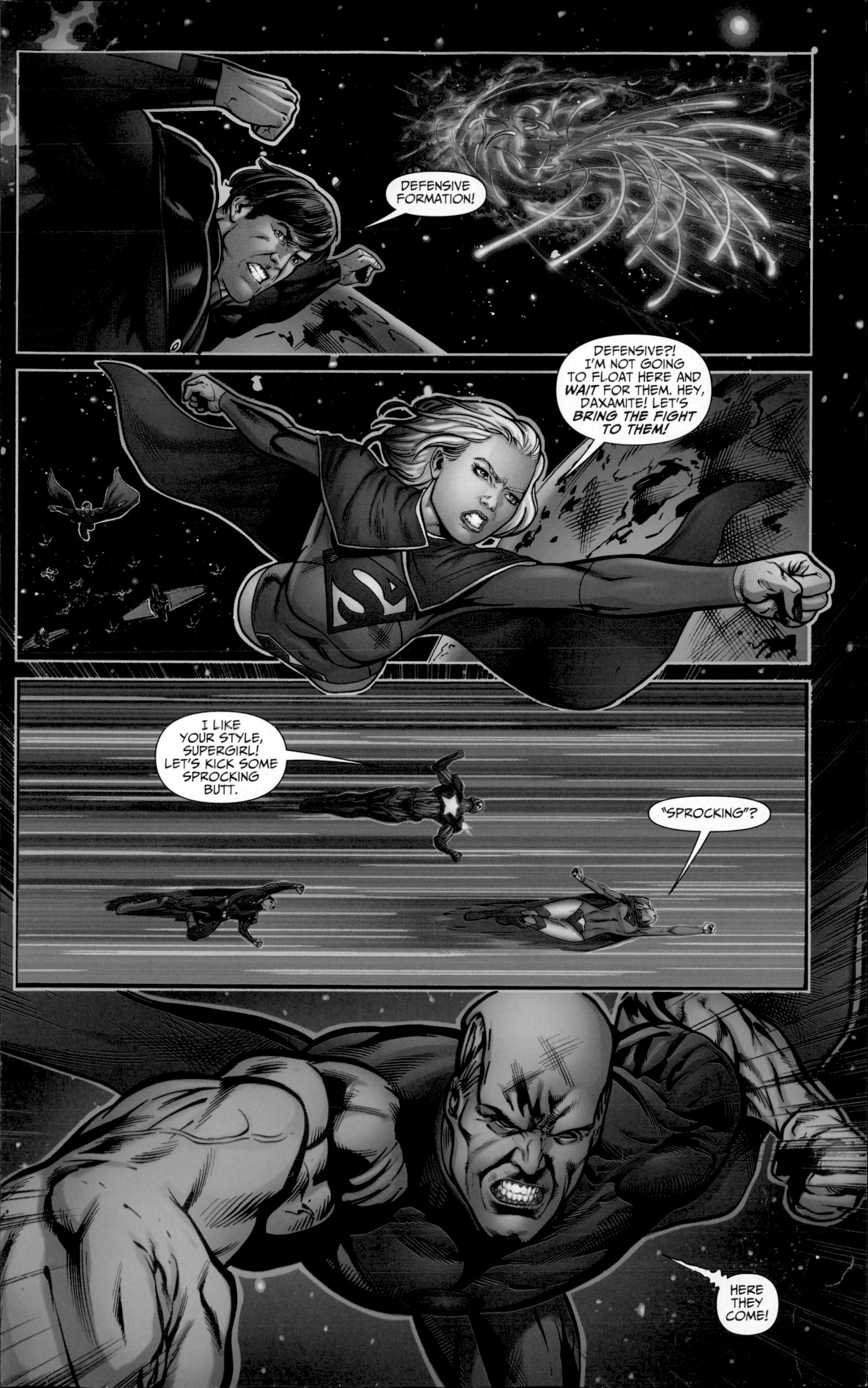
DEFENSIVE FORMATION!
DEFENSIVE?! I'M NOT GOING TO FLOAT HERE AND WAIT FOR THEM. HEY, DAXAMITE! LET'S BRING THE FIGHT TO THEM!
I LIKE YOUR STYLE, SUPERGIRL! LET'S KICK SOME SPROCKING BUTT.
"SPROCKING"?
HERE THEY COME!

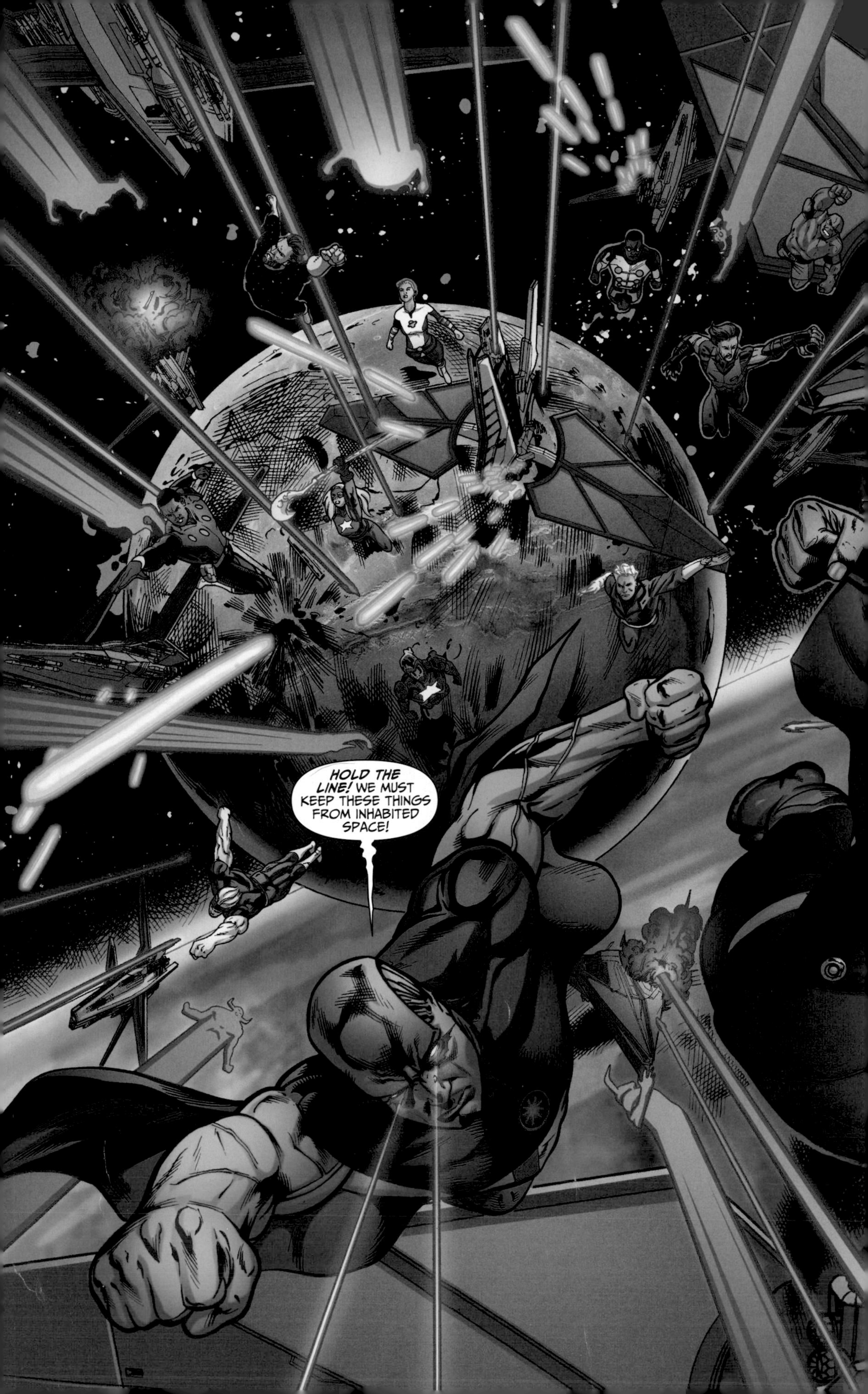
HOLD THE LINE! WE MUST KEEP THESE THINGS FROM INHABITED SPACE!

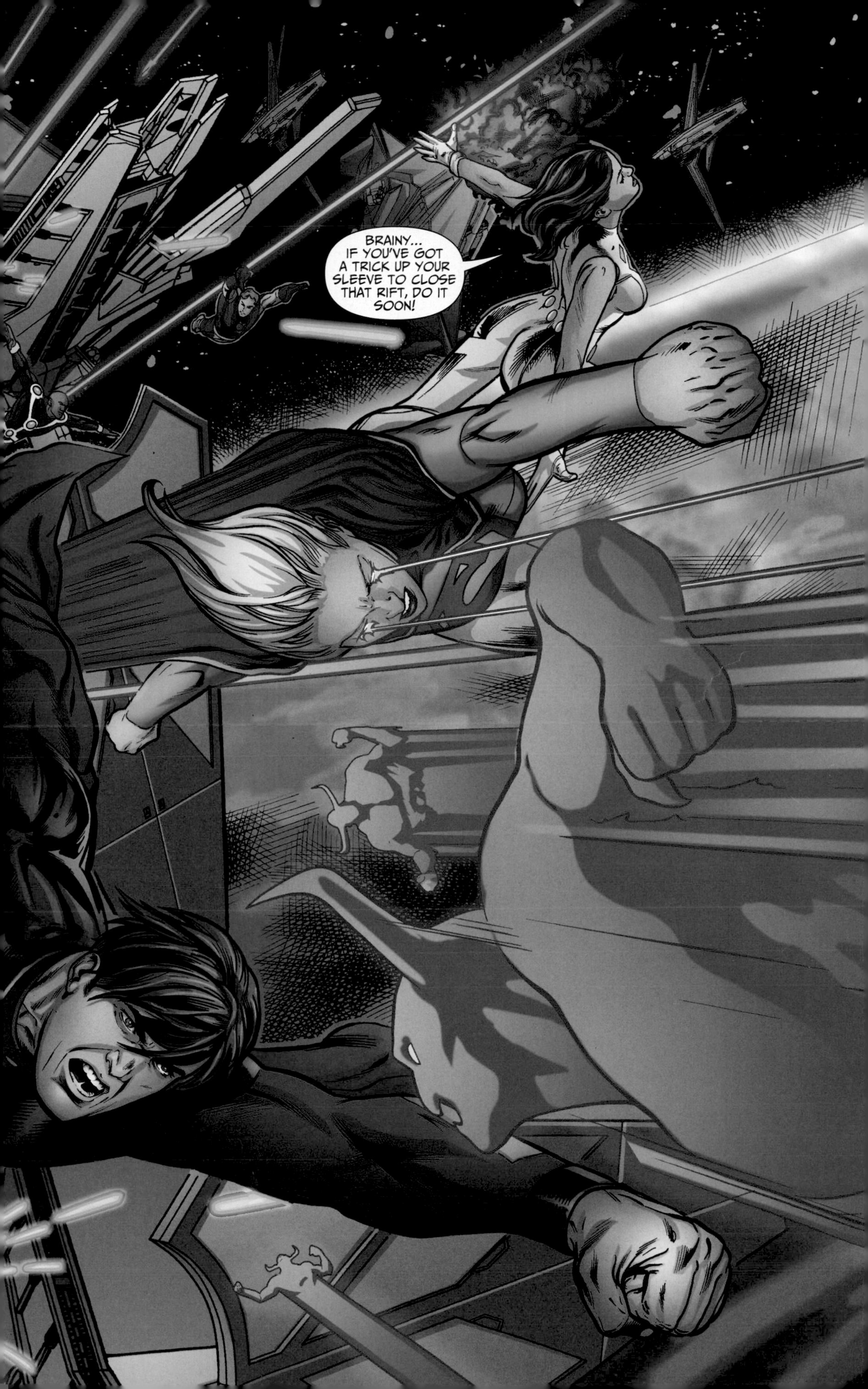
BRAINY... IF YOU'VE GOT A TRICK UP YOUR SLEEVE TO CLOSE THAT RIFT, DO IT SOON!

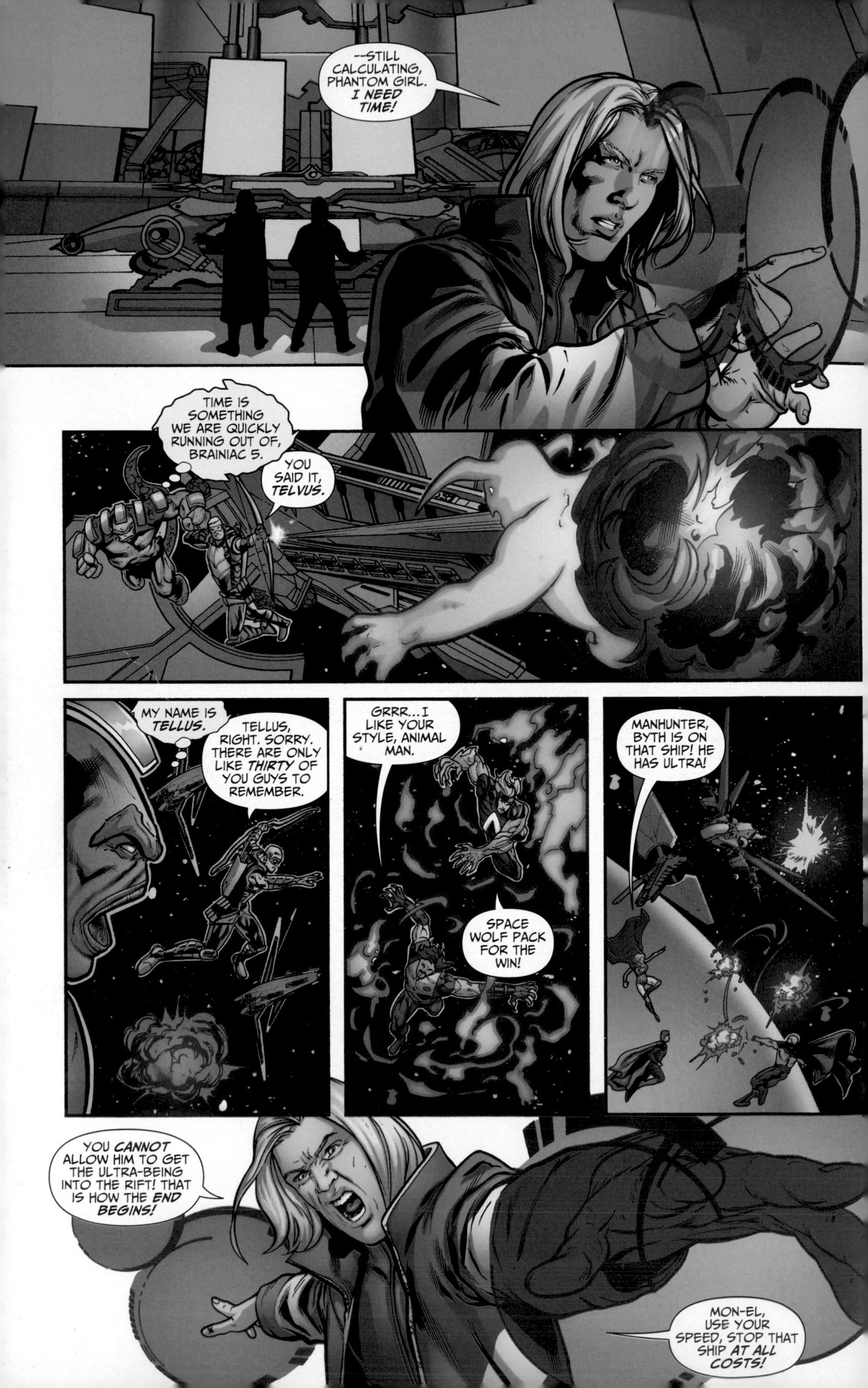
--STILL CALCULATING, PHANTOM GIRL. I NEED TIME!
TIME IS SOMETHING WE ARE QUICKLY RUNNING OUT OF, BRAINIAC 5.
YOU SAID IT, TELVUS.
MY NAME IS TELLUS.
TELLUS, RIGHT. SORRY. THERE ARE ONLY LIKE THIRTY OF YOU GUYS TO REMEMBER.
GRRR...I LIKE YOUR STYLE, ANIMAL MAN.
SPACE WOLF PACK FOR THE WIN!
MANHUNTER, BYTH IS ON THAT SHIP! HE HAS ULTRA!
YOU CANNOT ALLOW HIM TO GET THE ULTRA-BEING INTO THE RIFT! THAT IS HOW THE END BEGINS!
MON-EL, USE YOUR SPEED, STOP THAT SHIP AT ALL COSTS!

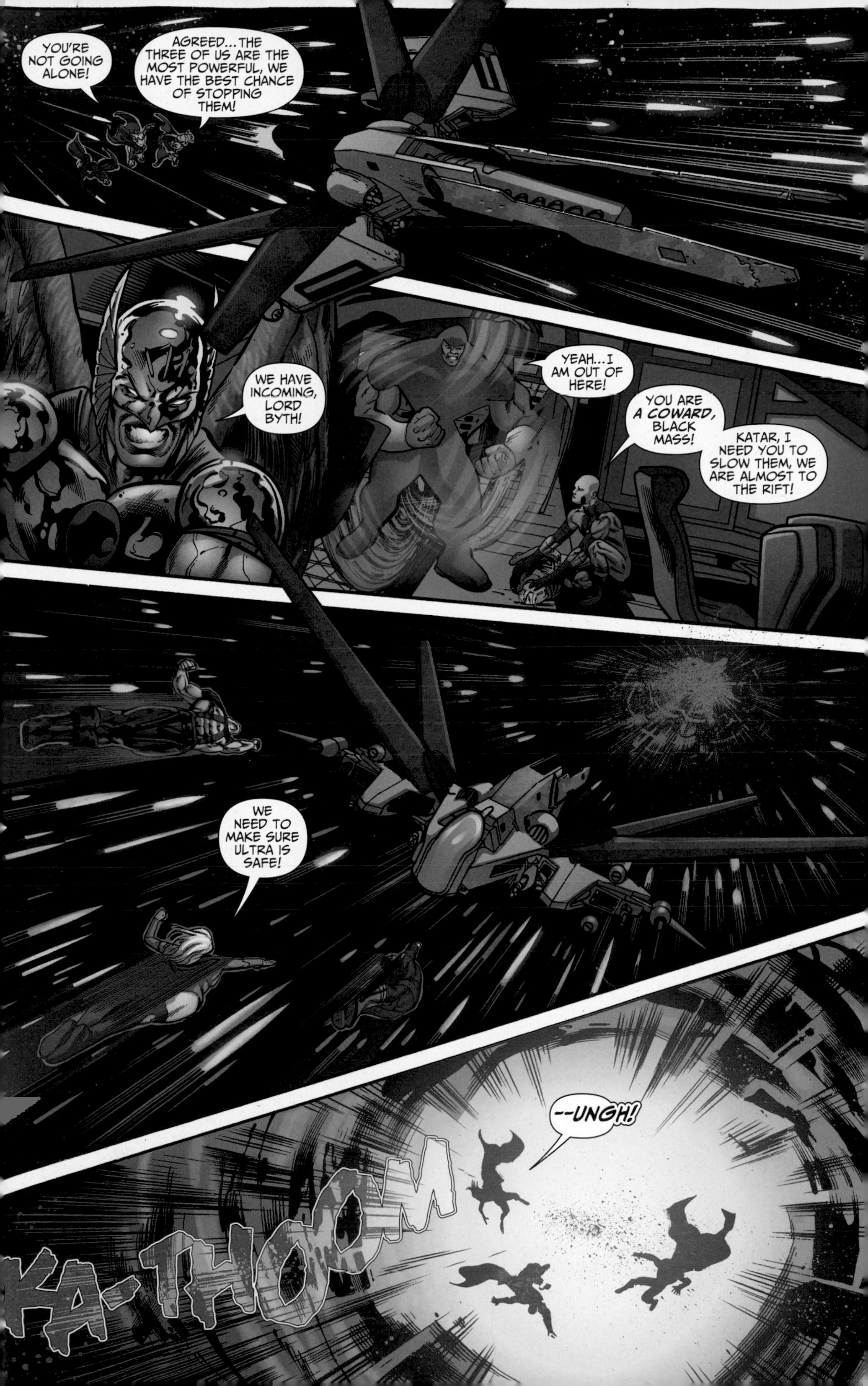
YOU'RE NOT GOING ALONE!
AGREED... THE THREE OF US ARE THE MOST POWERFUL, WE HAVE THE BEST CHANCE OF STOPPING THEM!
WE HAVE INCOMING, LORD BYTH!
YEAH... I AM OUT OF HERE!
YOU ARE A COWARD, BLACK MASS!
KATAR, I NEED YOU TO SLOW THEM, WE ARE ALMOST TO THE RIFT!
WE NEED TO MAKE SURE ULTRA IS SAFE!
--UNGH!
KA-THOOM

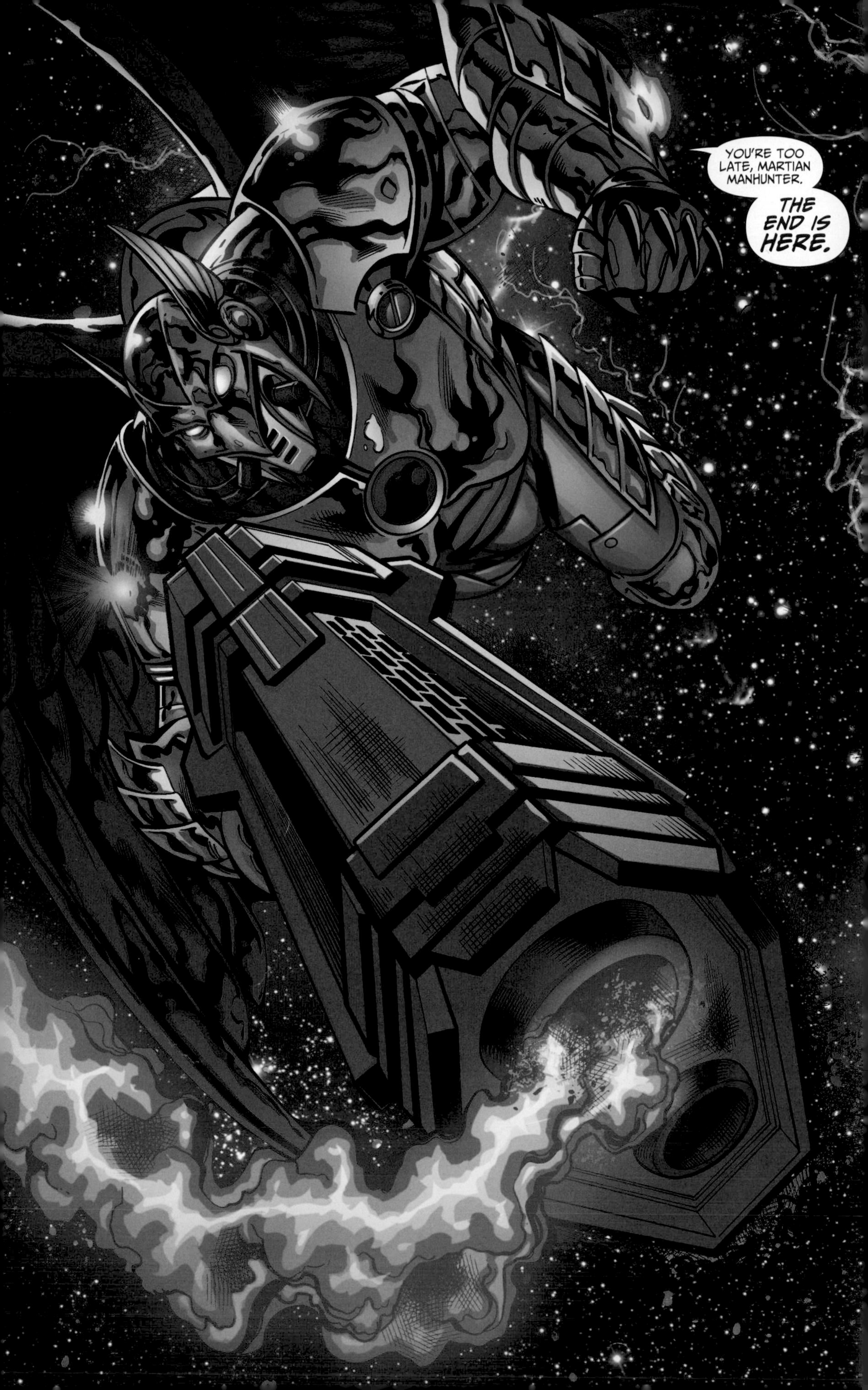
YOU'RE TOO LATE, MARTIAN MANHUNTER.
THE END IS HERE.

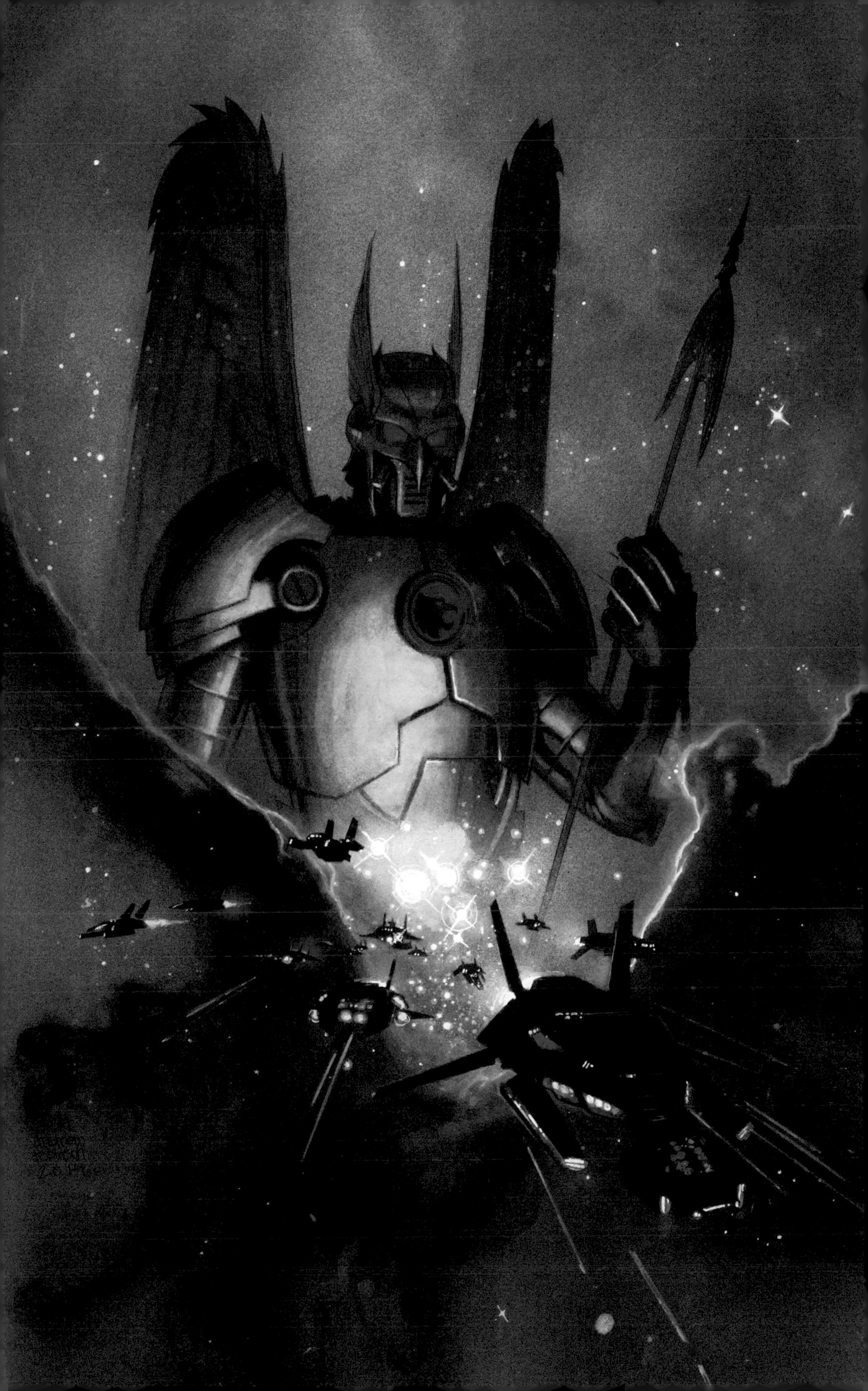

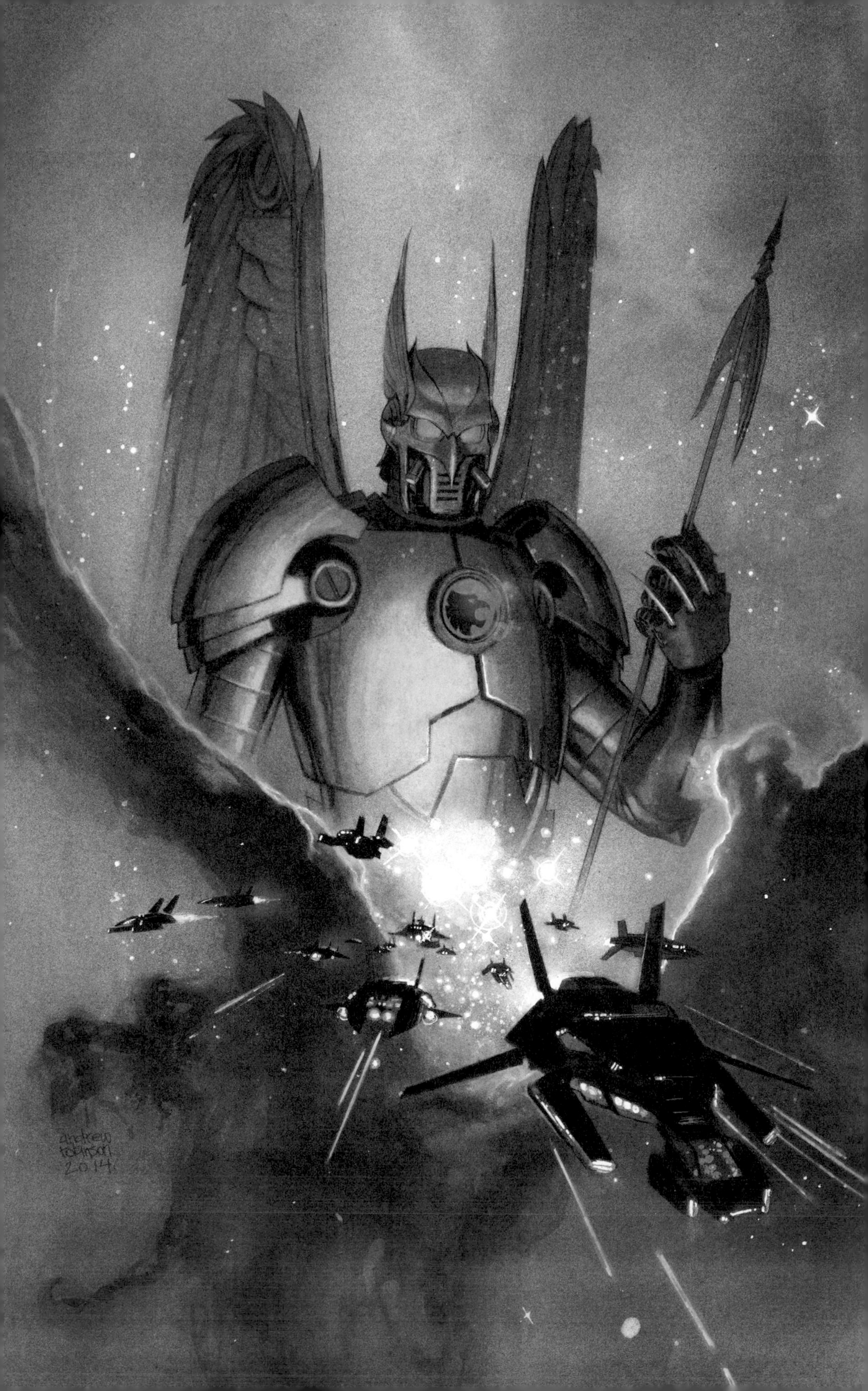
andrew robinson 2014

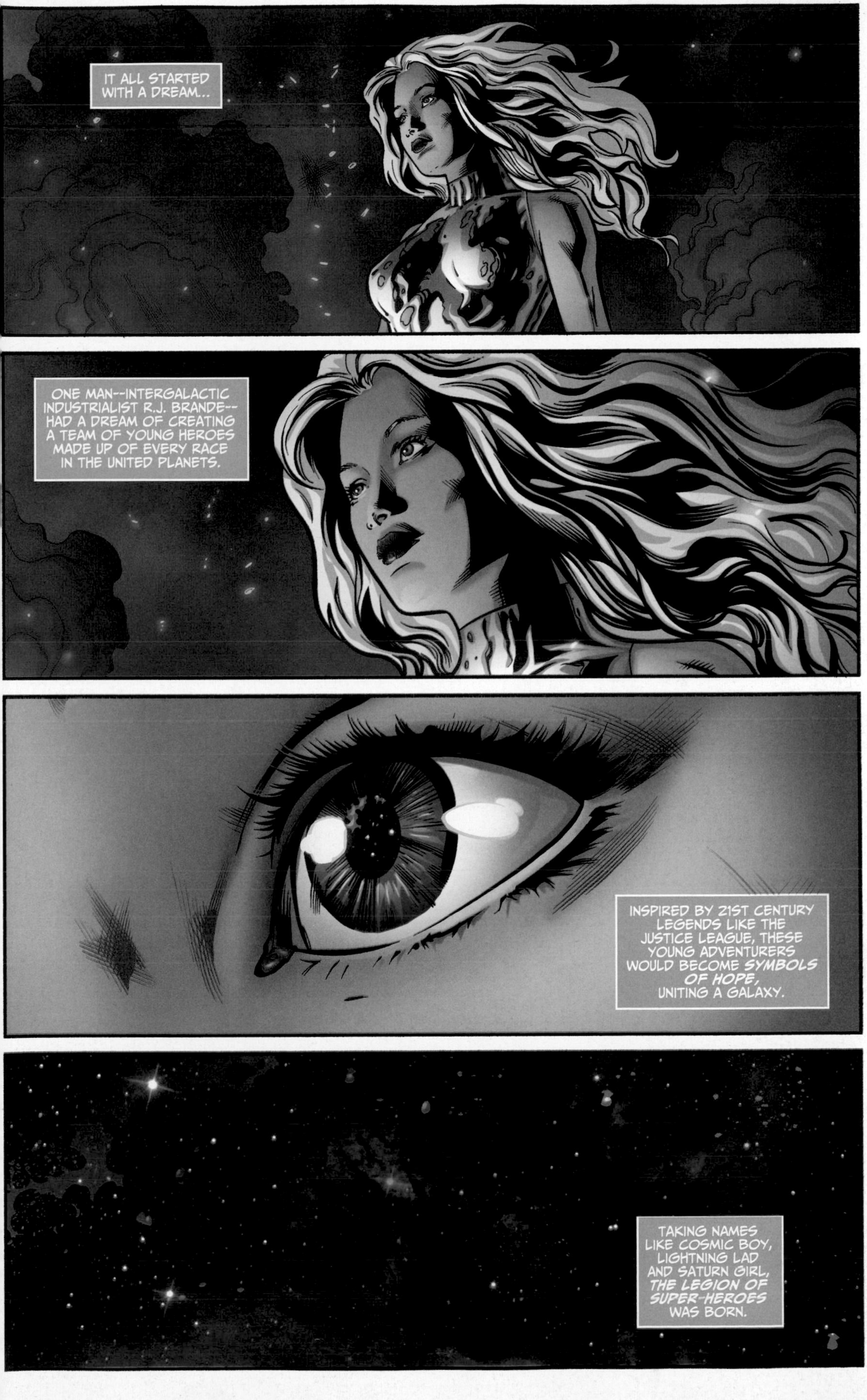
IT ALL STARTED WITH A DREAM...
ONE MAN--INTERGALACTIC INDUSTRIALIST R.J. BRANDE--HAD A DREAM OF CREATING A TEAM OF YOUNG HEROES MADE UP OF EVERY RACE IN THE UNITED PLANETS.
INSPIRED BY 21ST CENTURY LEGENDS LIKE THE JUSTICE LEAGUE, THESE YOUNG ADVENTURERS WOULD BECOME SYMBOLS OF HOPE, UNITING A GALAXY.
TAKING NAMES LIKE COSMIC BOY, LIGHTNING LAD AND SATURN GIRL, THE LEGION OF SUPER-HEROES WAS BORN.

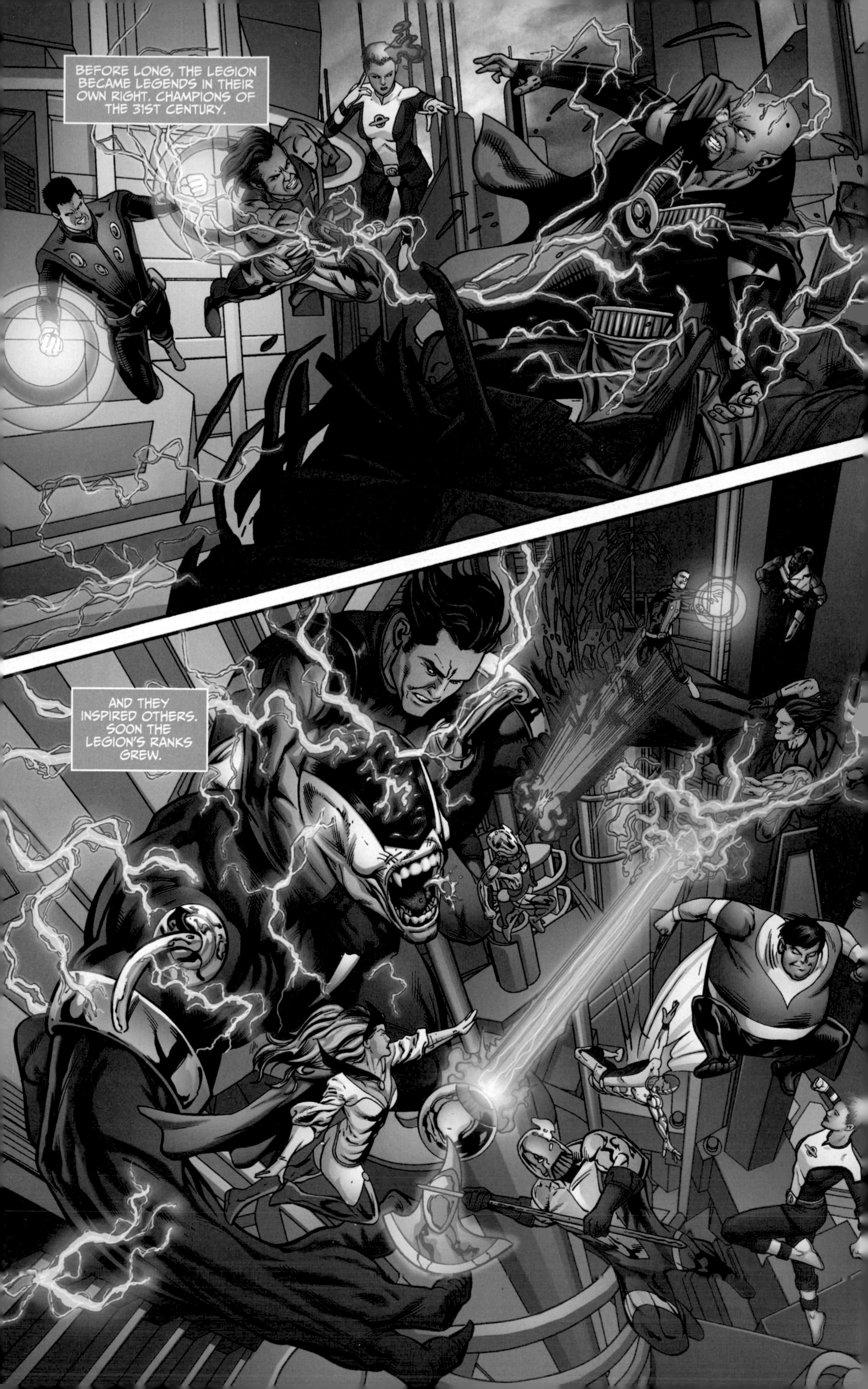
BEFORE LONG, THE LEGION BECAME LEGENDS IN THEIR OWN RIGHT. CHAMPIONS OF THE 31ST CENTURY.
AND THEY INSPIRED OTHERS. SOON THE LEGION'S RANKS GREW.

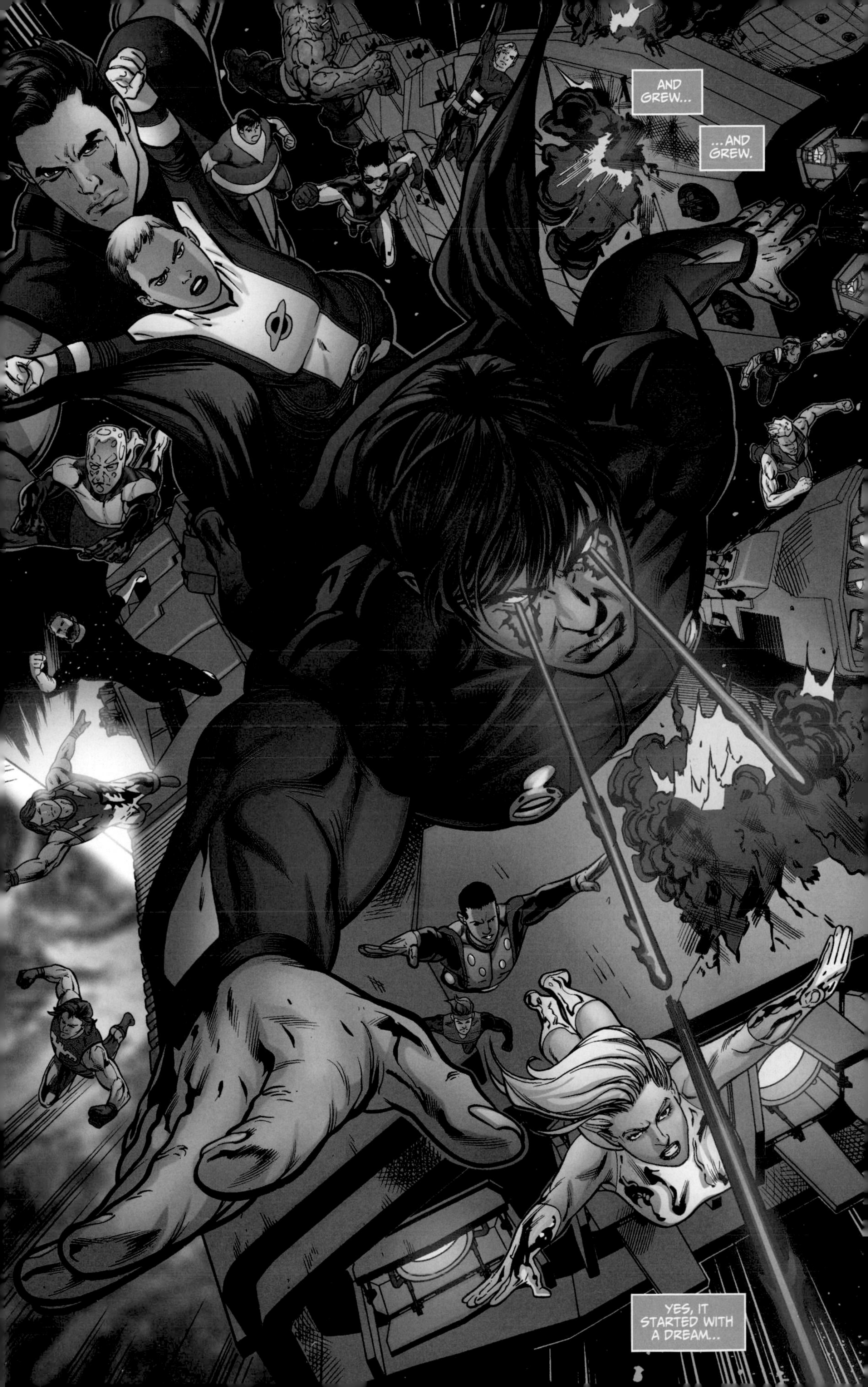
AND GREW...
...AND GREW.
YES, IT STARTED WITH A DREAM..

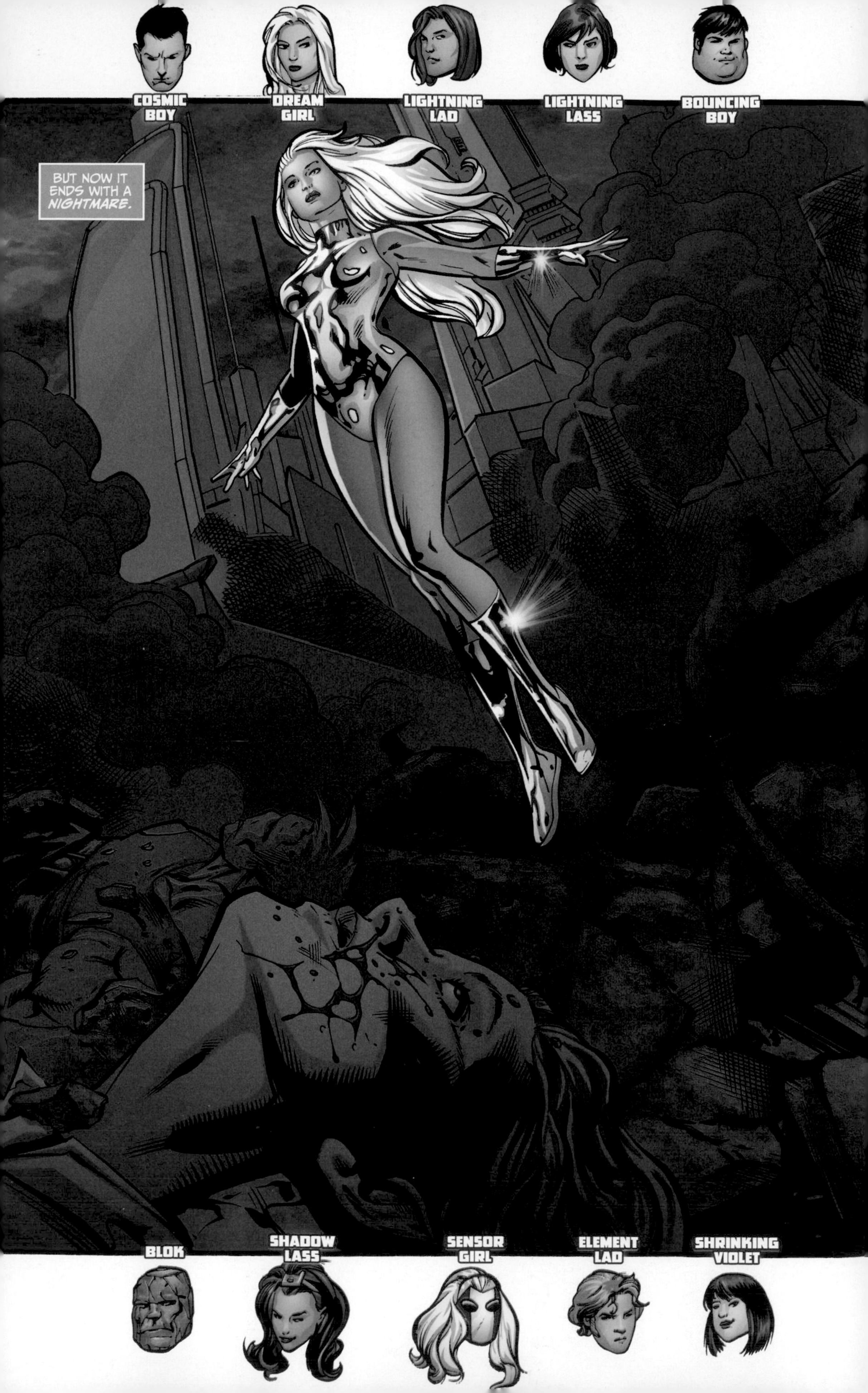
COSMIC BOY
DREAM GIRL
LIGHTNING LAD
LIGHTNING LASS
BOUNCING BOY
BUT NOW IT ENDS WITH A *NIGHTMARE.*
BLOK
SHADOW LASS
SENSOR GIRL
ELEMENT LAD
SHRINKING VIOLET

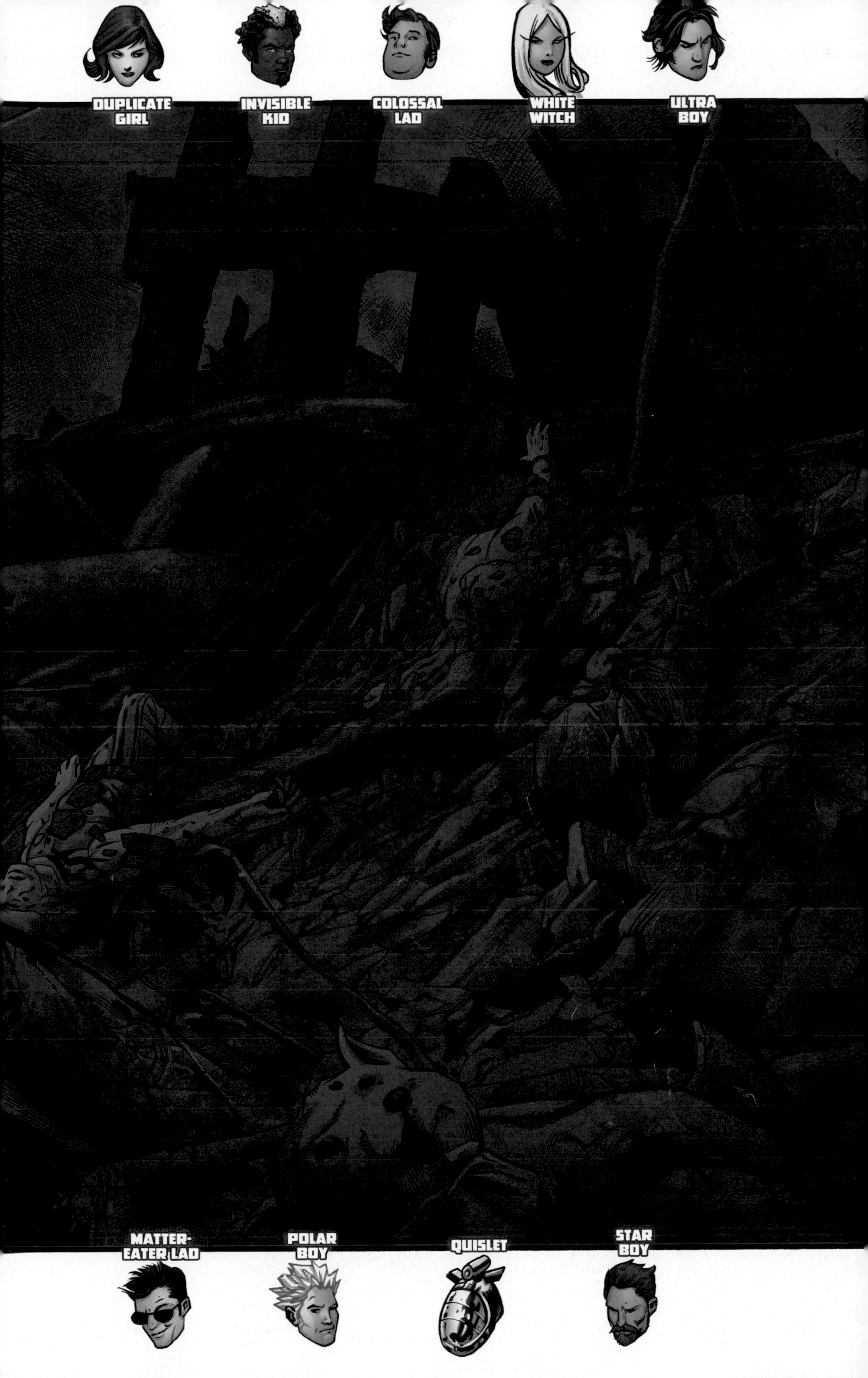
DUPLICATE GIRL
INVISIBLE KID
COLOSSAL LAD
WHITE WITCH
ULTRA BOY
MATTER-EATER LAD
POLAR BOY
QUISLET
STAR BOY

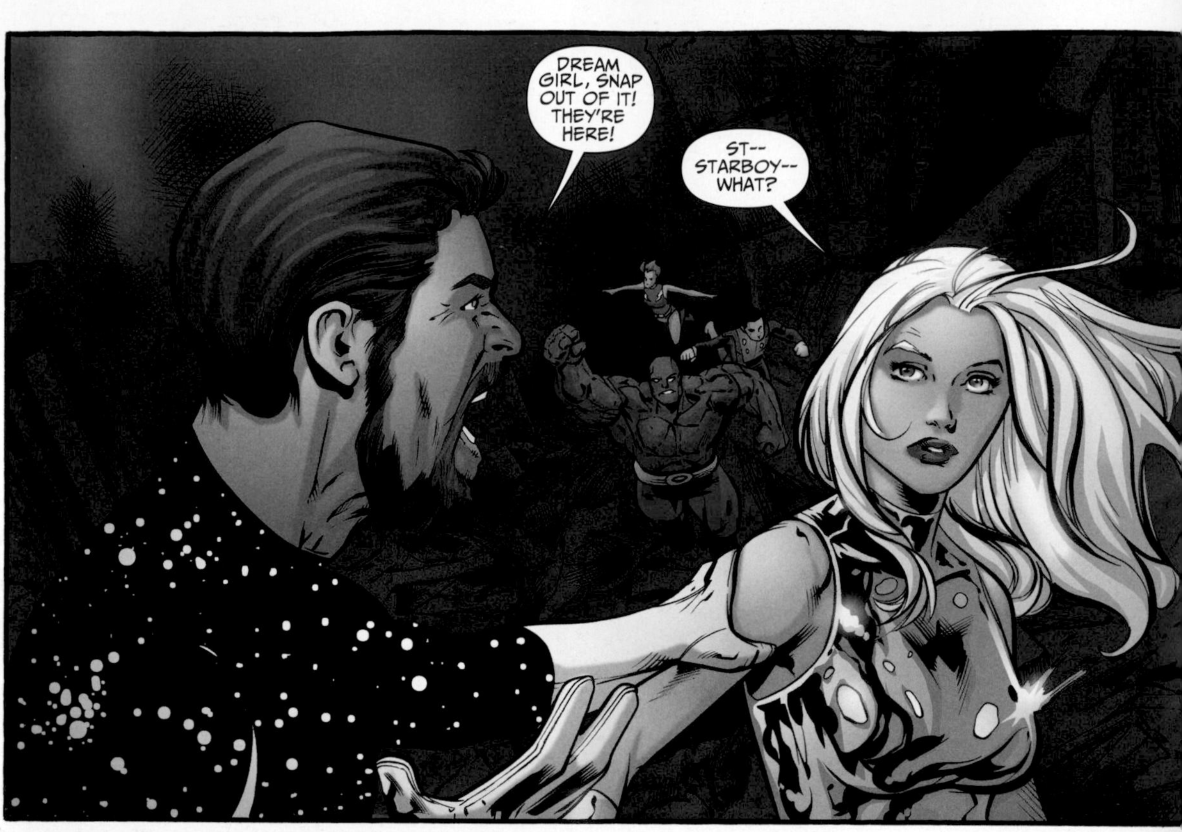
DREAM GIRL, SNAP OUT OF IT! THEY'RE HERE!
ST-- STARBOY-- WHAT?

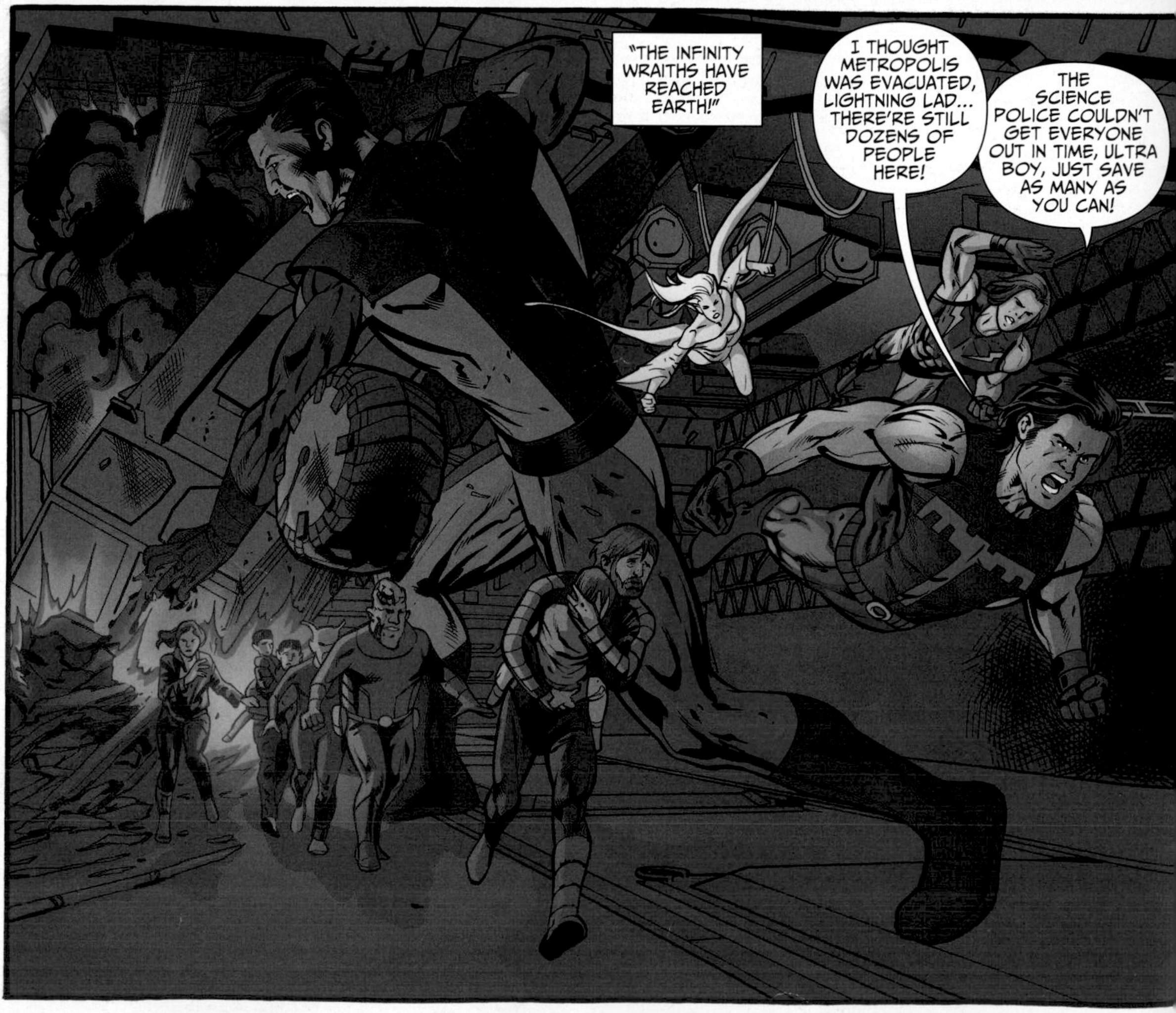
"THE INFINITY WRAITHS HAVE REACHED EARTH!"
I THOUGHT METROPOLIS WAS EVACUATED, LIGHTNING LAD... THERE'RE STILL DOZENS OF PEOPLE HERE!
THE SCIENCE POLICE COULDN'T GET EVERYONE OUT IN TIME, ULTRA BOY, JUST SAVE AS MANY AS YOU CAN!

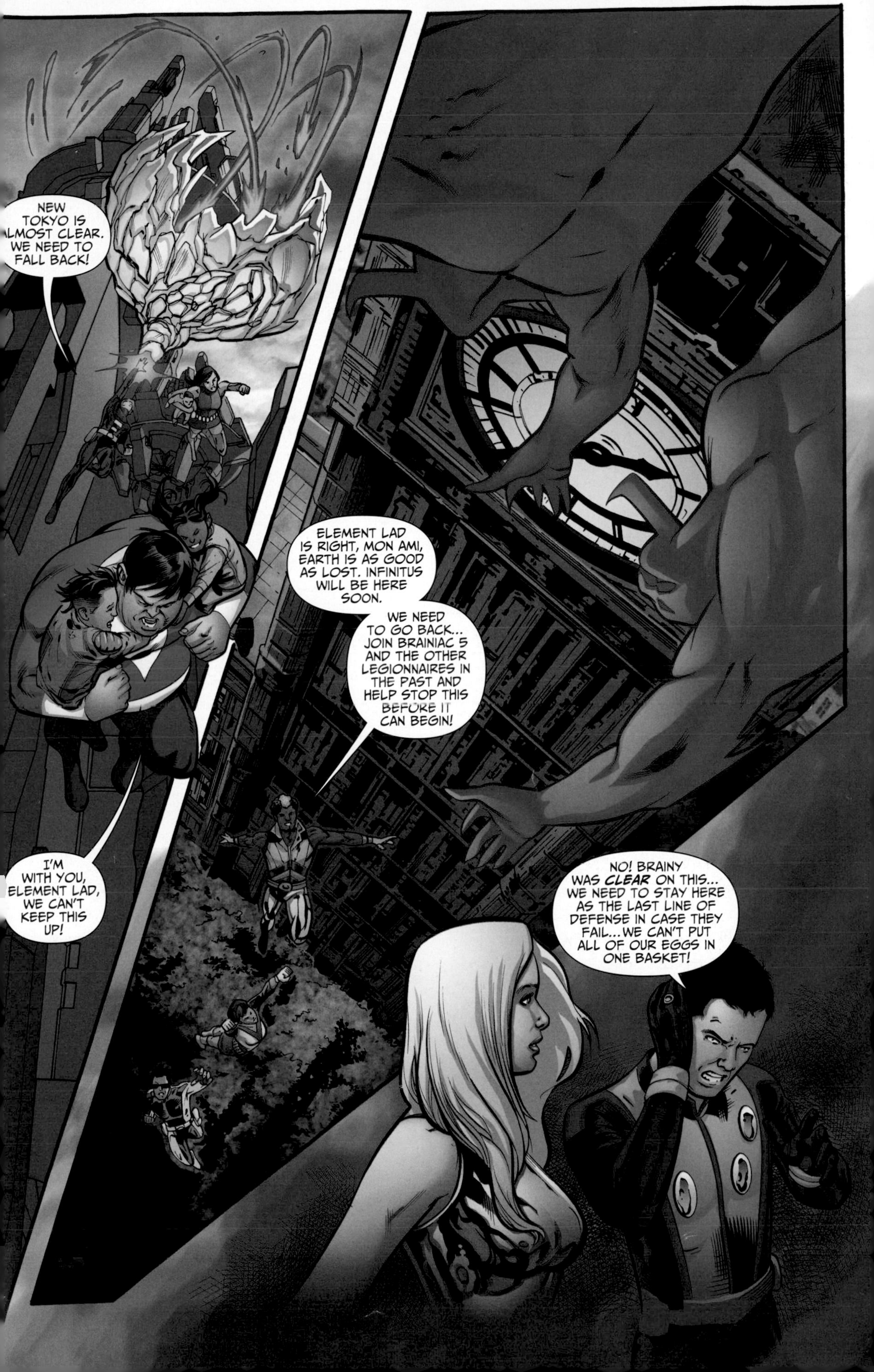
NEW TOKYO IS ALMOST CLEAR. WE NEED TO FALL BACK!
I'M WITH YOU, ELEMENT LAD, WE CAN'T KEEP THIS UP!
ELEMENT LAD IS RIGHT, MON AMI, EARTH IS AS GOOD AS LOST. INFINITUS WILL BE HERE SOON.
WE NEED TO GO BACK... JOIN BRAINIAC 5 AND THE OTHER LEGIONNAIRES IN THE PAST AND HELP STOP THIS BEFORE IT CAN BEGIN!
NO! BRAINY WAS CLEAR ON THIS... WE NEED TO STAY HERE AS THE LAST LINE OF DEFENSE IN CASE THEY FAIL... WE CAN'T PUT ALL OF OUR EGGS IN ONE BASKET!

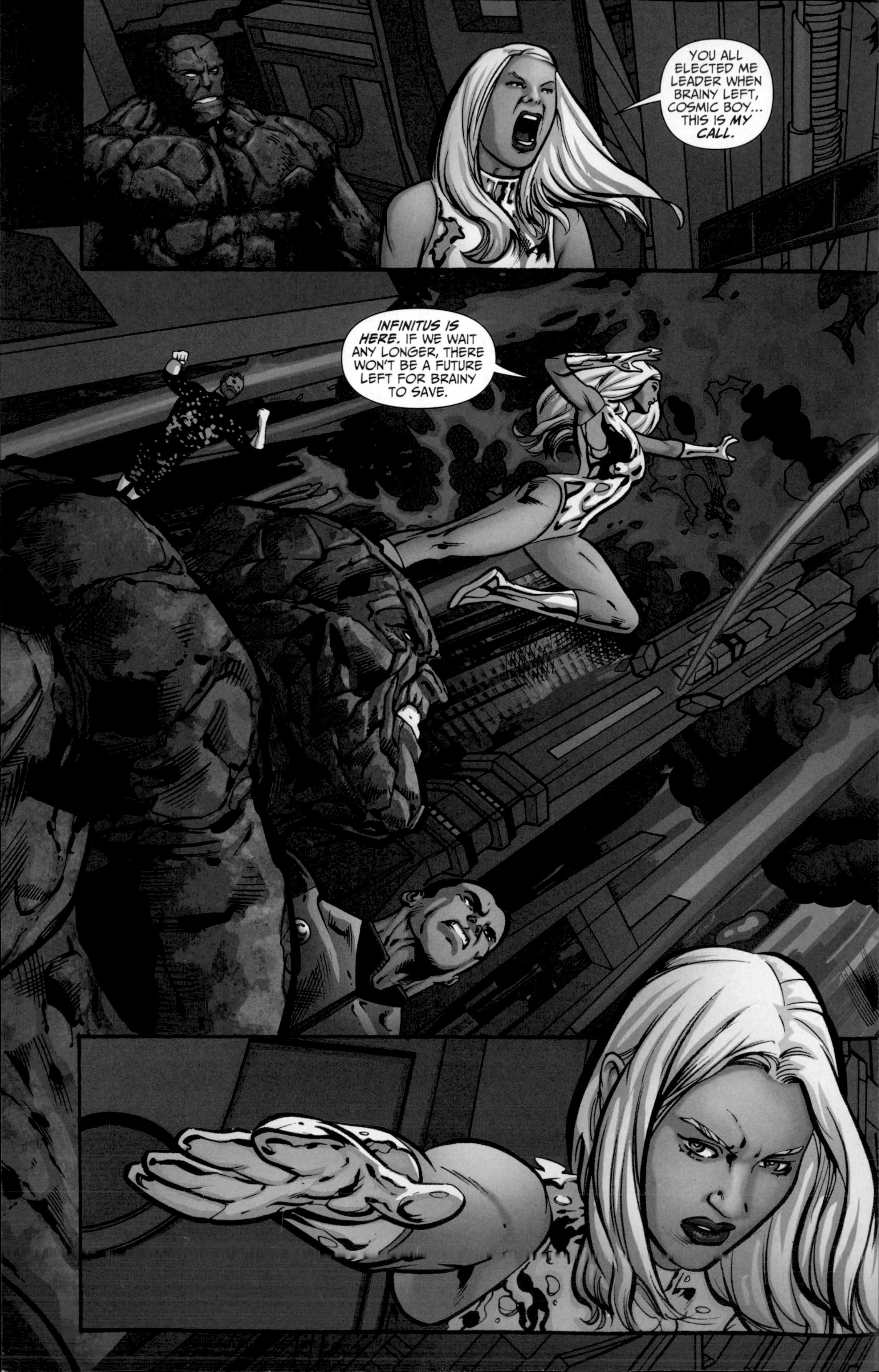
YOU ALL ELECTED ME LEADER WHEN BRAINY LEFT, COSMIC BOY... THIS IS MY CALL.
INFINITUS IS HERE. IF WE WAIT ANY LONGER, THERE WON'T BE A FUTURE LEFT FOR BRAINY TO SAVE.

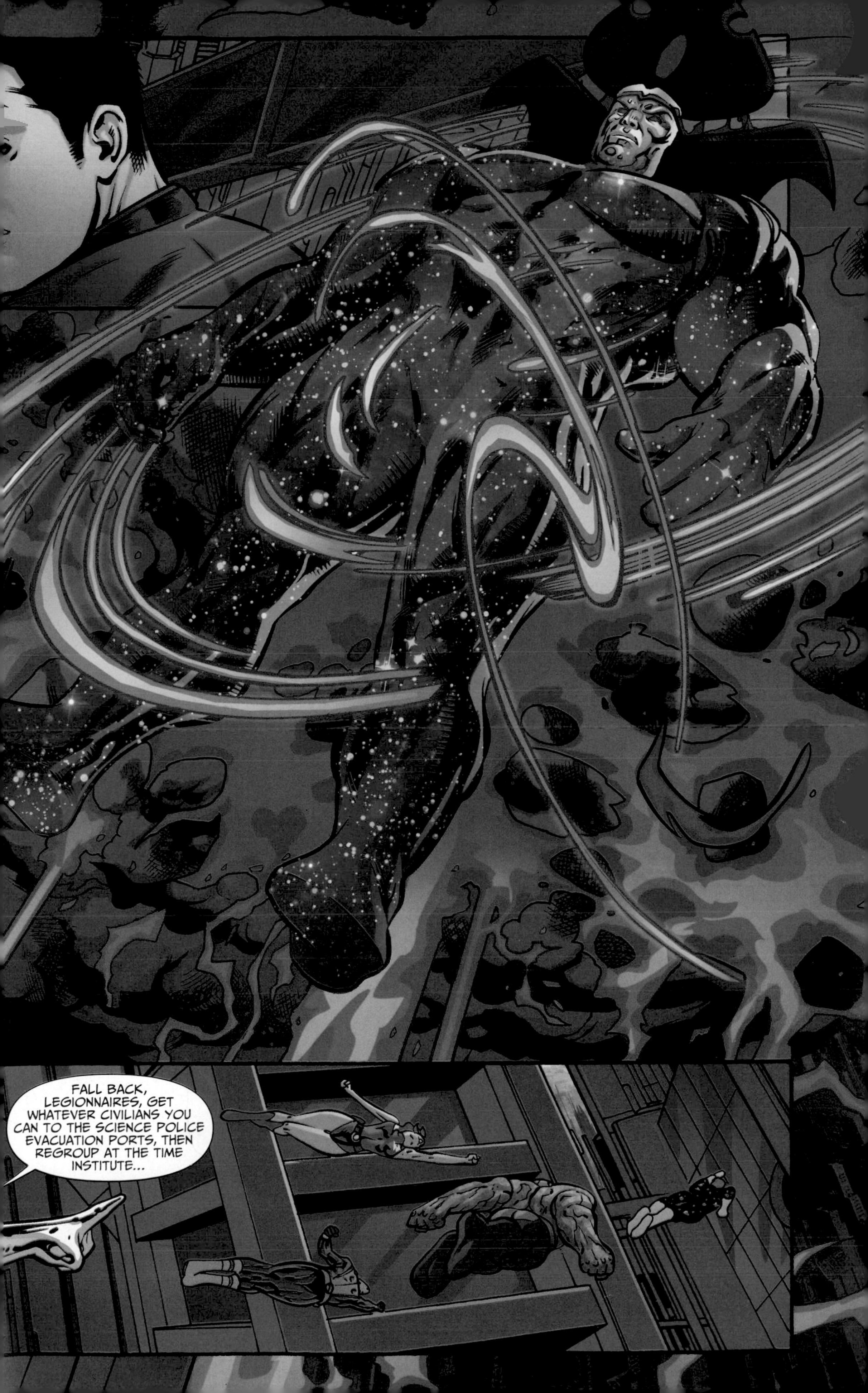
FALL BACK, LEGIONNAIRES, GET WHATEVER CIVILIANS YOU CAN TO THE SCIENCE POLICE EVACUATION PORTS, THEN REGROUP AT THE TIME INSTITUTE...

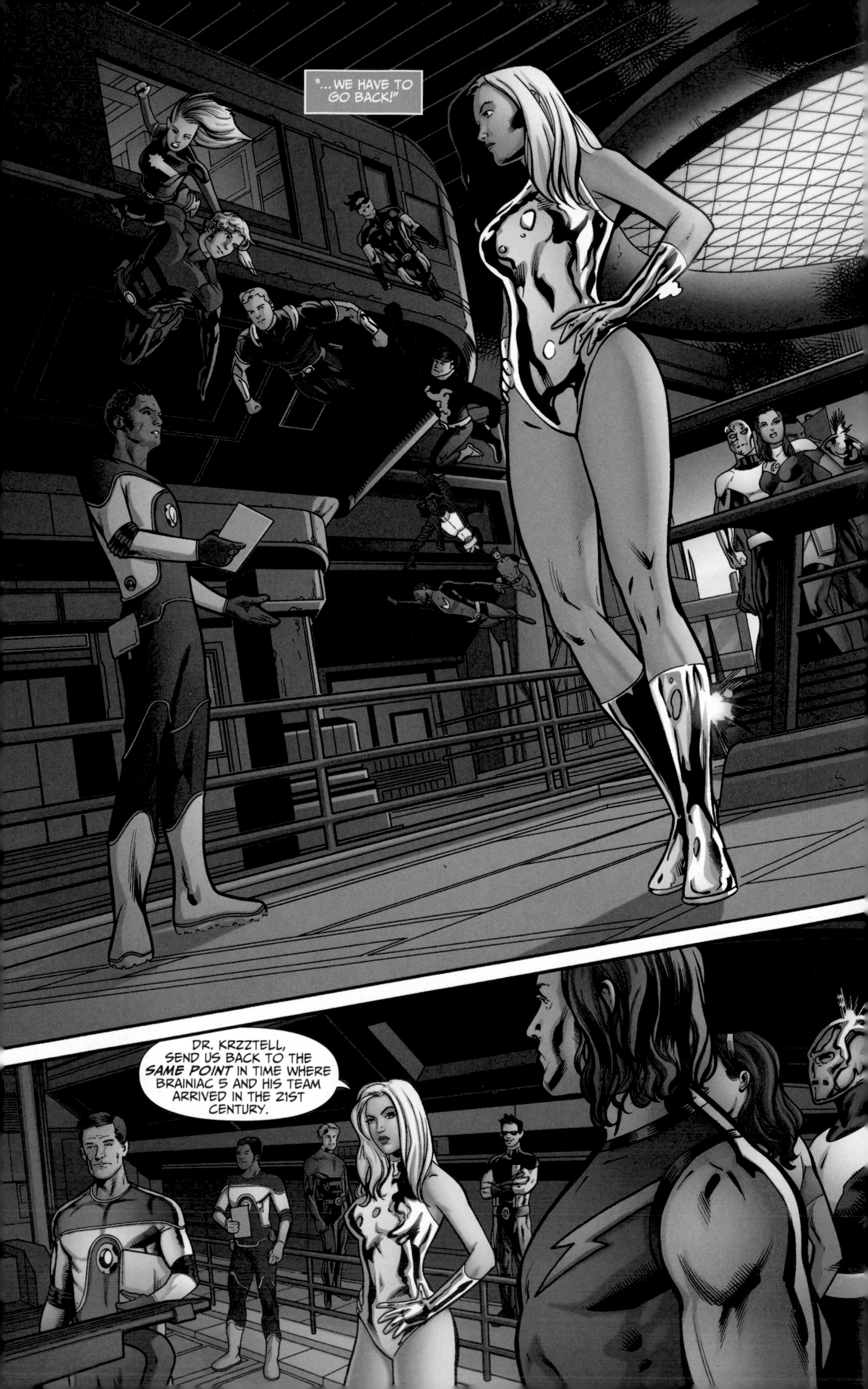
"...WE HAVE TO GO BACK!"
DR. KRZZTELL, SEND US BACK TO THE *SAME POINT* IN TIME WHERE BRAINIAC 5 AND HIS TEAM ARRIVED IN THE 21ST CENTURY.

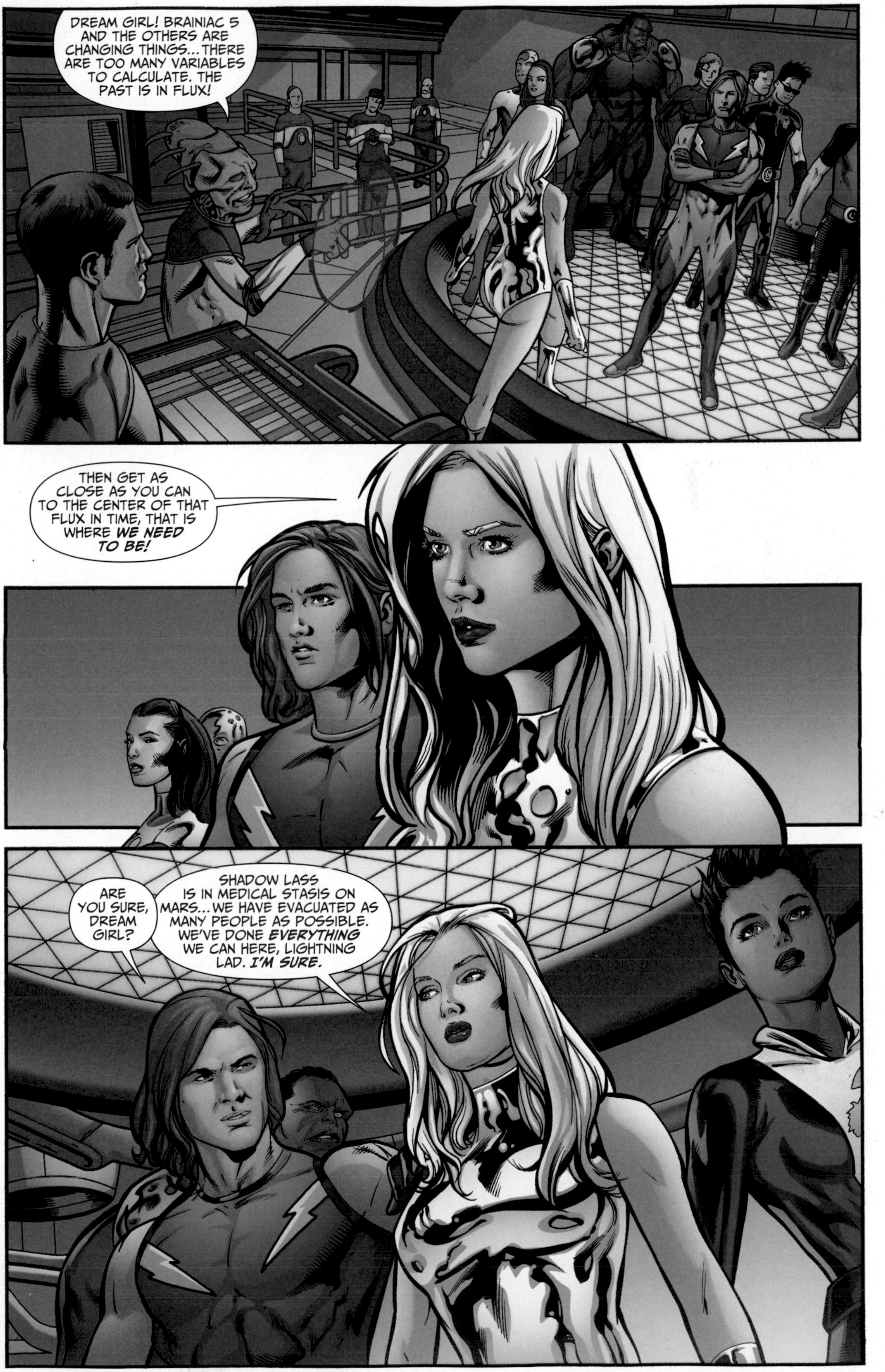
DREAM GIRL! BRAINIAC 5 AND THE OTHERS ARE CHANGING THINGS... THERE ARE TOO MANY VARIABLES TO CALCULATE. THE PAST IS IN FLUX!
THEN GET AS CLOSE AS YOU CAN TO THE CENTER OF THAT FLUX IN TIME, THAT IS WHERE ***WE NEED TO BE!***
ARE YOU SURE, DREAM GIRL?
SHADOW LASS IS IN MEDICAL STASIS ON MARS... WE HAVE EVACUATED AS MANY PEOPLE AS POSSIBLE. WE'VE DONE ***EVERYTHING*** WE CAN HERE, LIGHTNING LAD. ***I'M SURE.***

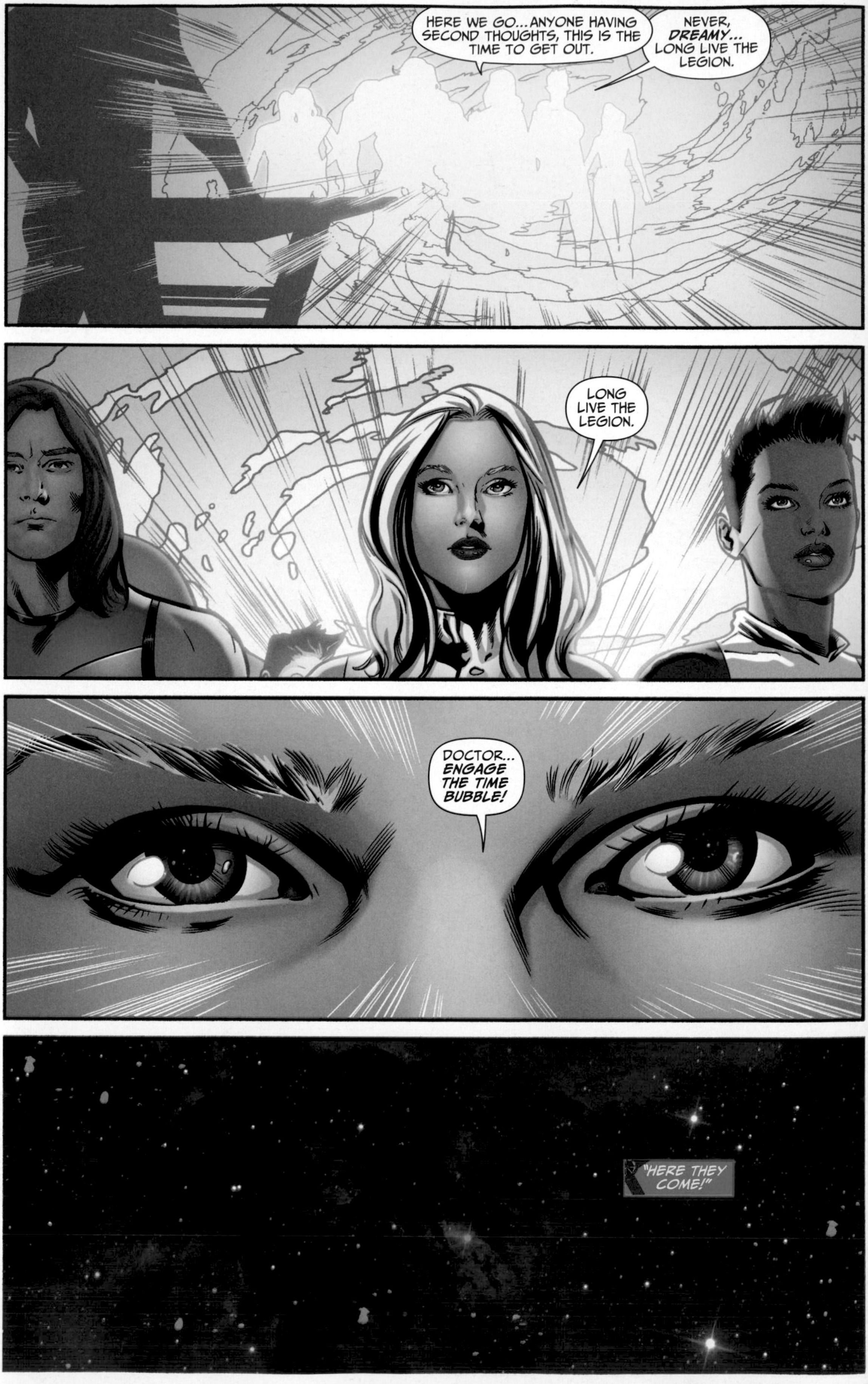
HERE WE GO...ANYONE HAVING SECOND THOUGHTS, THIS IS THE TIME TO GET OUT.
NEVER, DREAMY... LONG LIVE THE LEGION.
LONG LIVE THE LEGION.
DOCTOR... ENGAGE THE TIME BUBBLE!
"HERE THEY COME!"

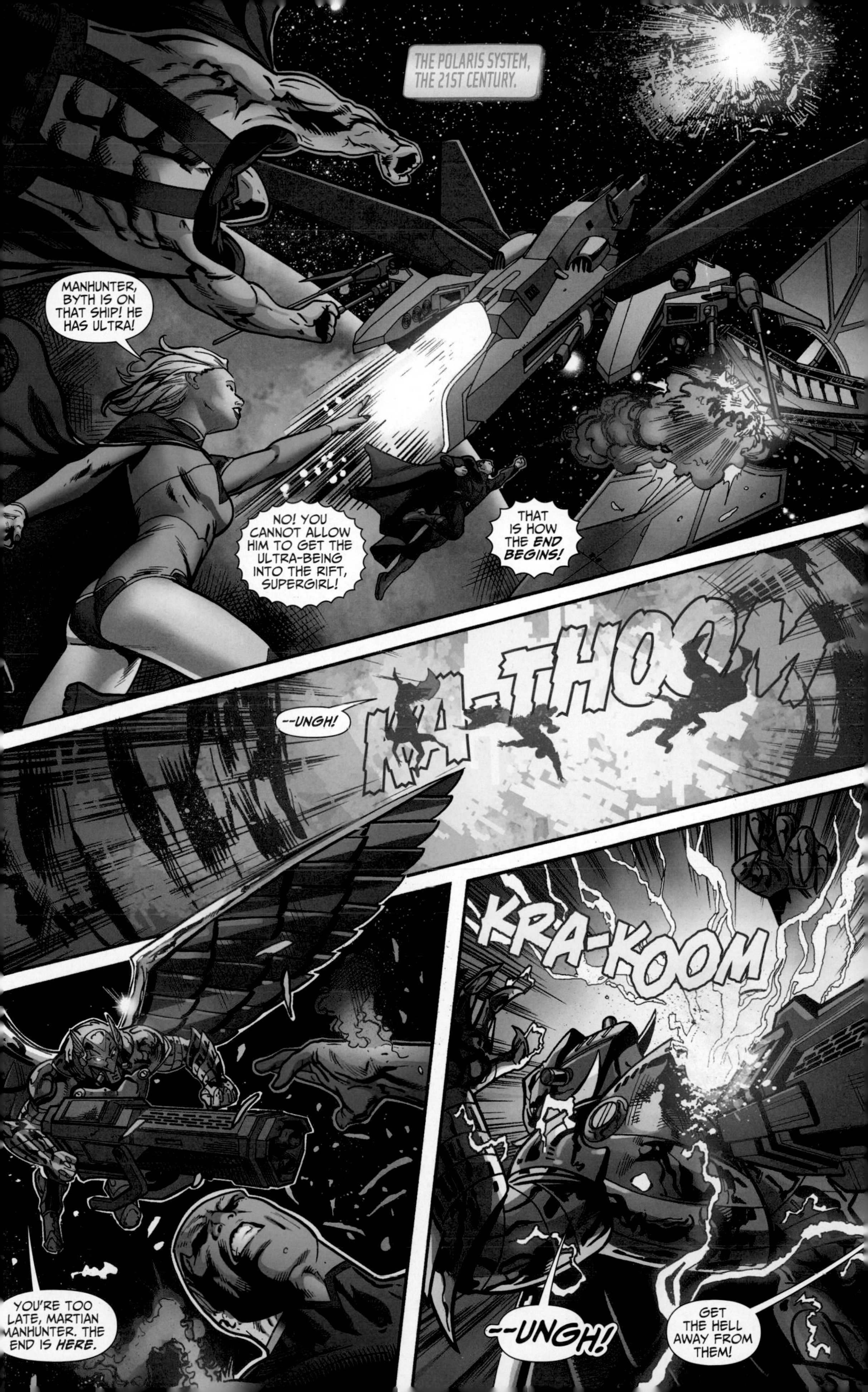
THE POLARIS SYSTEM, THE 21ST CENTURY.
MANHUNTER, BYTH IS ON THAT SHIP! HE HAS ULTRA!
NO! YOU CANNOT ALLOW HIM TO GET THE ULTRA-BEING INTO THE RIFT, SUPERGIRL!
THAT IS HOW THE *END BEGINS!*
--UNGH!
KA-THOOM
KRA-KOOM
YOU'RE TOO LATE, MARTIAN MANHUNTER. THE END IS *HERE.*
--UNGH!
GET THE HELL AWAY FROM THEM!

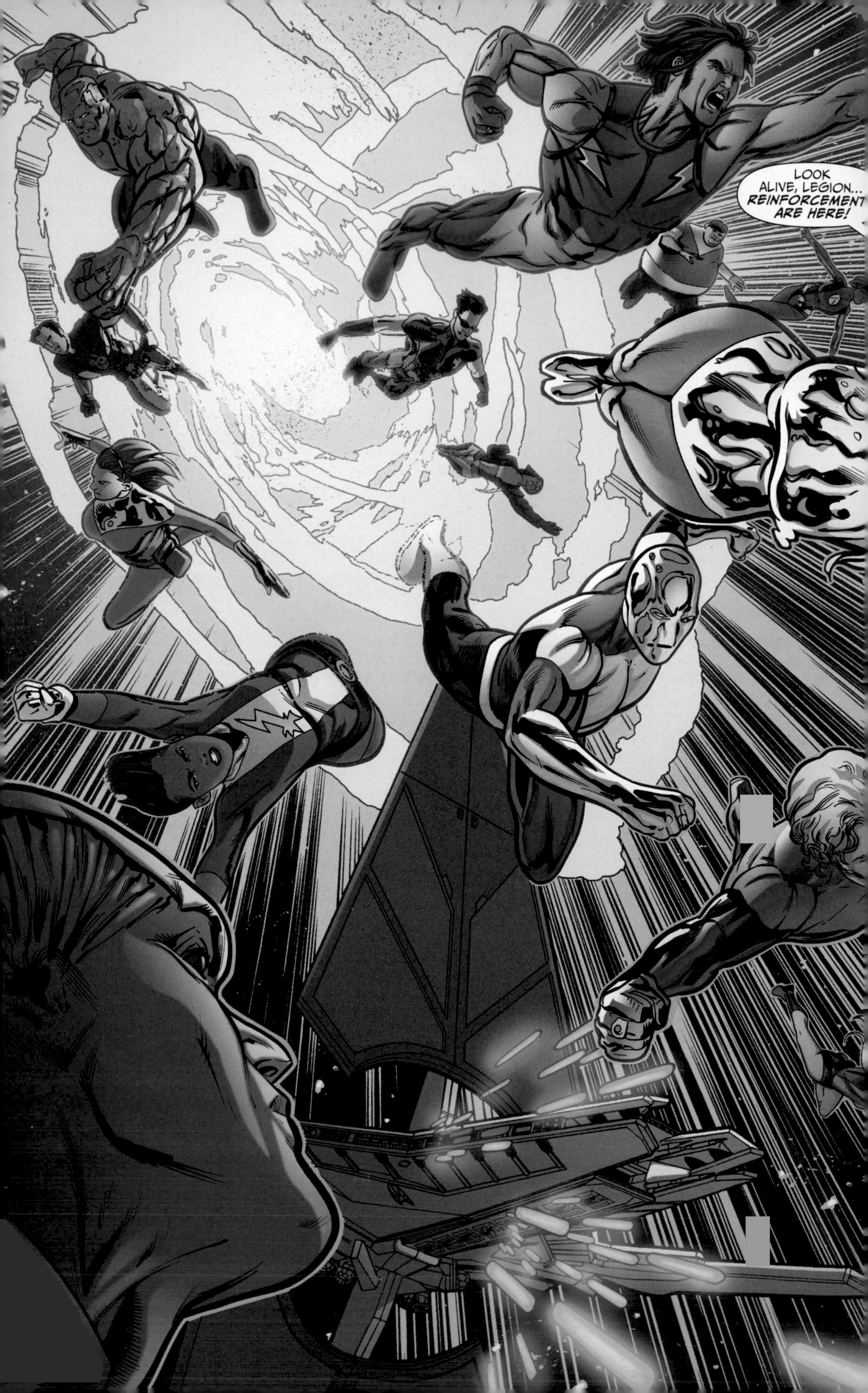
LOOK ALIVE, LEGION... REINFORCEMENT ARE HERE!

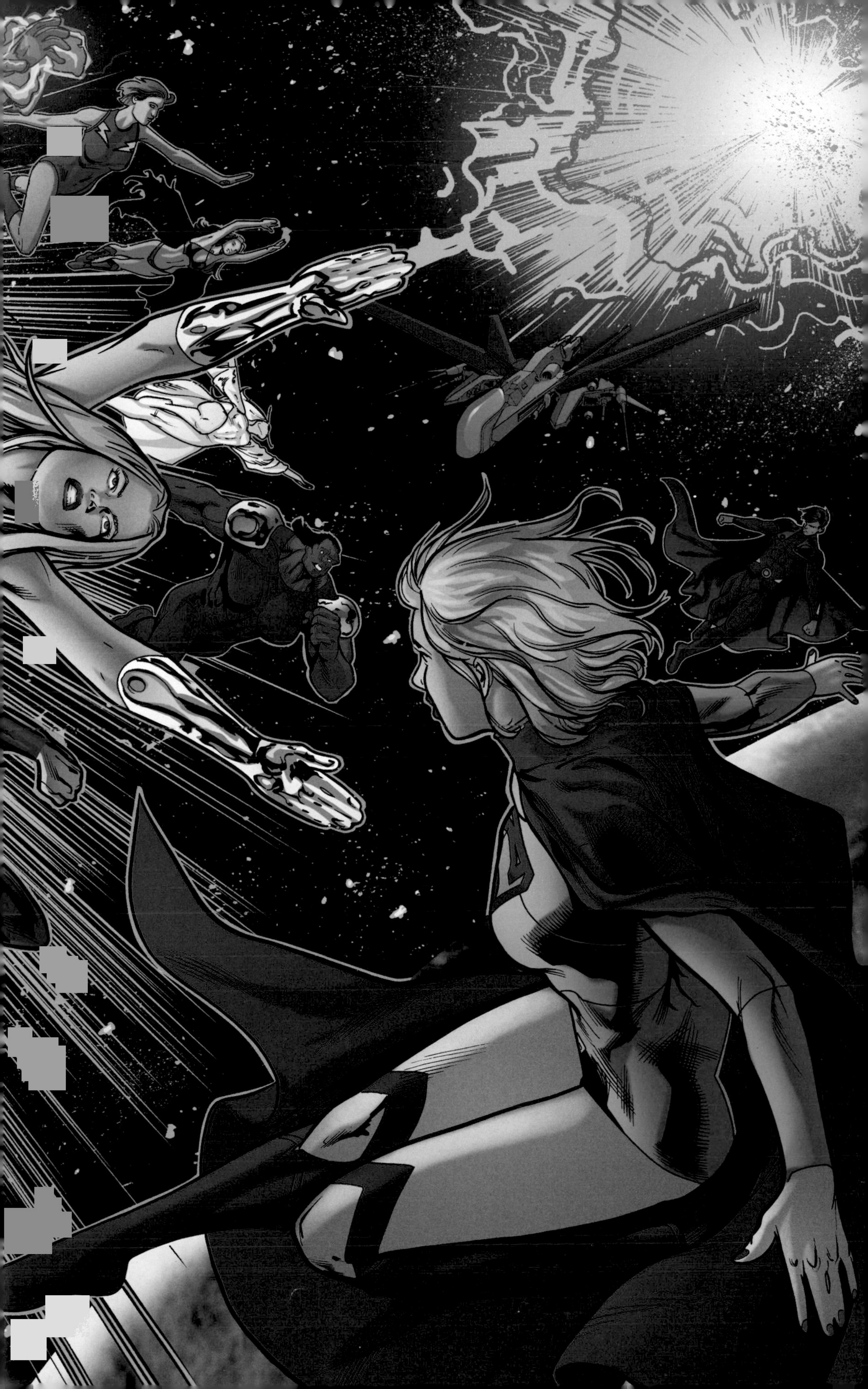

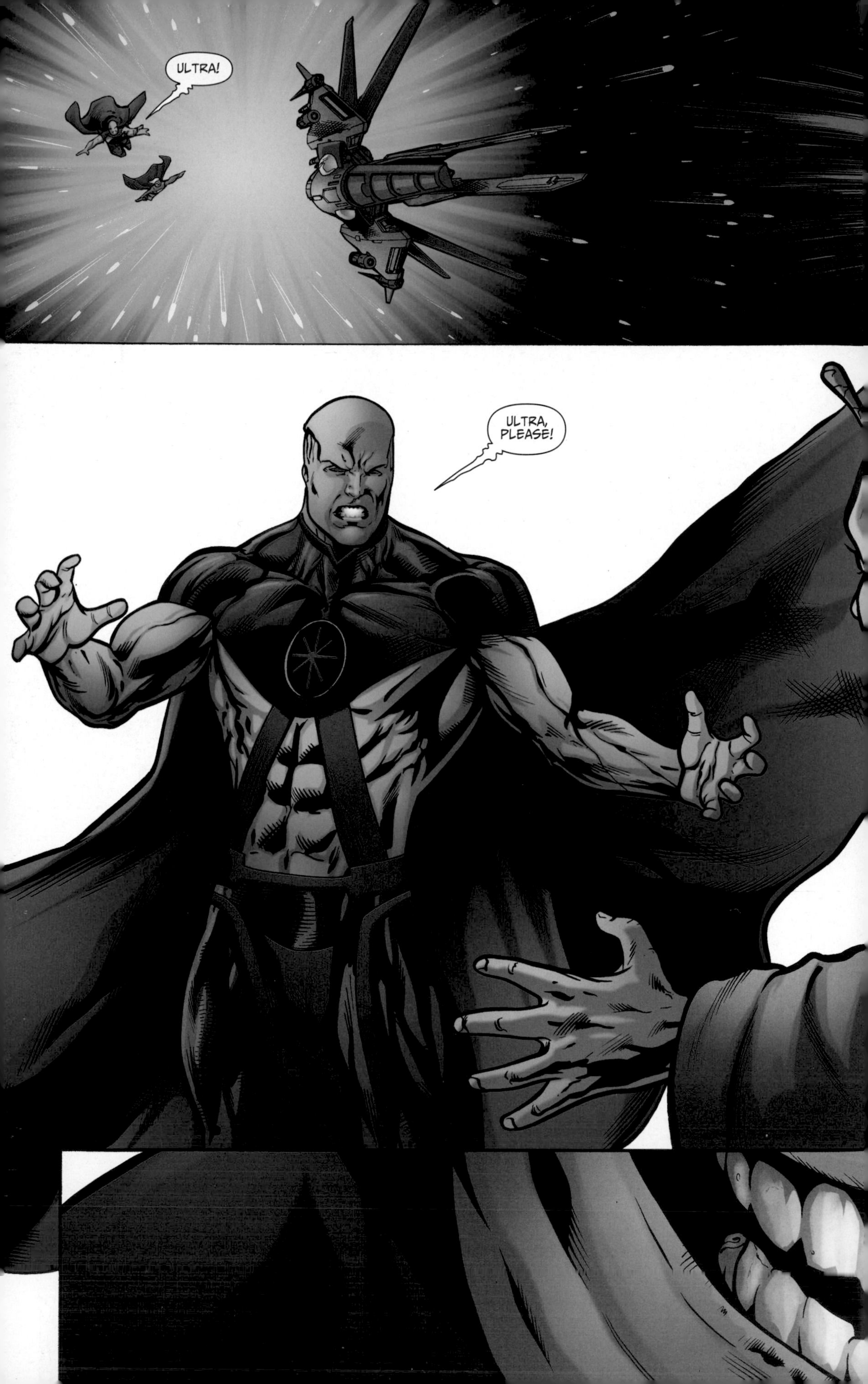
ULTRA!
ULTRA, PLEASE!

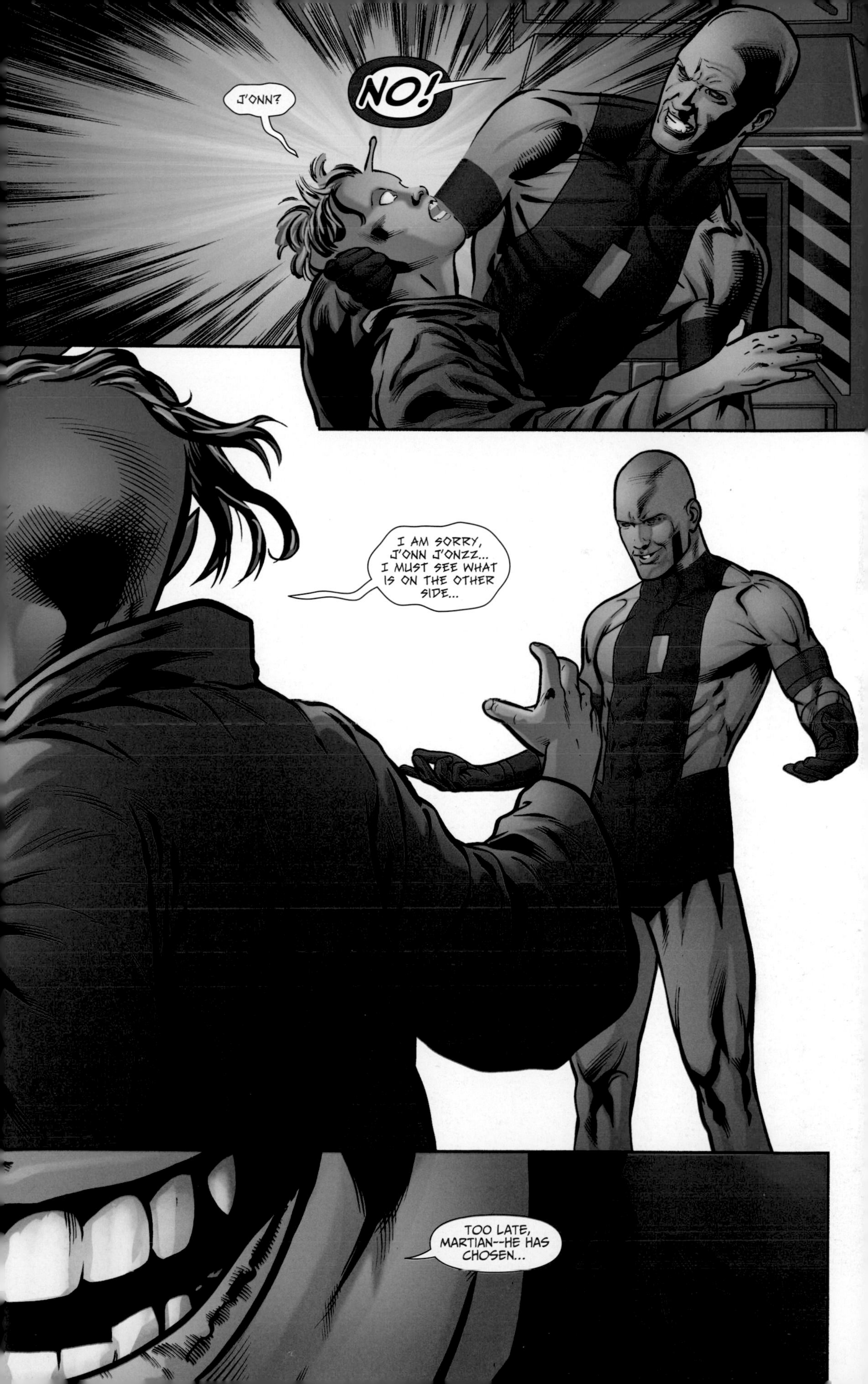
J'ONN?
NO!
I AM SORRY, J'ONN J'ONZZ... I MUST SEE WHAT IS ON THE OTHER SIDE...
TOO LATE, MARTIAN--HE HAS CHOSEN...

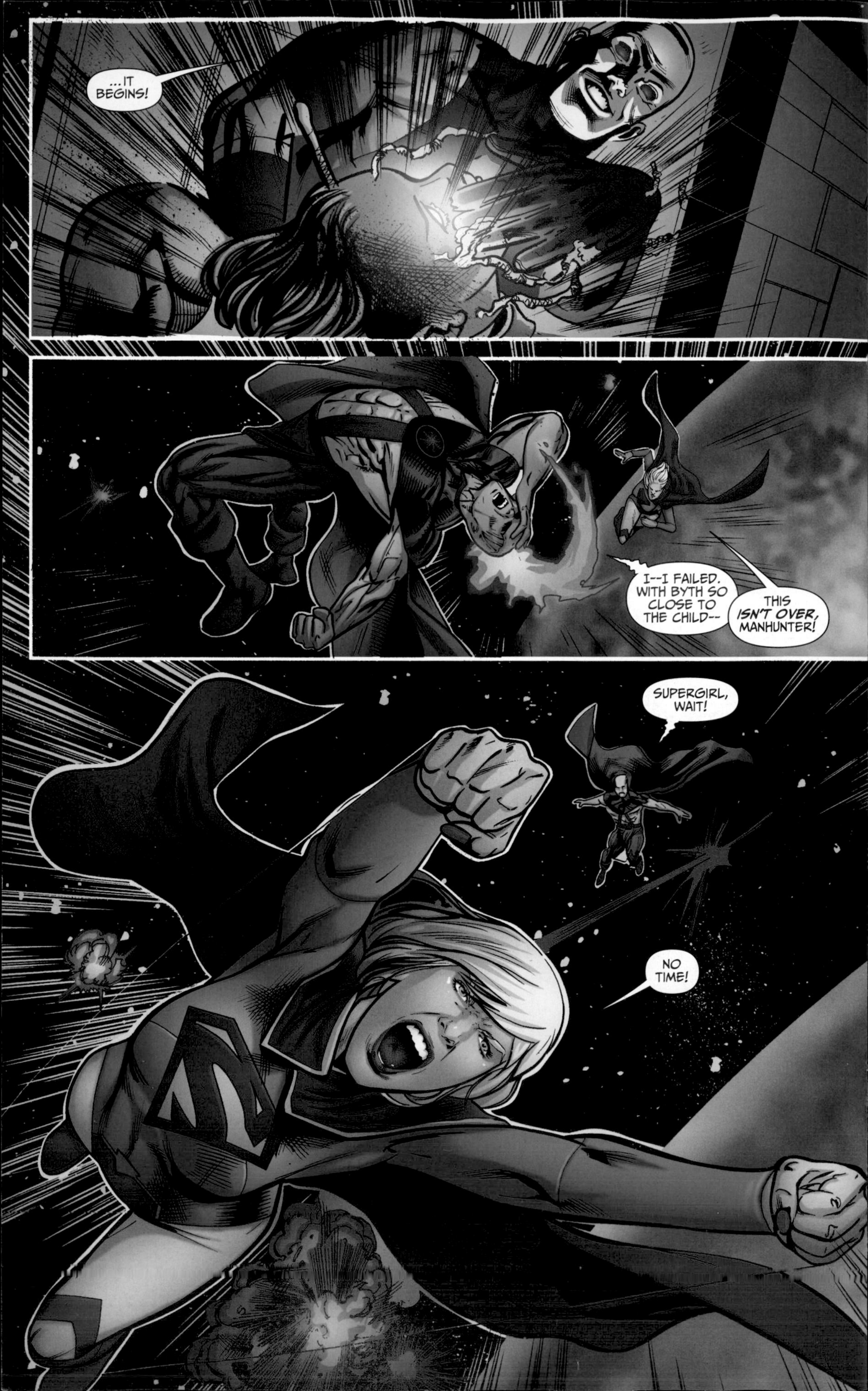
...IT BEGINS!
I--I FAILED. WITH BYTH SO CLOSE TO THE CHILD--
THIS ISN'T OVER, MANHUNTER!
SUPERGIRL, WAIT!
NO TIME!

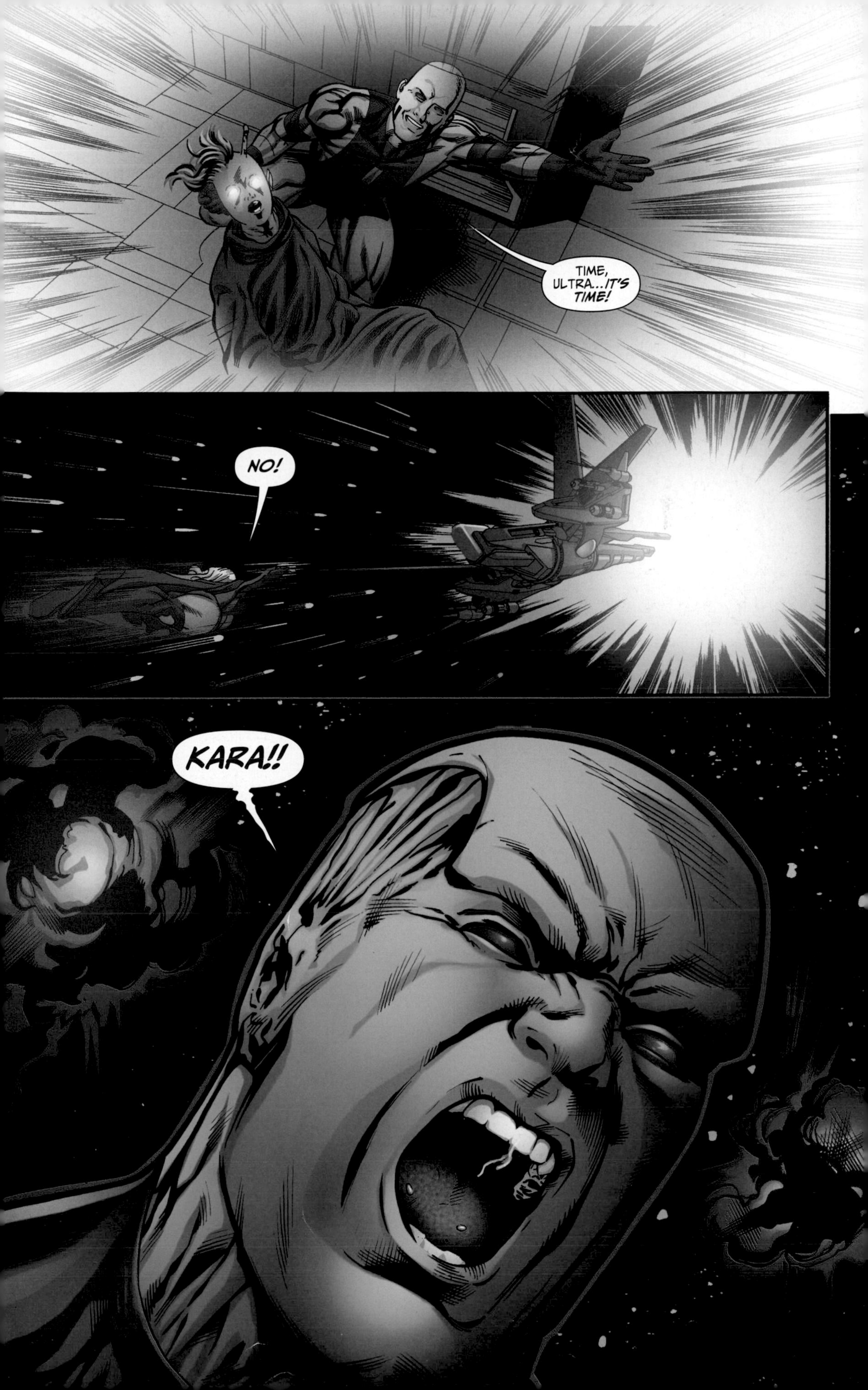
TIME, ULTRA...IT'S TIME!
NO!
KARA!!

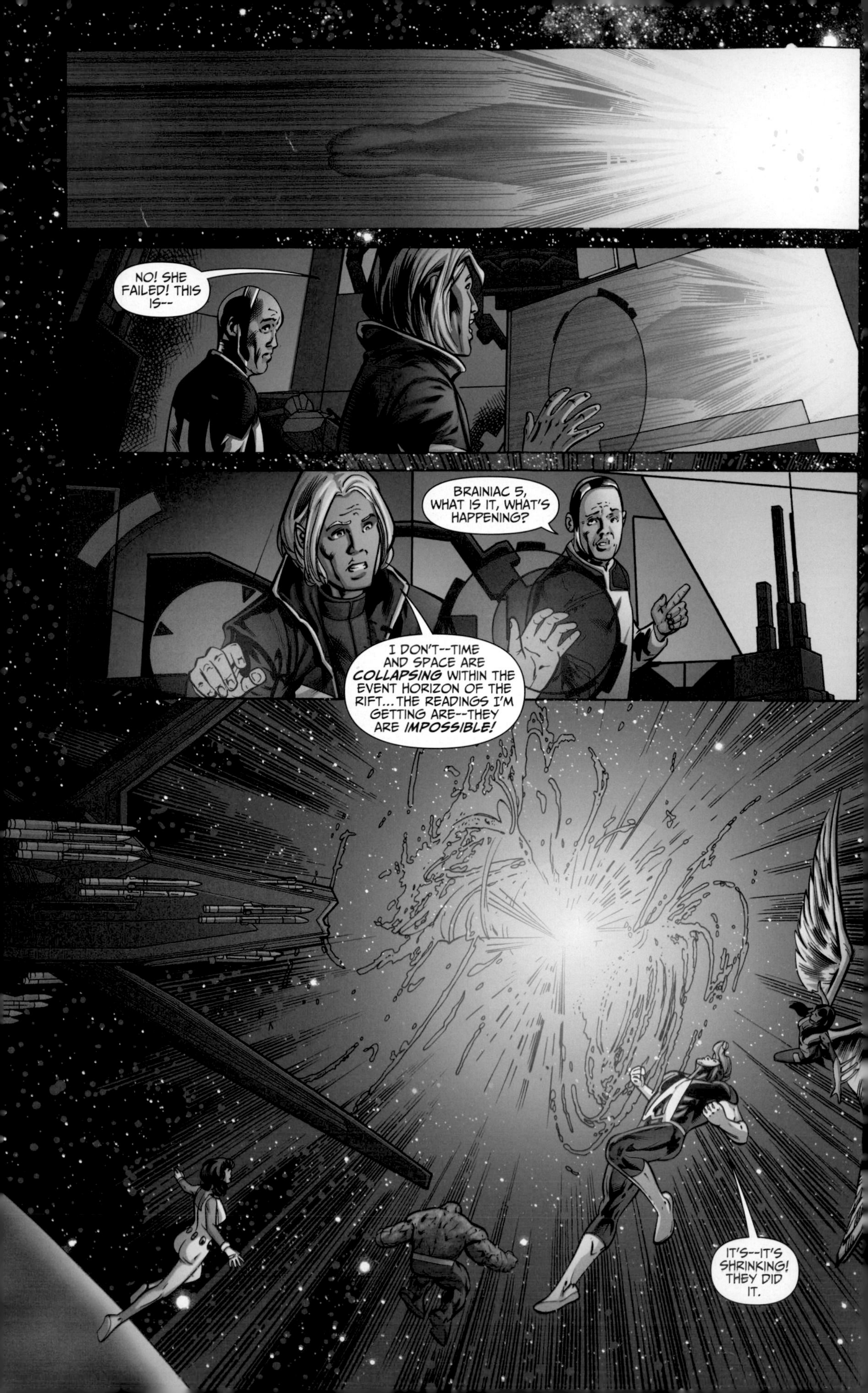
NO! SHE FAILED! THIS IS--
BRAINIAC 5, WHAT IS IT, WHAT'S HAPPENING?
I DON'T--TIME AND SPACE ARE COLLAPSING WITHIN THE EVENT HORIZON OF THE RIFT... THE READINGS I'M GETTING ARE--THEY ARE IMPOSSIBLE!
IT'S--IT'S SHRINKING! THEY DID IT.

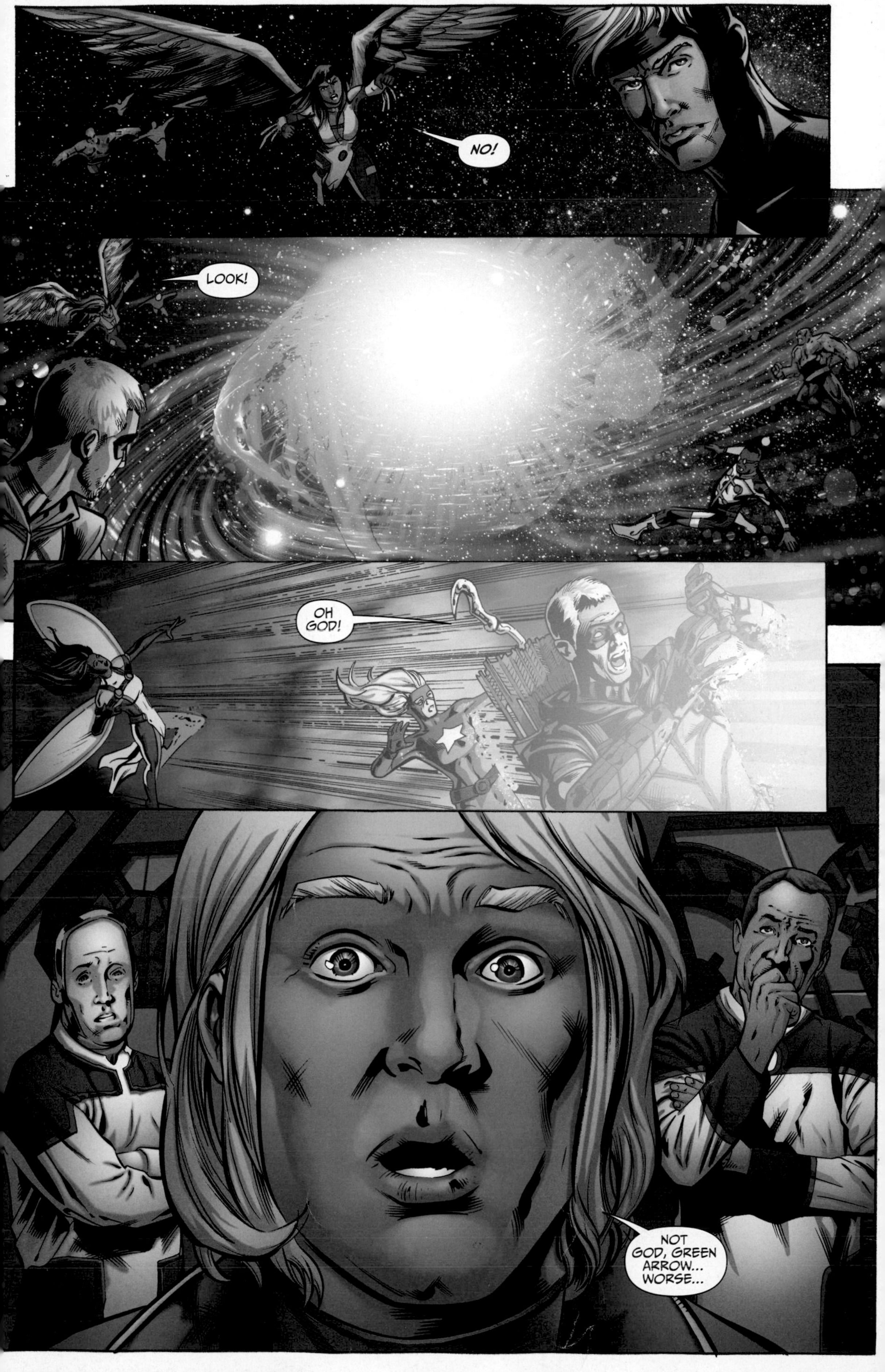
NO!
LOOK!
OH GOD!
NOT GOD, GREEN ARROW... WORSE...

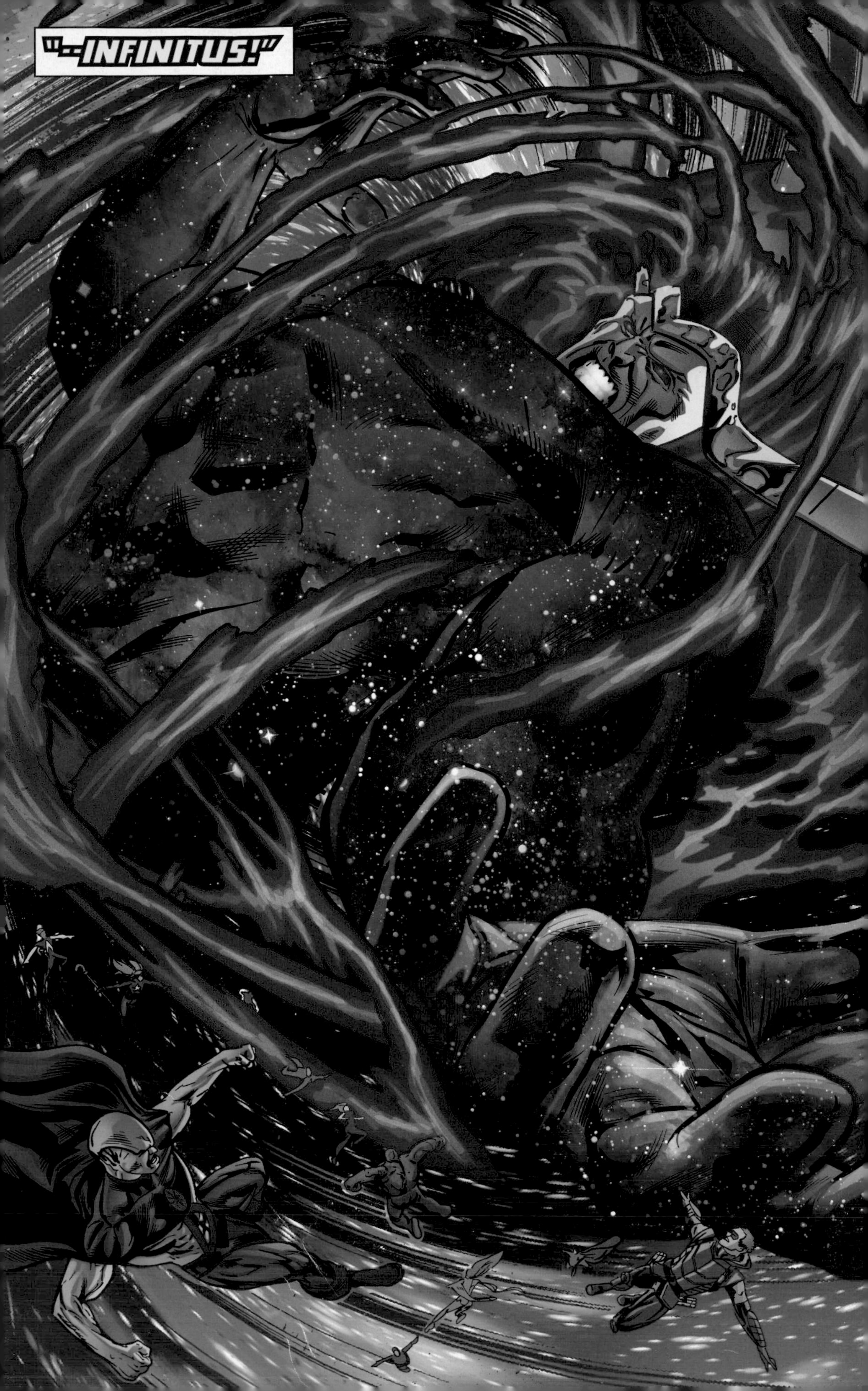
"--INFINITUS!"

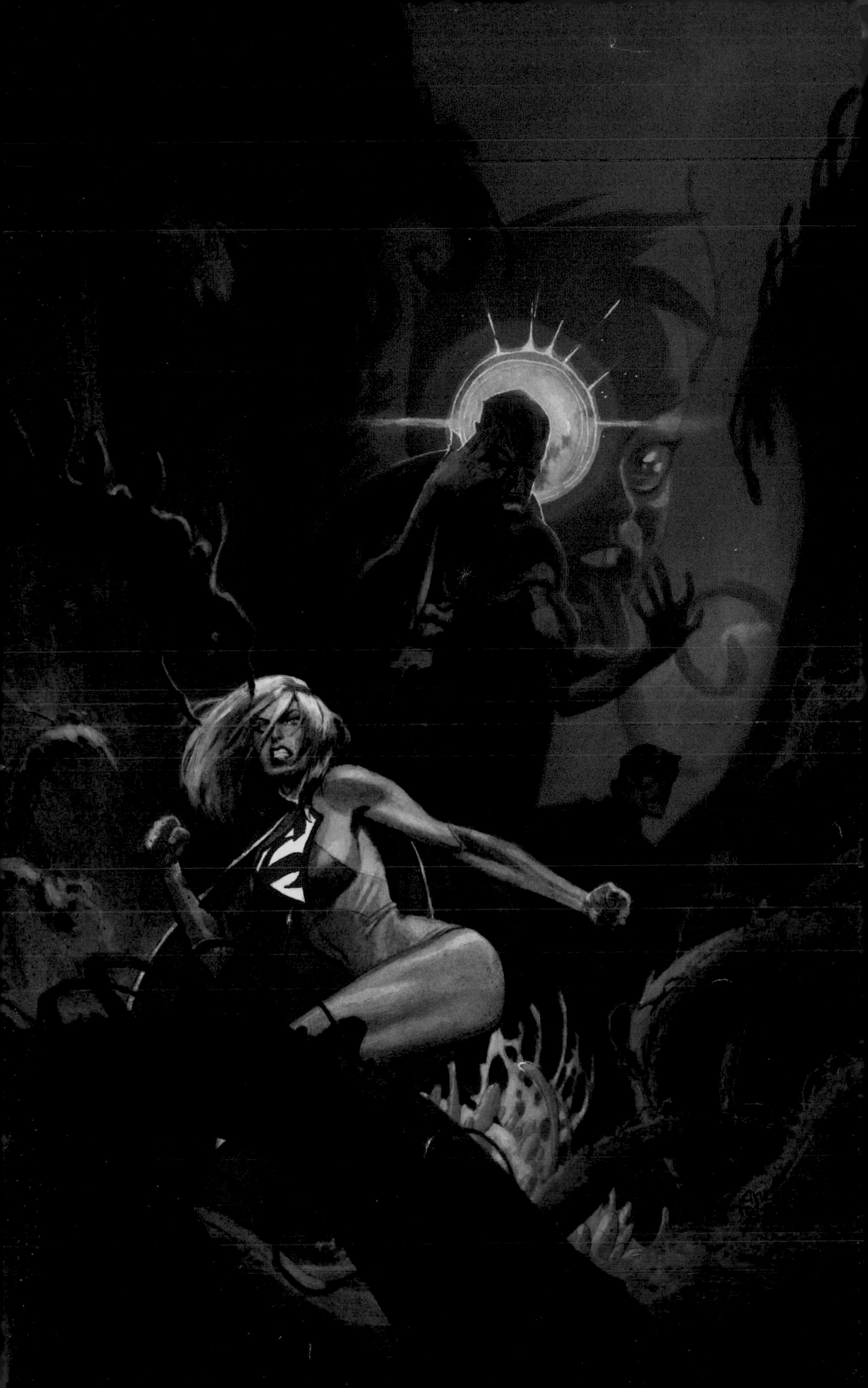

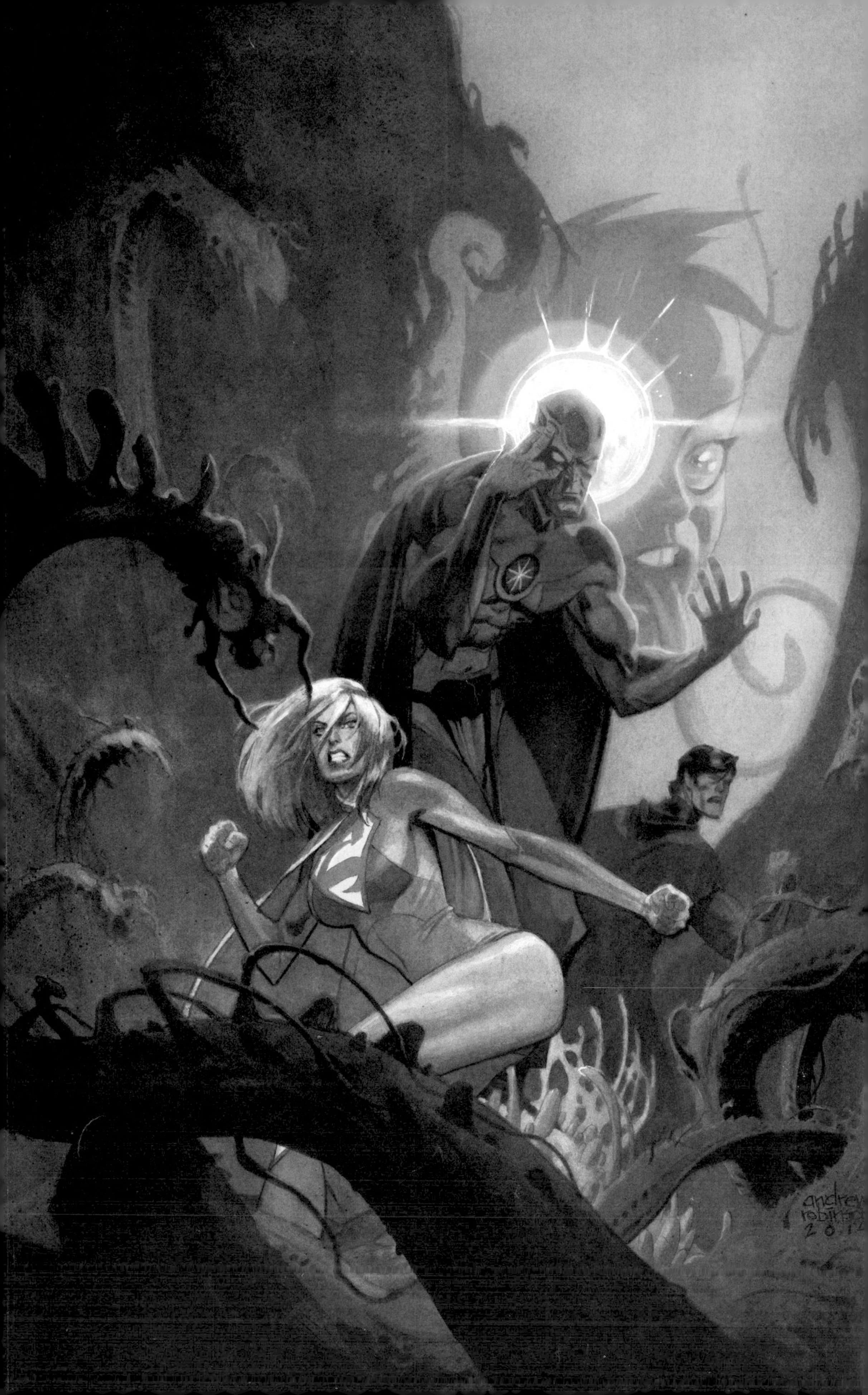

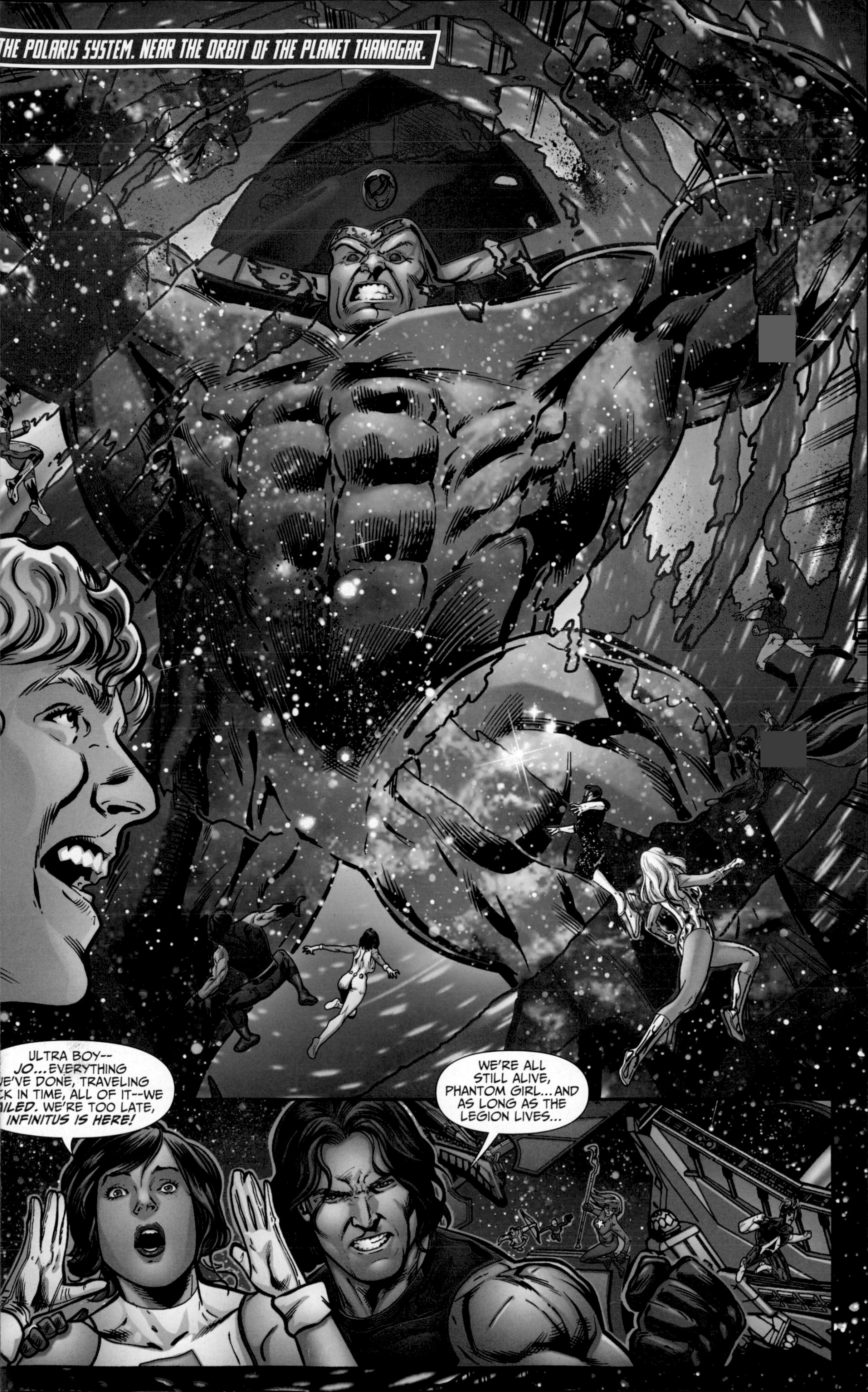
THE POLARIS SYSTEM. NEAR THE ORBIT OF THE PLANET THANAGAR.
ULTRA BOY-- JO...EVERYTHING E'VE DONE, TRAVELING CK IN TIME, ALL OF IT--WE AILED. WE'RE TOO LATE, INFINITUS IS HERE!
WE'RE ALL STILL ALIVE, PHANTOM GIRL...AND AS LONG AS THE LEGION LIVES...

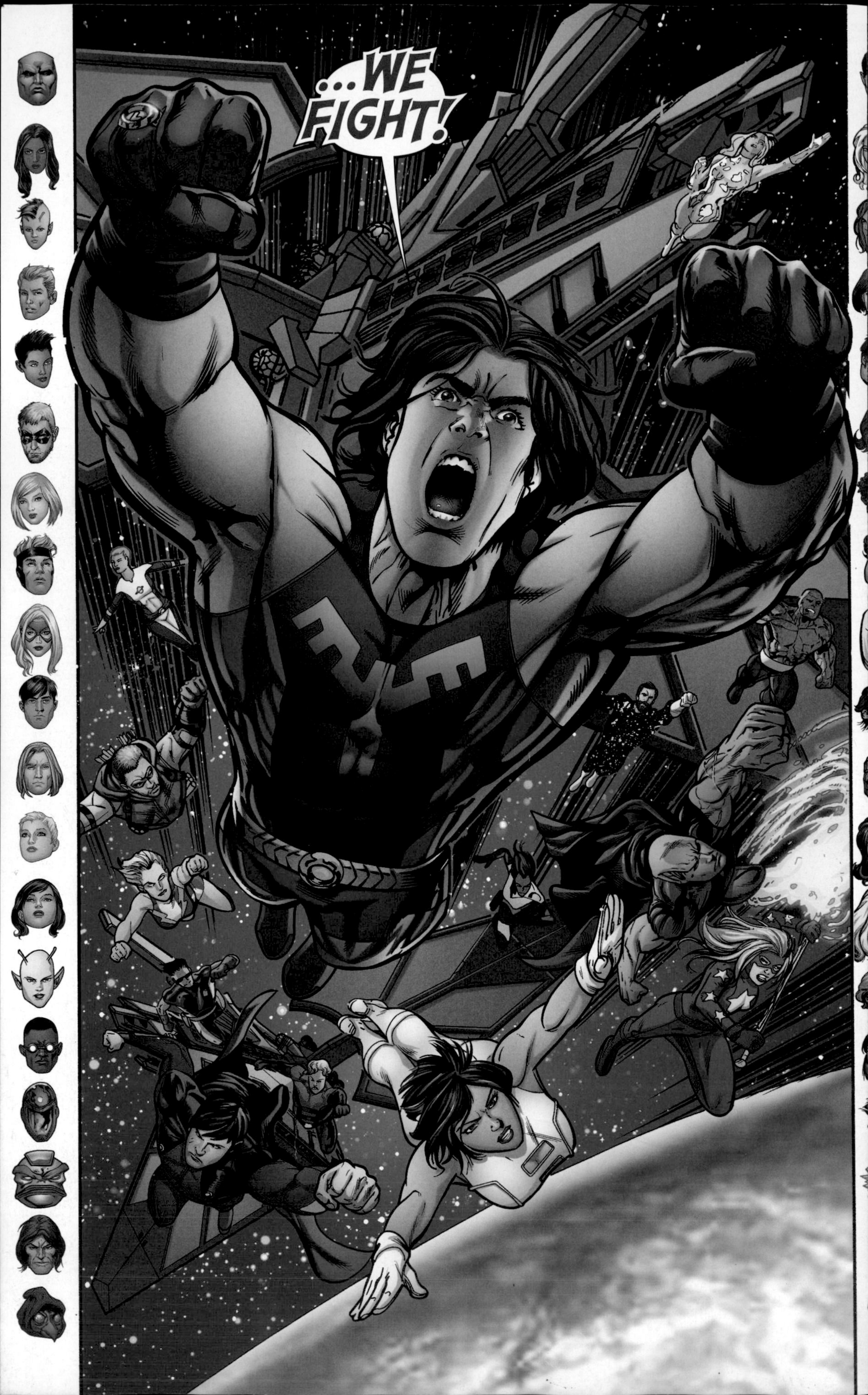
...WE FIGHT!

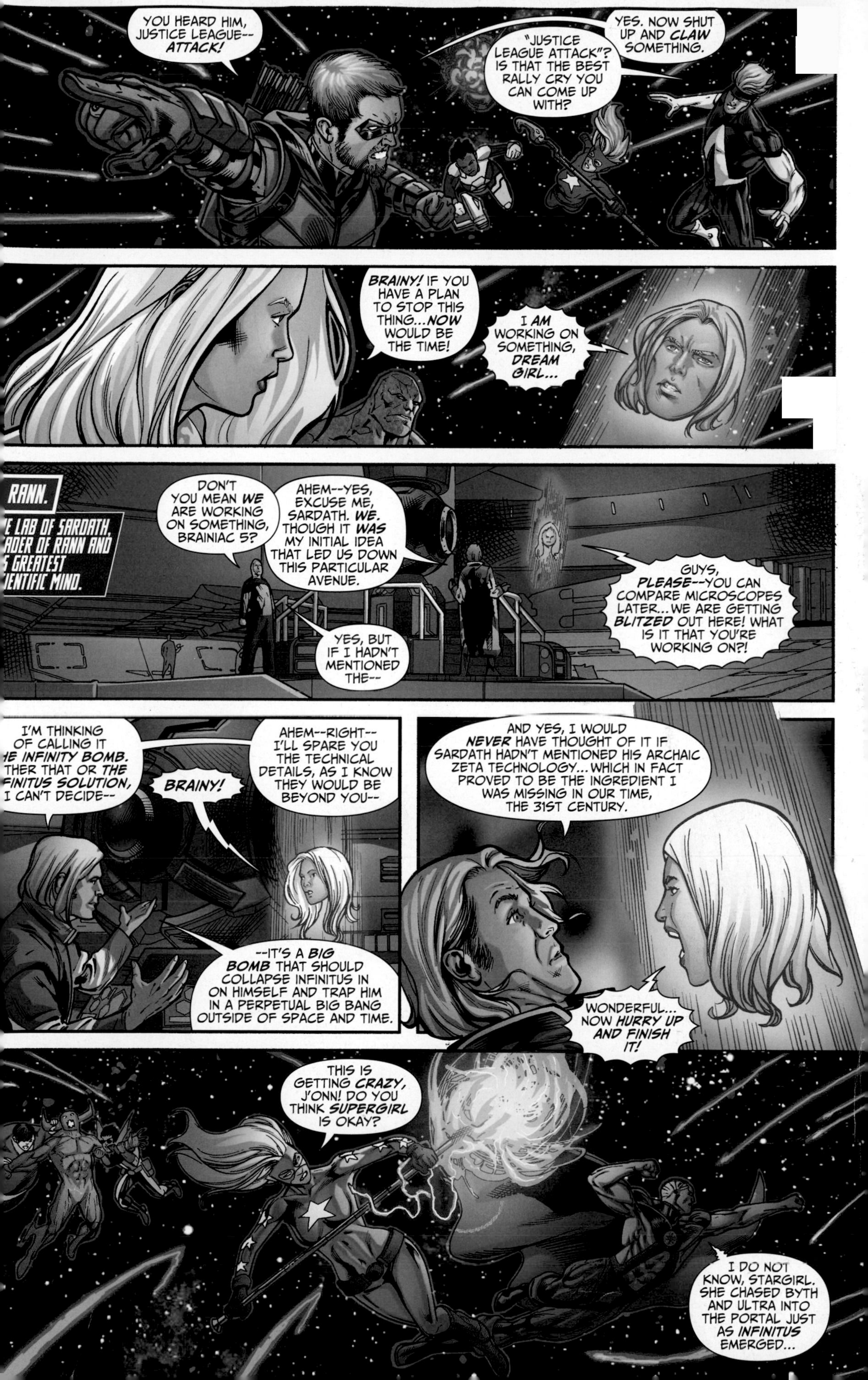
YOU HEARD HIM, JUSTICE LEAGUE-- ATTACK!
"JUSTICE LEAGUE ATTACK"? IS THAT THE BEST RALLY CRY YOU CAN COME UP WITH?
YES. NOW SHUT UP AND CLAW SOMETHING.
BRAINY! IF YOU HAVE A PLAN TO STOP THIS THING...NOW WOULD BE THE TIME!
I AM WORKING ON SOMETHING, DREAM GIRL...
RANN.
E LAB OF SARDATH, ADER OF RANN AND S GREATEST IENTIFIC MIND.
DON'T YOU MEAN WE ARE WORKING ON SOMETHING, BRAINIAC 5?
AHEM--YES, EXCUSE ME, SARDATH. WE. THOUGH IT WAS MY INITIAL IDEA THAT LED US DOWN THIS PARTICULAR AVENUE.
YES, BUT IF I HADN'T MENTIONED THE--
GUYS, PLEASE--YOU CAN COMPARE MICROSCOPES LATER...WE ARE GETTING BLITZED OUT HERE! WHAT IS IT THAT YOU'RE WORKING ON?!
AHEM--RIGHT-- I'LL SPARE YOU THE TECHNICAL DETAILS, AS I KNOW THEY WOULD BE BEYOND YOU--
--IT'S A BIG BOMB THAT SHOULD COLLAPSE INFINITUS IN ON HIMSELF AND TRAP HIM IN A PERPETUAL BIG BANG OUTSIDE OF SPACE AND TIME.
I'M THINKING OF CALLING IT HE INFINITY BOMB. THER THAT OR THE FINITUS SOLUTION, I CAN'T DECIDE--
BRAINY!
AND YES, I WOULD NEVER HAVE THOUGHT OF IT IF SARDATH HADN'T MENTIONED HIS ARCHAIC ZETA TECHNOLOGY...WHICH IN FACT PROVED TO BE THE INGREDIENT I WAS MISSING IN OUR TIME, THE 31ST CENTURY.
WONDERFUL... NOW HURRY UP AND FINISH IT!
THIS IS GETTING CRAZY, J'ONN! DO YOU THINK SUPERGIRL IS OKAY?
I DO NOT KNOW, STARGIRL. SHE CHASED BYTH AND ULTRA INTO THE PORTAL JUST AS INFINITUS EMERGED...

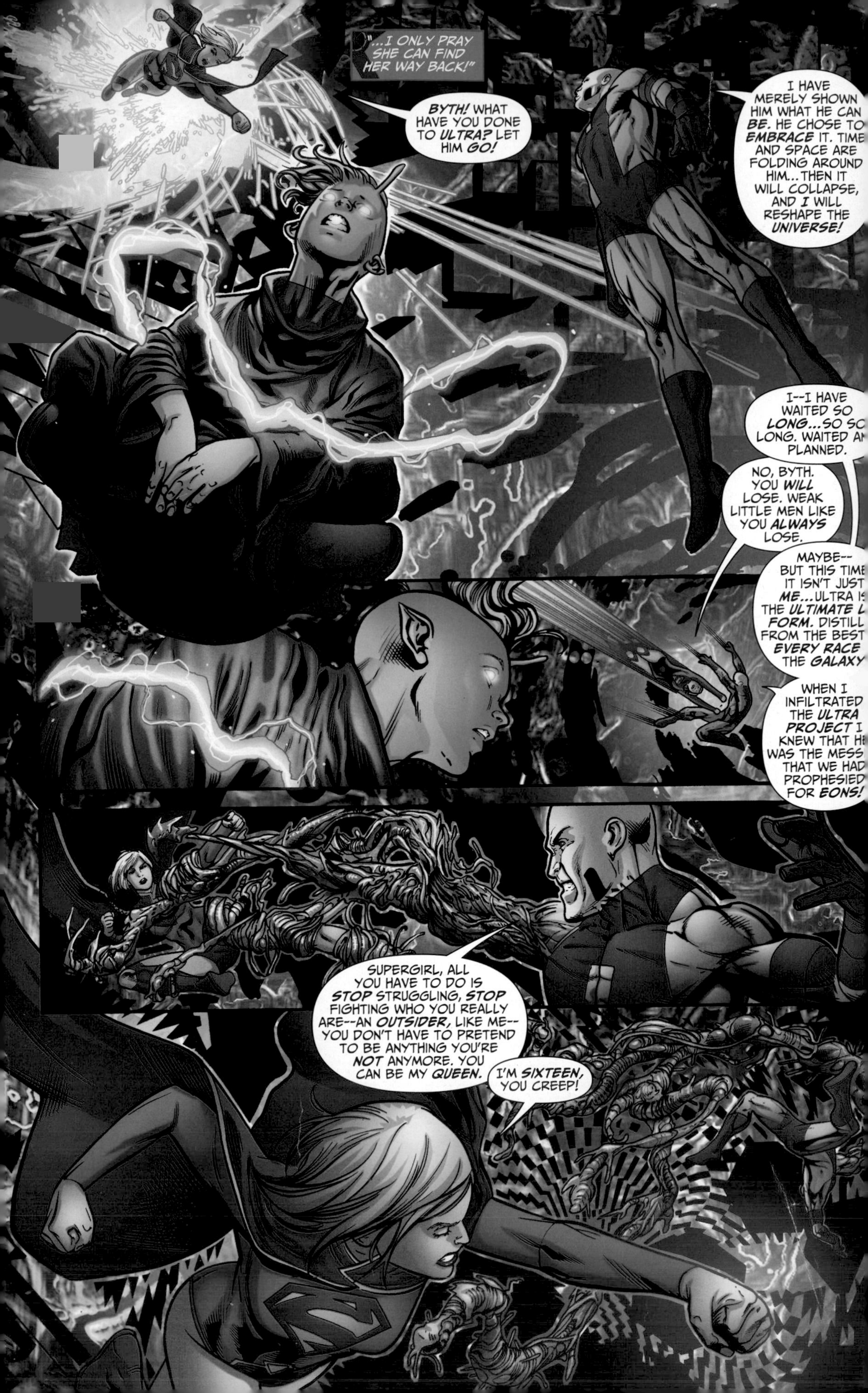
"...I ONLY PRAY SHE CAN FIND HER WAY BACK!"
BYTH! WHAT HAVE YOU DONE TO ULTRA? LET HIM GO!
I HAVE MERELY SHOWN HIM WHAT HE CAN BE. HE CHOSE TO EMBRACE IT. TIME AND SPACE ARE FOLDING AROUND HIM...THEN IT WILL COLLAPSE, AND I WILL RESHAPE THE UNIVERSE!
I--I HAVE WAITED SO LONG...SO SO LONG. WAITED A PLANNED.
NO, BYTH. YOU WILL LOSE. WEAK LITTLE MEN LIKE YOU ALWAYS LOSE.
MAYBE-- BUT THIS TIME IT ISN'T JUST ME...ULTRA IS THE ULTIMATE L FORM. DISTILL FROM THE BEST EVERY RACE THE GALAXY
WHEN I INFILTRATED THE ULTRA PROJECT I KNEW THAT H WAS THE MESS THAT WE HAD PROPHESIED FOR EONS!
SUPERGIRL, ALL YOU HAVE TO DO IS STOP STRUGGLING, STOP FIGHTING WHO YOU REALLY ARE--AN OUTSIDER, LIKE ME--YOU DON'T HAVE TO PRETEND TO BE ANYTHING YOU'RE NOT ANYMORE. YOU CAN BE MY QUEEN.
I'M SIXTEEN, YOU CREEP!

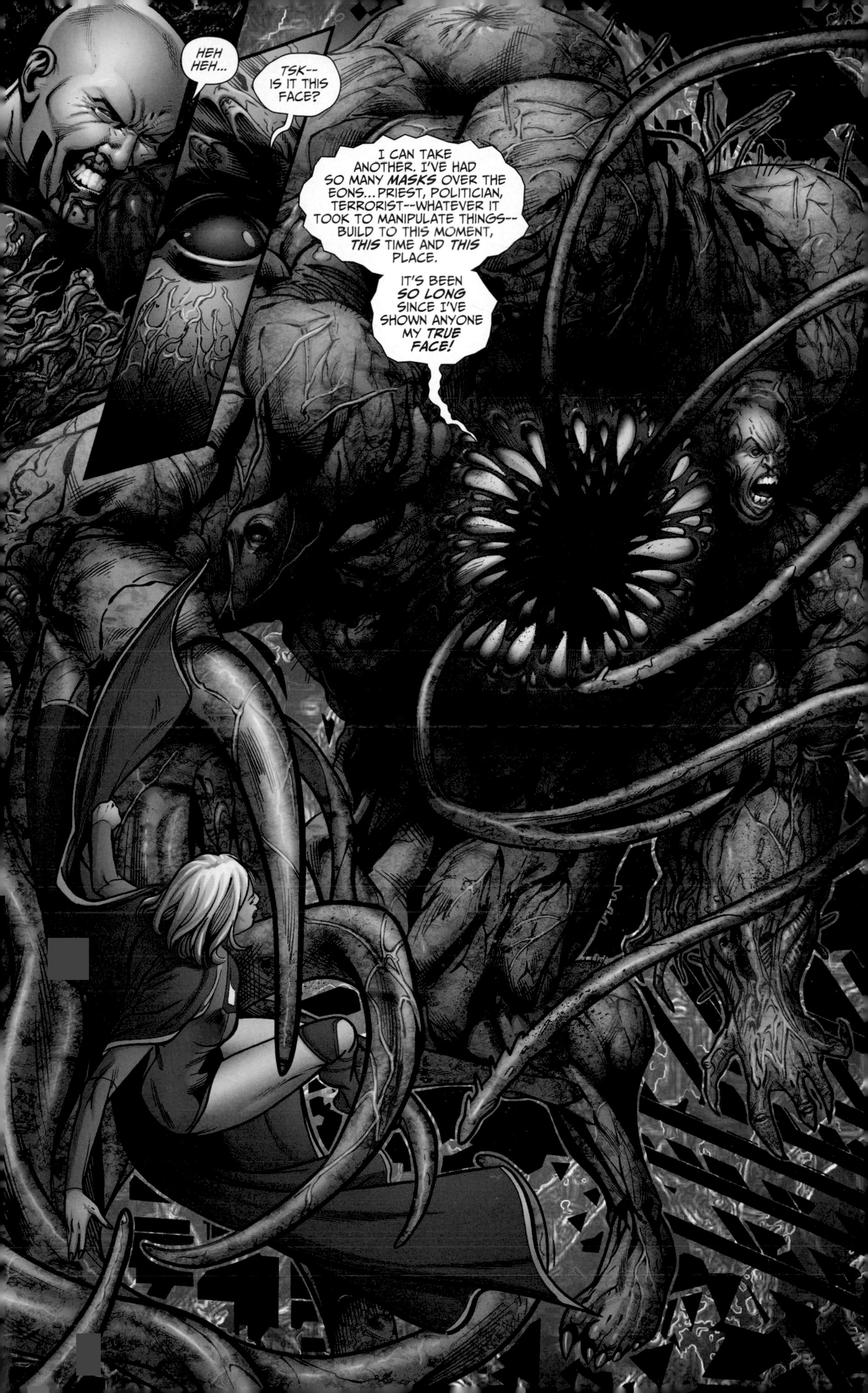
HEH HEH...
TSK-- IS IT THIS FACE?
I CAN TAKE ANOTHER. I'VE HAD SO MANY MASKS OVER THE EONS...PRIEST, POLITICIAN, TERRORIST--WHATEVER IT TOOK TO MANIPULATE THINGS-- BUILD TO THIS MOMENT, THIS TIME AND THIS PLACE.
IT'S BEEN SO LONG SINCE I'VE SHOWN ANYONE MY TRUE FACE!

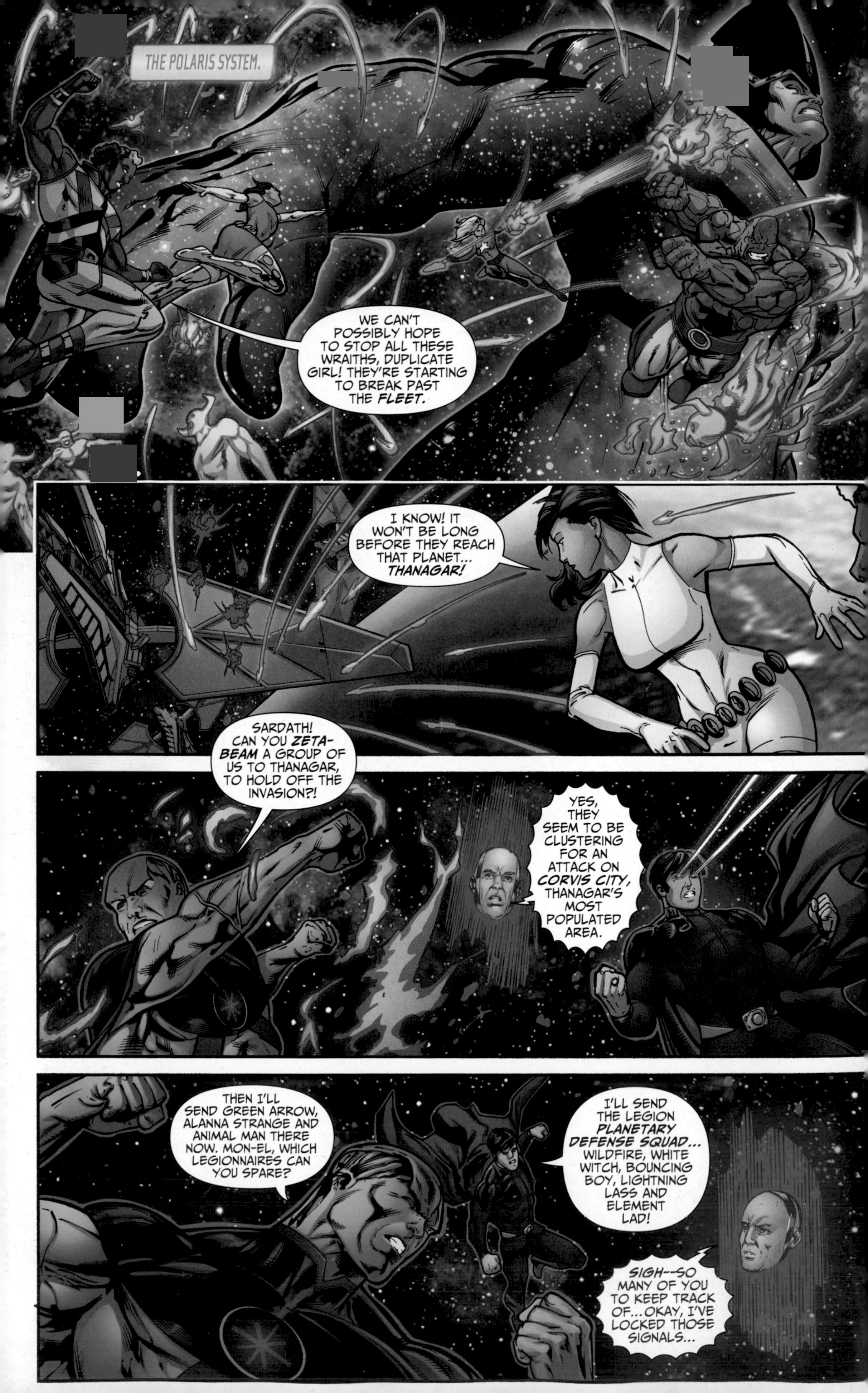
THE POLARIS SYSTEM.
WE CAN'T POSSIBLY HOPE TO STOP ALL THESE WRAITHS, DUPLICATE GIRL! THEY'RE STARTING TO BREAK PAST THE FLEET.
I KNOW! IT WON'T BE LONG BEFORE THEY REACH THAT PLANET... THANAGAR!
SARDATH! CAN YOU ZETA-BEAM A GROUP OF US TO THANAGAR, TO HOLD OFF THE INVASION?!
YES, THEY SEEM TO BE CLUSTERING FOR AN ATTACK ON CORVIS CITY, THANAGAR'S MOST POPULATED AREA.
THEN I'LL SEND GREEN ARROW, ALANNA STRANGE AND ANIMAL MAN THERE NOW. MON-EL, WHICH LEGIONNAIRES CAN YOU SPARE?
I'LL SEND THE LEGION PLANETARY DEFENSE SQUAD... WILDFIRE, WHITE WITCH, BOUNCING BOY, LIGHTNING LASS AND ELEMENT LAD!
SIGH--SO MANY OF YOU TO KEEP TRACK OF...OKAY, I'VE LOCKED THOSE SIGNALS...

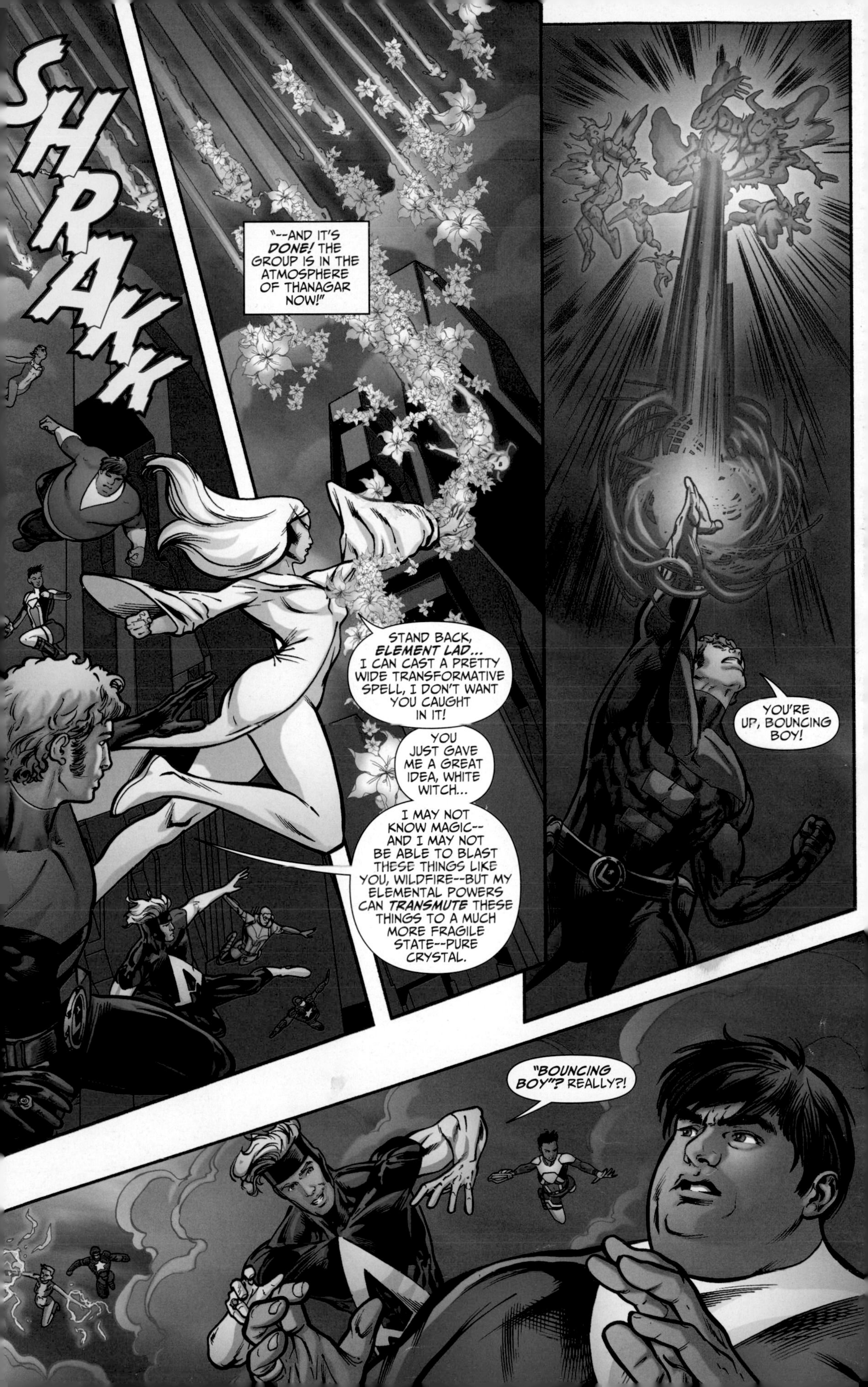
SHRAKK
"--AND IT'S DONE! THE GROUP IS IN THE ATMOSPHERE OF THANAGAR NOW!"
STAND BACK, ELEMENT LAD... I CAN CAST A PRETTY WIDE TRANSFORMATIVE SPELL, I DON'T WANT YOU CAUGHT IN IT!
YOU JUST GAVE ME A GREAT IDEA, WHITE WITCH...
I MAY NOT KNOW MAGIC--AND I MAY NOT BE ABLE TO BLAST THESE THINGS LIKE YOU, WILDFIRE--BUT MY ELEMENTAL POWERS CAN TRANSMUTE THESE THINGS TO A MUCH MORE FRAGILE STATE--PURE CRYSTAL.
YOU'RE UP, BOUNCING BOY!
"BOUNCING BOY"? REALLY?!

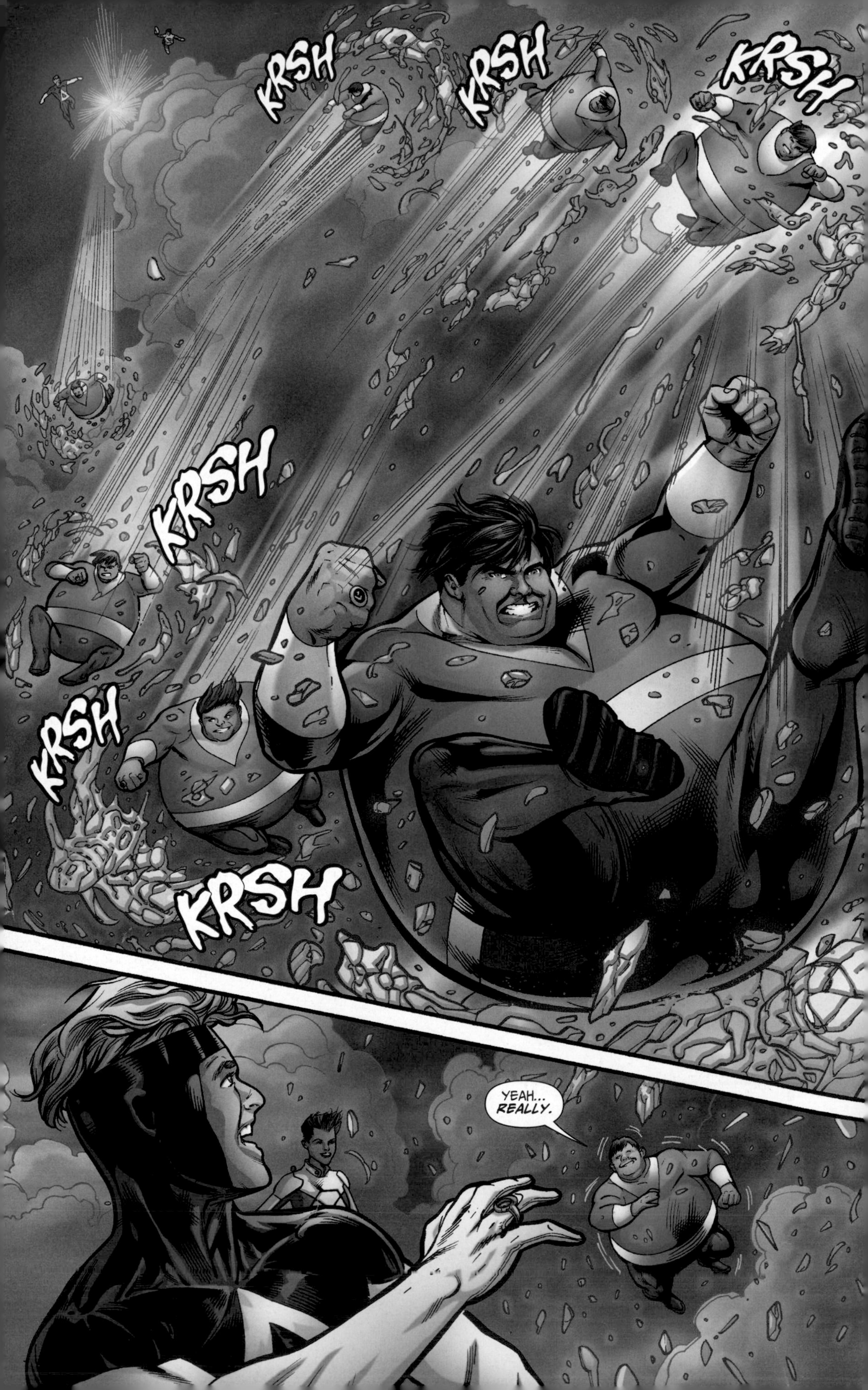
KRSH
KRSH
KRSH
KRSH
KRSH
KRSH
YEAH... REALLY.

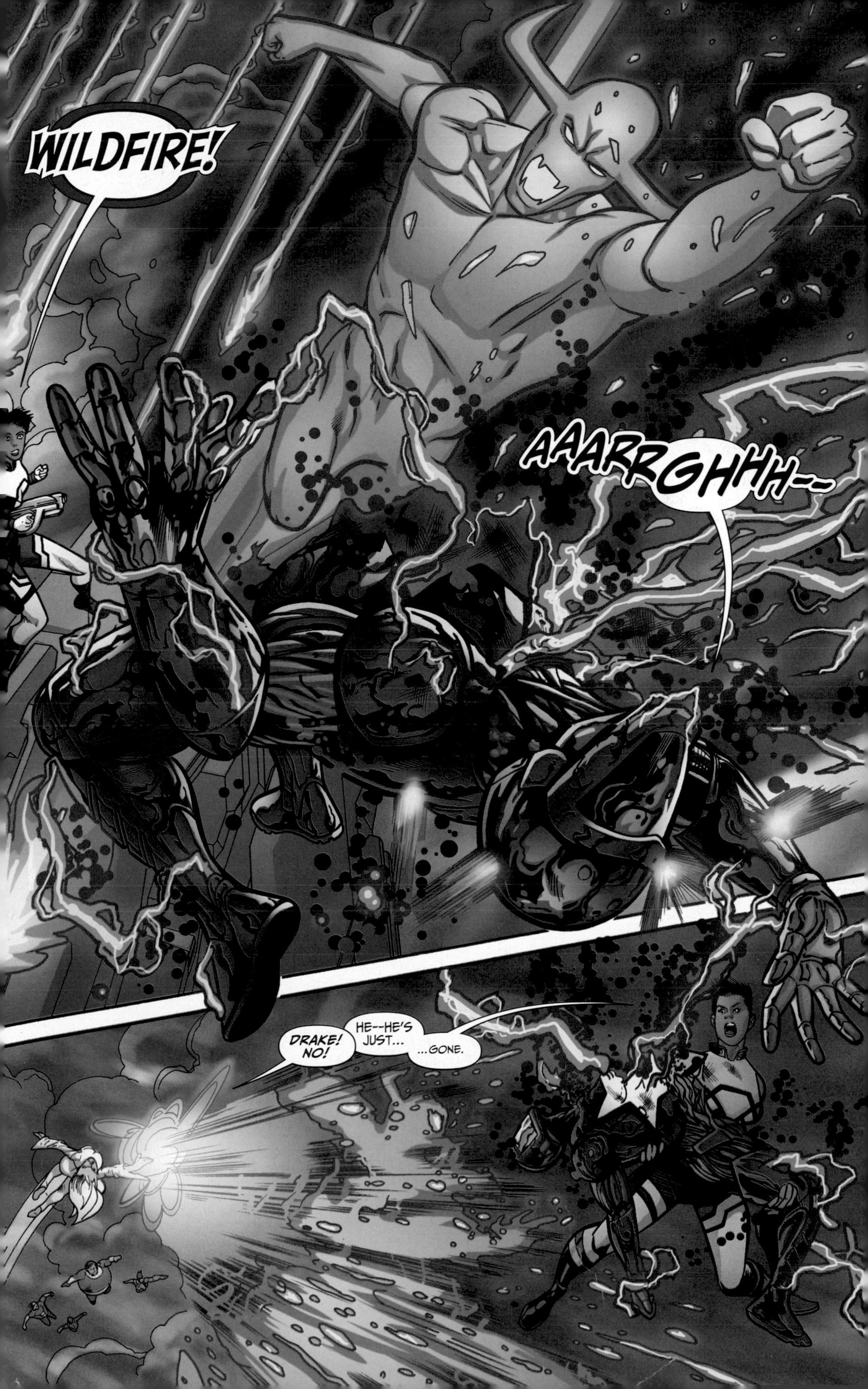
WILDFIRE!
AAARRGHHH--
DRAKE! NO!
HE--HE'S JUST...
...GONE.

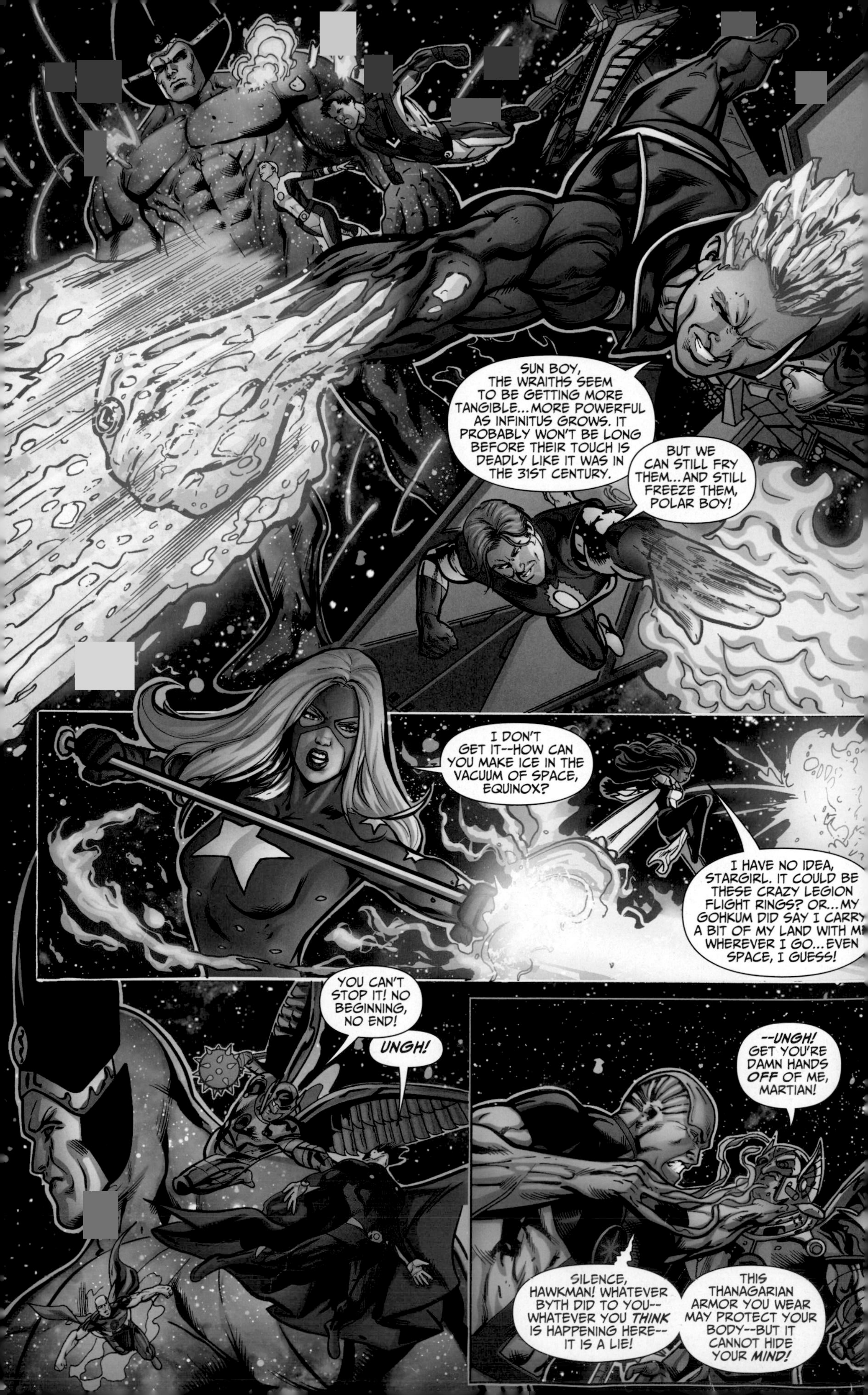

SUN BOY, THE WRAITHS SEEM TO BE GETTING MORE TANGIBLE...MORE POWERFUL AS INFINITUS GROWS. IT PROBABLY WON'T BE LONG BEFORE THEIR TOUCH IS DEADLY LIKE IT WAS IN THE 31ST CENTURY.
BUT WE CAN STILL FRY THEM...AND STILL FREEZE THEM, POLAR BOY!
I DON'T GET IT--HOW CAN YOU MAKE ICE IN THE VACUUM OF SPACE, EQUINOX?
I HAVE NO IDEA, STARGIRL. IT COULD BE THESE CRAZY LEGION FLIGHT RINGS? OR...MY GOHKUM DID SAY I CARRY A BIT OF MY LAND WITH M WHEREVER I GO...EVEN SPACE, I GUESS!
YOU CAN'T STOP IT! NO BEGINNING, NO END!
UNGH!
--UNGH! GET YOU'RE DAMN HANDS OFF OF ME, MARTIAN!
SILENCE, HAWKMAN! WHATEVER BYTH DID TO YOU-- WHATEVER YOU THINK IS HAPPENING HERE-- IT IS A LIE!
THIS THANAGARIAN ARMOR YOU WEAR MAY PROTECT YOUR BODY--BUT IT CANNOT HIDE YOUR MIND!

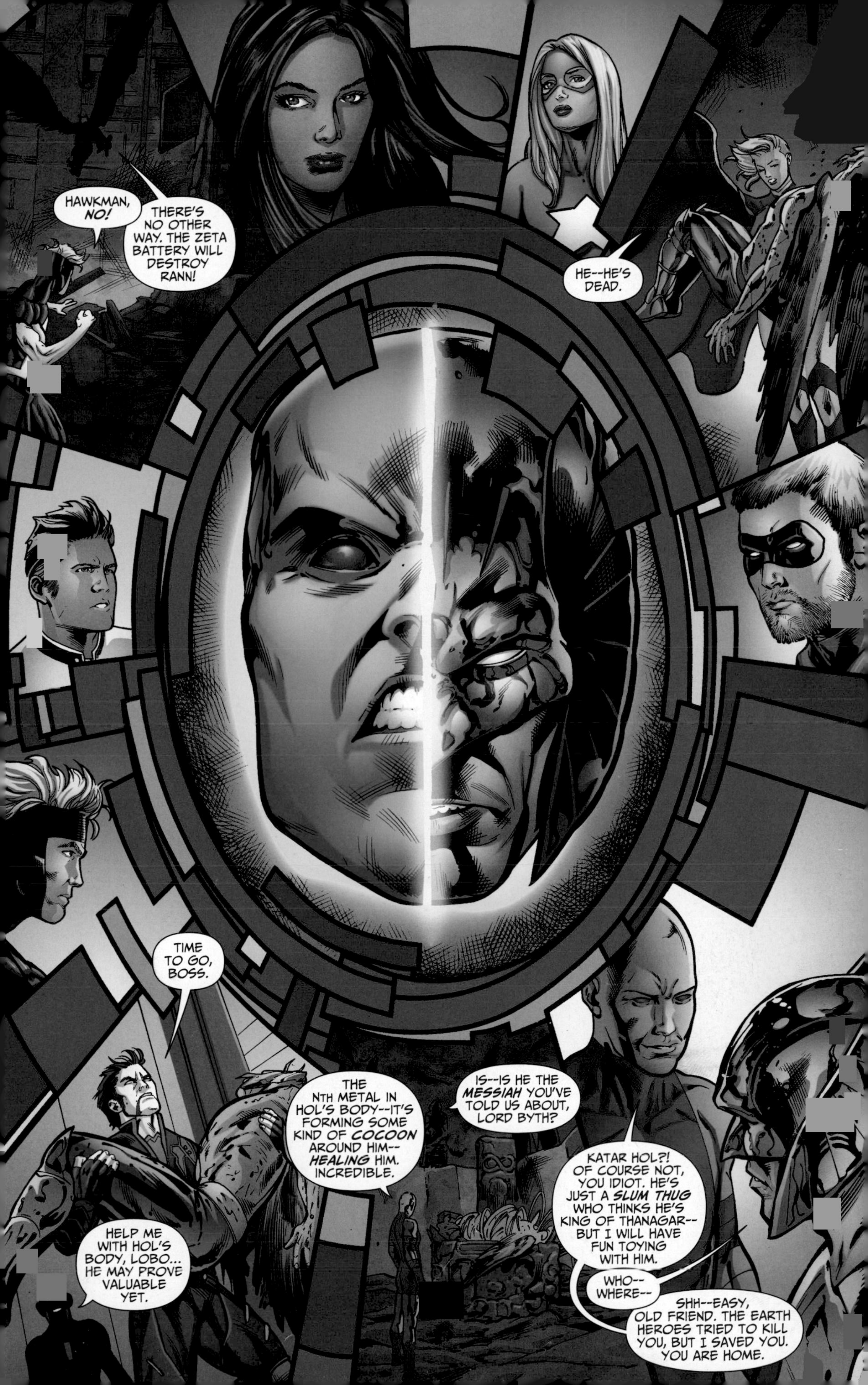
HAWKMAN, NO!
THERE'S NO OTHER WAY. THE ZETA BATTERY WILL DESTROY RANN!
HE--HE'S DEAD.
TIME TO GO, BOSS.
HELP ME WITH HOL'S BODY, LOBO... HE MAY PROVE VALUABLE YET.
THE Nth METAL IN HOL'S BODY--IT'S FORMING SOME KIND OF COCOON AROUND HIM--HEALING HIM. INCREDIBLE.
IS--IS HE THE MESSIAH YOU'VE TOLD US ABOUT, LORD BYTH?
KATAR HOL?! OF COURSE NOT, YOU IDIOT. HE'S JUST A SLUM THUG WHO THINKS HE'S KING OF THANAGAR--BUT I WILL HAVE FUN TOYING WITH HIM.
WHO-- WHERE--
SHH--EASY, OLD FRIEND. THE EARTH HEROES TRIED TO KILL YOU, BUT I SAVED YOU. YOU ARE HOME.

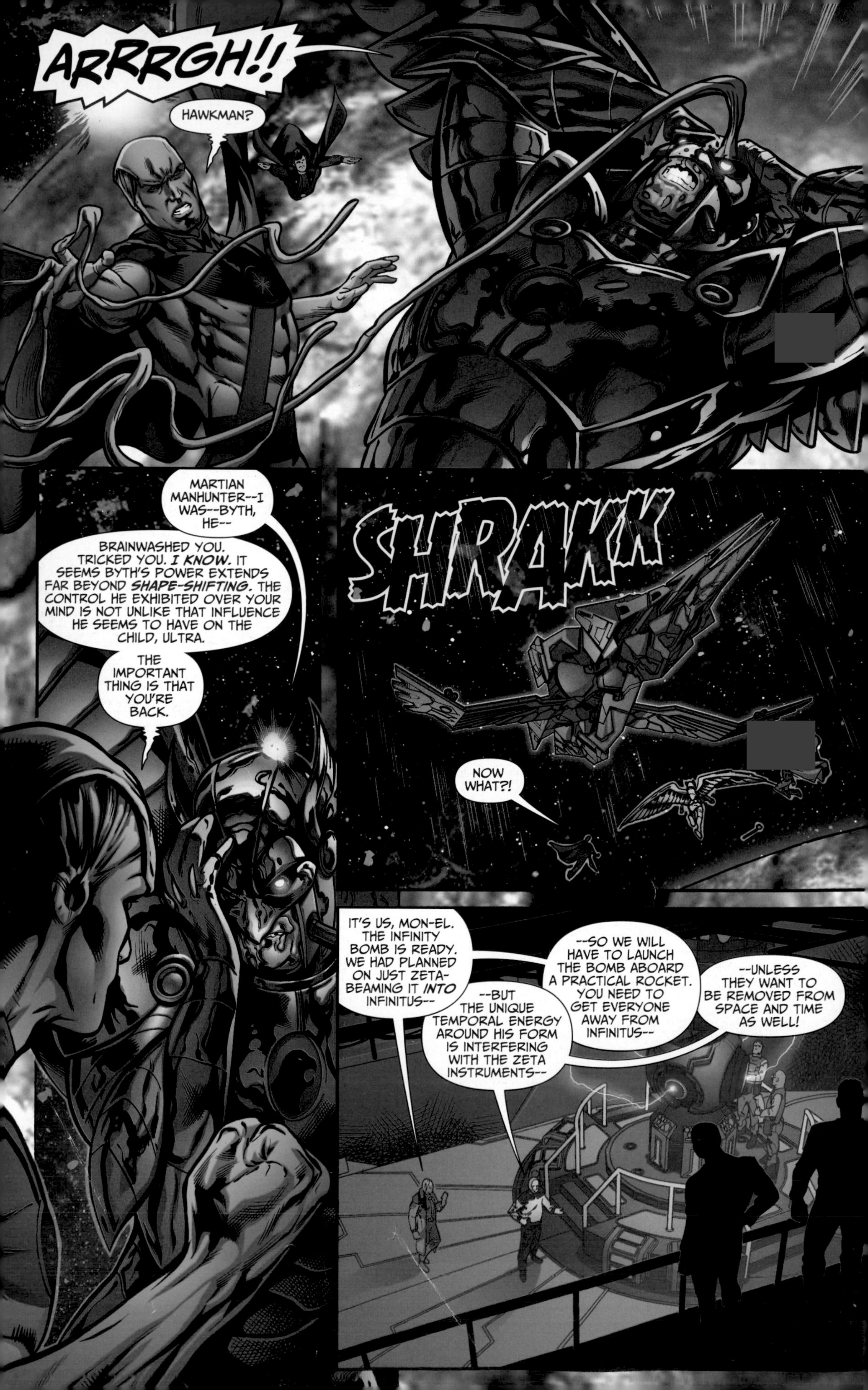
ARRRGH!!
HAWKMAN?
MARTIAN MANHUNTER--I WAS--BYTH, HE--
BRAINWASHED YOU. TRICKED YOU. I KNOW. IT SEEMS BYTH'S POWER EXTENDS FAR BEYOND SHAPE-SHIFTING. THE CONTROL HE EXHIBITED OVER YOUR MIND IS NOT UNLIKE THAT INFLUENCE HE SEEMS TO HAVE ON THE CHILD, ULTRA.
THE IMPORTANT THING IS THAT YOU'RE BACK.
SHRAKK
NOW WHAT?!
IT'S US, MON-EL. THE INFINITY BOMB IS READY. WE HAD PLANNED ON JUST ZETA-BEAMING IT INTO INFINITUS--
--BUT THE UNIQUE TEMPORAL ENERGY AROUND HIS FORM IS INTERFERING WITH THE ZETA INSTRUMENTS--
--SO WE WILL HAVE TO LAUNCH THE BOMB ABOARD A PRACTICAL ROCKET. YOU NEED TO GET EVERYONE AWAY FROM INFINITUS--
--UNLESS THEY WANT TO BE REMOVED FROM SPACE AND TIME AS WELL!

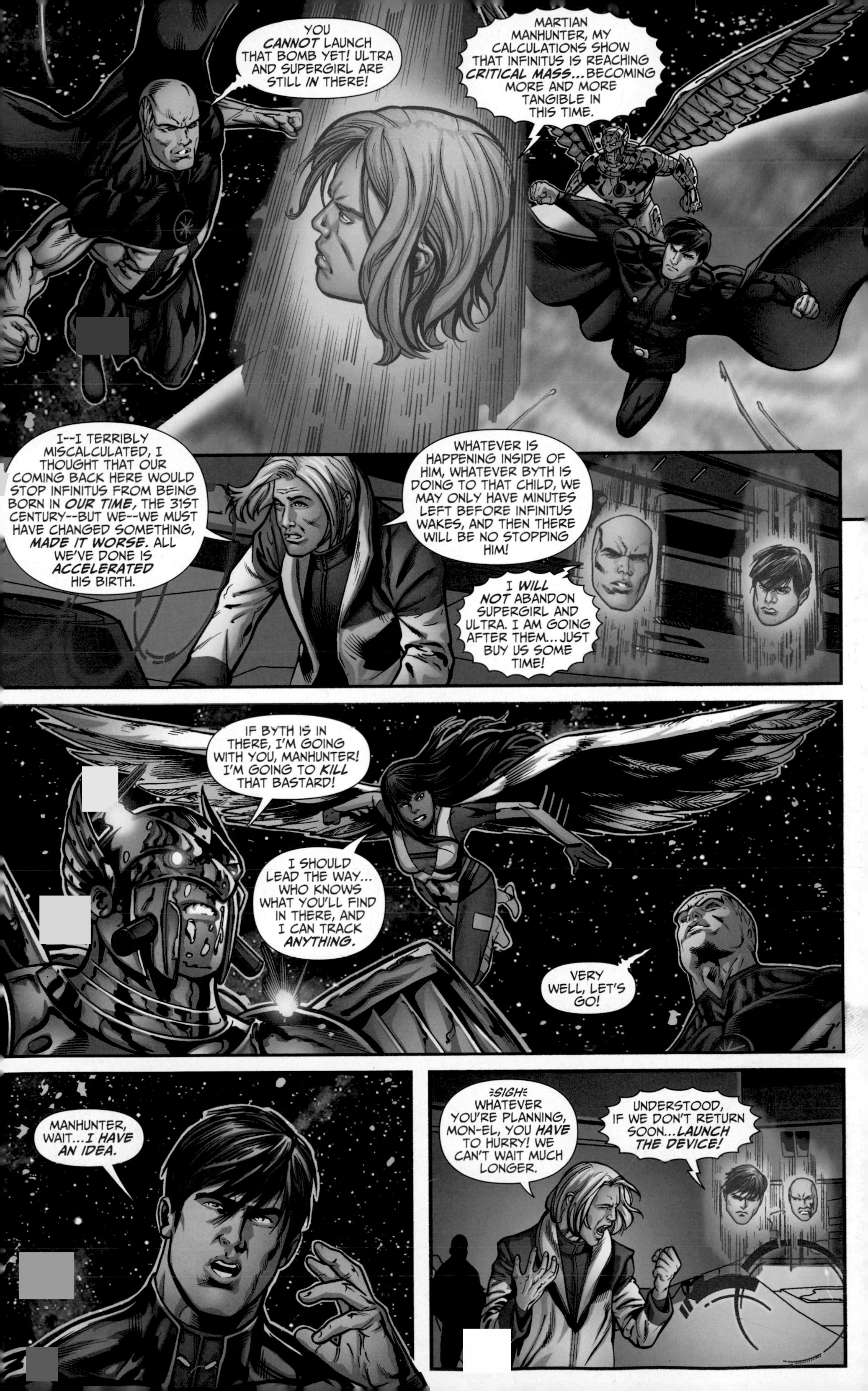
YOU CANNOT LAUNCH THAT BOMB YET! ULTRA AND SUPERGIRL ARE STILL IN THERE!
MARTIAN MANHUNTER, MY CALCULATIONS SHOW THAT INFINITUS IS REACHING CRITICAL MASS...BECOMING MORE AND MORE TANGIBLE IN THIS TIME.
I--I TERRIBLY MISCALCULATED, I THOUGHT THAT OUR COMING BACK HERE WOULD STOP INFINITUS FROM BEING BORN IN OUR TIME, THE 31ST CENTURY--BUT WE--WE MUST HAVE CHANGED SOMETHING, MADE IT WORSE. ALL WE'VE DONE IS ACCELERATED HIS BIRTH.
WHATEVER IS HAPPENING INSIDE OF HIM, WHATEVER BYTH IS DOING TO THAT CHILD, WE MAY ONLY HAVE MINUTES LEFT BEFORE INFINITUS WAKES, AND THEN THERE WILL BE NO STOPPING HIM!
I WILL NOT ABANDON SUPERGIRL AND ULTRA. I AM GOING AFTER THEM...JUST BUY US SOME TIME!
IF BYTH IS IN THERE, I'M GOING WITH YOU, MANHUNTER! I'M GOING TO KILL THAT BASTARD!
I SHOULD LEAD THE WAY... WHO KNOWS WHAT YOU'LL FIND IN THERE, AND I CAN TRACK ANYTHING.
VERY WELL, LET'S GO!
MANHUNTER, WAIT...I HAVE AN IDEA.
SIGH WHATEVER YOU'RE PLANNING, MON-EL, YOU HAVE TO HURRY! WE CAN'T WAIT MUCH LONGER.
UNDERSTOOD, IF WE DON'T RETURN SOON...LAUNCH THE DEVICE!

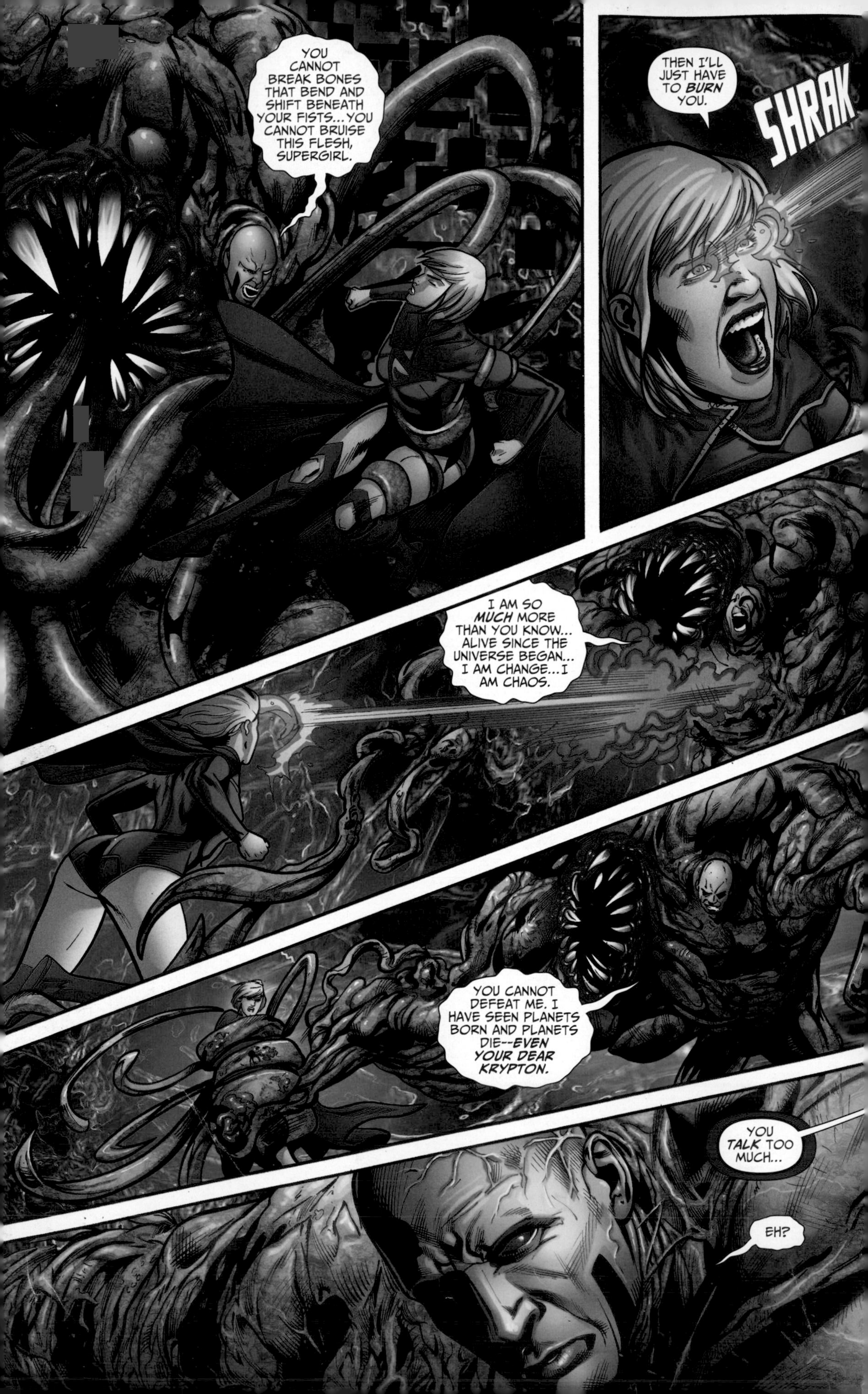
YOU CANNOT BREAK BONES THAT BEND AND SHIFT BENEATH YOUR FISTS...YOU CANNOT BRUISE THIS FLESH, SUPERGIRL.
THEN I'LL JUST HAVE TO BURN YOU.
SHRAK
I AM SO MUCH MORE THAN YOU KNOW... ALIVE SINCE THE UNIVERSE BEGAN... I AM CHANGE...I AM CHAOS.
YOU CANNOT DEFEAT ME. I HAVE SEEN PLANETS BORN AND PLANETS DIE--EVEN YOUR DEAR KRYPTON.
YOU TALK TOO MUCH...
EH?

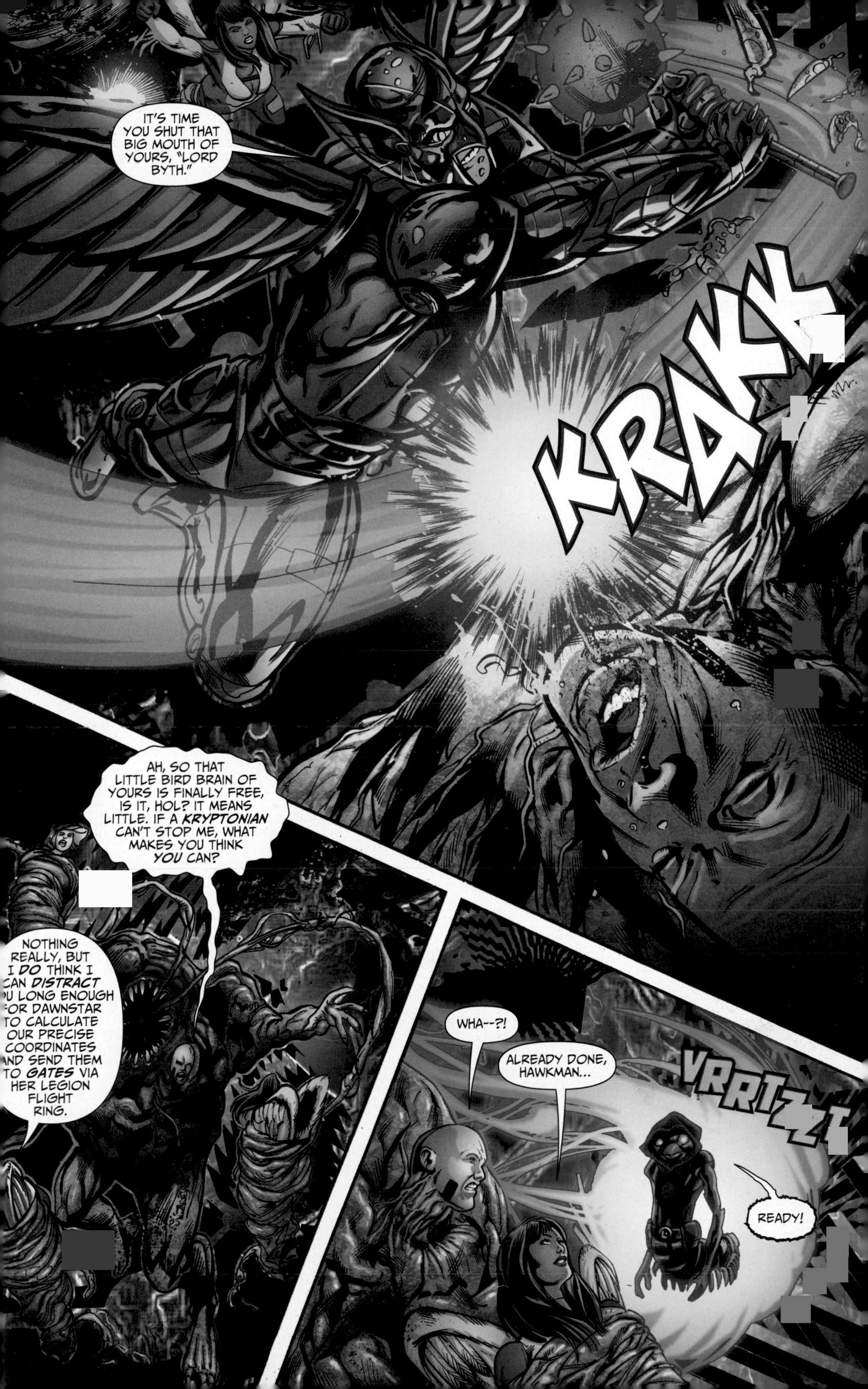
IT'S TIME YOU SHUT THAT BIG MOUTH OF YOURS, "LORD BYTH."
KRAKK
AH, SO THAT LITTLE BIRD BRAIN OF YOURS IS FINALLY FREE, IS IT, HOL? IT MEANS LITTLE. IF A KRYPTONIAN CAN'T STOP ME, WHAT MAKES YOU THINK YOU CAN?
NOTHING REALLY, BUT I DO THINK I CAN DISTRACT U LONG ENOUGH FOR DAWNSTAR TO CALCULATE OUR PRECISE COORDINATES AND SEND THEM TO GATES VIA HER LEGION FLIGHT RING.
WHA--?!
ALREADY DONE, HAWKMAN...
VRRTZZT
READY!

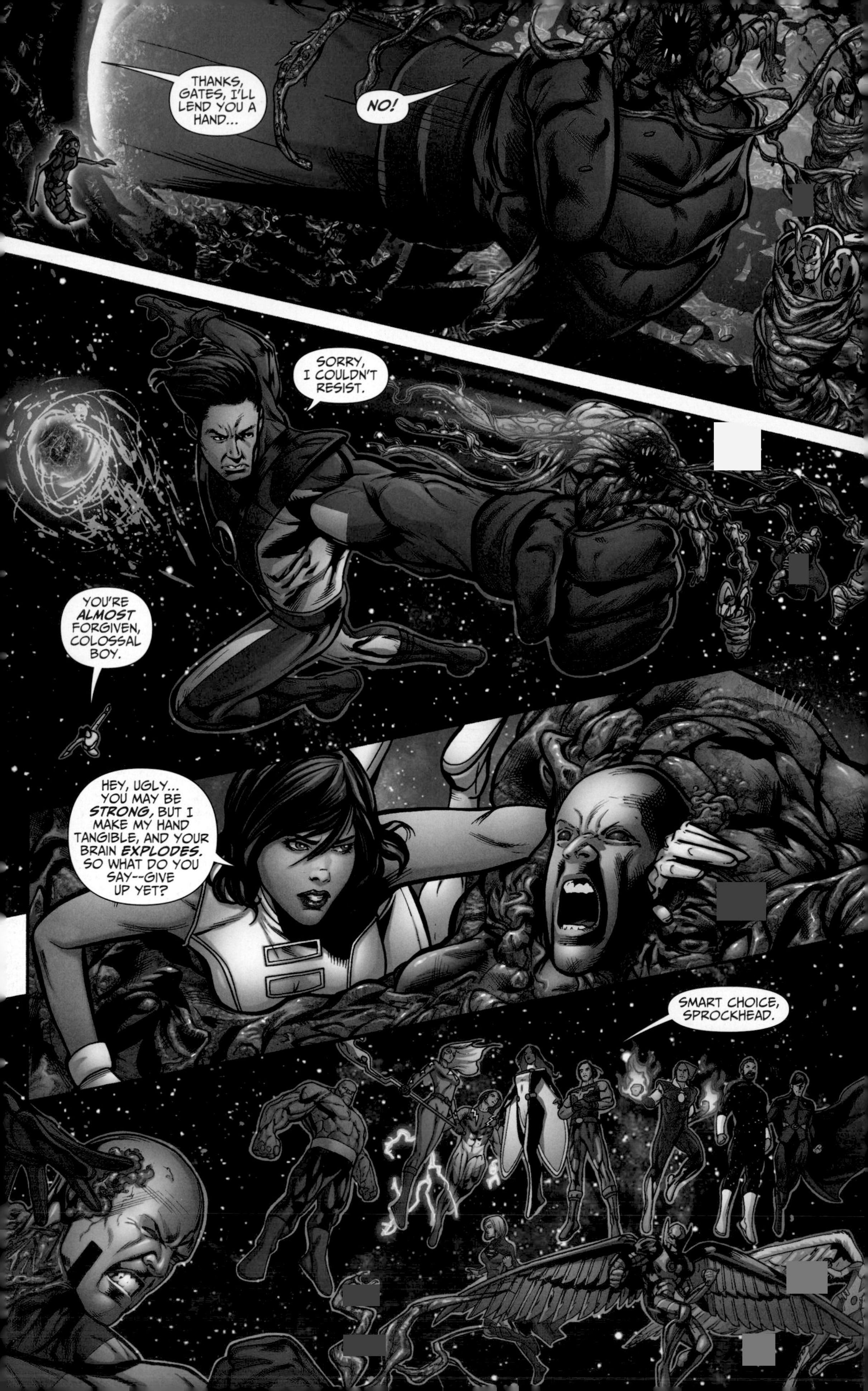
THANKS, GATES, I'LL LEND YOU A HAND...
NO!
SORRY, I COULDN'T RESIST.
YOU'RE ALMOST FORGIVEN, COLOSSAL BOY.
HEY, UGLY... YOU MAY BE STRONG, BUT I MAKE MY HAND TANGIBLE, AND YOUR BRAIN EXPLODES. SO WHAT DO YOU SAY--GIVE UP YET?
SMART CHOICE, SPROCKHEAD.

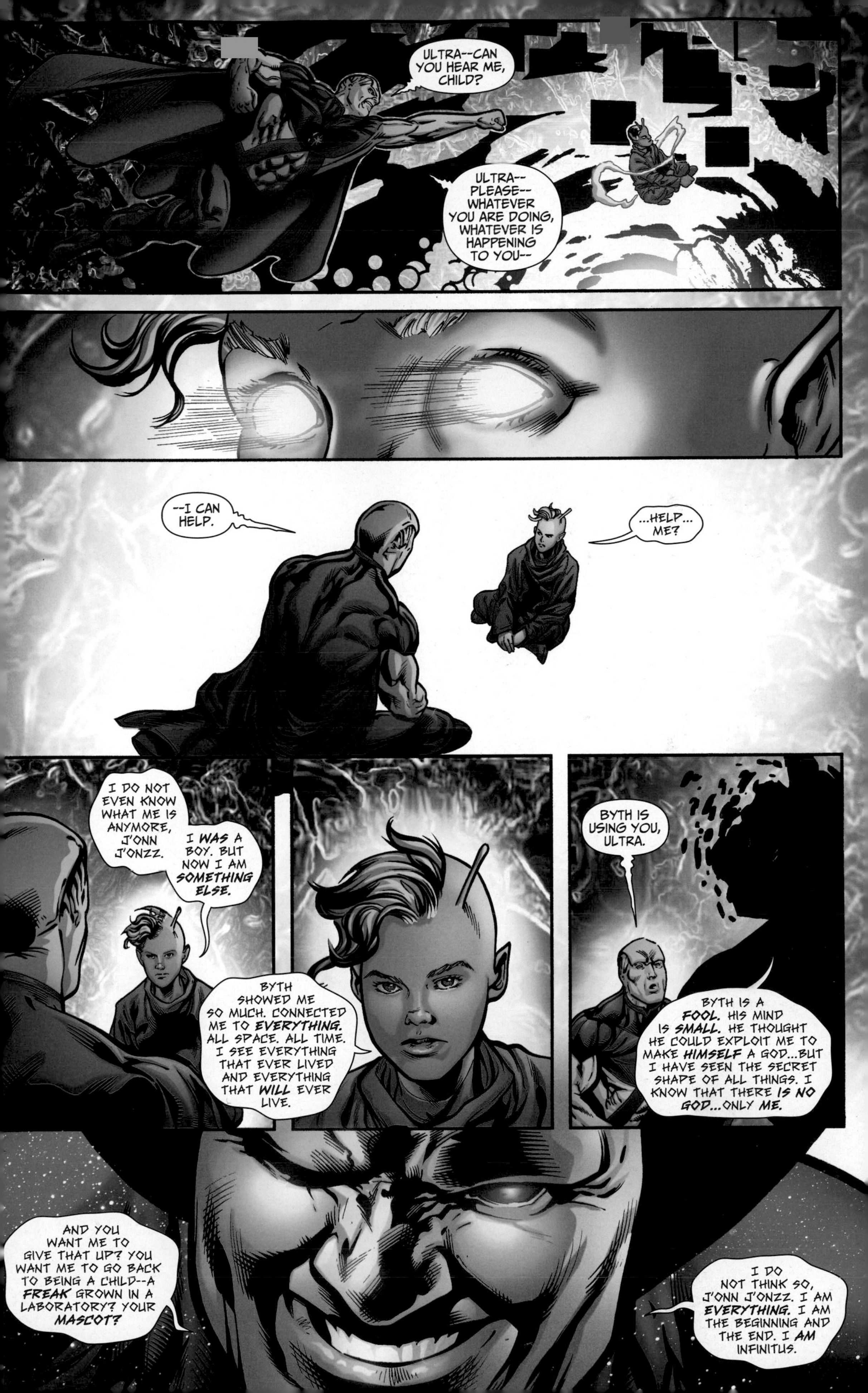
ULTRA--CAN YOU HEAR ME, CHILD?
ULTRA-- PLEASE-- WHATEVER YOU ARE DOING, WHATEVER IS HAPPENING TO YOU--
--I CAN HELP.
...HELP... ME?
I DO NOT EVEN KNOW WHAT ME IS ANYMORE, J'ONN J'ONZZ.
I **WAS** A BOY. BUT NOW I AM **SOMETHING ELSE.**
BYTH SHOWED ME SO MUCH. CONNECTED ME TO **EVERYTHING.** ALL SPACE. ALL TIME. I SEE EVERYTHING THAT EVER LIVED AND EVERYTHING THAT **WILL** EVER LIVE.
BYTH IS USING YOU, ULTRA.
BYTH IS A **FOOL.** HIS MIND IS **SMALL.** HE THOUGHT HE COULD EXPLOIT ME TO MAKE **HIMSELF** A GOD...BUT I HAVE SEEN THE SECRET SHAPE OF ALL THINGS. I KNOW THAT THERE **IS NO GOD...**ONLY **ME.**
AND YOU WANT ME TO GIVE THAT UP? YOU WANT ME TO GO BACK TO BEING A CHILD--A **FREAK** GROWN IN A LABORATORY? YOUR **MASCOT?**
I DO NOT THINK SO, J'ONN J'ONZZ. I AM **EVERYTHING.** I AM THE BEGINNING AND THE END. I **AM** INFINITUS.

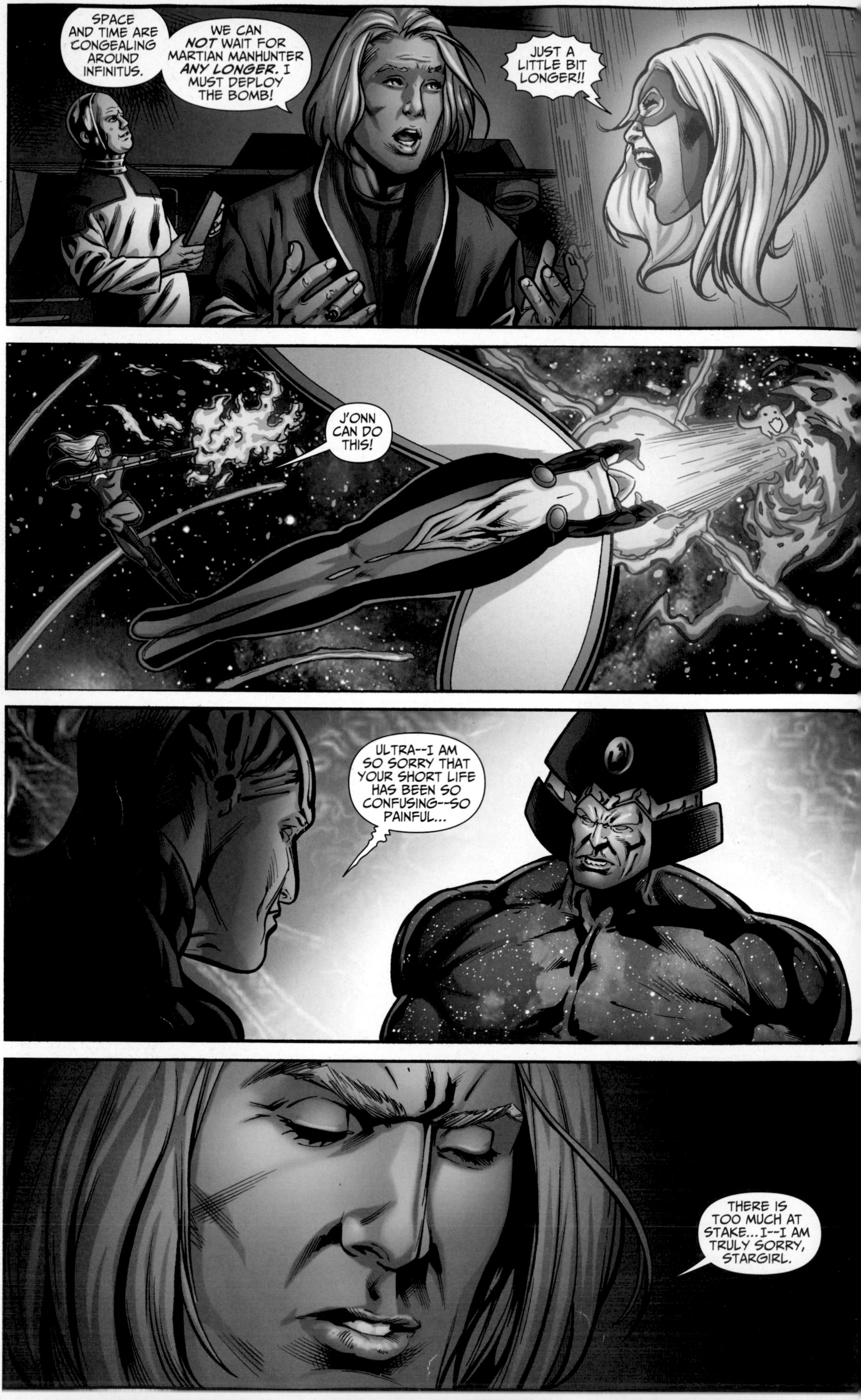
SPACE AND TIME ARE CONGEALING AROUND INFINITUS.
WE CAN NOT WAIT FOR MARTIAN MANHUNTER ANY LONGER. I MUST DEPLOY THE BOMB!
JUST A LITTLE BIT LONGER!!
J'ONN CAN DO THIS!
ULTRA--I AM SO SORRY THAT YOUR SHORT LIFE HAS BEEN SO CONFUSING--SO PAINFUL...
THERE IS TOO MUCH AT STAKE...I--I AM TRULY SORRY, STARGIRL.

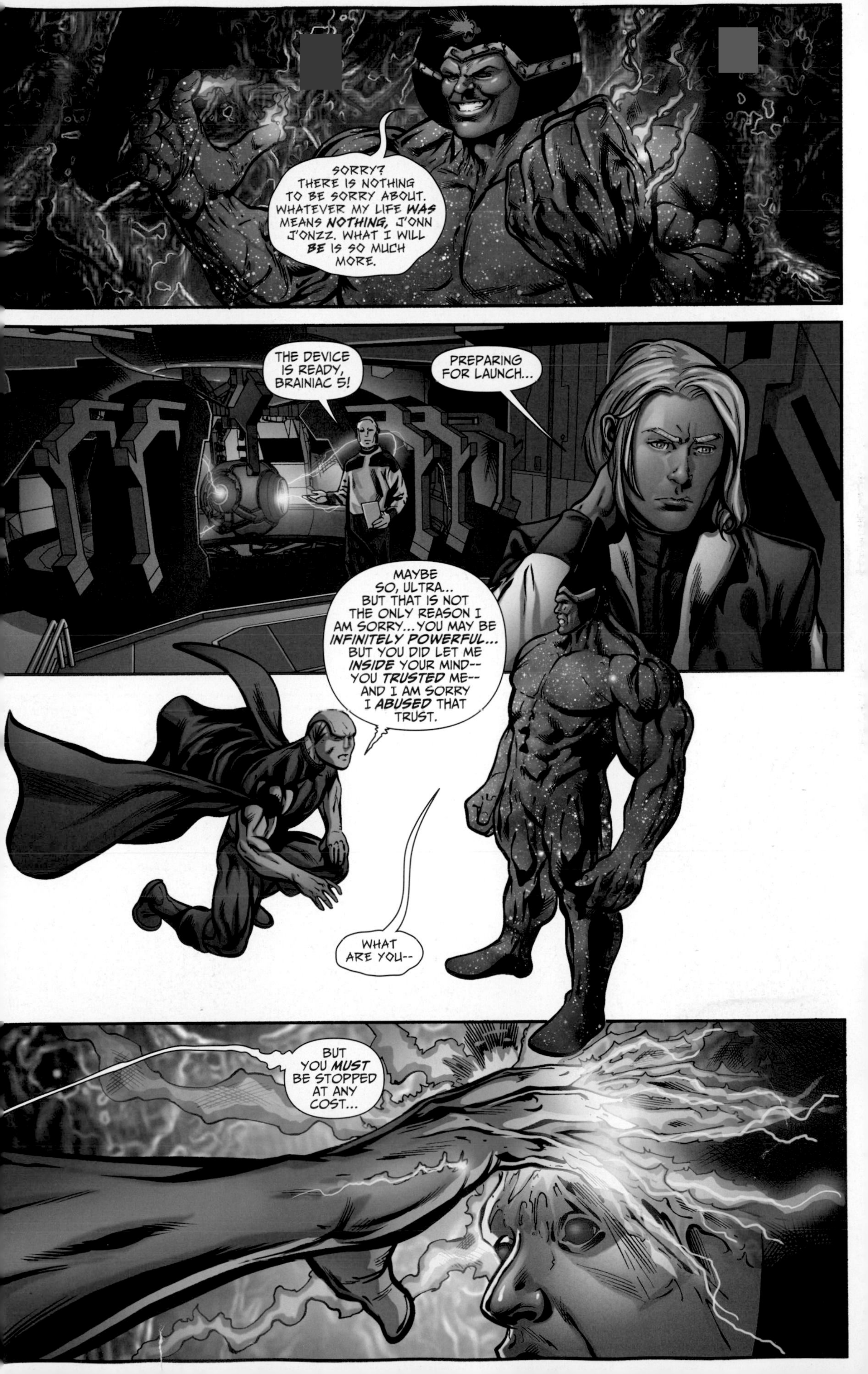

SORRY? THERE IS NOTHING TO BE SORRY ABOUT. WHATEVER MY LIFE *WAS* MEANS *NOTHING,* J'ONN J'ONZZ. WHAT I WILL *BE* IS SO MUCH MORE.
THE DEVICE IS READY, BRAINIAC 5!
PREPARING FOR LAUNCH...
MAYBE SO, ULTRA... BUT THE ONLY REASON I AM SORRY...YOU MAY BE *INFINITELY POWERFUL...* BUT YOU DID LET ME *INSIDE* YOUR MIND-- YOU *TRUSTED* ME-- AND I AM SORRY I *ABUSED* THAT TRUST.
WHAT ARE YOU--
BUT YOU *MUST* BE STOPPED AT ANY COST...

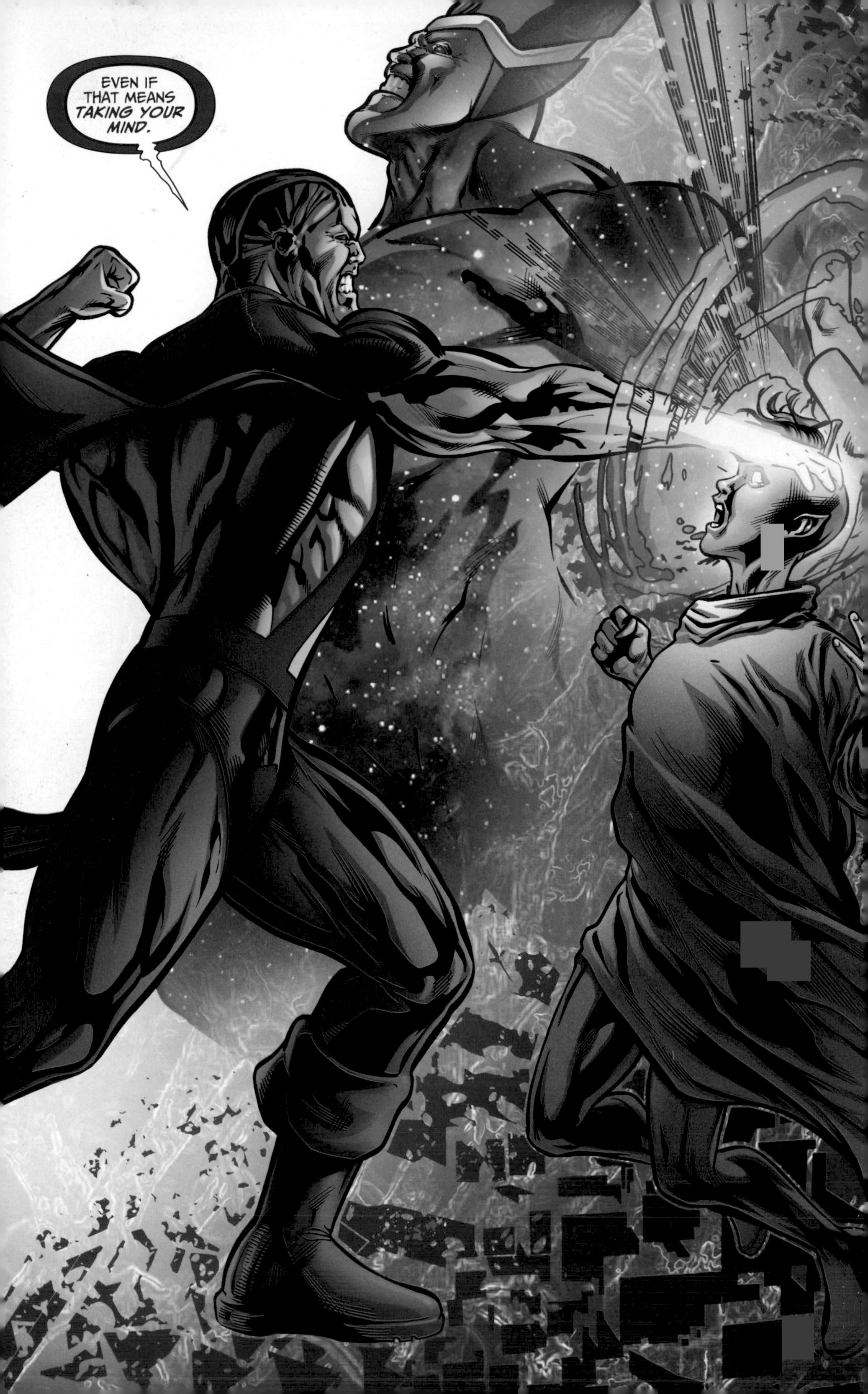
EVEN IF THAT MEANS TAKING YOUR MIND.

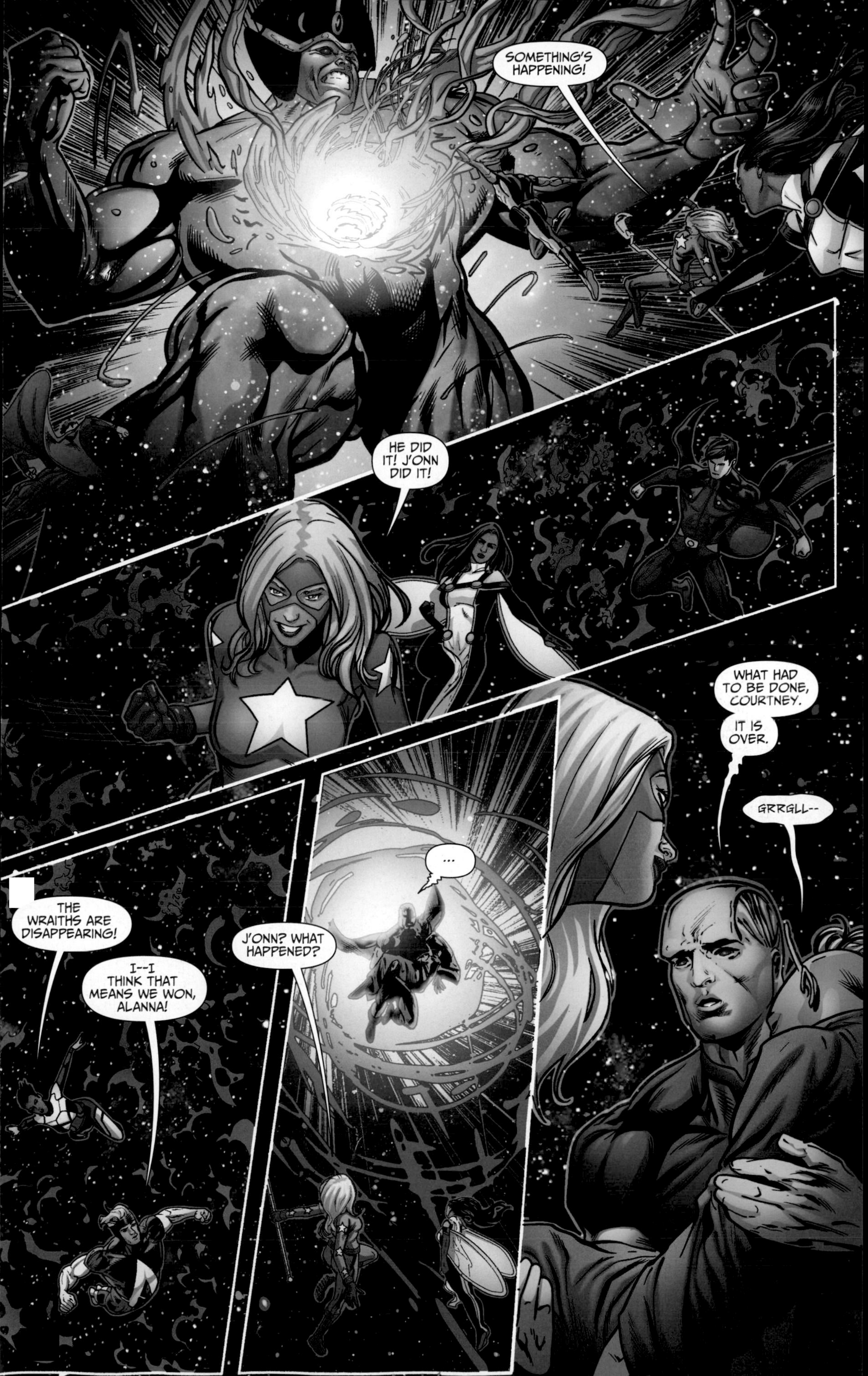
SOMETHING'S HAPPENING!
HE DID IT! J'ONN DID IT!
WHAT HAD TO BE DONE, COURTNEY.
IT IS OVER.
GRRGLL--
THE WRAITHS ARE DISAPPEARING!
I--I THINK THAT MEANS WE WON, ALANNA!
J'ONN? WHAT HAPPENED?
...

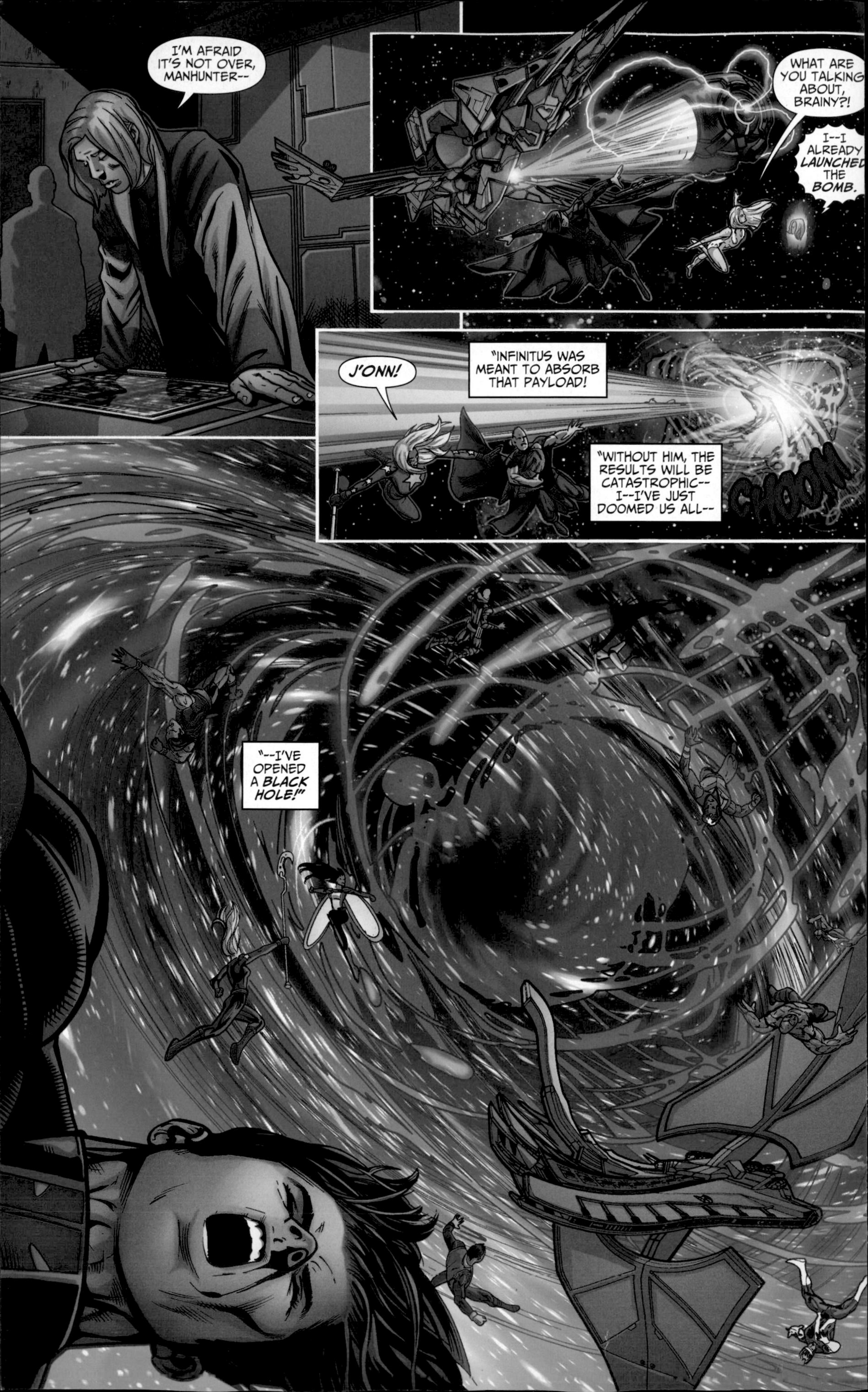
I'M AFRAID IT'S NOT OVER, MANHUNTER--
WHAT ARE YOU TALKING ABOUT, BRAINY?!
I--I ALREADY LAUNCHED THE BOMB.
"INFINITUS WAS MEANT TO ABSORB THAT PAYLOAD!
J'ONN!
"WITHOUT HIM, THE RESULTS WILL BE CATASTROPHIC-- I--I'VE JUST DOOMED US ALL--
CHOOM
"--I'VE OPENED A BLACK HOLE!"

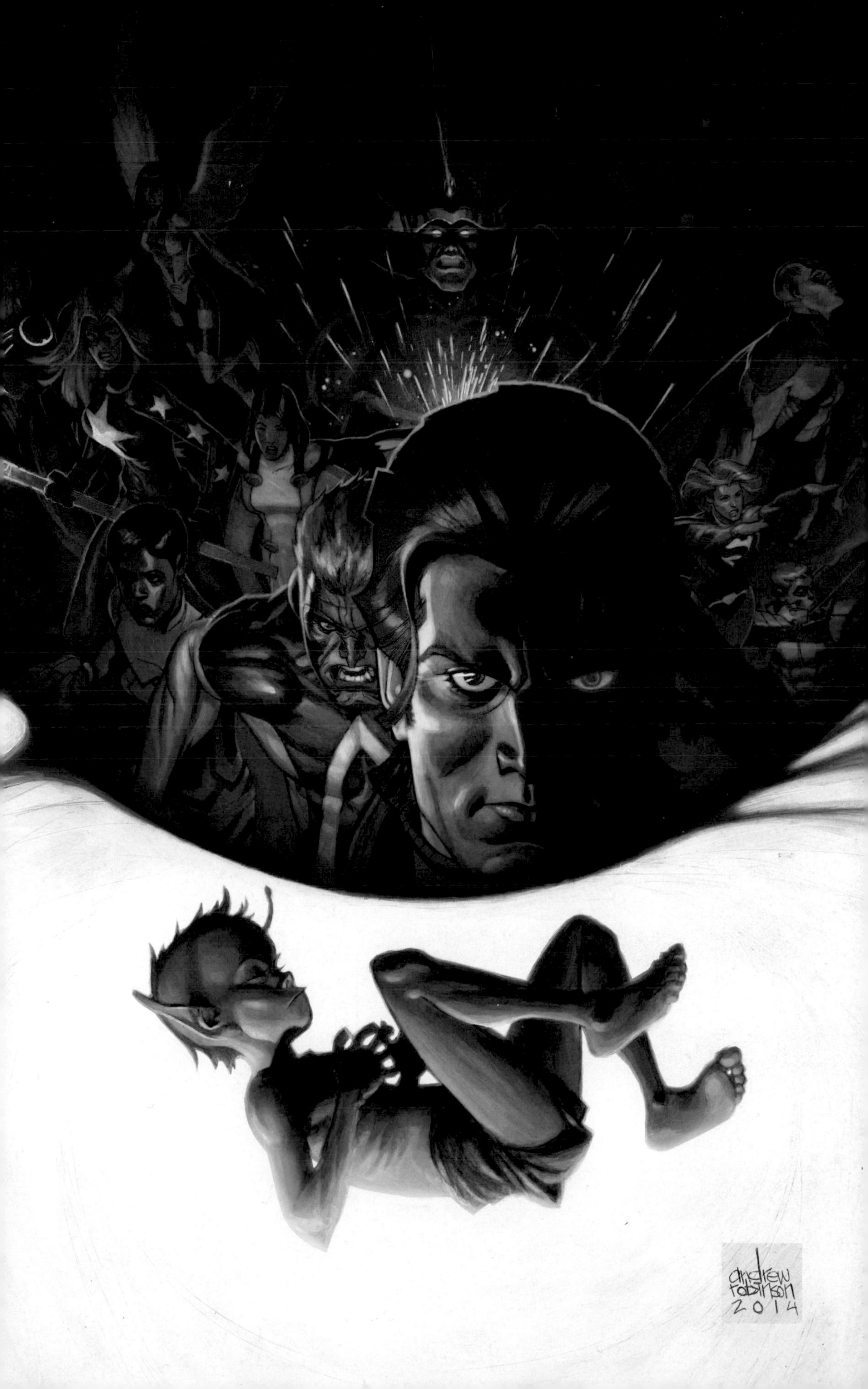
andrew robinson 2014

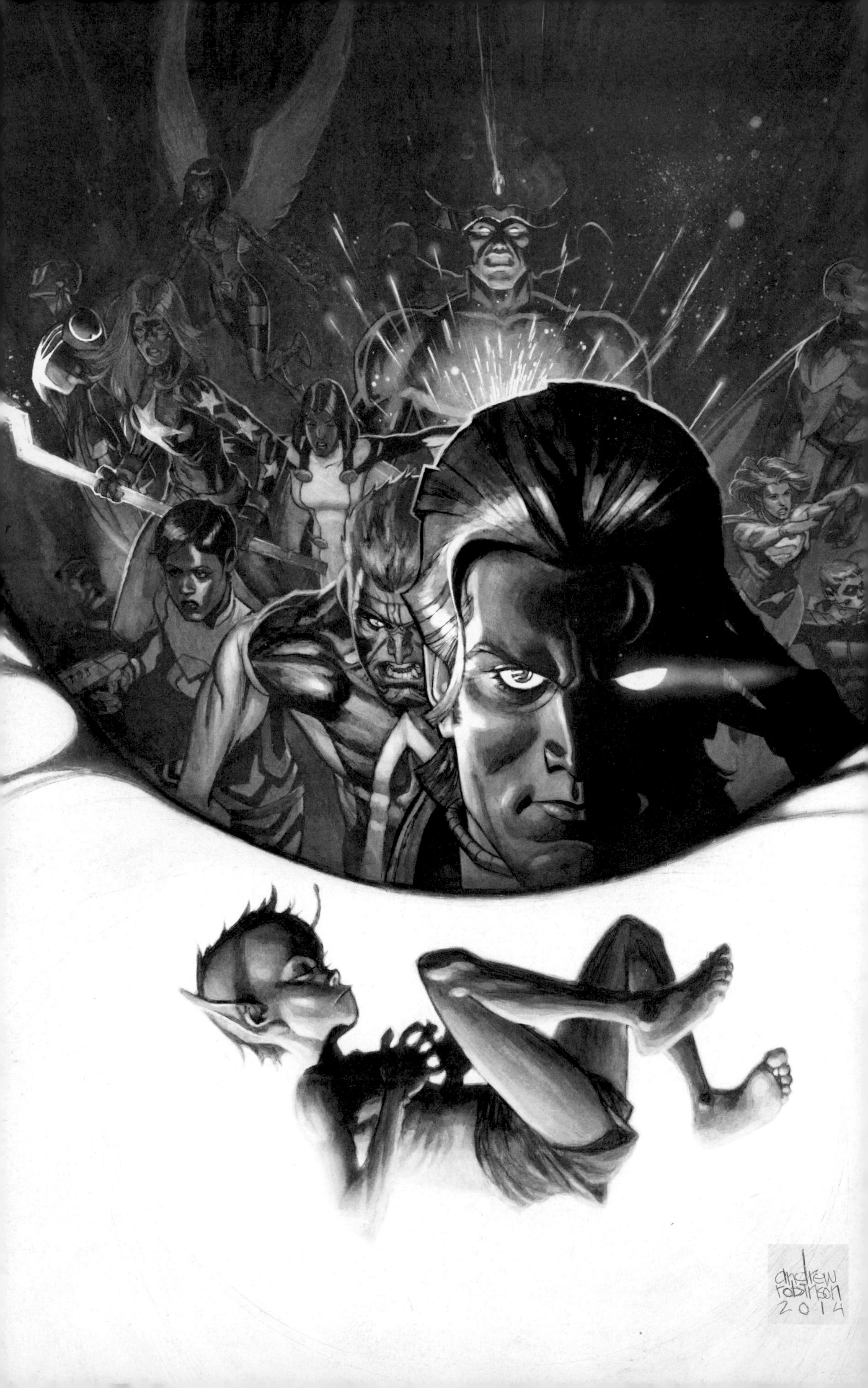
andrew robinson
2014

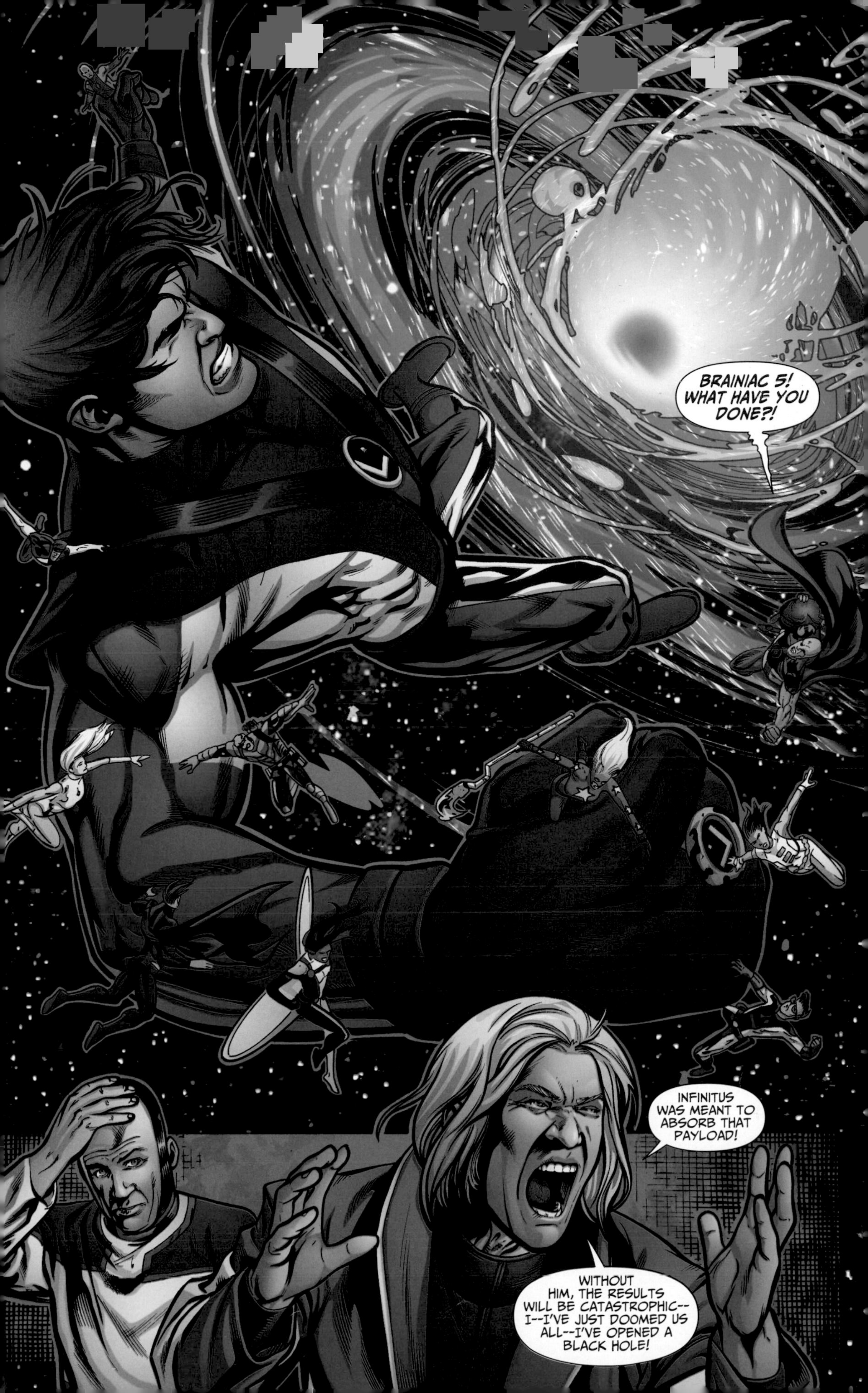
BRAINIAC 5! WHAT HAVE YOU DONE?!
INFINITUS WAS MEANT TO ABSORB THAT PAYLOAD!
WITHOUT HIM, THE RESULTS WILL BE CATASTROPHIC-- I--I'VE JUST DOOMED US ALL--I'VE OPENED A BLACK HOLE!

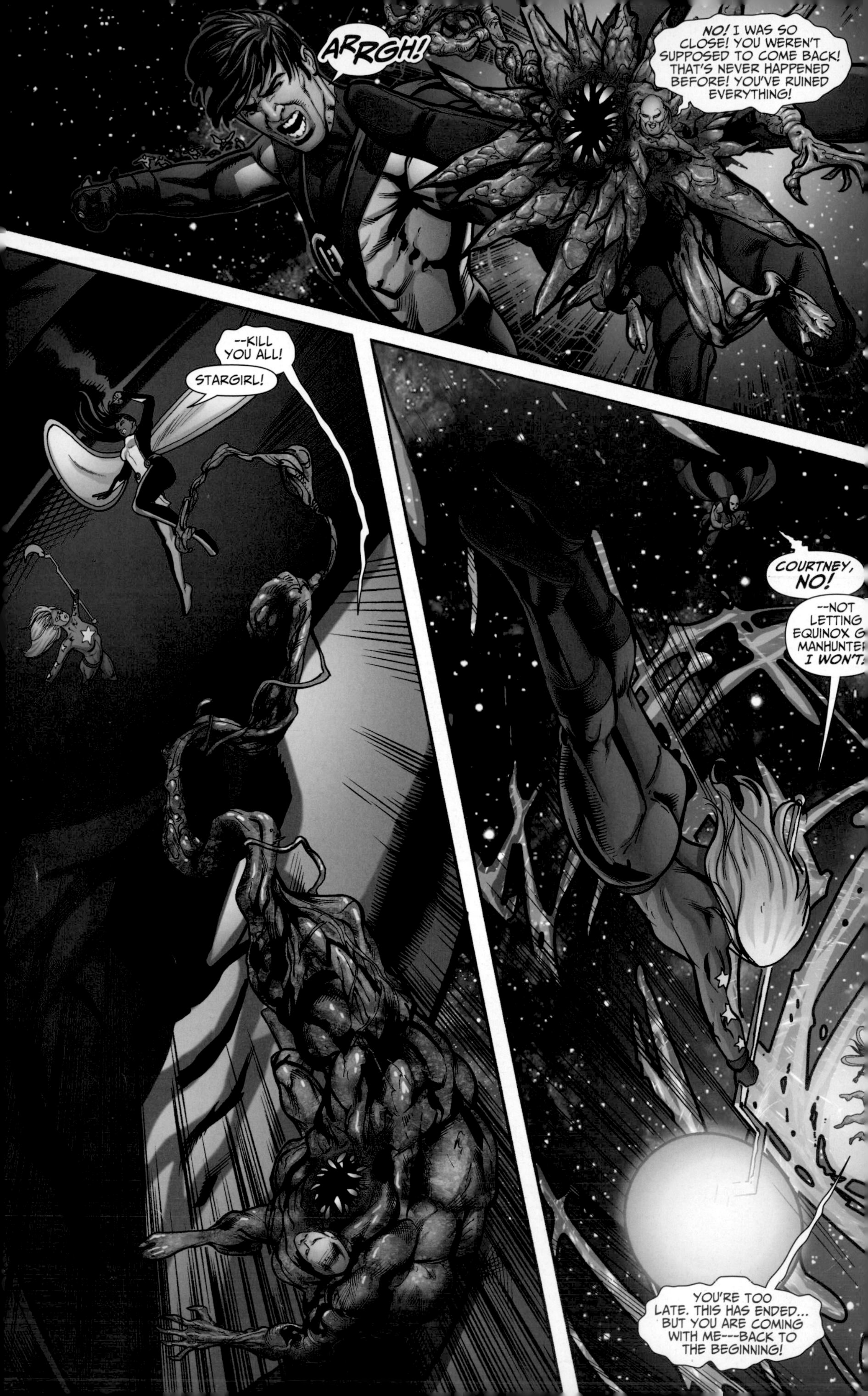
ARRGH!
NO! I WAS SO CLOSE! YOU WEREN'T SUPPOSED TO COME BACK! THAT'S NEVER HAPPENED BEFORE! YOU'VE RUINED EVERYTHING!
--KILL YOU ALL!
STARGIRL!
COURTNEY, NO!
--NOT LETTING EQUINOX G MANHUNTE I WON'T
YOU'RE TOO LATE. THIS HAS ENDED... BUT YOU ARE COMING WITH ME---BACK TO THE BEGINNING!

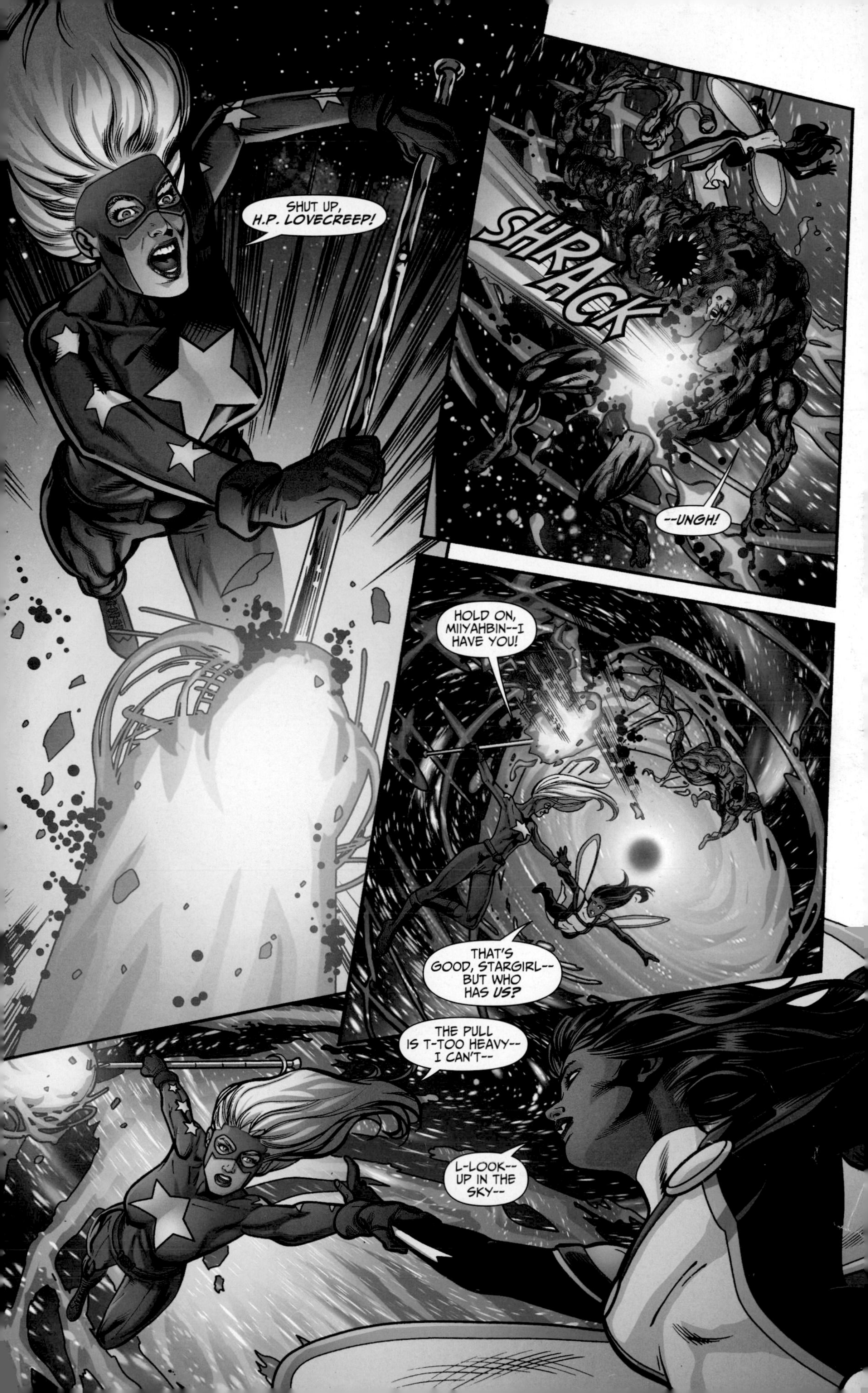
SHUT UP, H.P. LOVECREEP!
SHRACK
--UNGH!
HOLD ON, MIIYAHBIN--I HAVE YOU!
THAT'S GOOD, STARGIRL-- BUT WHO HAS US?
THE PULL IS T-TOO HEAVY-- I CAN'T--
L-LOOK-- UP IN THE SKY--

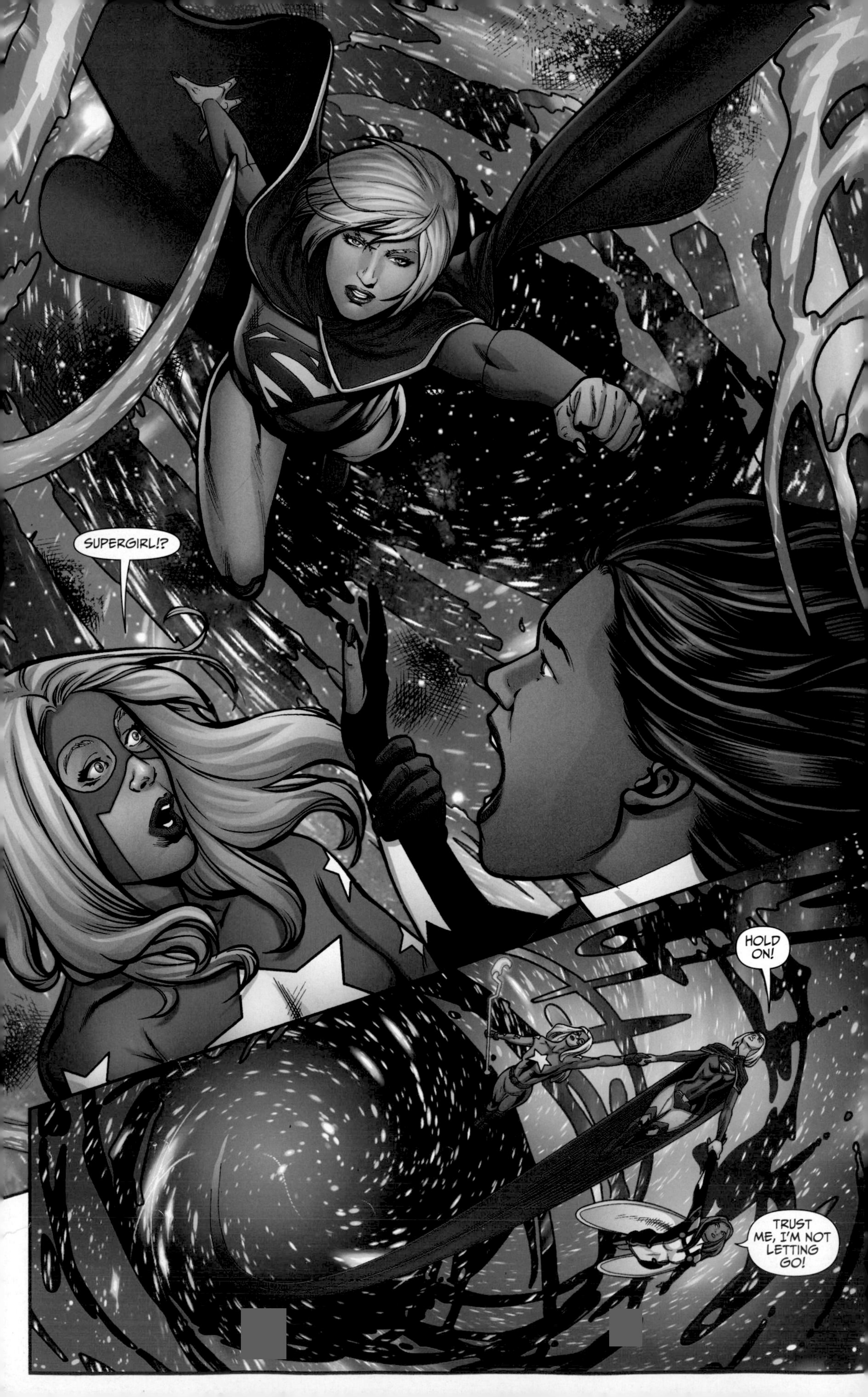
SUPERGIRL!?
HOLD ON!
TRUST ME, I'M NOT LETTING GO!

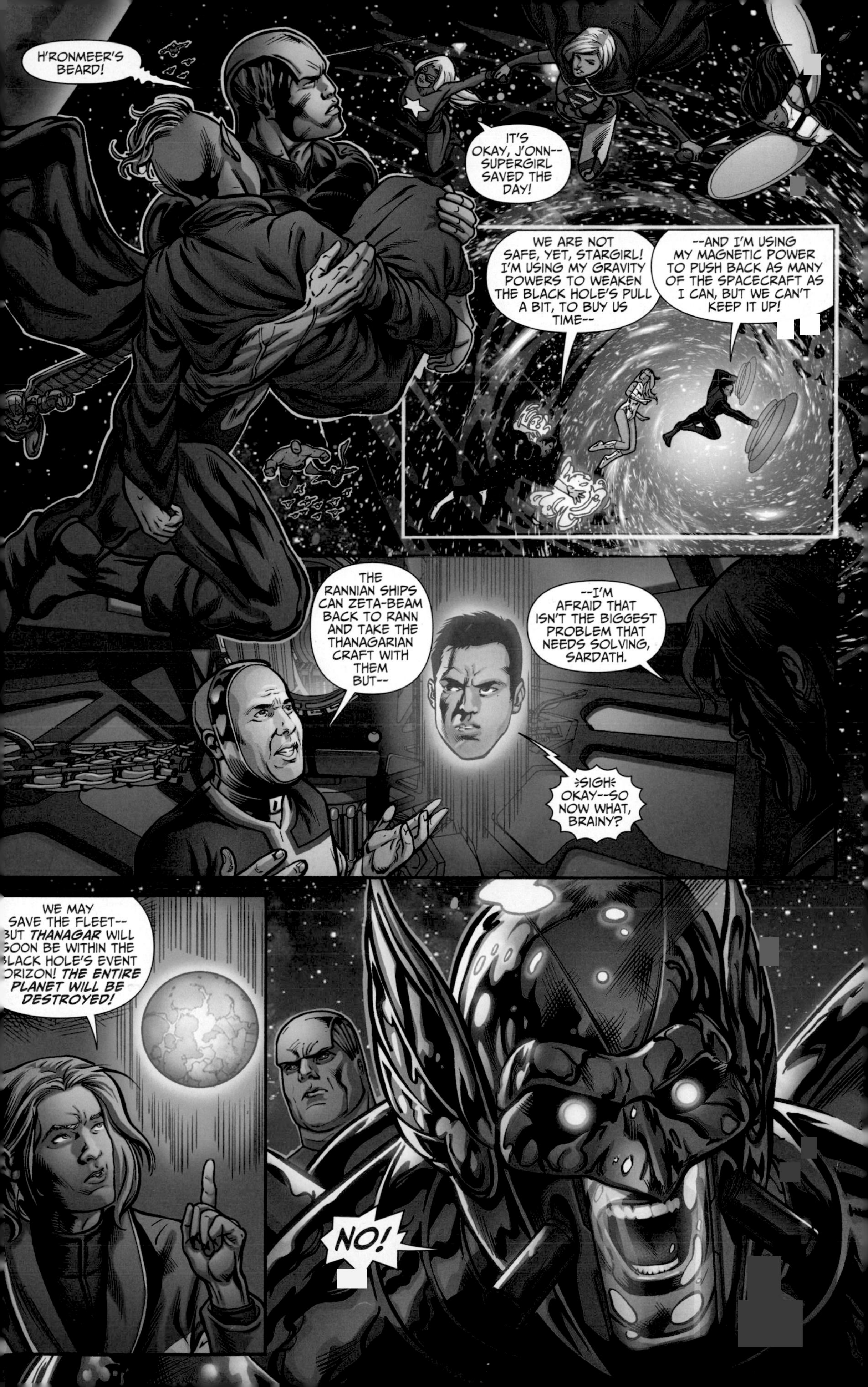
H'RONMEER'S BEARD!
IT'S OKAY, J'ONN-- SUPERGIRL SAVED THE DAY!
WE ARE NOT SAFE, YET, STARGIRL! I'M USING MY GRAVITY POWERS TO WEAKEN THE BLACK HOLE'S PULL A BIT, TO BUY US TIME--
--AND I'M USING MY MAGNETIC POWER TO PUSH BACK AS MANY OF THE SPACECRAFT AS I CAN, BUT WE CAN'T KEEP IT UP!
THE RANNIAN SHIPS CAN ZETA-BEAM BACK TO RANN AND TAKE THE THANAGARIAN CRAFT WITH THEM BUT--
--I'M AFRAID THAT ISN'T THE BIGGEST PROBLEM THAT NEEDS SOLVING, SARDATH.
SIGH OKAY--SO NOW WHAT, BRAINY?
WE MAY SAVE THE FLEET-- BUT THANAGAR WILL SOON BE WITHIN THE BLACK HOLE'S EVENT HORIZON! THE ENTIRE PLANET WILL BE DESTROYED!
NO!

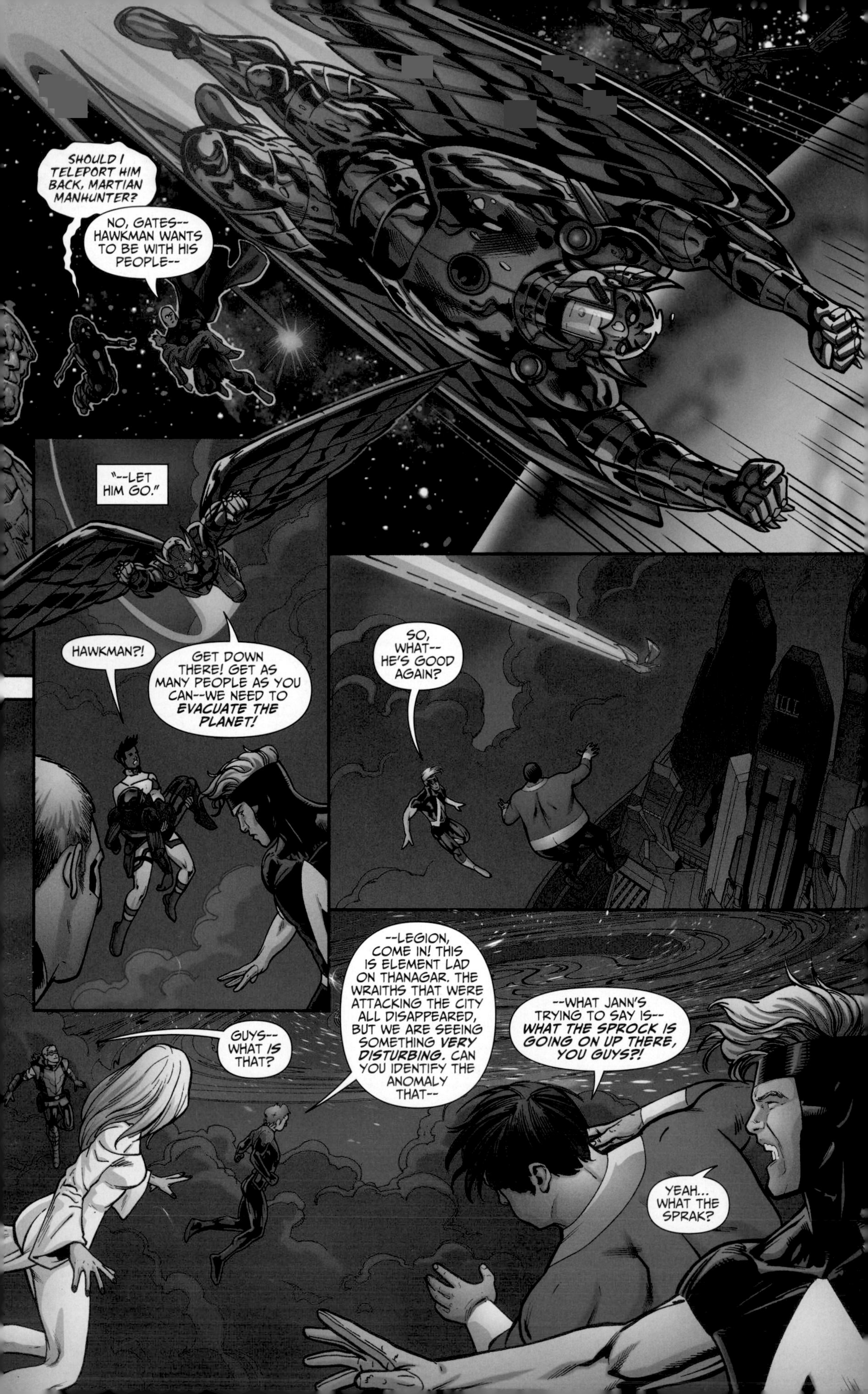

SHOULD I TELEPORT HIM BACK, MARTIAN MANHUNTER?
NO, GATES-- HAWKMAN WANTS TO BE WITH HIS PEOPLE--
"--LET HIM GO."
HAWKMAN?!
GET DOWN THERE! GET AS MANY PEOPLE AS YOU CAN--WE NEED TO EVACUATE THE PLANET!
SO, WHAT-- HE'S GOOD AGAIN?
GUYS-- WHAT IS THAT?
--LEGION, COME IN! THIS IS ELEMENT LAD ON THANAGAR. THE WRAITHS THAT WERE ATTACKING THE CITY ALL DISAPPEARED, BUT WE ARE SEEING SOMETHING VERY DISTURBING. CAN YOU IDENTIFY THE ANOMALY THAT--
--WHAT JANN'S TRYING TO SAY IS-- WHAT THE SPROCK IS GOING ON UP THERE, YOU GUYS?!
YEAH... WHAT THE SPRAK?

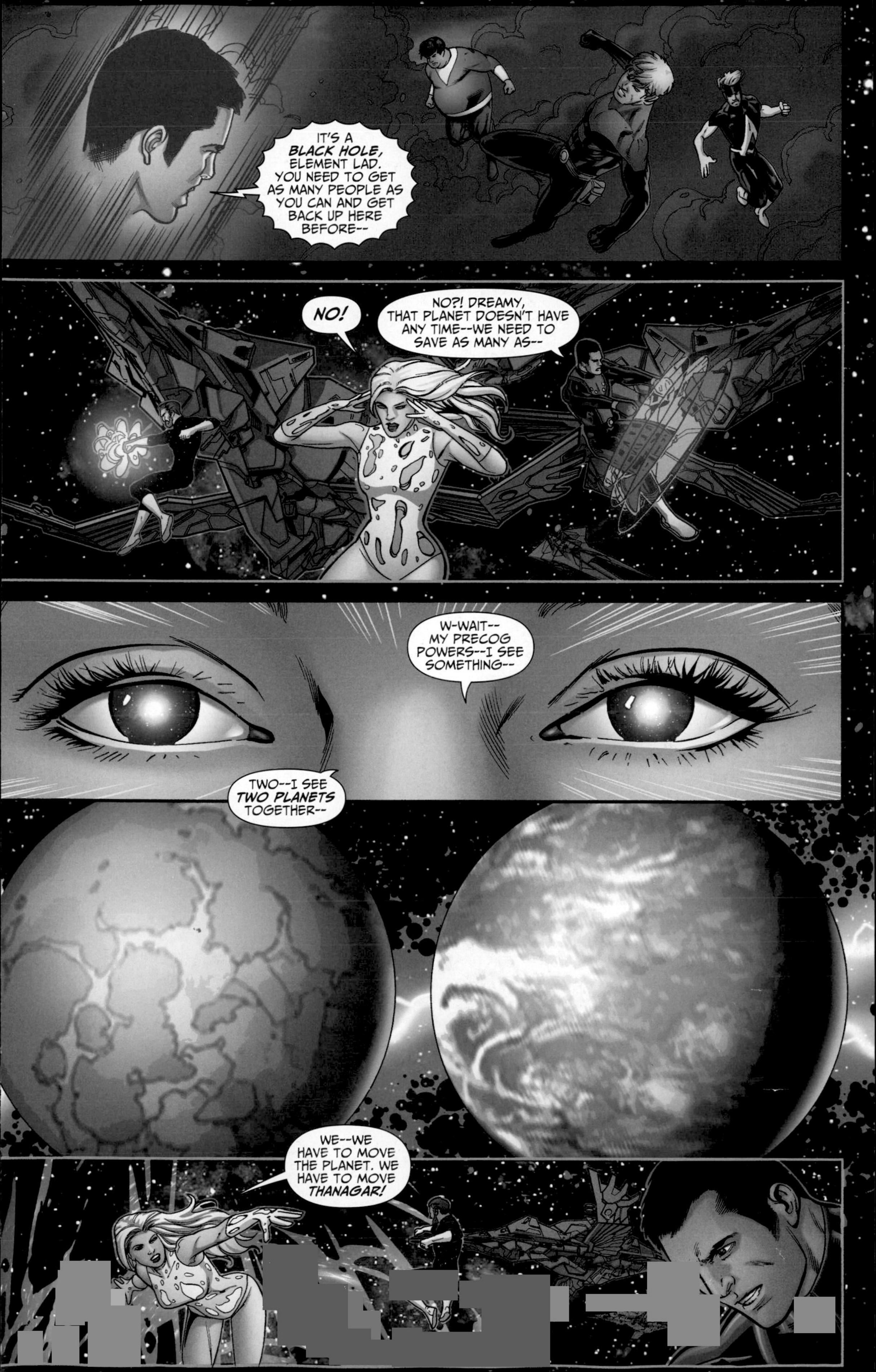
IT'S A **BLACK HOLE,** ELEMENT LAD. YOU NEED TO GET AS MANY PEOPLE AS YOU CAN AND GET BACK UP HERE BEFORE--
NO!
NO?! DREAMY, THAT PLANET DOESN'T HAVE ANY TIME--WE NEED TO SAVE AS MANY AS--
W-WAIT-- MY PRECOG POWERS--I SEE SOMETHING--
TWO--I SEE ***TWO PLANETS*** TOGETHER--
WE--WE HAVE TO MOVE THE PLANET. WE HAVE TO MOVE ***THANAGAR!***

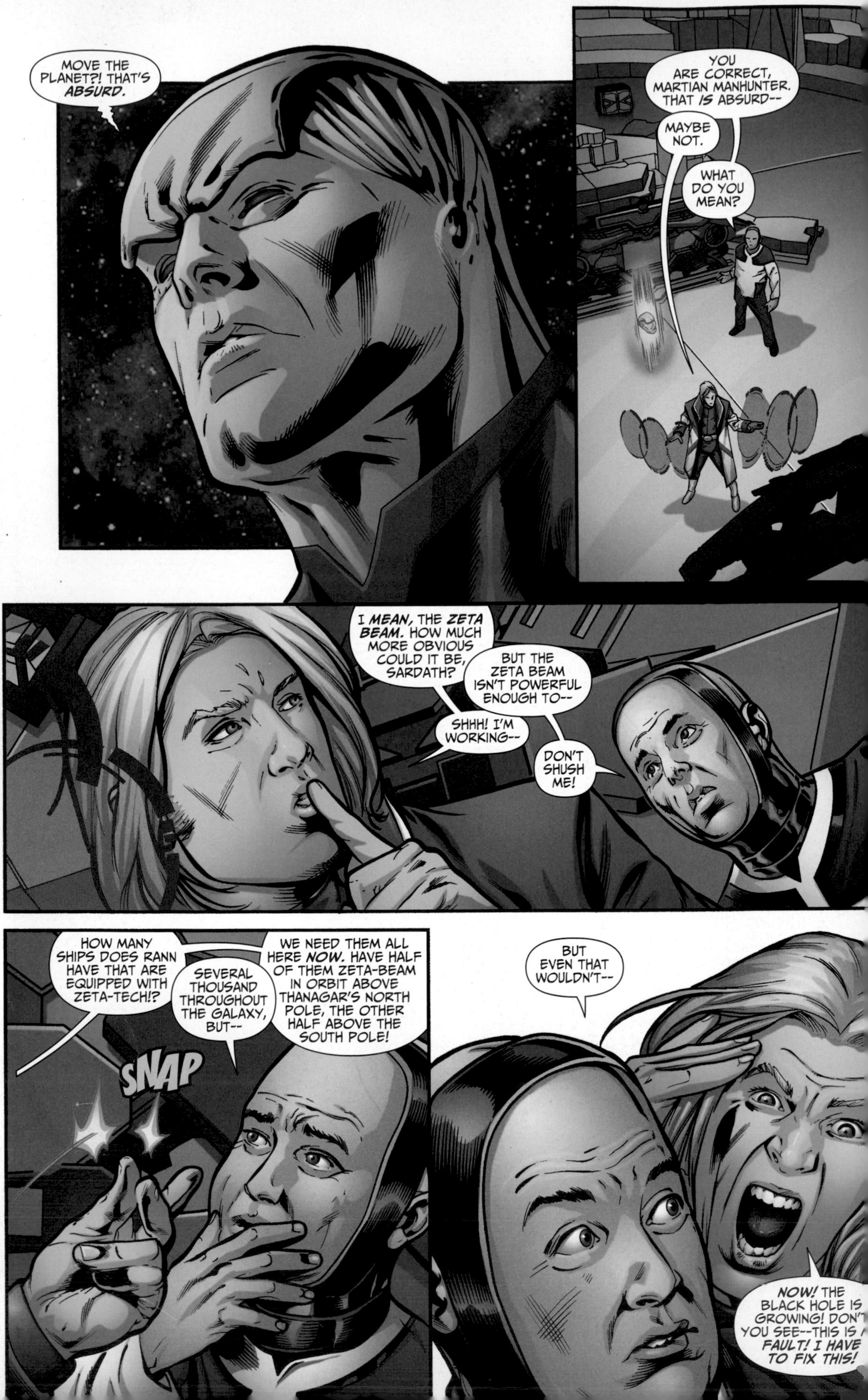
MOVE THE PLANET?! THAT'S ABSURD.
YOU ARE CORRECT, MARTIAN MANHUNTER. THAT IS ABSURD--
MAYBE NOT.
WHAT DO YOU MEAN?
I MEAN, THE ZETA BEAM. HOW MUCH MORE OBVIOUS COULD IT BE, SARDATH?
BUT THE ZETA BEAM ISN'T POWERFUL ENOUGH TO--
SHHH! I'M WORKING--
DON'T SHUSH ME!
HOW MANY SHIPS DOES RANN HAVE THAT ARE EQUIPPED WITH ZETA-TECH!?
SEVERAL THOUSAND THROUGHOUT THE GALAXY, BUT--
WE NEED THEM ALL HERE NOW. HAVE HALF OF THEM ZETA-BEAM IN ORBIT ABOVE THANAGAR'S NORTH POLE, THE OTHER HALF ABOVE THE SOUTH POLE!
SNAP
BUT EVEN THAT WOULDN'T--
NOW! THE BLACK HOLE IS GROWING! DON'T YOU SEE--THIS IS FAULT! I HAVE TO FIX THIS!

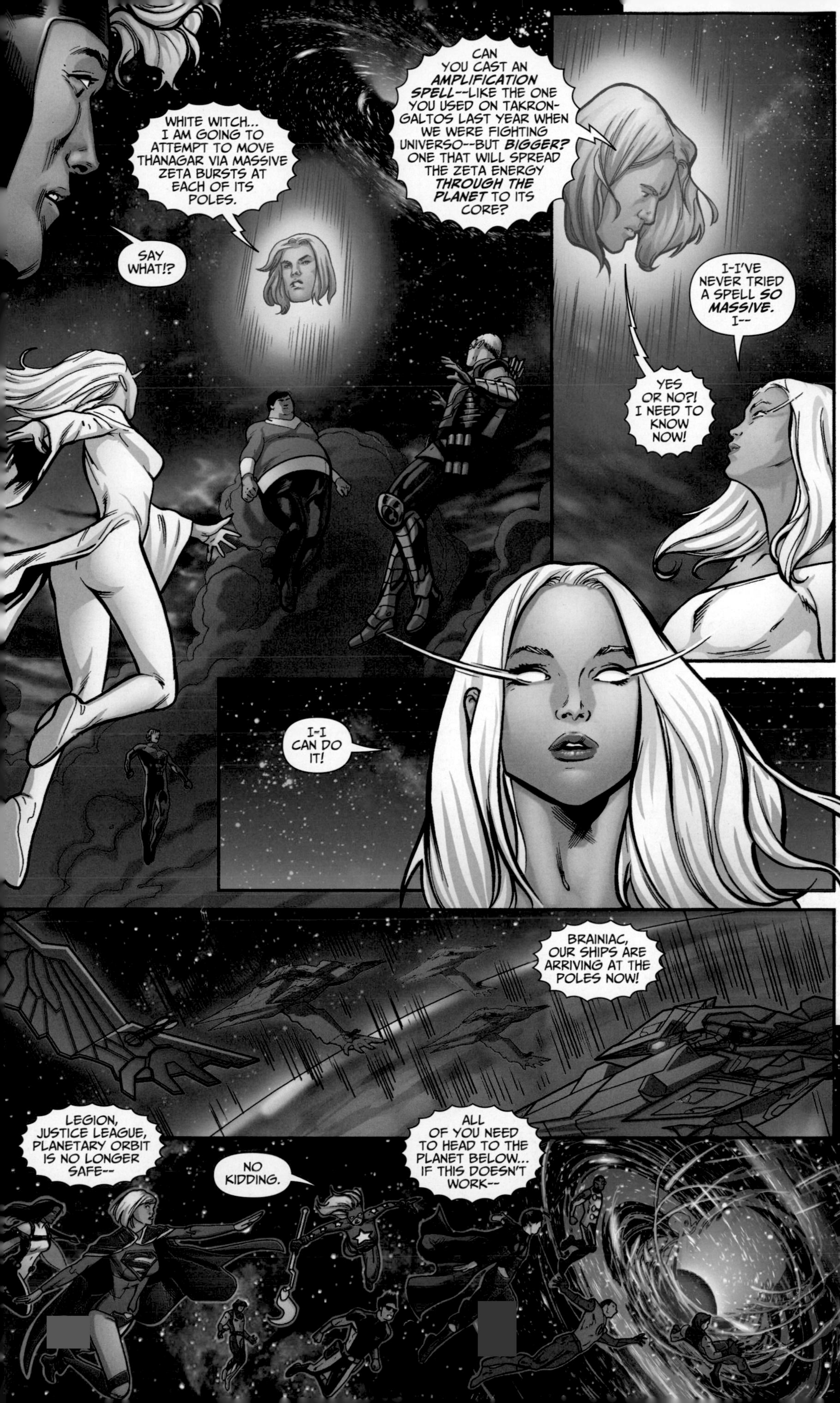
WHITE WITCH... I AM GOING TO ATTEMPT TO MOVE THANAGAR VIA MASSIVE ZETA BURSTS AT EACH OF ITS POLES.
SAY WHAT!?
CAN YOU CAST AN AMPLIFICATION SPELL--LIKE THE ONE YOU USED ON TAKRON-GALTOS LAST YEAR WHEN WE WERE FIGHTING UNIVERSO--BUT BIGGER? ONE THAT WILL SPREAD THE ZETA ENERGY THROUGH THE PLANET TO ITS CORE?
I-I'VE NEVER TRIED A SPELL SO MASSIVE. I--
YES OR NO?! I NEED TO KNOW NOW!
I-I CAN DO IT!
BRAINIAC, OUR SHIPS ARE ARRIVING AT THE POLES NOW!
LEGION, JUSTICE LEAGUE, PLANETARY ORBIT IS NO LONGER SAFE--
NO KIDDING.
ALL OF YOU NEED TO HEAD TO THE PLANET BELOW... IF THIS DOESN'T WORK--

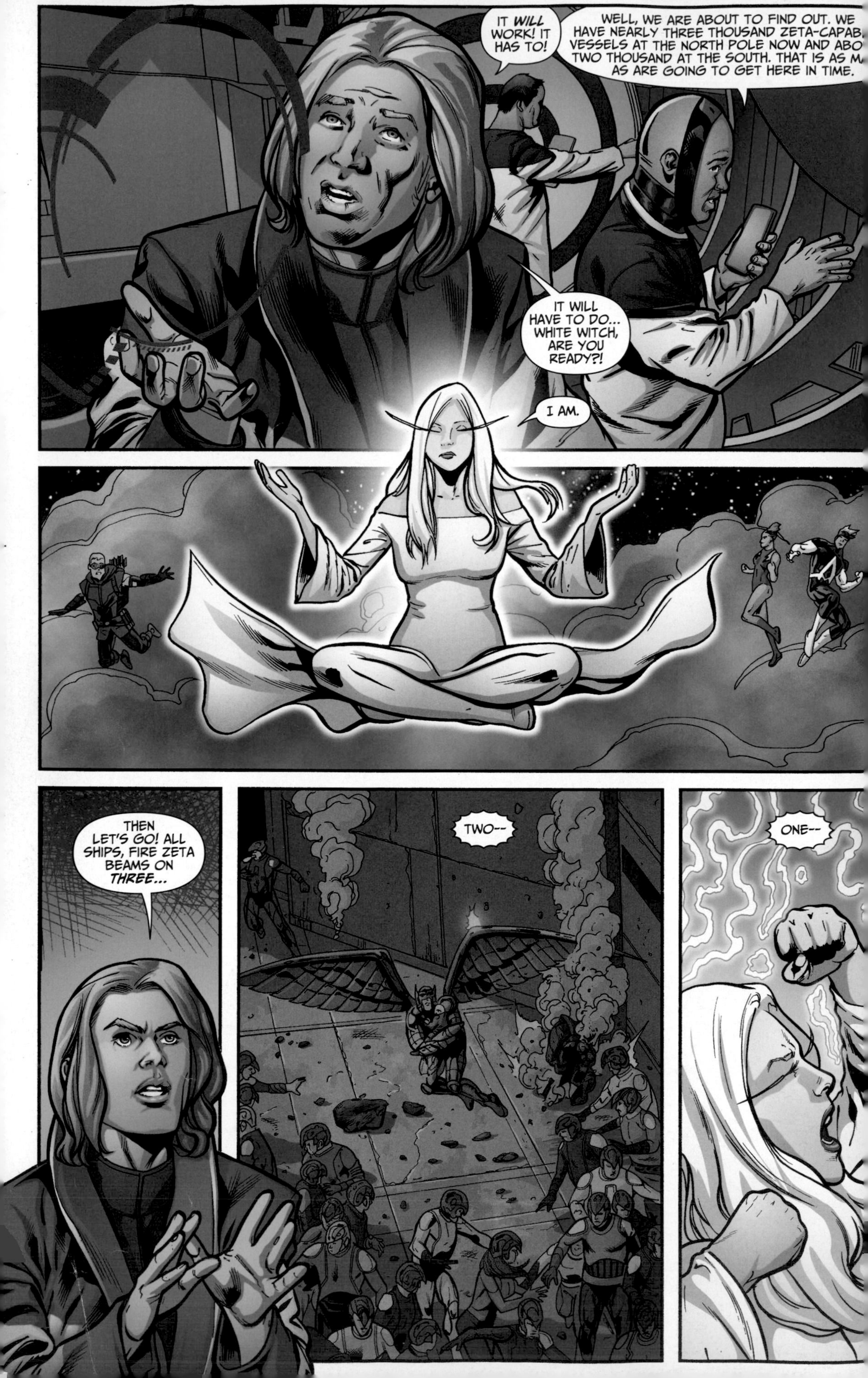
IT WILL WORK! IT HAS TO!
WELL, WE ARE ABOUT TO FIND OUT. WE HAVE NEARLY THREE THOUSAND ZETA-CAPAB VESSELS AT THE NORTH POLE NOW AND ABO TWO THOUSAND AT THE SOUTH. THAT IS AS M AS ARE GOING TO GET HERE IN TIME.
IT WILL HAVE TO DO... WHITE WITCH, ARE YOU READY?!
I AM.
THEN LET'S GO! ALL SHIPS, FIRE ZETA BEAMS ON THREE...
TWO--
ONE--

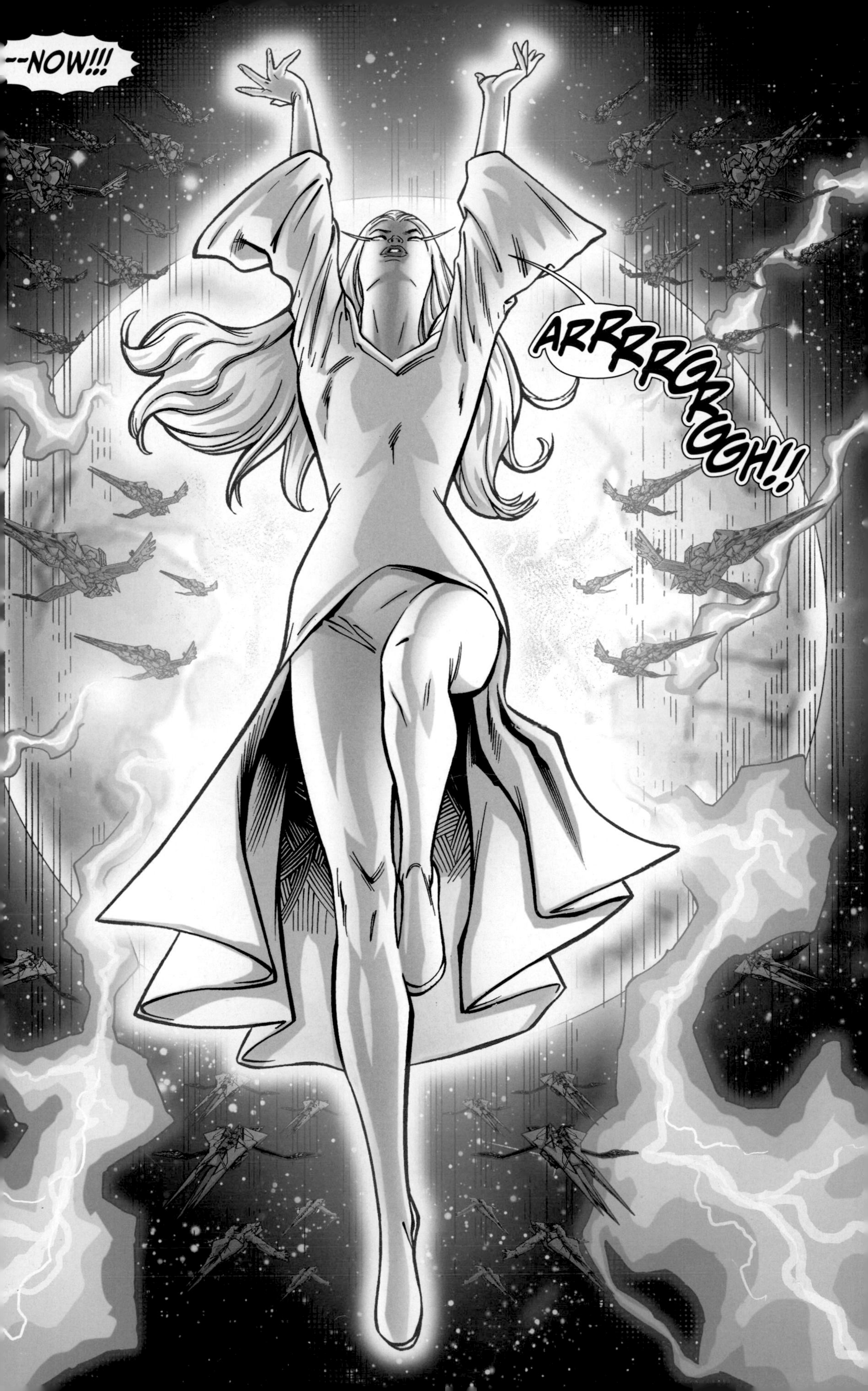
--NOW!!!
ARRRRRGGGGH!!

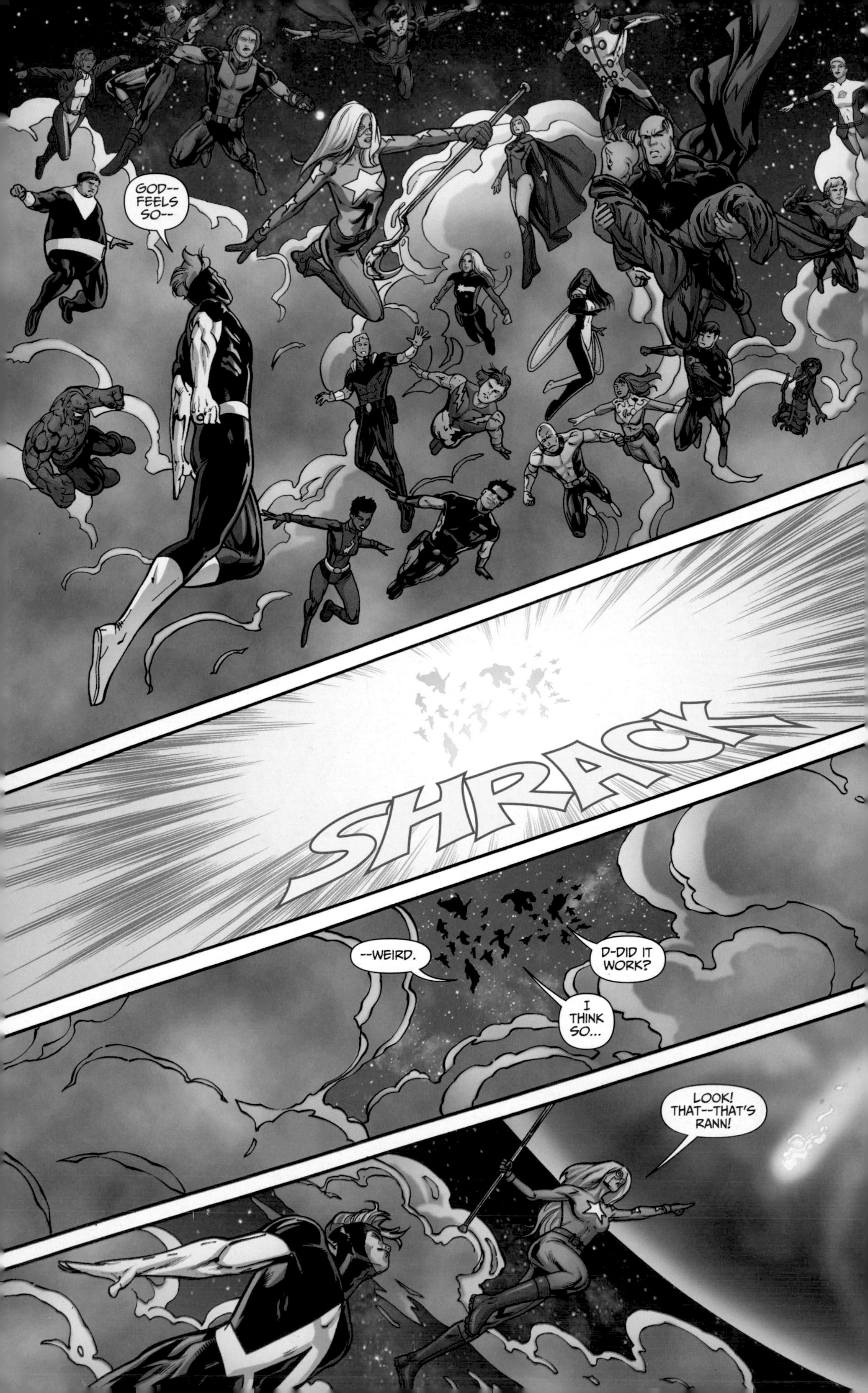

GOD--
FEELS
SO--
SHRACK
--WEIRD.
D-DID IT
WORK?
I
THINK
SO...
LOOK!
THAT--THAT'S
RANN!

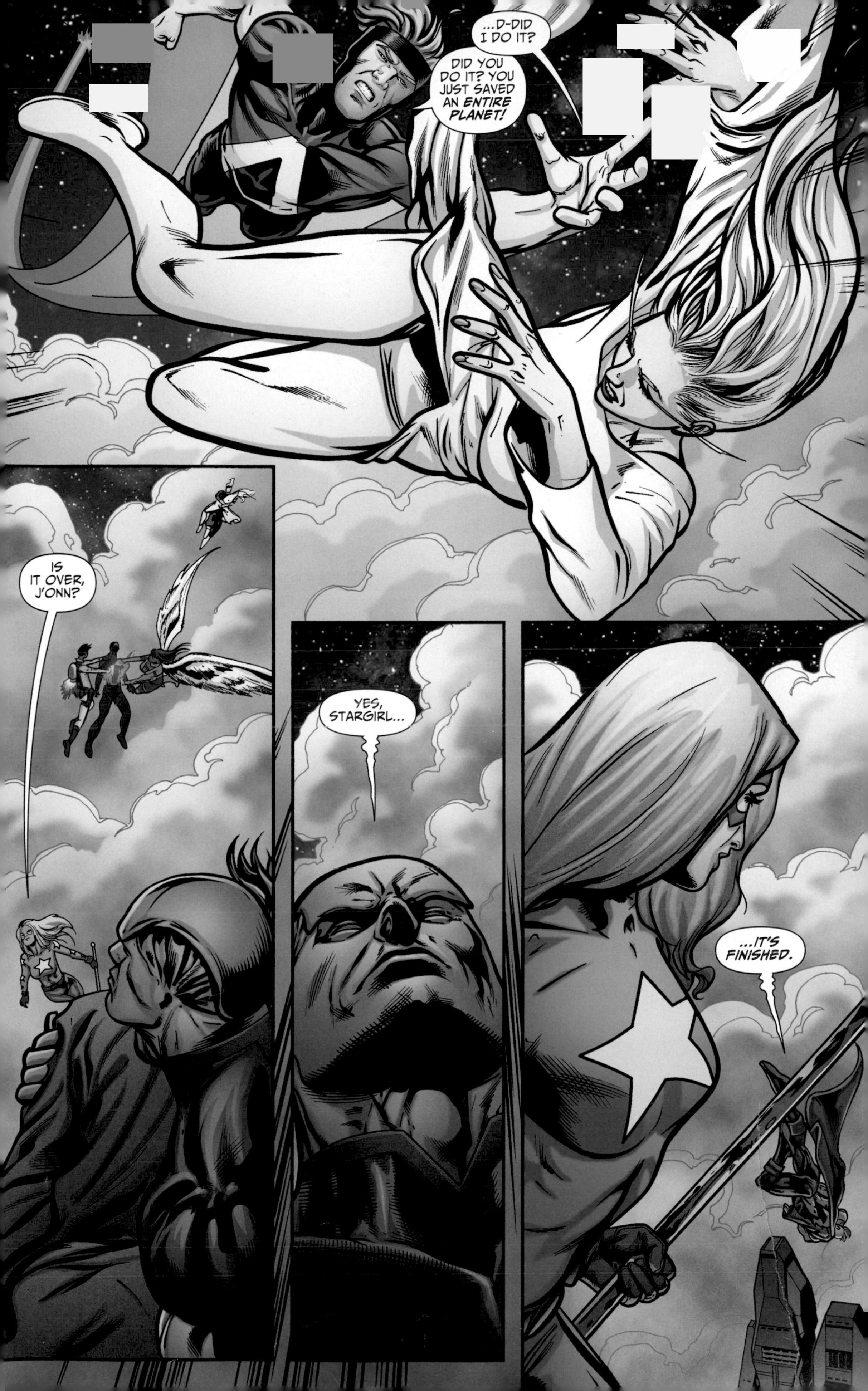
...D-DID I DO IT?
DID YOU DO IT? YOU JUST SAVED AN ENTIRE PLANET!
IS IT OVER, J'ONN?
YES, STARGIRL...
...IT'S FINISHED.

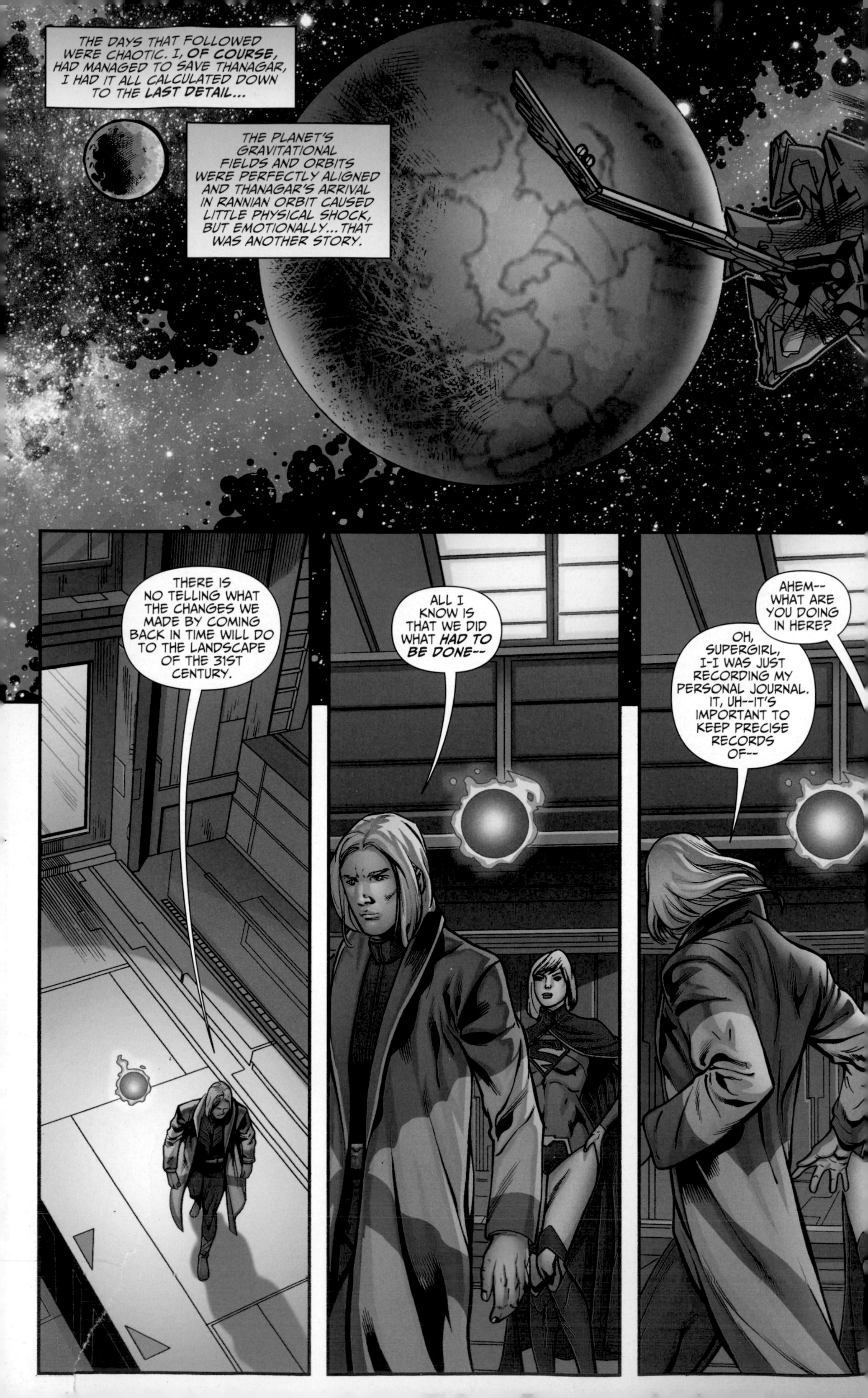
THE DAYS THAT FOLLOWED WERE CHAOTIC. I, OF COURSE, HAD MANAGED TO SAVE THANAGAR, I HAD IT ALL CALCULATED DOWN TO THE LAST DETAIL...
THE PLANET'S GRAVITATIONAL FIELDS AND ORBITS WERE PERFECTLY ALIGNED AND THANAGAR'S ARRIVAL IN RANNIAN ORBIT CAUSED LITTLE PHYSICAL SHOCK, BUT EMOTIONALLY...THAT WAS ANOTHER STORY.
THERE IS NO TELLING WHAT THE CHANGES WE MADE BY COMING BACK IN TIME WILL DO TO THE LANDSCAPE OF THE 31ST CENTURY.
ALL I KNOW IS THAT WE DID WHAT HAD TO BE DONE--
AHEM-- WHAT ARE YOU DOING IN HERE?
OH, SUPERGIRL, I-I WAS JUST RECORDING MY PERSONAL JOURNAL. IT, UH--IT'S IMPORTANT TO KEEP PRECISE RECORDS OF--

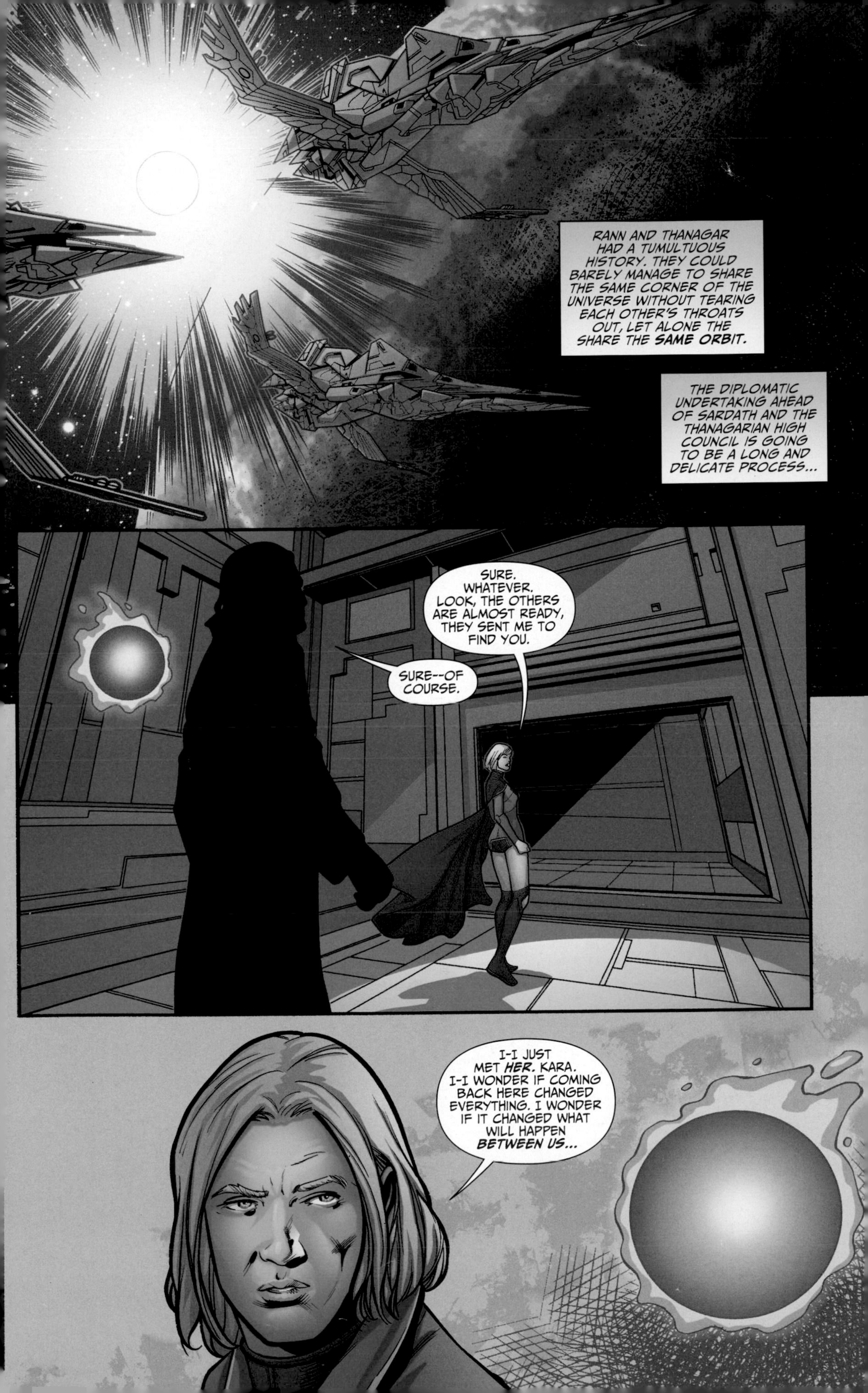
RANN AND THANAGAR HAD A TUMULTUOUS HISTORY. THEY COULD BARELY MANAGE TO SHARE THE SAME CORNER OF THE UNIVERSE WITHOUT TEARING EACH OTHER'S THROATS OUT, LET ALONE THE SHARE THE SAME ORBIT.
THE DIPLOMATIC UNDERTAKING AHEAD OF SARDATH AND THE THANAGARIAN HIGH COUNCIL IS GOING TO BE A LONG AND DELICATE PROCESS...
SURE. WHATEVER. LOOK, THE OTHERS ARE ALMOST READY, THEY SENT ME TO FIND YOU.
SURE--OF COURSE.
I-I JUST MET HER. KARA. I-I WONDER IF COMING BACK HERE CHANGED EVERYTHING. I WONDER IF IT CHANGED WHAT WILL HAPPEN BETWEEN US...

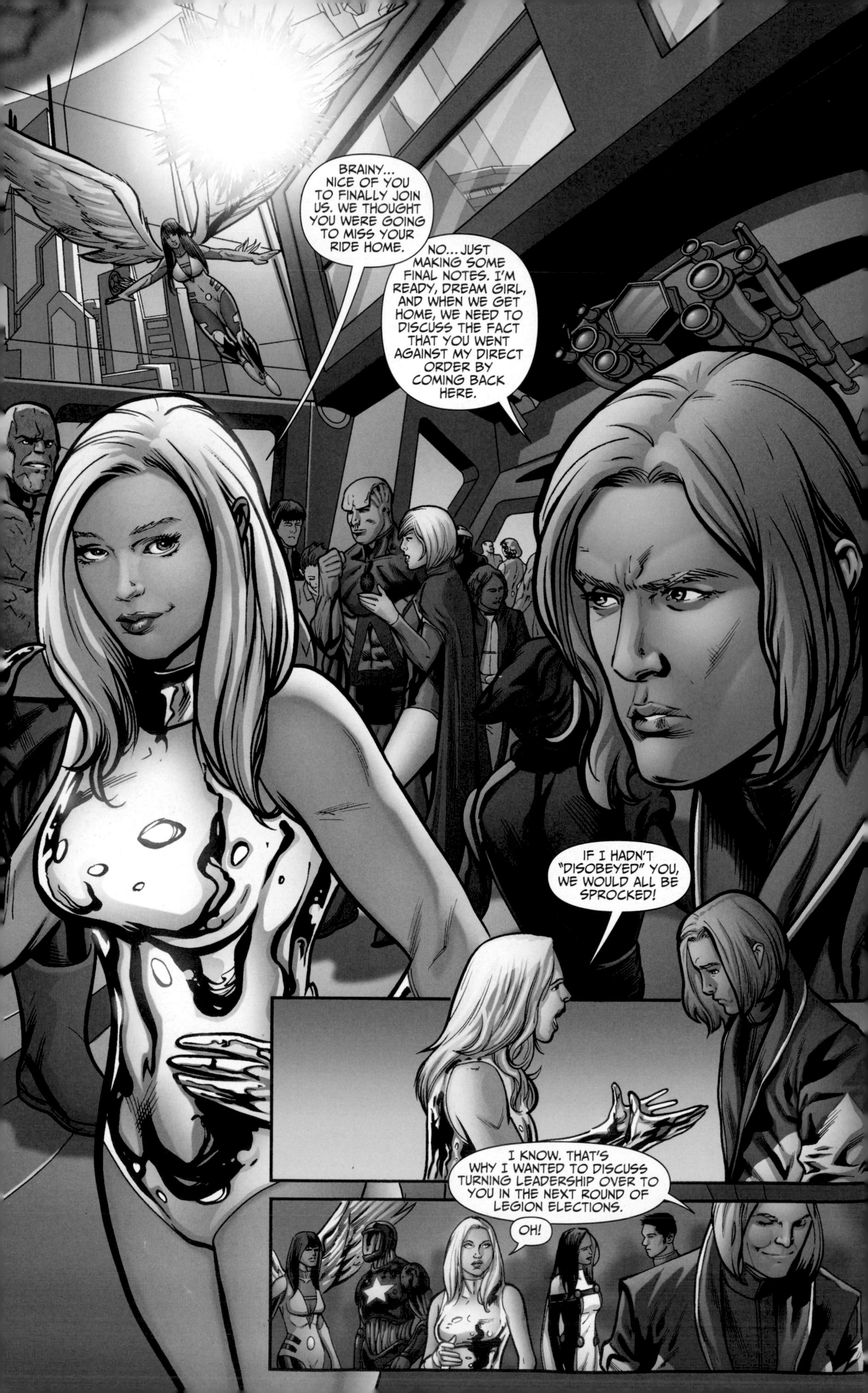
BRAINY... NICE OF YOU TO FINALLY JOIN US. WE THOUGHT YOU WERE GOING TO MISS YOUR RIDE HOME.
NO... JUST MAKING SOME FINAL NOTES. I'M READY, DREAM GIRL, AND WHEN WE GET HOME, WE NEED TO DISCUSS THE FACT THAT YOU WENT AGAINST MY DIRECT ORDER BY COMING BACK HERE.
IF I HADN'T "DISOBEYED" YOU, WE WOULD ALL BE SPROCKED!
I KNOW. THAT'S WHY I WANTED TO DISCUSS TURNING LEADERSHIP OVER TO YOU IN THE NEXT ROUND OF LEGION ELECTIONS.
OH!

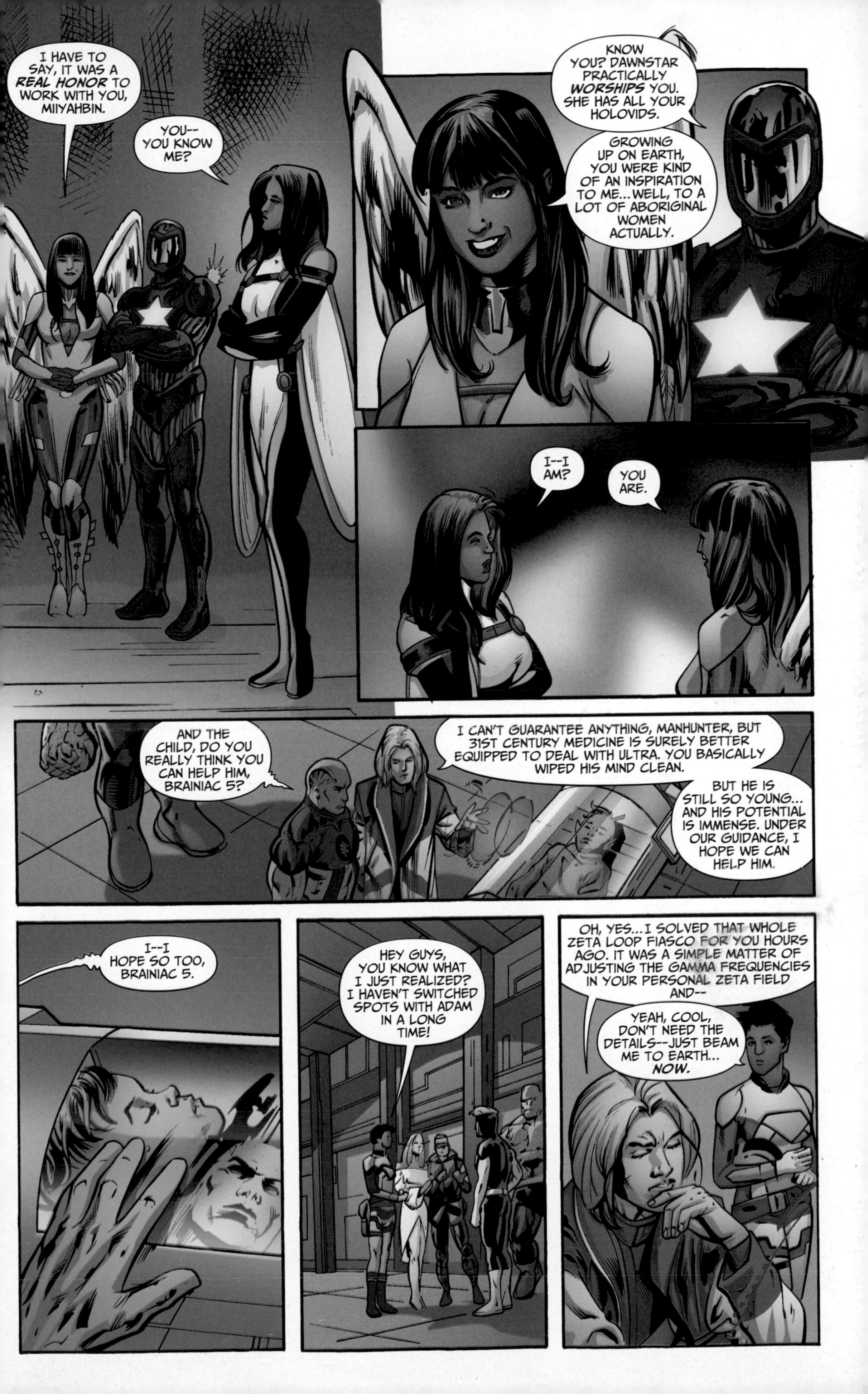
I HAVE TO SAY, IT WAS A **REAL HONOR** TO WORK WITH YOU, MIIYAHBIN.
YOU-- YOU KNOW ME?
KNOW YOU? DAWNSTAR PRACTICALLY **WORSHIPS** YOU. SHE HAS ALL YOUR HOLOVIDS.
GROWING UP ON EARTH, YOU WERE KIND OF AN INSPIRATION TO ME...WELL, TO A LOT OF ABORIGINAL WOMEN ACTUALLY.
I--I AM?
YOU ARE.
AND THE CHILD, DO YOU REALLY THINK YOU CAN HELP HIM, BRAINIAC 5?
I CAN'T GUARANTEE ANYTHING, MANHUNTER, BUT 31ST CENTURY MEDICINE IS SURELY BETTER EQUIPPED TO DEAL WITH ULTRA. YOU BASICALLY WIPED HIS MIND CLEAN.
BUT HE IS STILL SO YOUNG... AND HIS POTENTIAL IS IMMENSE. UNDER OUR GUIDANCE, I HOPE WE CAN HELP HIM.
I--I HOPE SO TOO, BRAINIAC 5.
HEY GUYS, YOU KNOW WHAT I JUST REALIZED? I HAVEN'T SWITCHED SPOTS WITH ADAM IN A LONG TIME!
OH, YES...I SOLVED THAT WHOLE ZETA LOOP FIASCO FOR YOU HOURS AGO. IT WAS A SIMPLE MATTER OF ADJUSTING THE GAMMA FREQUENCIES IN YOUR PERSONAL ZETA FIELD AND--
YEAH, COOL, DON'T NEED THE DETAILS--JUST BEAM ME TO EARTH... **NOW.**

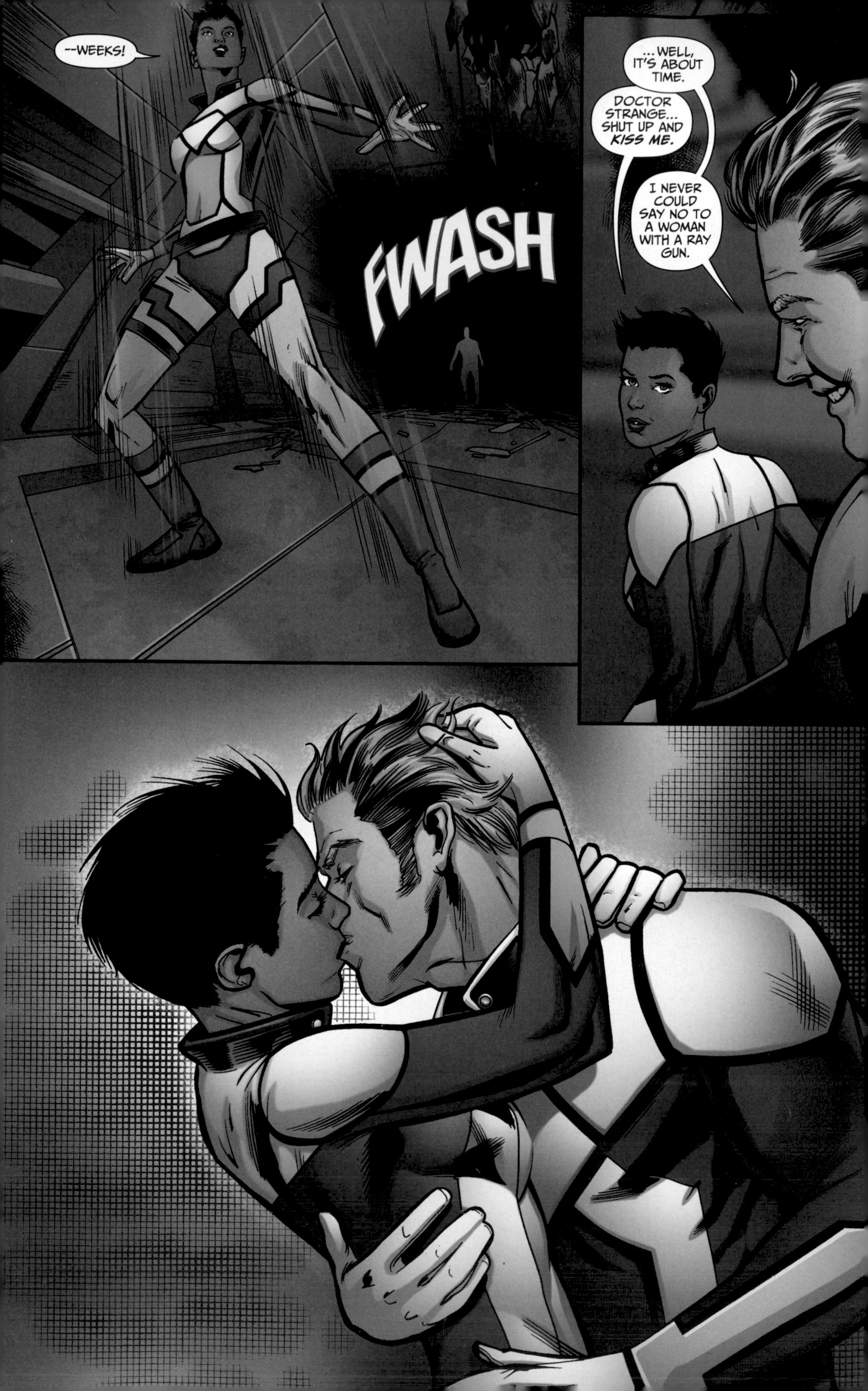
--WEEKS!
FWASH
...WELL, IT'S ABOUT TIME.
DOCTOR STRANGE... SHUT UP AND KISS ME.
I NEVER COULD SAY NO TO A WOMAN WITH A RAY GUN.

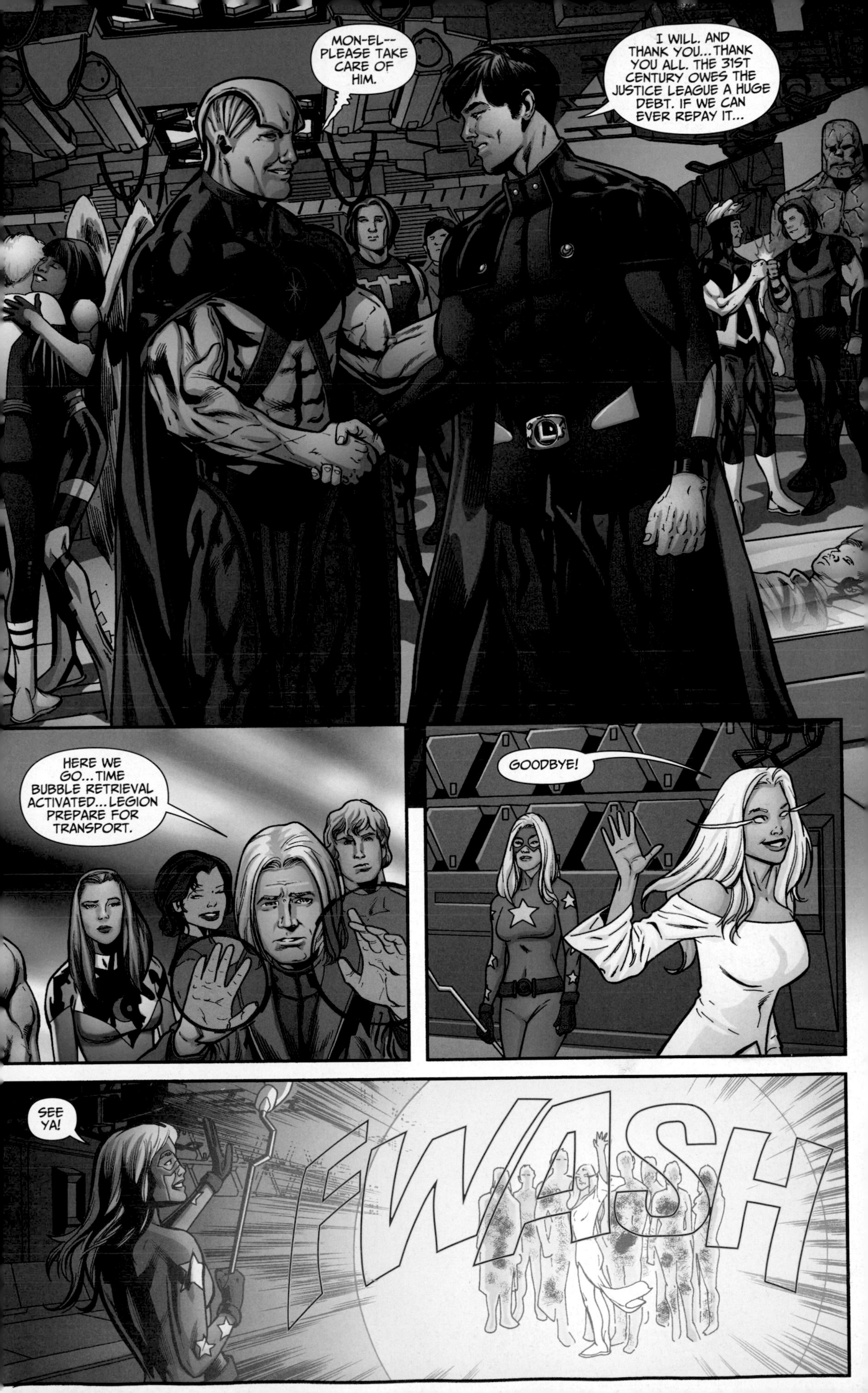
MON-EL--
PLEASE TAKE CARE OF HIM.
I WILL. AND THANK YOU... THANK YOU ALL. THE 31ST CENTURY OWES THE JUSTICE LEAGUE A HUGE DEBT. IF WE CAN EVER REPAY IT...
HERE WE GO... TIME BUBBLE RETRIEVAL ACTIVATED... LEGION PREPARE FOR TRANSPORT.
GOODBYE!
SEE YA!
FWASH

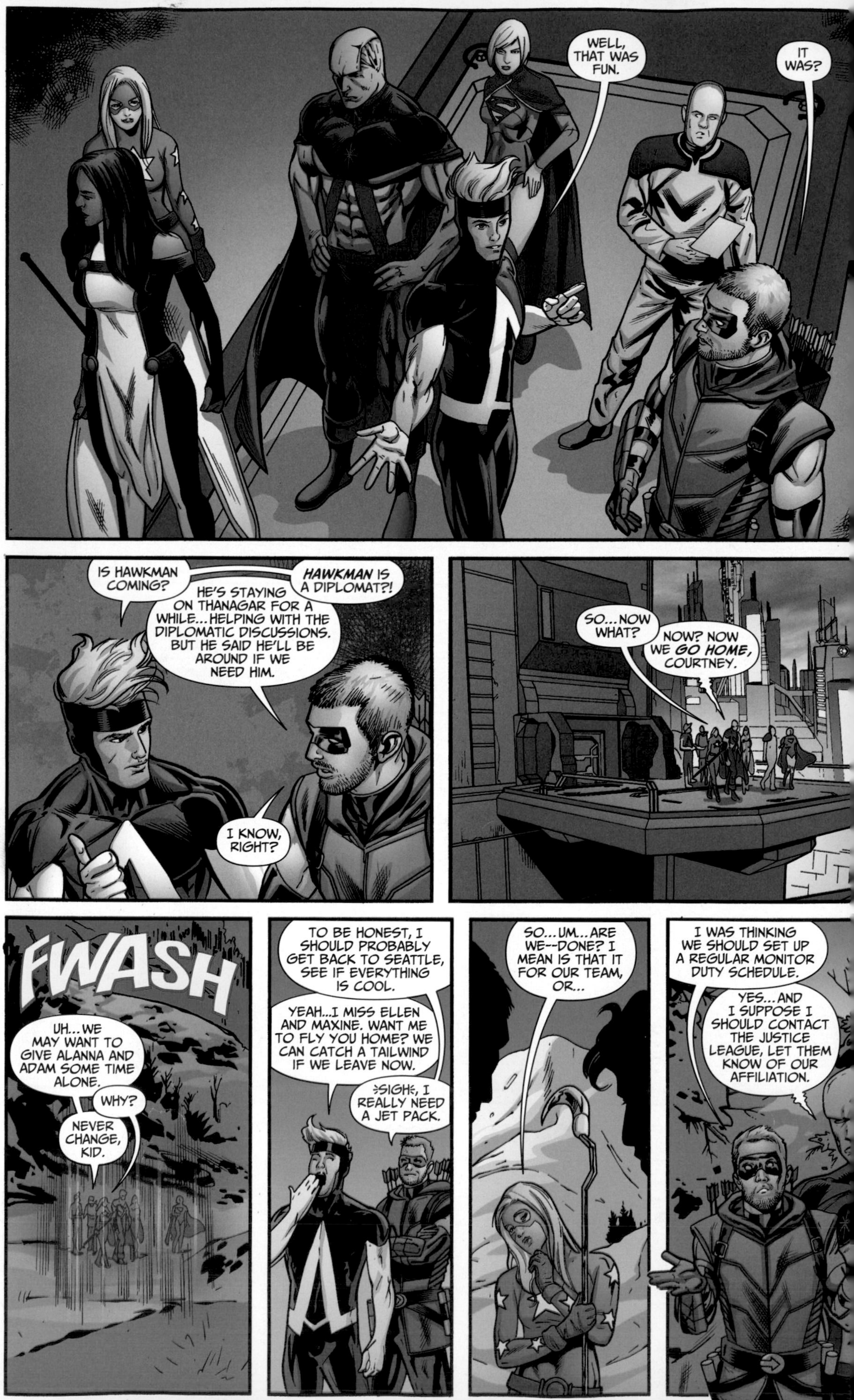
WELL, THAT WAS FUN.
IT WAS?
IS HAWKMAN COMING?
HE'S STAYING ON THANAGAR FOR A WHILE...HELPING WITH THE DIPLOMATIC DISCUSSIONS. BUT HE SAID HE'LL BE AROUND IF WE NEED HIM.
HAWKMAN IS A DIPLOMAT?!
I KNOW, RIGHT?
SO...NOW WHAT?
NOW? NOW WE GO HOME, COURTNEY.
FWASH
UH...WE MAY WANT TO GIVE ALANNA AND ADAM SOME TIME ALONE.
WHY?
NEVER CHANGE, KID.
TO BE HONEST, I SHOULD PROBABLY GET BACK TO SEATTLE, SEE IF EVERYTHING IS COOL.
YEAH...I MISS ELLEN AND MAXINE. WANT ME TO FLY YOU HOME? WE CAN CATCH A TAILWIND IF WE LEAVE NOW.
SIGH, I REALLY NEED A JET PACK.
SO...UM...ARE WE--DONE? I MEAN IS THAT IT FOR OUR TEAM, OR...
I WAS THINKING WE SHOULD SET UP A REGULAR MONITOR DUTY SCHEDULE.
YES...AND I SUPPOSE I SHOULD CONTACT THE JUSTICE LEAGUE, LET THEM KNOW OF OUR AFFILIATION.

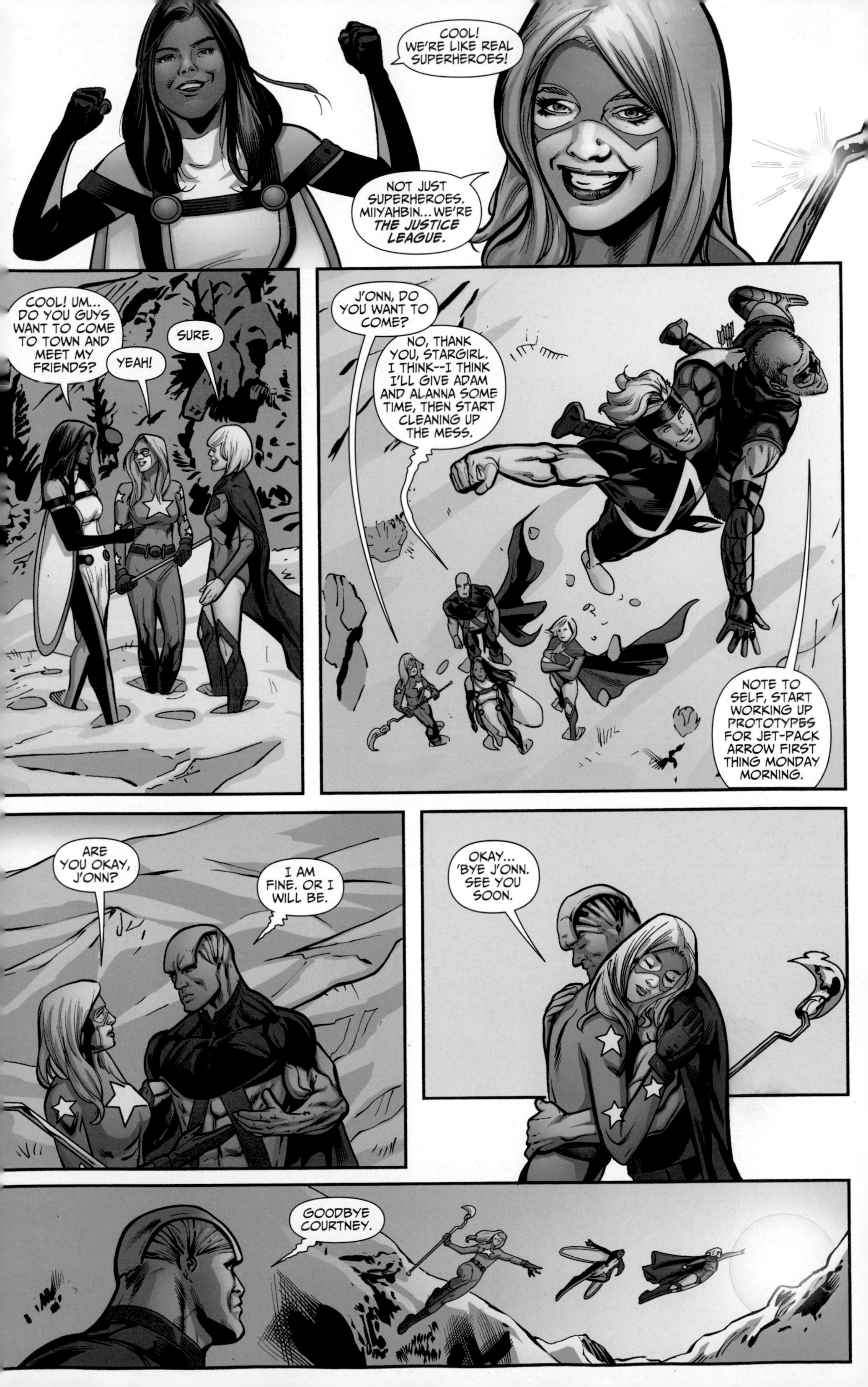
COOL! WE'RE LIKE REAL SUPERHEROES!
NOT JUST SUPERHEROES. MIIYAHBIN...WE'RE *THE JUSTICE LEAGUE.*
COOL! UM... DO YOU GUYS WANT TO COME TO TOWN AND MEET MY FRIENDS?
YEAH!
SURE.
J'ONN, DO YOU WANT TO COME?
NO, THANK YOU, STARGIRL. I THINK--I THINK I'LL GIVE ADAM AND ALANNA SOME TIME, THEN START CLEANING UP THE MESS.
NOTE TO SELF, START WORKING UP PROTOTYPES FOR JET-PACK ARROW FIRST THING MONDAY MORNING.
ARE YOU OKAY, J'ONN?
I AM FINE. OR I WILL BE.
OKAY... 'BYE J'ONN. SEE YOU SOON.
GOODBYE COURTNEY.

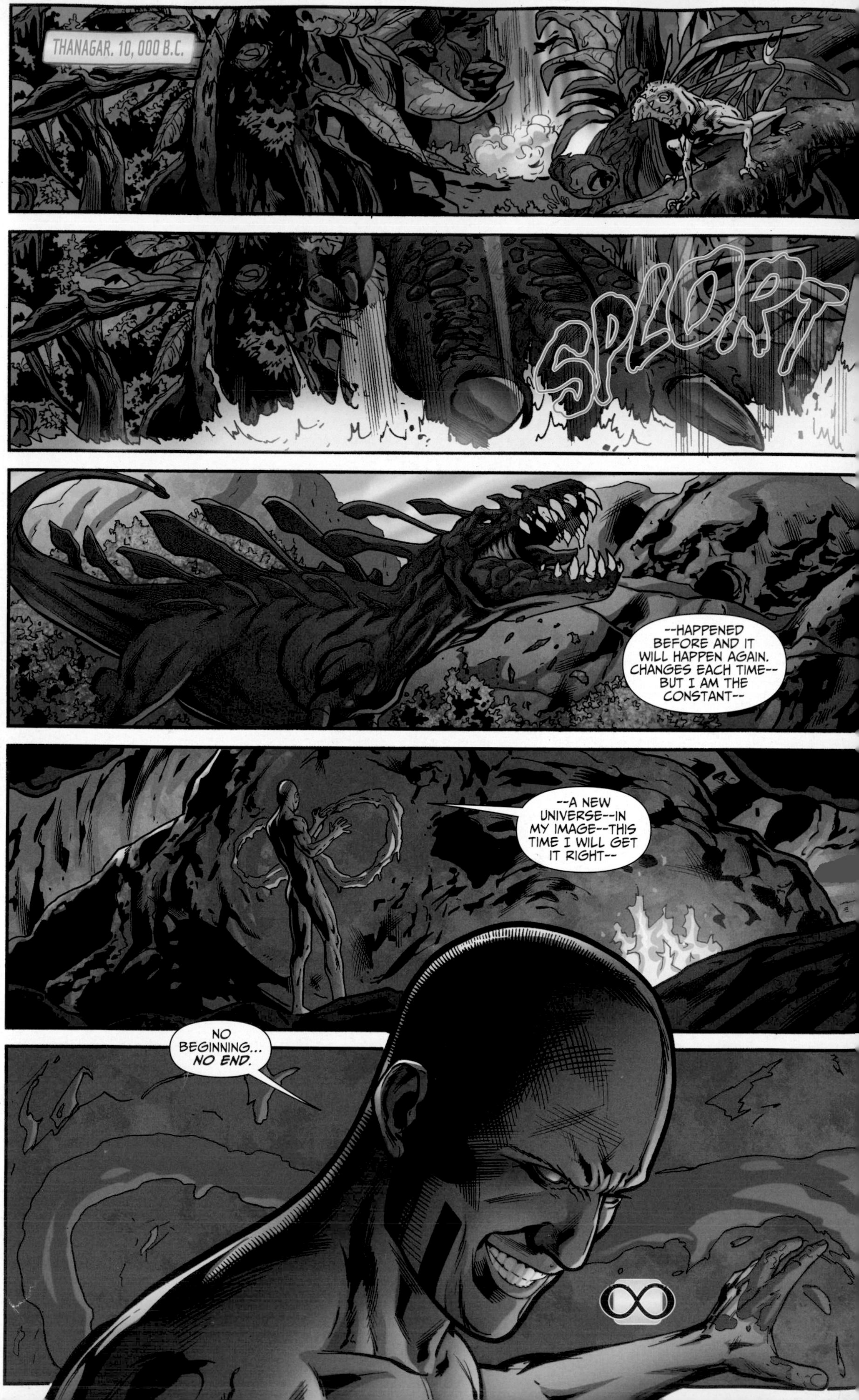
THANAGAR. 10, 000 B.C.
SPLORT
--HAPPENED BEFORE AND IT WILL HAPPEN AGAIN. CHANGES EACH TIME-- BUT I AM THE CONSTANT--
--A NEW UNIVERSE--IN MY IMAGE--THIS TIME I WILL GET IT RIGHT--
NO BEGINNING... NO END.

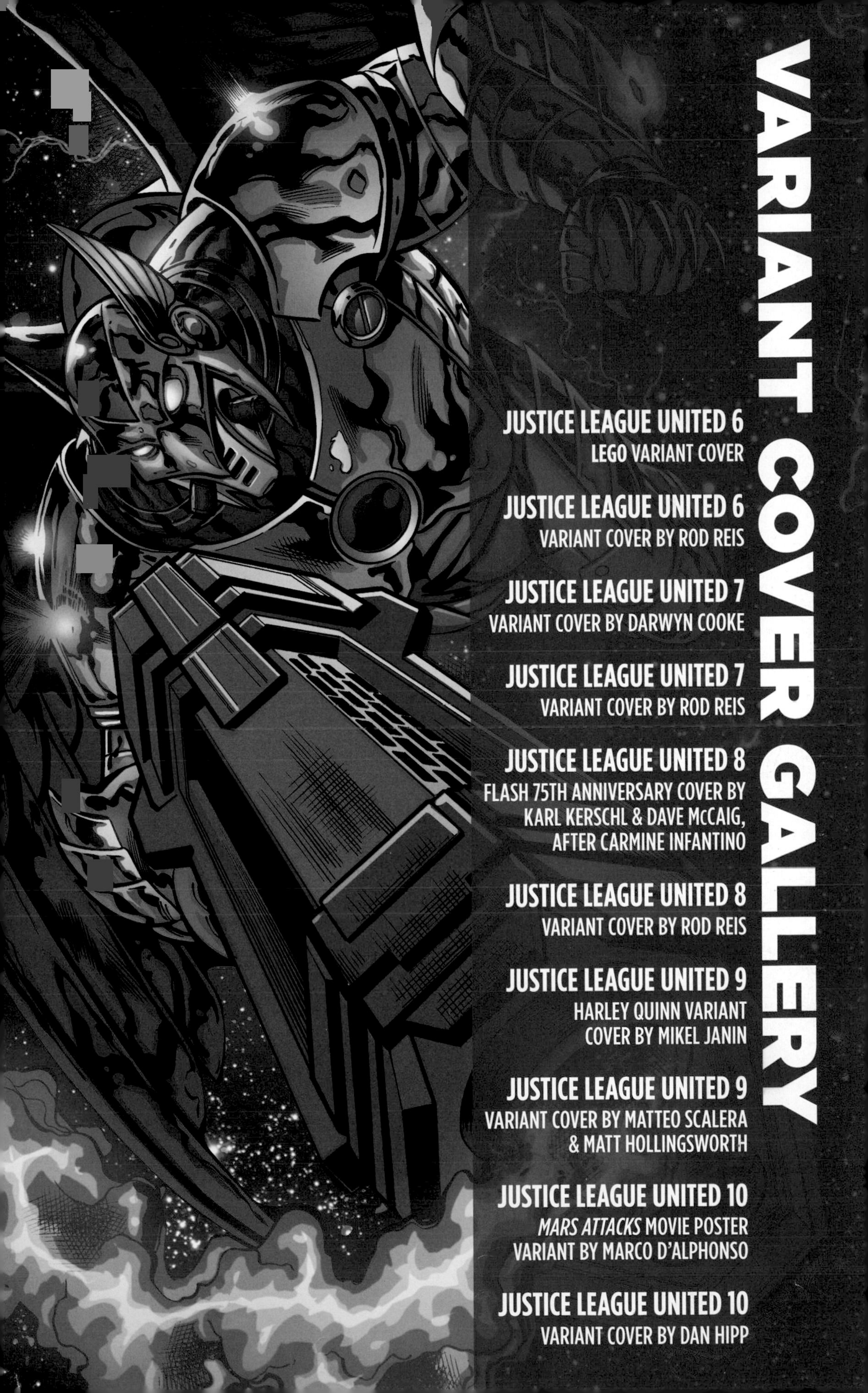

VARIANT COVER GALLERY

JUSTICE LEAGUE UNITED 6
LEGO VARIANT COVER

JUSTICE LEAGUE UNITED 6
VARIANT COVER BY ROD REIS

JUSTICE LEAGUE UNITED 7
VARIANT COVER BY DARWYN COOKE

JUSTICE LEAGUE UNITED 7
VARIANT COVER BY ROD REIS

JUSTICE LEAGUE UNITED 8
FLASH 75TH ANNIVERSARY COVER BY KARL KERSCHL & DAVE McCAIG, AFTER CARMINE INFANTINO

JUSTICE LEAGUE UNITED 8
VARIANT COVER BY ROD REIS

JUSTICE LEAGUE UNITED 9
HARLEY QUINN VARIANT COVER BY MIKEL JANIN

JUSTICE LEAGUE UNITED 9
VARIANT COVER BY MATTEO SCALERA & MATT HOLLINGSWORTH

JUSTICE LEAGUE UNITED 10
MARS ATTACKS MOVIE POSTER VARIANT BY MARCO D'ALPHONSO

JUSTICE LEAGUE UNITED 10
VARIANT COVER BY DAN HIPP

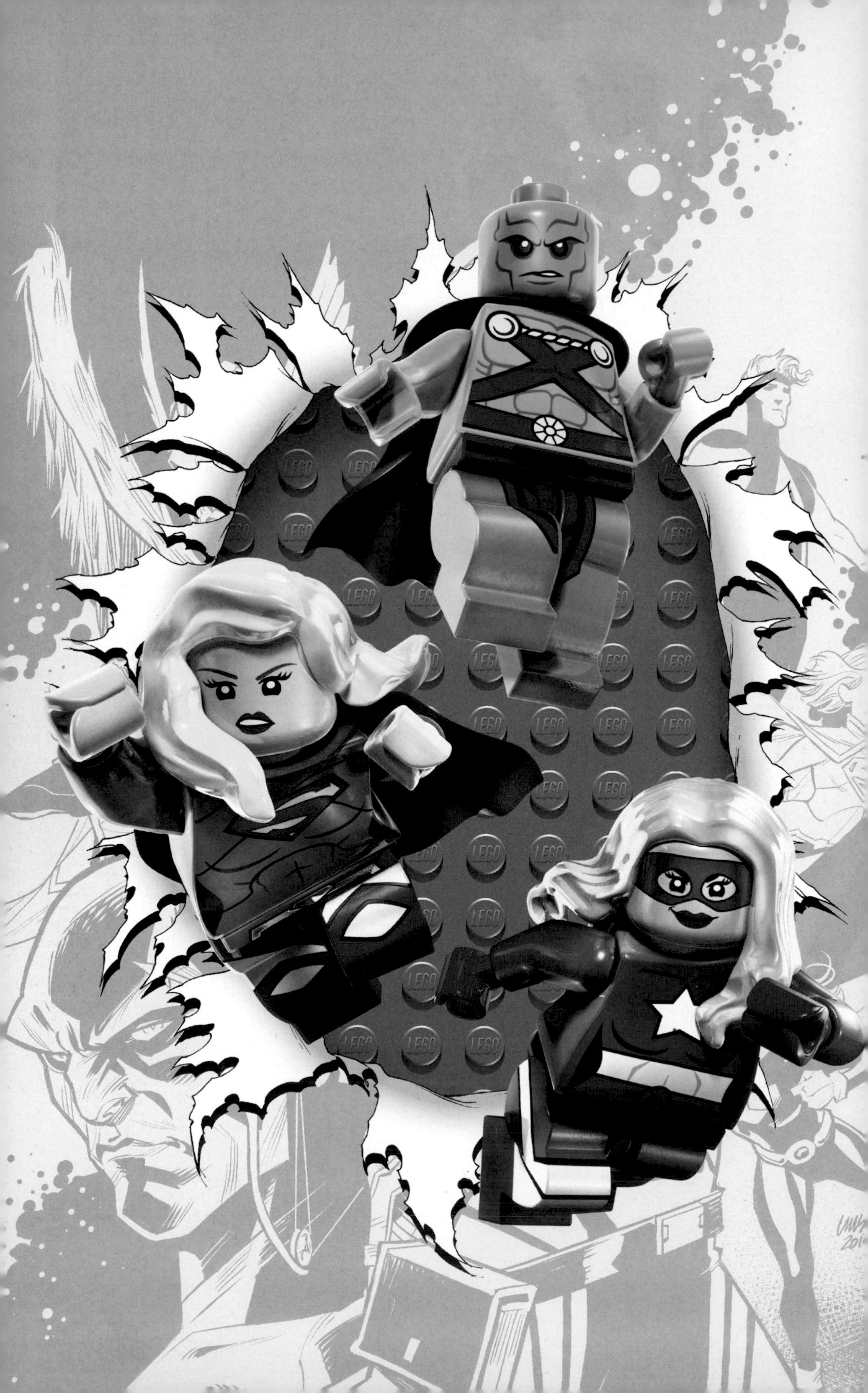

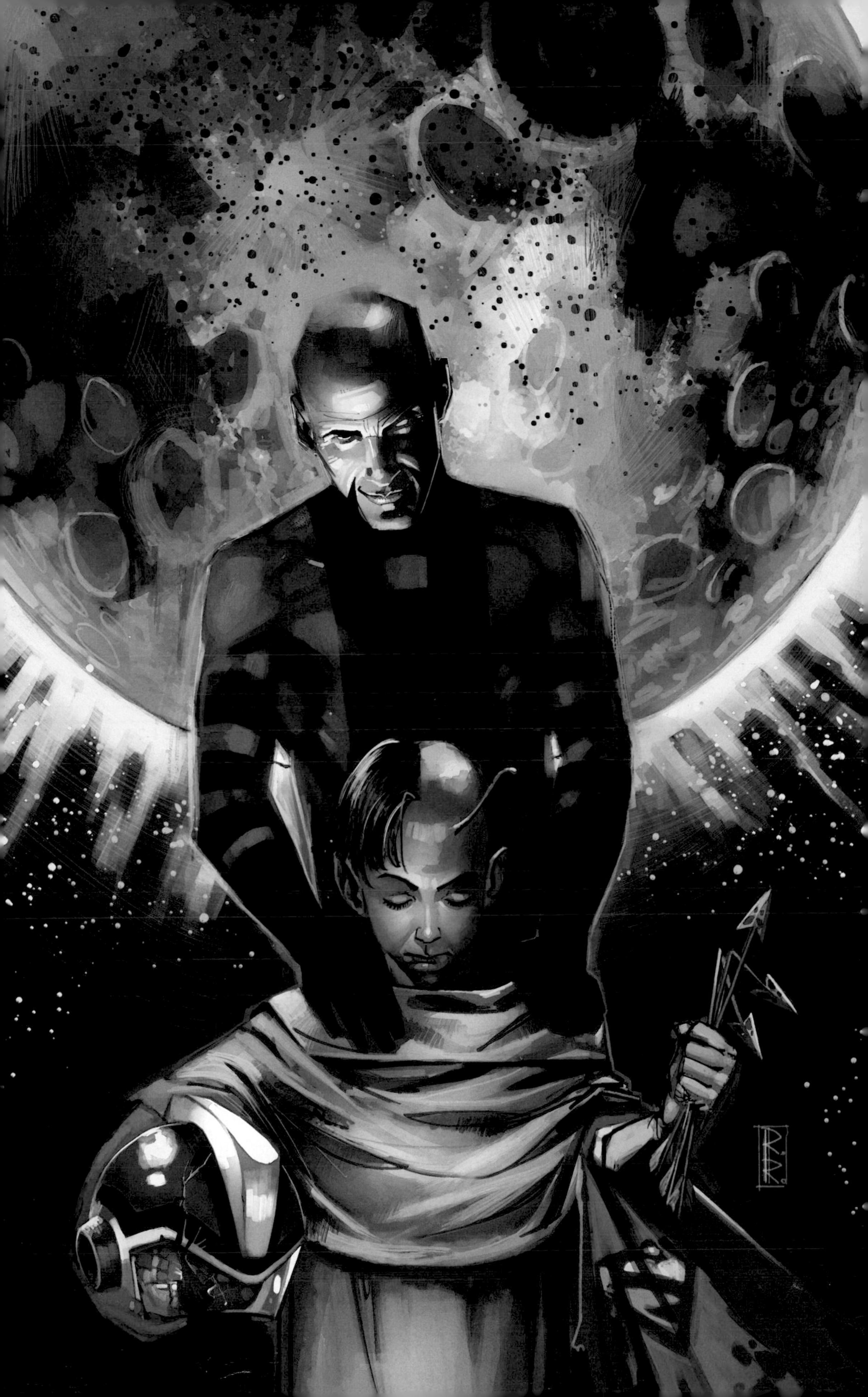

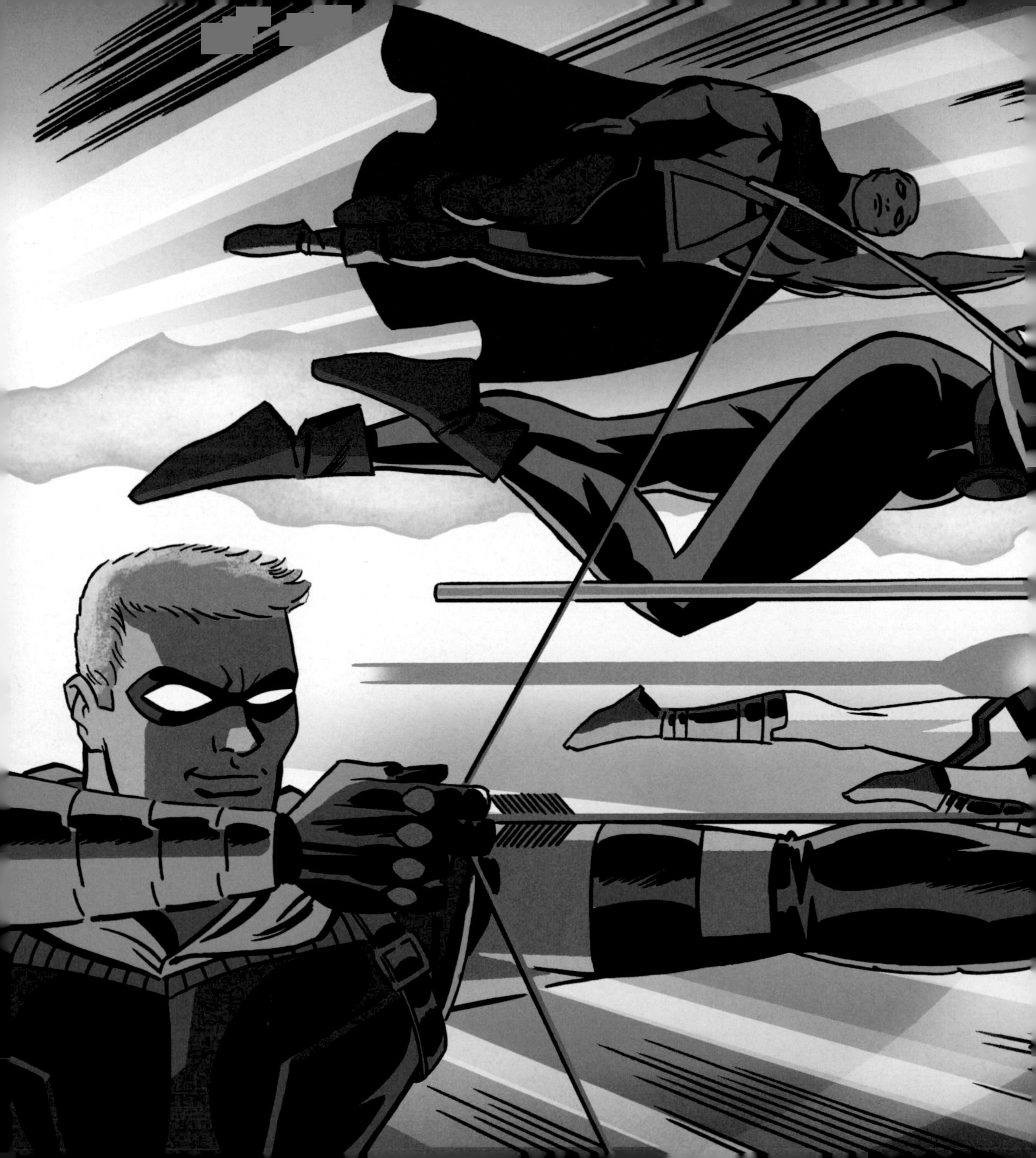

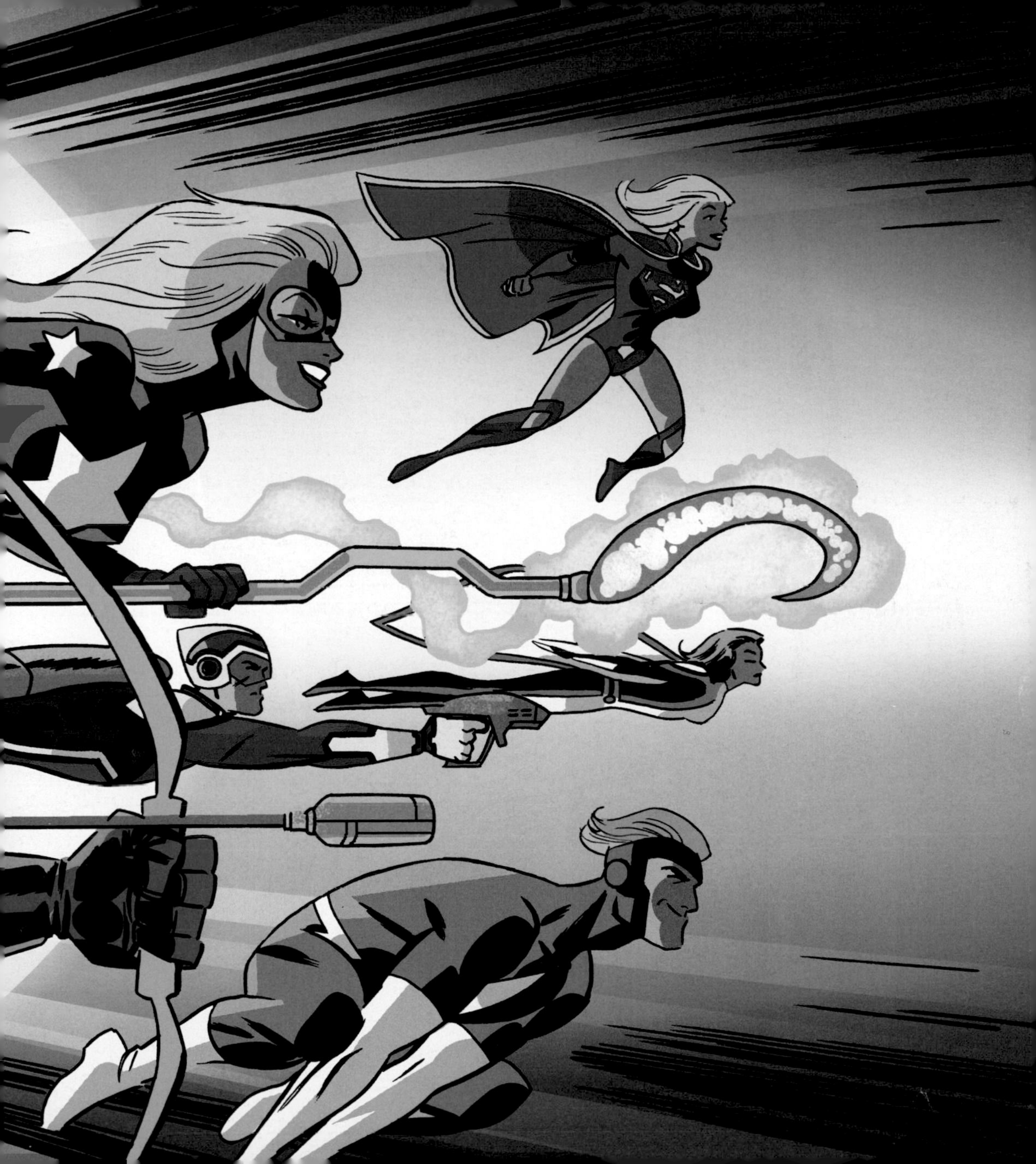

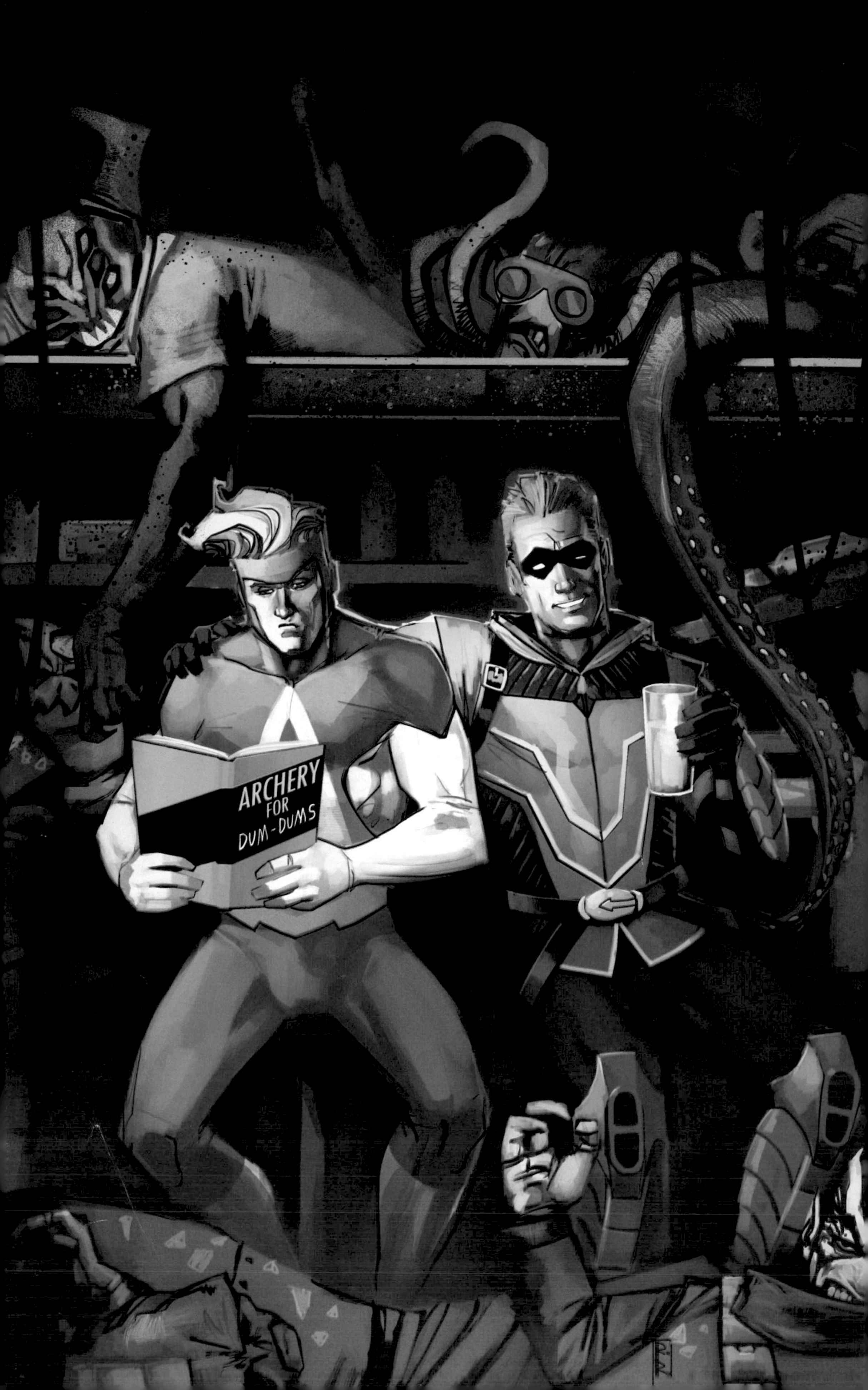
ARCHERY FOR DUM-DUMS

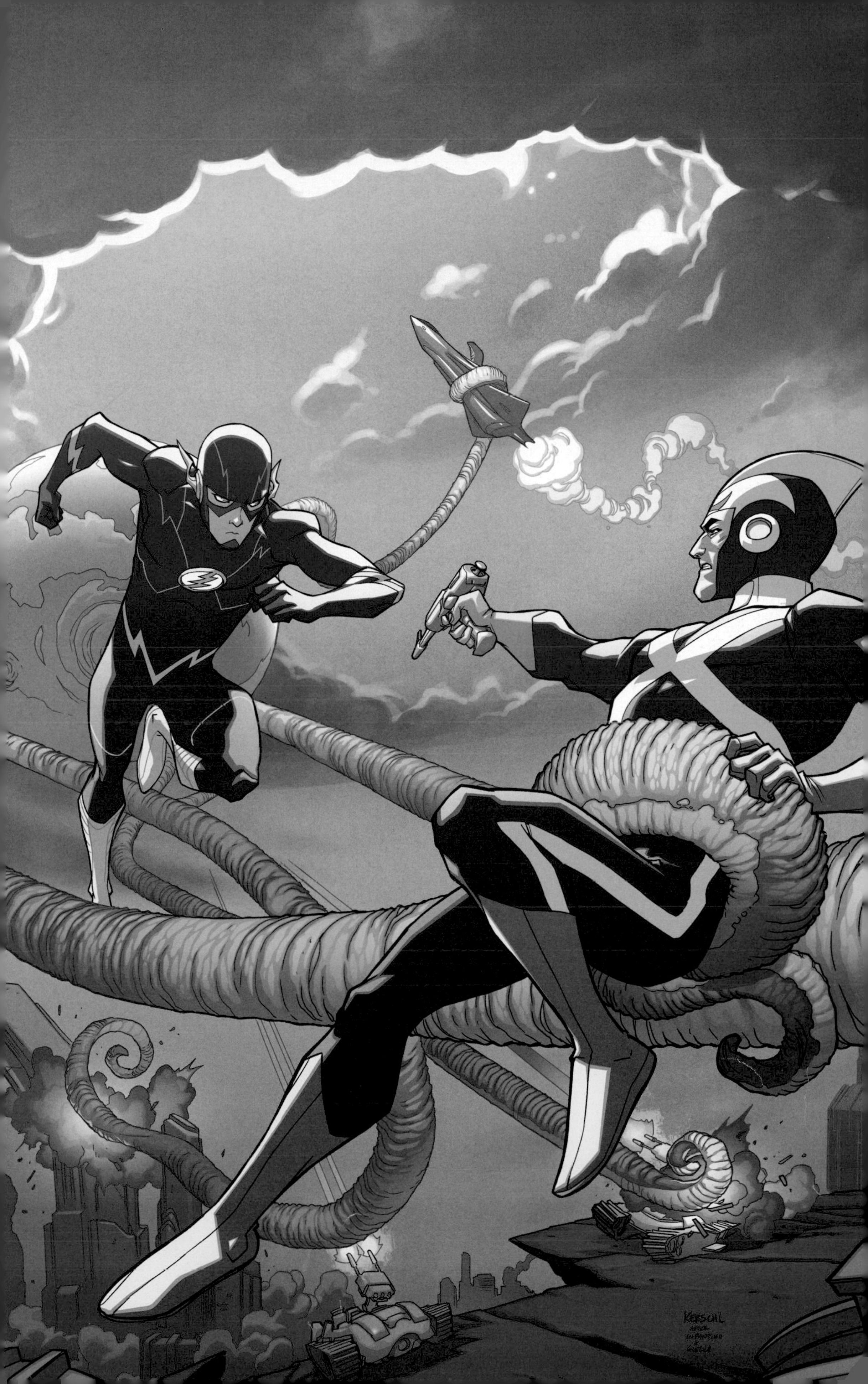

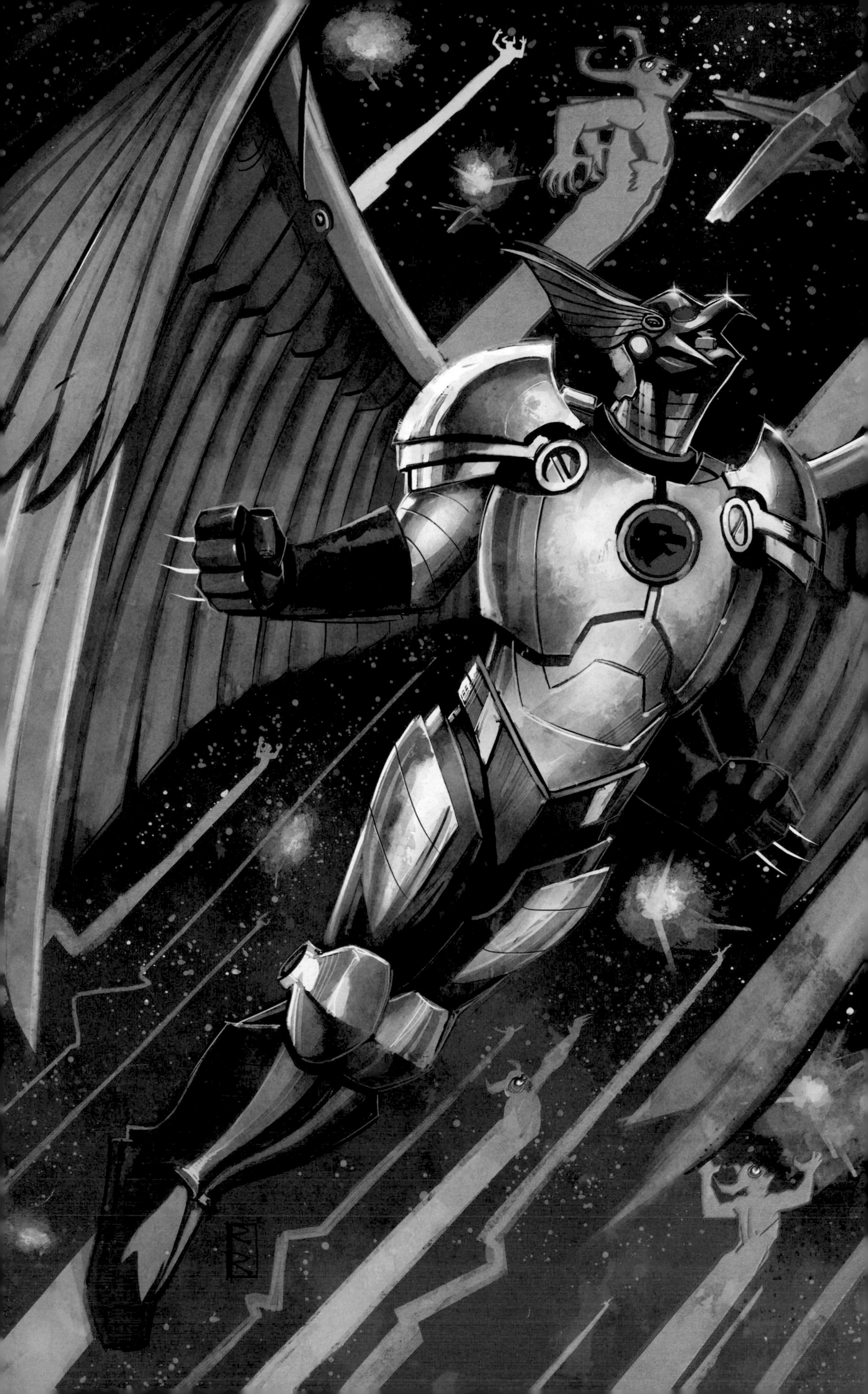

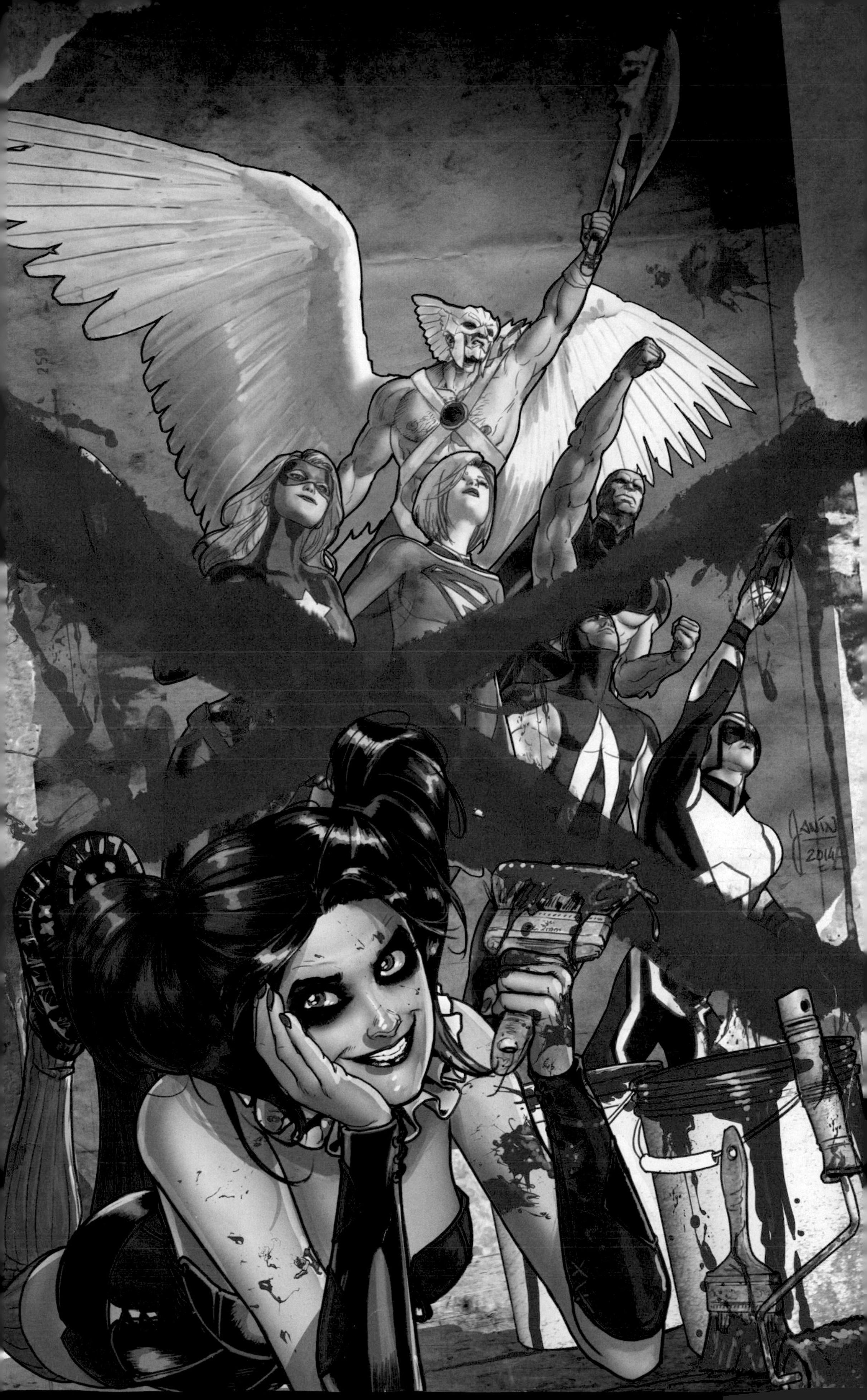

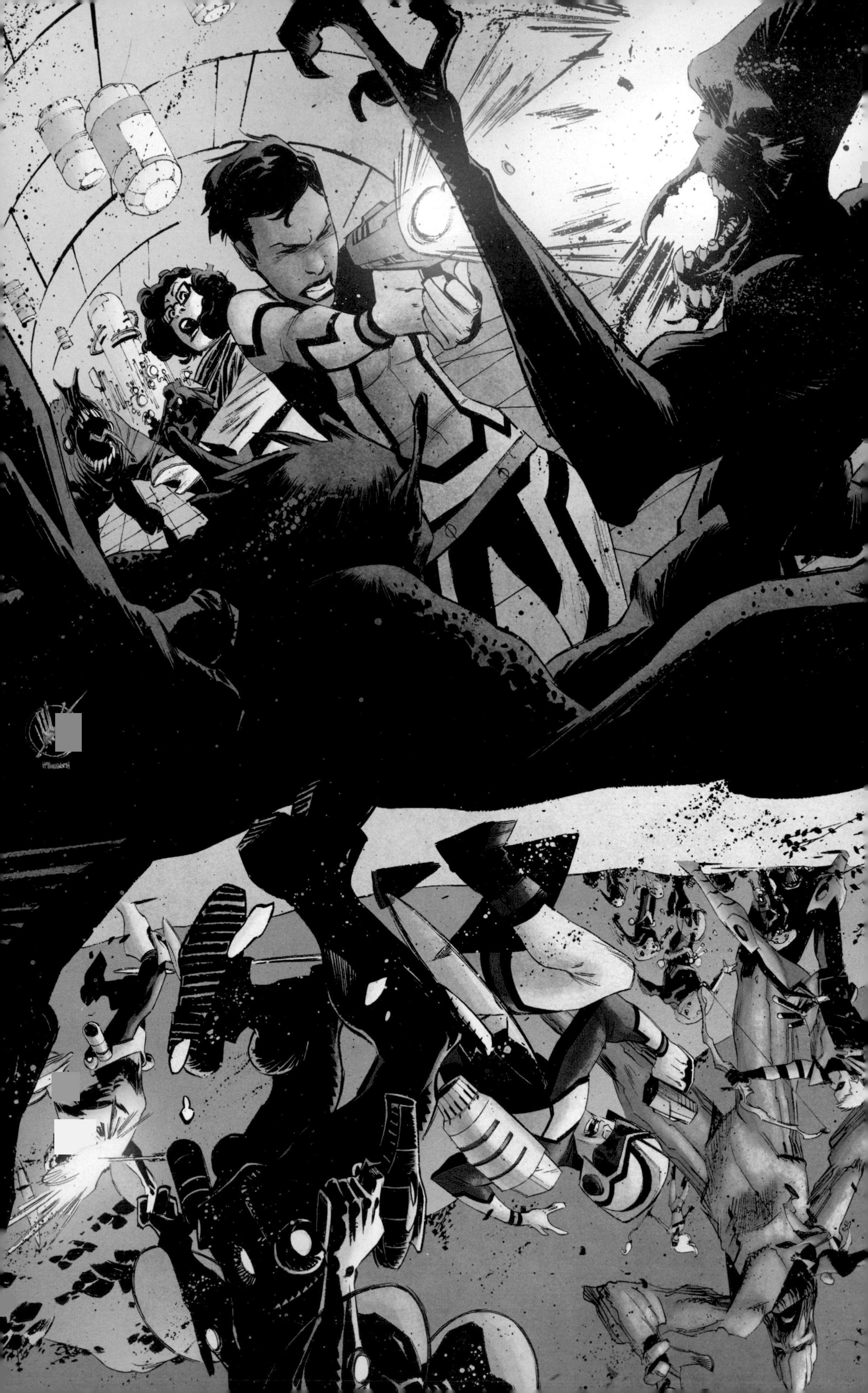

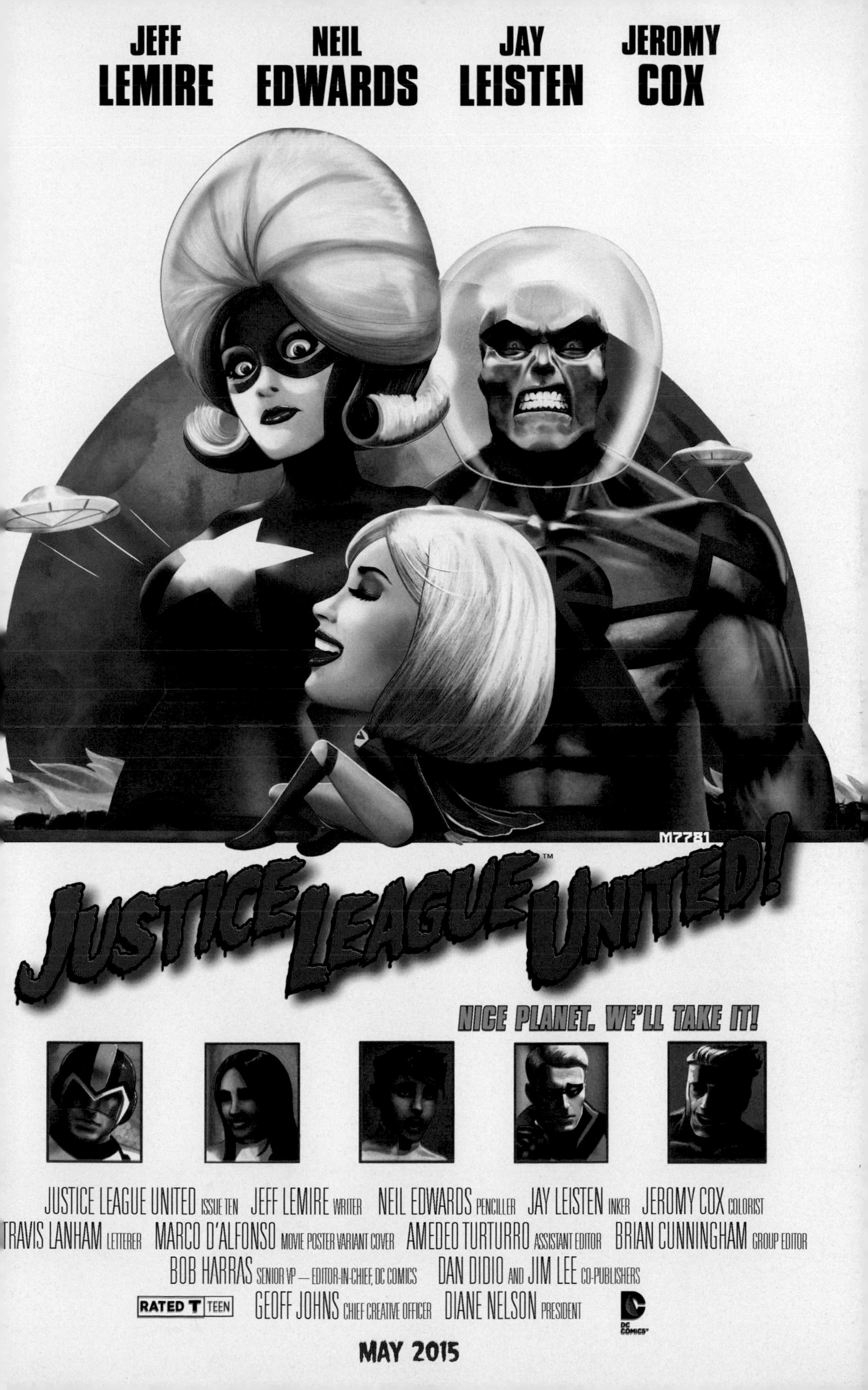
JEFF LEMIRE
NEIL EDWARDS
JAY LEISTEN
JEROMY COX
JUSTICE LEAGUE UNITED!™
NICE PLANET. WE'LL TAKE IT!
JUSTICE LEAGUE UNITED ISSUE TEN JEFF LEMIRE WRITER NEIL EDWARDS PENCILLER JAY LEISTEN INKER JEROMY COX COLORIST
TRAVIS LANHAM LETTERER MARCO D'ALFONSO MOVIE POSTER VARIANT COVER AMEDEO TURTURRO ASSISTANT EDITOR BRIAN CUNNINGHAM GROUP EDITOR
BOB HARRAS SENIOR VP — EDITOR-IN-CHIEF, DC COMICS DAN DIDIO AND JIM LEE CO-PUBLISHERS
RATED T TEEN
GEOFF JOHNS CHIEF CREATIVE OFFICER DIANE NELSON PRESIDENT
DC COMICS
MAY 2015

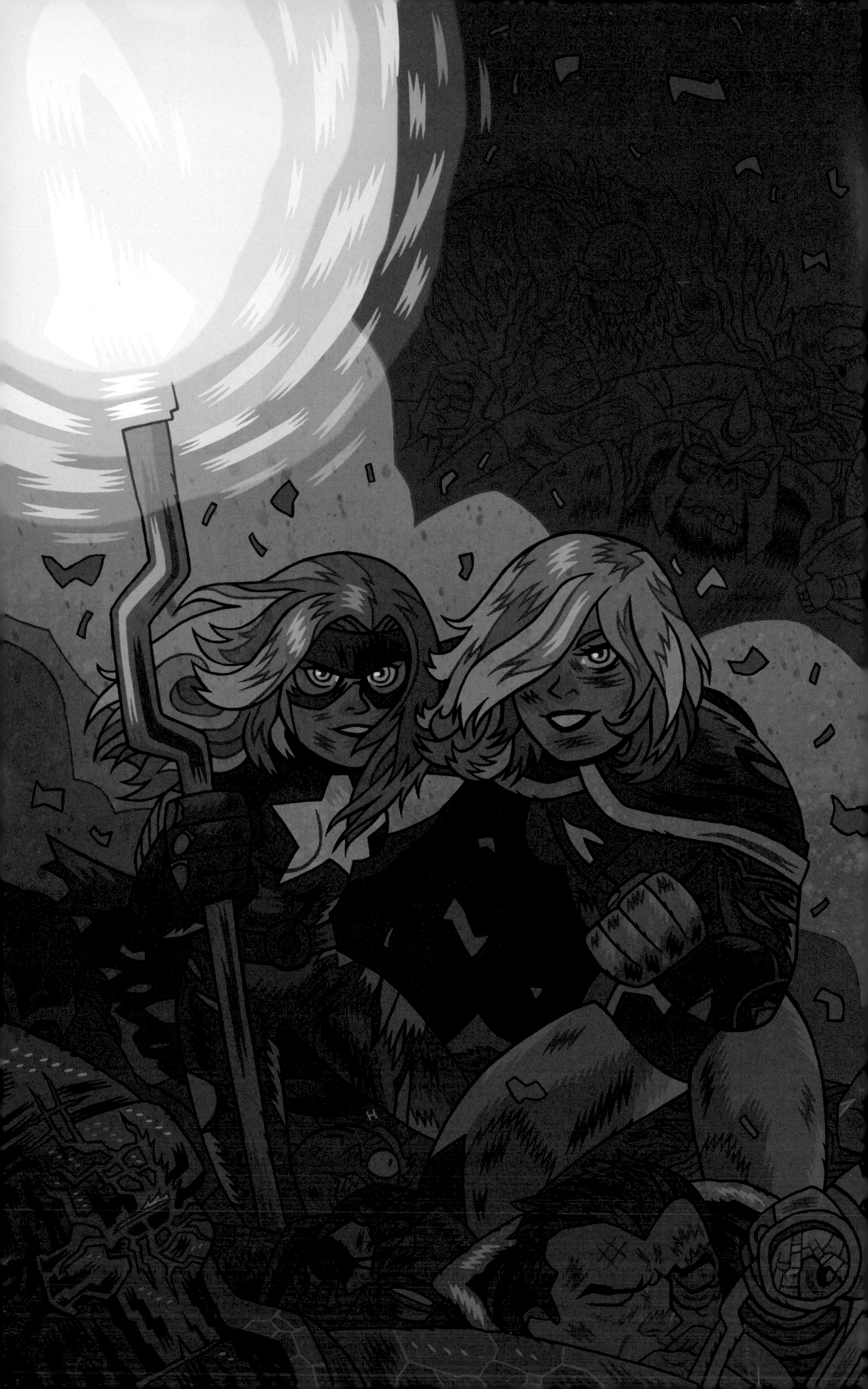

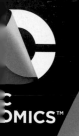

DC COMICS™

"Writer Geoff Johns and artist Jim Lee toss you–and their heroes–into the action from the very start and don't put on the brakes. DC's über-creative team craft an inviting world for those who are trying out a comic for the first time. Lee's art is stunning."—USA TODAY

"A fun ride."—IGN

START AT THE BEGINNING!

JUSTICE LEAGUE VOLUME 1: ORIGIN

GEOFF JOHNS and JIM LEE

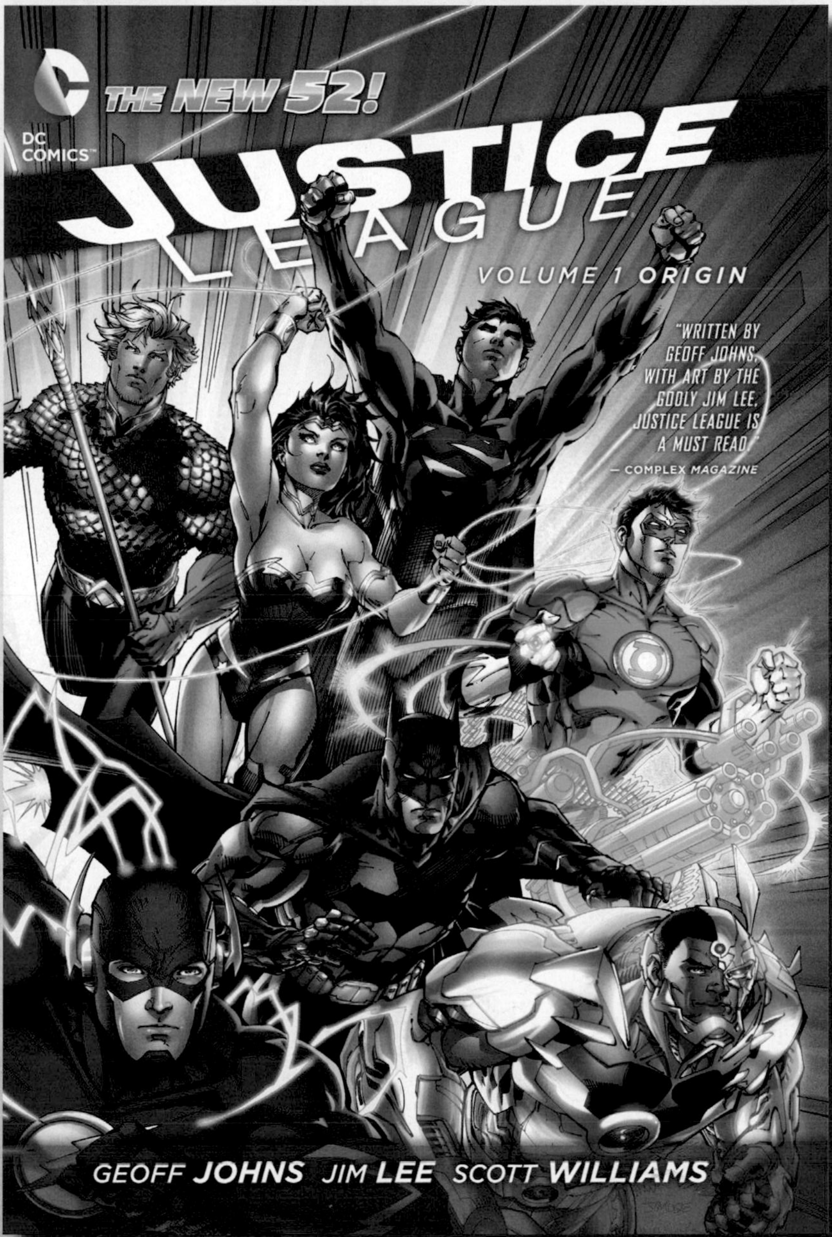

THE NEW 52!
DC COMICS™
JUSTICE LEAGUE
VOLUME 1 ORIGIN
"WRITTEN BY GEOFF JOHNS, WITH ART BY THE GODLY JIM LEE, JUSTICE LEAGUE IS A MUST READ."
— COMPLEX MAGAZINE
GEOFF JOHNS JIM LEE SCOTT WILLIAMS

JUSTICE LEAGUE VOL. 2: THE VILLAIN'S JOURNEY

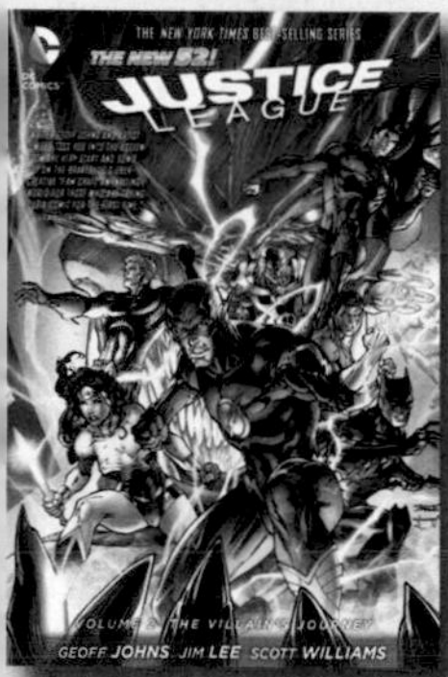

JUSTICE LEAGUE
GEOFF JOHNS JIM LEE SCOTT WILLIAMS

JUSTICE LEAGUE VOL. 3: THRONE OF ATLANTIS

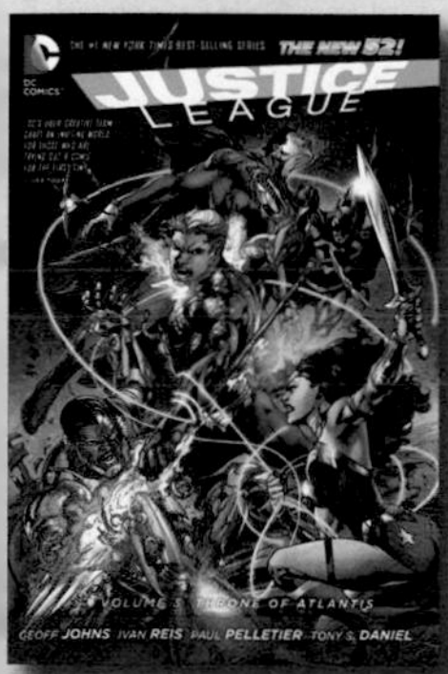

THE NEW 52!
JUSTICE LEAGUE
GEOFF JOHNS IVAN REIS PAUL PELLETIER TONY S. DANIEL

JUSTICE LEAGUE OF AMERICA VOL. 1: WORLD'S MOST DANGEROUS

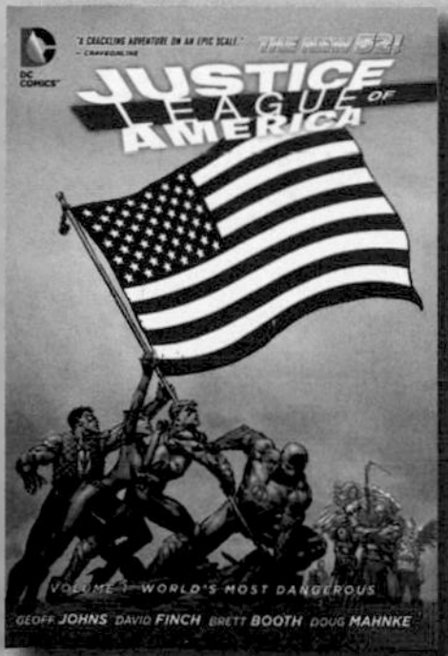

THE NEW 52!
JUSTICE LEAGUE OF AMERICA
VOLUME 1 WORLD'S MOST DANGEROUS
GEOFF JOHNS DAVID FINCH BRETT BOOTH DOUG MAHNKE

DC COMICS™

FROM THE WRITER OF ALL-STAR SUPERMAN AND BATMAN & ROBIN

GRANT MORRISON
with HOWARD PORTER

JLA VOL. 2

with HOWARD PORTER

JLA VOL. 3

with HOWARD PORTER

JLA VOL. 4

with HOWARD PORTER,
MARK WAID, and MARK
PAJARILLO

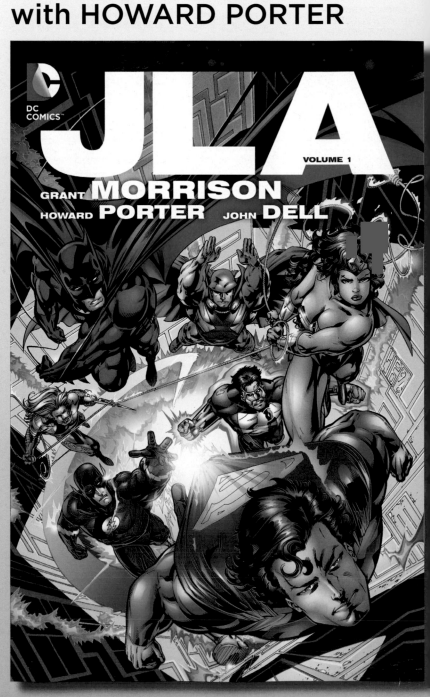

DC COMICS™

JLA
VOLUME 1

GRANT MORRISON
HOWARD PORTER   JOHN DELL

DC COMICS™

"Drips with energy."
—IGN

"Grade A."
—USA TODAY

START AT THE BEGINNING!

TEEN TITANS VOLUME 1: IT'S OUR RIGHT TO FIGHT

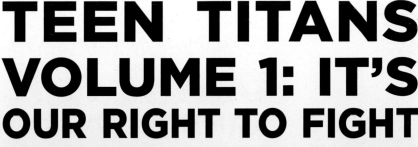

LEGION OF SUPER-HEROES VOLUME 1: HOSTILE WORLD

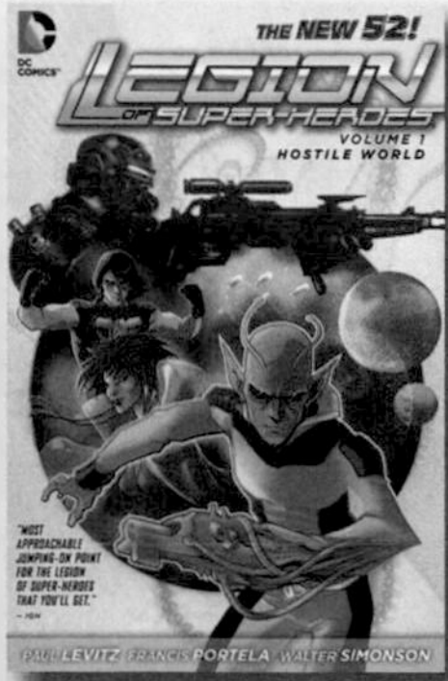
THE NEW 52!
LEGION OF SUPER-HEROES
VOLUME 1
HOSTILE WORLD
PAUL LEVITZ FRANCIS PORTELA WALTER SIMONSON

LEGION LOST VOLUME 1: RUN FROM TOMORROW

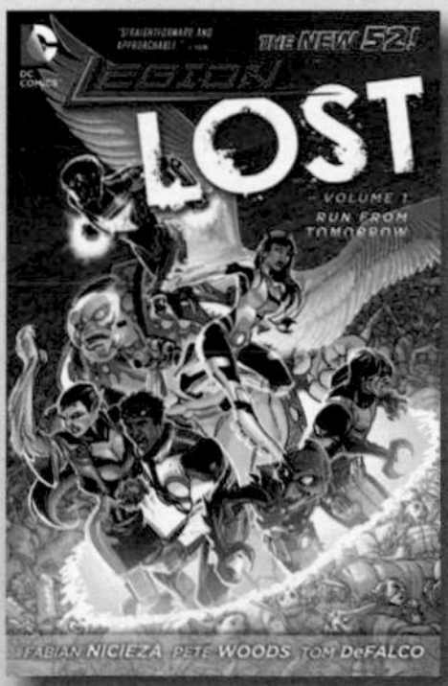
THE NEW 52!
LEGION LOST
VOLUME 1
RUN FROM TOMORROW
FABIAN NICIEZA PETE WOODS TOM DeFALCO

STATIC SHOCK VOLUME 1: SUPERCHARGED

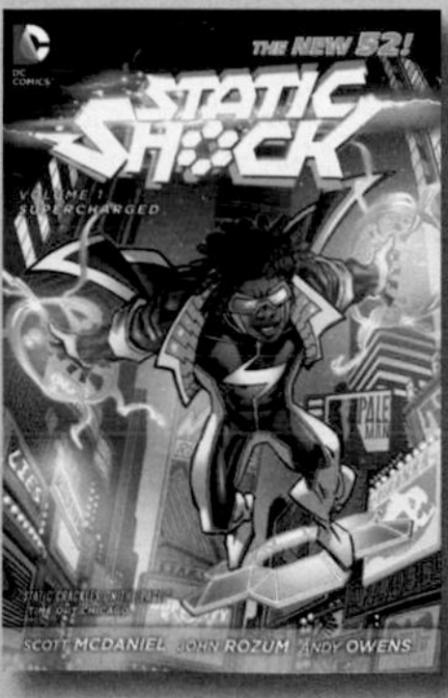
THE NEW 52!
STATIC SHOCK
SUPERCHARGED
SCOTT McDANIEL JOHN ROZUM ANDY OWENS

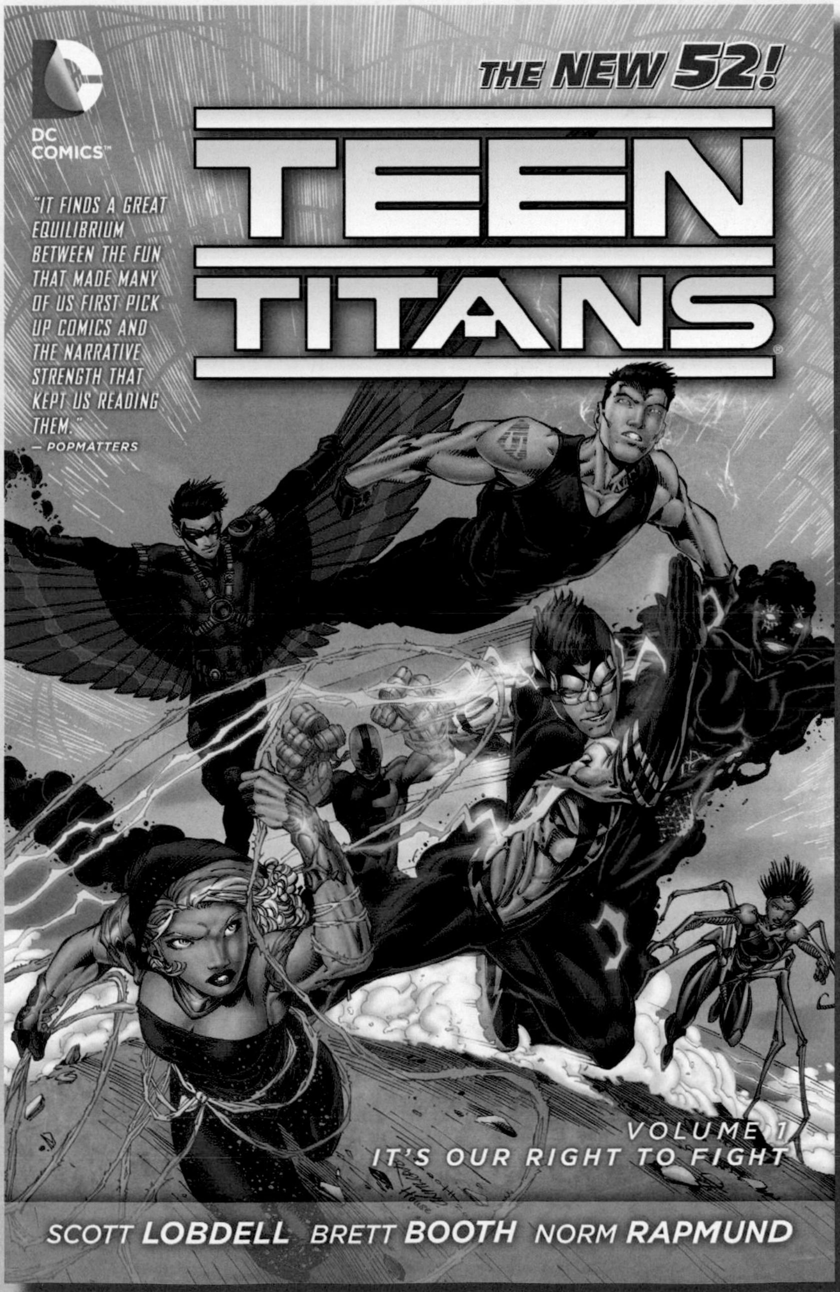
DC COMICS
THE NEW 52!
TEEN TITANS
"IT FINDS A GREAT EQUILIBRIUM BETWEEN THE FUN THAT MADE MANY OF US FIRST PICK UP COMICS AND THE NARRATIVE STRENGTH THAT KEPT US READING THEM."
— POPMATTERS
VOLUME 1
IT'S OUR RIGHT TO FIGHT
SCOTT LOBDELL BRETT BOOTH NORM RAPMUND